PEOPLE, PLACES, THINGS

PEOPLE, PLACES, THINGS

ESSAYS BY ELIZABETH BOWEN

EDITED WITH AN INTRODUCTION BY
ALLAN HEPBURN

Edinburgh University Press

© Curtis Brown Ltd, London, Literary Executors of The Estate
of Elizabeth Bowen, 2008
Selection and Editorial material © Allan Hepburn, 2008

Transferred to Digital Print 2011

Edinburgh University Press Ltd
22 George Square, Edinburgh

Typeset in Optima
by Norman Tilley Graphics Ltd, Northampton

Printed and bound by CPI Group (UK) Ltd, Croydon, CR0 4YY

A CIP record for this book is available
from the British Library

ISBN 978 0 7486 3568 9 (hardback)
ISBN 978 0 7486 3569 6 (paperback)

Published with the support of the Edinburgh University
Scholarly Publishing Initiatives Fund.

Contents

CONTENTS

Acknowledgements

When I first began collecting Elizabeth Bowen's ungathered essays, I had no plan to edit them for publication. With an eye to writing a critical book about Bowen's fiction, I photocopied or transcribed material in various libraries while I was researching other projects. Pages mounted up. My collecting became more deliberate. I found Bowen's essays at the National Library of Ireland in Dublin, the British Library in London, the Library of Congress in Washington, Firestone Library at Princeton University, the McLennan Library at McGill University, the Cornell University Library, the Toronto Reference Library, the Robarts Library at the University of Toronto, the Bibliothèque Nationale du Québec, Library and Archives Canada, and other libraries that I have, in the five years that it took me to bring these materials together, nearly forgotten. Reference librarians applied their considerable powers of deduction to locating obscure mid-century journals and newspapers. I am grateful to the librarians at McGill University who patiently fielded questions and obtained documents from other libraries. In particular, Lonnie Weatherby has been generous with his time and expertise. A month-long Mellon Fellowship at the Harry Ransom Center at the University of Texas at Austin in June 2006 helped me to make substantial progress towards completing this book. The staff at the Harry Ransom Center, especially Patricia Fox, Robert Fulton, Richard Oram, Molly Schwartzburg, and Tom Staley, win my heartfelt thanks for their gracious welcome. A research grant from the Arts Insights programme in the Faculty of Arts at McGill University defrayed pre-production costs. A Standard Research Grant from the Social Sciences and Humanities Research Council of Canada allowed me to hire research assistants and to travel to archives. The Fonds du Québec pour la Recherche en Sciences et Culture also funded a semester of research assistance. Two research assistants, Robin Feenstra and Liisa Stephenson, have been involved in this project almost as long as I have; their expertise as detectives, transcribers, editors, commentators, and proofreaders helped speed this book to completion. When I lost some computer files, Charlotte Nunes graciously verified facts at the Harry Ransom Center. Many friends have sustained this project with their conversation and wisdom; I wish especially to thank Phyllis Lassner, Patrick Moran, and Barbara Morris. Jackie Jones at Edinburgh University Press has encouraged me with timely words. Lastly, I thank the Estate of Elizabeth Bowen for permission to publish these essays, which, I hope, will find the audience that they deserve.

Introduction

Elizabeth Bowen, best known for her short stories and novels, wrote essays on literary, political, and personal subjects throughout her career. Some of these essays convey her opinions about writing; others address broad cultural questions. Whether meditating on the state of fiction in postwar Britain or incandescent lights, her favourite topics tend to be nouns: people, places, things. She is attracted to strangeness in physical entities, even prior to knowing what constitutes their uniqueness. Familiar things – a house or a toy – possess an element of unusualness, all the more so because they are familiar. Recognizing that strangeness appeals to her imagination, Bowen remarks in "First Writing" that, as a novice, she aimed "to register the hazy queerness places and persons had for me" (119). Written between the 1920s and 1960s, the essays in this volume, as attempts to describe "hazy queerness," span everything from the genius of Jane Austen to Cold War politics. Each of these essays, in its own way, engages with the reality of the physical world. The allure of physical objects and places did not prevent Bowen from speculation on metaphysical subjects, especially human relations and the passage of time. In her later essays, she tallies, with profound regret, pleasures outlived and youth exhausted. As a genre, the essay accommodates diversity. Using the essay as an instrument of enquiry and explanation, Bowen confronts difficult subjects, such as disappointment, ageing, and eccentricity, that no one cares to think about, or to think about enough.

An improvised genre, the essay defies precise definition. Of almost any length, it blends information with personal observation. The good essayist isolates a topic that others may have noticed but have never expressed in so many words. Amenable to almost any subject, the essay succeeds through perspicacity. Michel de Montaigne, whose forays into the genre combine wisdom with wit, found plenty to say about thumbs, smells, prayers, Rome, and the reasonableness of letting business wait until tomorrow. Following suit, Bowen writes insightfully about painting, James Joyce, pre-posterous heroines, toys, teenagers, eccentricity, and other topics. What she sees and senses – an encounter with reality that leaves an impression – germinates into an idea. An essay thus embodies knowledge as lived experience. In this sense, the genre, certainly as Bowen practises it, contains an element of autobiography, or more precisely autobiography at a distance, for the essayist observes her own behaviour as part of an abstract pattern. Within the essay, where conjecture and large claims have their place, individual experience broadens into human truth.

Bowen never brought together the essays in this volume as a collection. She did compile two books of essays during her lifetime: *Collected Impressions* (1950) and *Afterthought: Pieces About Writing* (1962). A third volume, *Pictures and Conversations* (1974), was assembled posthumously by Bowen's friend and literary execu-tor, Spencer Curtis Brown. Hermione Lee selected material from *Collected Impressions*, *Afterthought*, and *Pictures and Conver-sations*, and added four previously uncollected essays in *The Mulberry Tree* (1986), along with a sampling of correspondence. Those four essays – "Tipperary Woman," "Coming to London," "Eire," and the preface to *Frost in May* – have not been reprinted in this volume because they are already available. In keeping with her passion for places and buildings, Bowen also wrote several non-fictional books: *Bowen's Court* (1942), *The Shelbourne* (1951) and *A Time in Rome* (1960). The very short and charming *Seven Winters* (1942) is as much a recollection of Dublin circa 1900 as it is a memoir of Bowen's early childhood. All of her non-fiction registers the immediacy of particular places, which she calls their "climate." Bowen invariably conceives of the present moment as historical in its implications. By imperceptible degrees, historical events alter the climate of a place in so far as those events are lived out and lived through.

Although Bowen never finished the autobiographical section of *Pictures and Conversations*, she planned the book to be about the relationship between "living and writing" (61). For Bowen, living and writing amount to the same thing, or almost. Hardworking, conscientious, she never ceased to write to earn a living. As interviews and publicity notices make clear, Bowen viewed herself as a professional writer who logged long, regular hours at her desk. The necessity of paying household bills spurred productivity. From 1935, she and her husband, Alan Cameron, kept a house on Clarence Terrace, on the outer ring of Regent's Park in London, as well as Bowen's Court, the country house in County Cork that Bowen inherited from her father in 1930. With royalties from *The Death of the Heart* (1938), she installed an electrical generator and indoor lighting at Bowen's Court. Bowen wrote to William Plomer on 30 October 1939: "We now have the telephone, and Jim Gates (do you remember) is busy putting in electric light for me here. As I am simply having old lamps wired for electricity, it does not change the effect of the lighting much" (Plomer Archive, MSS 19/1). Bowen and her husband gave up the house in London after Christmas 1951 and moved permanently to Ireland. When Alan Cameron died suddenly in August 1952, the upkeep of Bowen's Court fell entirely on her shoulders.

Written to measure, Bowen's journalism brought in some money, but never enough. Answering "The Cost of Letters," a questionnaire created by Cyril Connolly in *Horizon* in 1946, Bowen estimated, with good humour and high optimism, that she needed £3,500 net per year. In all, twenty-one authors answered Connolly's set of six questions; Bowen's estimate of "the cost of letters" outstripped everyone else's. In his reply, George Orwell calculates that £1,000 per year would suffice, although he also mentions the sums of £10 after tax for a married man and £6 per week for an unmarried man. V. S. Pritchett guesses that £1,200–£1,400 gross would do. More modestly, William Sansom thinks that a minimum of £400–£500 per year would buy him privacy; he does not, needless to say, set a maximum. Rose Macaulay avoids the question altogether and urges aspiring writers to support themselves with other jobs. Dylan Thomas reasons that a writer "needs as much money as he wants to spend" (Connolly 121).

Although Bowen hoped for £3,500 after taxes, her income in the postwar years never rose that high. After the Labour Party won the

1945 elections in a landslide, they levied dizzying levels of income tax. Like other people, Bowen felt pinched by these measures that ushered in the welfare state. To satisfy auditors, she created a summary of her earnings through the latter half of the 1940s. In the fiscal year 1944–5, her royalties amounted to £352.6.11. Weekly book reviews for the *Tatler* brought in £546; journalism grossed £50; other income amounted to £130. Expenses that year included £150 for a secretary and £30 for oddments. Revenue thus totalled a few shillings over £1,078, minus £180 in expenses. Revenues in 1945–6 were £1,550.4.5; expenses were £200. In 1946–7, revenues were £2,164.15.1; expenses, £215. In 1947–8, her income crested at £2,133.17.7, while expenses crept up to £230 (HRC 12.5–6). During these years, she relied on the *Tatler* for about £500 of annual income. But earning a wage from the *Tatler* required herculean efforts: every week, in addition to other obligations, Bowen read three or four books and submitted a synoptic review. Time-consuming as journalism may have been, it was a stop-gap measure rather than a full-time occupation. In any event, her income never climbed to the vaunted heights of £3,500 that she claimed to need.

By the late 1930s, Bowen had earned an international reputation. Throughout the 1940s, her reputation grew further because of unstinting hard work: she wrote essays for money; she wrote in aid of charities. She wrote to pay for repairs to the house on Clarence Terrace, which was twice damaged by bombs during the war. Her output of short stories and non-fiction was prodigious, but she scarcely had time for novels. Solicited from all sides, she hired a secretary to deal with business correspondence. Secretarial help alone could not stem the tide of queries and demands. On 3 July 1946, Spencer Curtis Brown, Bowen's literary agent since 1927, advised her to direct all business, not just negotiations for books, through his office. Requests for articles, broadcasts, and adaptations, he proposed, could be handled by his staff. He played on Bowen's worries about sacrificing fiction-writing to energy-dispersing non-fiction:

I have been thinking more about your worries with editors and others who consistently approach you direct. As you know I am much opposed to any policy by which you would delay the writing of novels through undertaking a number of small commissions, either for magazines or for the B.B.C. Your standing with the public depends ultimately on your books, and the dispersal of time on small committments [sic] is I think, not only uneconomical financially, but a bad policy for you as a writer. Any editor will of course phone you up or write to you direct if possible, for they have a good idea that if they are sufficiently persistent you will in the end agree – if only to get rid of them. (HRC 11.2)

Agents in both London and New York, working tirelessly to place Bowen's essays, obtained top fees for her fiction and non-fiction. She in turn looked to Curtis Brown for more than literary guidance and interventions on her behalf; the agency occasionally advanced her money to pay taxes.

Notwithstanding her considerable output as an essayist, Bowen felt uneasy about the enduringness of her non-fiction. In a letter written to John Lehmann on 14 October 1950, she expressed concern about the uneven quality of her first volume of essays: "I am most awfully glad to know you enjoyed Collected Impressions – I had been tentative about publishing it, in the first place. It's unequal value, as a collection, I think; but there are one or two things in it I've been glad to preserve" (HRC John Lehmann Collection). Despite evidence to the contrary, Bowen persisted in believing that her essays and prefaces were inferior to her fiction. In her view, criticism remained subordinate to creativity. In an "Autobiographical Note" drafted in the late 1940s and revised in 1952, she denies her credentials as a critic: "I do not really consider myself a critic – I do not think, really, that a novelist *should* be a critic; but, by some sort of irresistible force, criticism seems to come almost every novelist's way. I write, at intervals, for the New Statesman, the Listener, Vogue, Harper's Bazaar; and do request articles, from time to time, for papers too diverse to enumerate" (HRC 1.5).

In the foreword to *Collected Impressions*, Bowen clarifies that "Notes on Writing a Novel" and some of her prefaces "put forward claims with which time has nothing to do" and therefore qualify as "serious work" (vi). In the same foreword, she expresses scepticism about novelists taking on the role of critics: "It might be argued that the habitual story-teller would do better not to enter the critical field at all" (v). Criticism, in the strict sense of the term, is a judgement upon the success or failure of a work of art. As Bowen asserts in *Afterthought*, criticism invites "reflectiveness" about writing: "One may not exactly know what one has (finally) written till one has finished it – and then only after a term of time" (9). As time passes, one's own writing becomes more and more strange, to the point that its unfamiliarity requires explanation. Criticism accounts for self-estrangements.

Bowen's pronouncements on fiction should not be undervalued, for they sum up modernist assumptions about character and plot on the one hand, and, on the other, Bowen's personal convictions about what she intends to do and what she has already done. She advocates that authors strive for freshness of expression. Clichés will not do. Describing plot, she resorts to metaphors of tautness, pressure, grip, as if inexorability were the desideratum of the novelist. If Bowen advises other writers how to proceed, she does so as a working writer who keeps in mind readers' expectations. In "Notes on Writing a Novel," she lays down a series of dicta about the speed of narration, the angle – both moral and visual – of narrative presentation, the relevance of events within the telling of a story. "It is the palpable presence of the alternatives that gives action interest," Bowen asserts (*Afterthought* 251). She fires off other aphorisms with a sniper's precision: "Speech is what the characters *do to each other*" (*Afterthought* 255). Locale affects events: "Nothing can happen nowhere" (*Afterthought* 253). Although her pronouncements are not usually so epigrammatic, Bowen feels compelled to defend the writer's strategic manœuvres with no margin for ambiguity. In this regard, the essays and critical writings provide invaluable commentary on the art of fiction.

The title of her first collection of essays, *Collected Impressions*, articulates one aspect of Bowen's aesthetic: the impression. Sensitive to atmospheres and places, she renders them visually, in terms of light and image. An impression is an insight or a glimpse, by necessity ephemeral. The strength of Bowen's writing follows from her ability to define, through gesture and mood, the undercurrents that motivate human interactions. In her journalistic essays, she stresses that she does not deliver factual information so much as record fleeting states of being. Each of the three newspaper reports filed about the 1946 Paris Peace Conference bears the subtitle "Some Impressions." A radio broadcast in 1948 is likewise called "Impressions of Czechoslovakia." The word returns in other contexts. In "Hungary," written in the autumn of 1948, she sets down "the impression of being in an occupied country, in which any genuine life was being lived surreptitiously" (HRC 6.2), even though the war has ended and no foreign regime has taken control of the country. Travel induces unsettling impressions. In "Ireland," she acknowledges that travellers "carry away a strange and sometimes disturbing blend of impressions" (92). The impression intrudes into consciousness. It disconcerts, and ought to.

In Bowen's sense of the term, an "impression" does not entail imprecision. The impression captures what cannot be fully acknowledged in the present. Other influences – invisible, unspoken – bear upon the passing impression. In wartime London, with every nerve stretched taut, she "received impressions of happening things; impressions that stored themselves up and acquired force without being analysed or considered" (*Collected Impressions* 52). Intuition marks the impression, a hunch that something not yet articulated within a scene remains to be understood. In her introduction to *Pride and Prejudice*, Bowen, recalling that Jane Austen's initial title for that book was "First [or, False] Impressions," remarks, "The subject, it must be remembered, of the entire story is the false, or misleading, nature of first impressions" (vii, xi). If an impression creates a margin of doubt, it also establishes the conditions for longing. One is left with a fleeting impression only when one wishes the impression had lasted longer, or had developed into more than an impression, as when Bowen as a young girl sees the violet, distant coast of France and yearns to go there. As she acknowledges in "The Idea of France," the impression yields to a welter of detail when Bowen crosses the English Channel. Second, third, and subsequent impressions correct the first. To collect one's impressions is, therefore, to compile one's judgements and to reckon their accuracy as intuitions or partial glimpses.

The impression has political implications. A witness to history, Bowen turns to the essay to convey firsthand impressions of upheavals in the twentieth century. Indeed, her non-fiction offers a profile of her political thinking as a series of impressions. Although Bowen is conservative by class and persuasion, other factors inflect and modify her conservatism. In the 1930s and 1940s, Isaiah Berlin, the liberal philosopher, figured among her closest friends. She had a long and intimate relation with Charles Ritchie, the Canadian diplomat and ambassador. The scion of a conservative family, Ritchie cagily guarded his political allegiances but made no bones about preferring Liberal Lester B. Pearson over Conservative John Diefenbaker as successive prime ministers in Canada (*Diplomatic Passport* 185). Conversation with Ritchie could not but have influenced Bowen's understanding of mid-century politics. According to Ritchie's diaries, he and Bowen spoke about everything from West German politics to the Suez Crisis and the role of the United Nations. She lived in a milieu of informed opinions. After the war, Bowen befriended the popular historian C. V. Wedgwood, who published extensively on the English civil war and Restoration. Not university-trained herself, Bowen was surrounded by professors and dons, including Maurice Bowra and David Cecil. Alan Cameron, Bowen's husband, served as Director of Education in Oxford, and later worked at the BBC. Her friendships, her reading, and her inherited prerogatives shaped her views on class and politics.

Hermione Lee, commenting on Bowen's convictions, notes that her critique of middle-class values never settled into complacency. When it comes to the English middle classes, Bowen "is the spy inside the gates" (Lee 225). As if in concentric circles, affiliations with the Anglo-Irish Ascendancy, Ireland, England, Europe, and, in the latter decades of her life, the United States complicate her political allegiances by degrees. In the first of these affiliations, Bowen sometimes acts as an apologist for Ireland and sometimes as a critic of Irish policy. The essays about Ireland – sardonic, fond, unsympathetic, explanatory – present that country by turns as a tourist destination and as an oppressed colony. According to Lee, Bowen's political position vis-à-vis Ireland falls within the Burkean tradition of "enlightened imperialism" (26). This characterisation does not do full justice to the contradictions that inhere in Bowen's stance. Living between English and Irish culture, she positioned herself as an outsider to both, as the rhetorical slippage between "we" to mean "the Irish" and "we" to mean "the English" betrays. Speaking in her Irish persona, which is to say with irony, Bowen asserts in "Portrait of a Woman Reading" that Ireland is frightfully dull, with not a story anywhere to be had in the endless farmhouses that dot the countryside: "One's better off doing what Sheridan does or what I try to do – swoop down on the English" (10).

By virtue of being an outsider, Bowen can indeed swoop down on the English. On the principle of fairness, she occasionally reverses tactics and swoops down on the Irish. Explaining Irish neutrality during the war to a dubious British readership, her political commentary preserves level-headedness without sacrificing nuance. She concedes that the Irish point of view is, in the true meaning of the word, insular: "On the whole, Eire's sequestration from Europe is (for her) the principal ill of her neutrality: it may go to create a national childishness, a lack of grasp on the general scheme of the world" ("Eire" 383). Bowen's awareness of being the last of a line colours her Anglo-Irishness; she was an only child and she had no children. She saw herself as a lone survivor of the Ascendancy class from which she sprang. A profound sense of obligation informs her essays about Ireland and about Bowen's Court as a big house: "Inherent in this way of life, as in all others, is responsibility; the sense of one's debt to society" ("Ireland Makes Irish" 217).

National politics aside, she sees an intimate correlation between public events and private lives. This principle holds true for Irish history as much as it holds true for international history. There is no history that is not a lived history. Maud Ellmann observes that Bowen's "fiction examines how world-historical events penetrate the shadows of private life, transforming the ways that people talk, shop, move, dress, work, love, and kill" (5). *The Shelbourne*, an account of a stately hotel in Dublin, illustrates the integration of public history with culture. Not just a quaint assessment of Irish social life, the book touches on crucial episodes in the history of the country – the Easter Uprising, the Troubles, the two world wars – in terms of enduring architecture. "Siege, shooting and military occupation had left their mark both outside and in," Bowen claims about the years of unrest in Dublin and its effects on the hotel (*Shelbourne* 146). History leaves its marks, and those marks tell a story. First and foremost, political history materialises as lived and personalised history.

More than any other historical event, the Second World War left a lasting imprint on Bowen's sensibility. As the stories in *The Demon Lover* (1945) and the novel *The Heat of the Day* (1949) attest, the war called out Bowen's creative powers. In her preface to *The Demon Lover*, she asserts that she saw war "more as a territory than as a page of history" (*Collected Impressions* 48). She does not mean that the war was an event outside history; rather, the war assumed immense proportions that had no edge and no end. In this regard, duty, guilt, shock, enmity, survival, disbelief, and heroism create political magnitude in her wartime writing. Her essays from the 1940s, including "Britain in Autumn" and "Calico Windows," document calamity with acute feeling. Life during the war was lived at a pitch of intensity. By the same token, that intensity quelled a full recognition of catastrophe. The war tore private lives apart and induced degrees of numbness. In the poignant essay "Opening up the House," survivors, stunned by six years of warfare, slowly awaken to "an eternity of loss and change" (75).

Bowen did not, however, cease to learn political lessons during the war. In "London, 1940," dislocated, bombed-out Londoners trade what information they have about devastated neighbourhoods and rough nights; across the ruins, they greet each other as survivors. A community forms around those who stay on in the city despite bombardments. In Bowen's opinion, a different kind of democracy emerges at the height of the war. In "Britain in Autumn," a draft version of "London, 1940," she writes, "We have almost stopped talking about Democracy because, for the first time, *we are a democracy*. We are more, we are almost a commune [. . .] But the thing goes deeper than this: we could not see as we do see it without feeling the force of a revolution in Britain that has already started and must accomplish itself. Bombs only mark the material end of things" (HRC 2.2). Bowen's comments about democracy emerge from a specific context. Because the government passed the Emergency Powers (Defence) Act in May 1940, democracy per se did not obtain in Great Britain during the war. Under martial law, as Clement Attlee told the nation on the radio, "Parliament has given to the Government full power to control all persons and property. There is no distinction between rich and poor, between worker and employer; between man and woman; the services and property of all must be at the disposal of the Government for the common task" (Attlee 1036). Attlee advocates "the common task," and Bowen glimpses a "commune" in the war effort. The priority given to national defence, even to the point of suspending civil law, creates equality, with the understanding that the government does not intend to abuse the powers that it has arrogated. While preparing "London, 1940," Bowen cancelled the passage about the democratic levelling that wartime fighting created. The censor, moreover, cut passages from the essay. Perhaps as a consequence of the censor's disapproval, Bowen moderated her apocalyptic tone; the direness of the situation had led her to false prophecies. The "people's war" did not create revolution, nor even the possibility of revolution. War simply rallied patriots to fight for the cause of democracy.

Believing in the cause of democracy, Bowen lived out her principles. Volunteering as an Air Raid Precautions warden, she participated directly in the war effort. Her wartime conception of the nation as a democracy verging on a commune derived in part from her work for the public good, with all the nationalist implications that such work entailed. Unlike other modernist writers who fled to Switzerland, or planned to commit suicide against a possible German invasion, or ranted madly on the radio, Bowen refused to surrender to futility. As she said during a radio interview in 1959, "Just as in an air raid, if you were a warden, which I was, you stump up and down the streets making a clatter with the boots you are wearing, knowing you can't prevent a bomb falling, but thinking, 'At any rate I'm taking part in this, I may be doing some good'" (HRC 2.3). Civic obligation determines her political outlook. She holds herself responsible for the public good. In this regard, her politics are not élitist. As Spencer Curtis Brown puts it, Bowen "saw this obligation in proportion to her duties imposed from outside whether by individuals or events, but the fulfilling of such outside duties did not, in her opinion, exempt her from her obligations to writing" (*Pictures and Conversations* xviii). No one, however, is obliged to write. For Bowen, writing webs the author into social relations. Writing is an assumption of obligation. Her non-fictional essays in particular manifest her sense of duty and allegiance. Writing, as a strategy of resistance to war, keeps alive democratic responsibilities.

In her postwar essays, Bowen constructs a passage to the future, which she views as worldly and pan-European, at least in its ideal incarnation. In "Autobiographical Note," Bowen recalls her prewar affiliation with Western Europe: "Now that the war is over and Europe 'open' again, I am filled, like almost everyone else, with an insatiable longing for travel" (HRC 1.5). Realising her wish, Bowen travelled extensively throughout Central Europe between 1946 and 1955, at a time when postwar austerities and restrictions kept most British citizens at home. These trips revealed to her the widening rifts of the Cold War. In 1946, she attended the Paris Peace Conference as a reporter for the *Cork Examiner*. Attuned to breaches of diplomacy during negotiations over frontiers and reparations, she hones in on the bullying tactics of the Russians; as she subsequently had reason to observe, the Paris Peace Conference was a trial run for Soviet tactics of stalling and arguing over procedure in the international arena.

While writing dispatches about the conference, Bowen may also have been gathering intelligence. Bowen never made a secret of being employed by the Ministry of Information in the early part of the war. She casually mentions her work for the government in various publicity notices, and articles in *Collected Impressions* are identified as Ministry of Information contributions. Critics have commented at length about these activities in 1940–2 (Bryant 98–104; Lee 149–50; Lane 5–9). Tax records, however, reveal that the Ministry of Information also paid Bowen between 1944 and 1947. In 1944–5, she earned £115 from the Ministry. The next year, she earned £117.12.0. At the end of her employment in 1946–7, she received a mere £21.3.0 (HRC 12.5–6). Whereas intelligence-gathering in 1940–2 took her to Eire, the nature of her work between 1944 and 1947 remains unspecified.

In multiple trips to the continent, Bowen gave public addresses on literature under the auspices of the British Council. She toured Austria, Hungary, Czechoslovakia, and West Germany, but she declined an invitation to Serbo-Croatia. In May 1954, the British Council invited her to lecture in South America. D. E. Noel-Paton, who issued the invitation, suggested a trip lasting "from two to three months" with the choice of countries left to Bowen: "It would take in as many of the countries in South America where we have representation as you would agree to visit. These countries are Brazil, Uruguay, Argentina, Chile, Peru and Columbia" (HRC 10.6). Bowen's prestige was such that she could pick and choose destinations. In a letter dated 4 January 1949 to Blanche Knopf, her publisher and friend, Bowen gives details about her travels:

I have, I know, been very bad about writing. The autumn seems to have gone by in a flash. My fortnight in Hungary was exceedingly interesting and I was fascinated by the country and the people. The Iron Curtain atmosphere was so much more to be felt at some times than at others: I think I resented most of all the restraint on people so naturally spontaneous. They are so handsome and one feels should be so naturally happy: even under the repressiveness of the present rule, so many graces and courtesies have remained. Although I highly esteemed the Czechs, I must say I really *enjoyed* meeting the Hungarians – quite a distinction that! I saw quite a fair amount of the country during one long weekend drive, but otherwise was in Budapest. (HRC Knopf Collection 685.14)

A cluster of essays recounts these European excursions: "Prague and the Crisis," "Hungary," and "Without Coffee, Cigarettes, or Feeling." Narrated with a novelist's eye for atmosphere and dialogue, these pieces grapple with the complexities of the Cold War. Talking with citizens and officials, Bowen hopes that rationality will prevail. She puts faith in students, who might engineer a workable future notwithstanding Soviet interference. In Bowen's view, the youth of Europe possess the energy and will to imagine a better political life for themselves. In these essays, she views nationalism with suspicion while recognizing that British nationalism constitutes resistance during the Cold War, just as it had during the Second World War. At the same time, she understands that cooperation could have a positive impact on the political future of Europe.

To lecture for the British Council was tacitly to avow that the Cold War could be won through culture. Discussing literature written in English with European audiences, Bowen encouraged cultural exchange and contact among nations. In return, she reported to British audiences her sense of what was happening on the continent. In the broadcast entitled "Impressions of Czechoslovakia," Bowen extols the "vivid examples of social and cultural life," with emphasis on the "modern [Czech] housing and industrial buildings [. . .] The organisation of public libraries, and their obvious popularity with a great host of readers, particularly impressed me" (HRC 2.3). In an undated letter to Isaiah Berlin, almost certainly posted in 1948, Bowen mentions that she "spoke to a newly-formed society [in Salzburg], and a beautiful dignified man came up afterwards in tears & said, 'This is the first evening of true culture we have had since 1937.' So I burst into tears too. As a matter of fact I spent much of my 3 weeks in Central Europe in floods of tears" (MSS Berlin 245). These floods may be tears of grief that so much was lost during the war, or tears of relief that some vestiges of culture survived the war. The scene recalls the Viennese audience in *The Third Man* who show up to hear a lecture by a Henry James-like novelist. As in Greene's novella, Bowen thought that the best chance for cultural liberty in Austria, and by extension political freedom, lay with Britain.

The theme of maintaining contact with European countries sounds throughout the postwar essays. In "Hungary," Bowen sorts information about the relation of Central Europe to England:

> It was clear to me that, if only for commercial reasons, the present Hungarian government is anxious that knowledge of the English language should not lapse. I gather that, therefore, little intimidation against attendance at English lectures exists – provided that the lecturer is ideologically harmless. As against that, it obviously required courage for any Hungarian to have *social* contact with any British person. It was surprising, considering the system of espionage and notation of every individual's movements, how many Hungarians did take the initiative where I was concerned – or, at least, accept invitations to meet me. (HRC 6.2)

Observing the "incalculable pressure" and nerves "near the breaking-point" that Hungarians experience, Bowen concludes that the average person in Budapest longs to retain contact with the West: "I may be pardoned for speaking intuitively, even sentimentally, when I say that I felt that 'Do not let us go!' was the prevailing Hungarian attitude. It was conveyed to me not only in my direct contacts with people but in small ways, by strangers" (HRC 6.2). After commenting on propaganda and the restructuring of the universities, which effectively halted education, Bowen concludes that "The lessening of any cultural ties that we *can* maintain with Hungary would be, I am convinced, not only a blunder but a betrayal" (HRC 6.2).

In her essays about Central Europe, Bowen wonders what access Hungarian, Czech, or German students have to books and how much they allow themselves to be influenced by ideas from other nations. Books, she supposes, have political and humanising efficacy. Many of the essays in this volume dwell on the nature of reading: who reads, for what reason, under what circumstances. Reading increased during the Second World War; according to Cyril Connolly in a *Horizon* editorial in late 1949, "there was very little to do in the blackout but read" (Connolly 212). In *The Heat of the Day*, Stella Rodney reads while the anti-aircraft guns thud in the background. Reading informs, even as it engages with political realities.

Bowen's essays sustain a concentrated questioning of books and reading. Once read, a book guides the reader to unsuspected realms of experience. Bowen repeatedly conjures reality from books. Before she travels to France, she imagines what the country must be like by reading *Madame Bovary*. So, too, before she moves to London, she reads about the city in books. "Nothing made full sense to me that was not in print," Bowen claims about her childhood and her habit of calibrating life as a sub-species of literature ("Coming to London" 77). Bowen, who translated passages from Marcel Proust's *Le Temps retrouvé* in the early 1930s, adapts his insight that real life merely occupies worlds represented in literature: "La vraie vie, la vie enfin découverte et éclaircie, la seule vie par conséquent pleinement vécue, c'est la littérature" (202). In C. K. Scott Moncrieff's translation of this passage, emphasis falls on the laying bare of reality in literature, rather than its imaginative enchantments: "Real life, life at last laid bare and illuminated – the only life in consequence which can be said to be really lived – is literature" (931). But the passage also means that life is fully lived through literature. Literature touches the secret well-springs of existence; literature irradiates and enhances life. Bowen abides by the principle that literature precedes life, while adding a twist to that principle. Writing, in whatever form, traces possibilities; alternative realities emerge from the imagined worlds found in books. Books conjure impressions in relation to which people live their lives. Like writing, reading is a mode of living.

Books have complex histories that encompass their writing, their production, their scarcity, their desecration, and their endurance. A book is an object, a "thing-in-itself," as she notes in "Alfred Knopf" (HRC 1.2). The physical qualities of covers and the texture of paper compel readers to take up books. "The format itself, fawn-grey binding indented prettily with a gilt pattern, nice-looking thick paper and large print, was promising and beguiling," she claims about E. M. Forster's *The Celestial Omnibus*, which she discovered as a schoolgirl ("A Passage to E. M. Forster" 1). Although the book has a material existence, that existence yields to intangible orders of meaning. In a valise in her aunt's attic, Bowen finds *Howards End* with two "bedfellows," volumes of poetry by Walt Whitman and W. E. Henley ("A Passage to E. M. Forster" 2). In this regard, Bowen's many introductions to others' books – by Rose Macaulay, John Ruskin, William Sansom, Nigel Kneale, Sheridan Le Fanu, Jane Austen, Angela Thirkell – describe first impressions and re-discoveries over time. Angela Thirkell's novels remind her of "the atmosphere, manners, morals, conversational idiom and general outlook on life of the early 1930s in England," as she claims in the introduction to *An Angela Thirkell Omnibus* (viii). Avenues to the past, books catalyse the imagination. More than that, they document culture and its transformation.

The war radically altered book culture. Libraries disappeared in the blitz. Paper rationing slowed book production nearly to a halt. In "Opening up the House," Bowen uses a book as a metaphor for the hiatus in time inflicted by war. Those who return in 1945 to houses evacuated five or six years earlier discover the strangeness of habitats once familiar: "The marker waits in the half-read book – a blade of grass of the summer of 1939" ("Opening Up the House" 75). The book, with a blade of grass tucked in its pages, embodies broken-off time, the time of reading. In a variation on this motif in "Calico Windows," a sofa leg, blasted off during an air-raid, wedges open the pages of a book. As physical objects, books attest to a history of interruption and wreckage. After years of global conflict, who will resume interrupted reading? Has the anonymous reader survived the war? Some interruptions may be so complete that a return to the marked page and forgotten story is impossible; life cannot pick up where it left off. "Nothing undoes the years," Bowen mourns in "Opening up the House" (75). No matter how they help people to live, books offer only the slenderest barricade against catastrophe. On the other hand, after the disarray that war has imposed on all aspects of civilian life, books may be the only bridge back to 1939.

Bowen does not advocate reading books neutrally or nostalgically. She has a firm conviction of the pastness of the past. Like Proust, from whom she learned a great deal, Bowen's theme is time, and more particularly the penalties that time exacts. Time regained is always time transformed. Books embody time – the time of Stella's reading and listening to guns – but that time is not always accessible. "Books offer illimitable wealth," Bowen writes in "Mental Annuity," but she admits that books do not invariably find adequate readers: "A difficulty of reading is not only selection but continuity – disjected fragments of literature, like torn pages flapping around in a draughty attic, may settle to nothing within one, so go to waste" (109).

The essays in this volume have been brought down from the attic, so to speak. After decades of going unread, they need not go to waste. On the contrary, Bowen's essays retain vitality because of their perceptiveness and range. They assume their proper place alongside T. S. Eliot's, Virginia Woolf's, and George Orwell's nonfiction. Like those other modernists, Bowen cuts a broad swath through key events in the cultural life of the twentieth century. At the same time, her commentary – engaged, penetrating, alert to general ideas – has a great deal in common with essays by Cyril Connolly, V. S. Pritchett, Angus Wilson, and Doris Lessing. Observing the disappearance of reticence and the rise of the teenager, she takes social changes in her stride. No matter what the subject, curiosity never deserts her. As a young girl, Bowen associated writing with grown-ups. Continuing to write is her way of growing up, of behaving responsibly towards the world. Wise and provocative, her essays provide reports from the middle of the twentieth century about the impact of war, the state of literature, and the inevitable passage to the future.

Editorial Practices

I have arranged Bowen's essays thematically and, whenever possible, chronologically. "Modern Lighting," Bowen's first published essay, stands at the head of the volume; "The Thread of Dreams," her last-known essay, provides a conclusion. Within sections, the arrangement is also, by and large, chronological. Certain juxtapositions create agreeable surprises and continuities. When feasible, I have devised section titles that resemble Bowen's – concrete nouns. In the present volume, I have not included broadcasts or essays based on public addresses. Nor did I include Bowen's autobiographical writings, newspaper questionnaires, or promotional blurbs for books. She wrote several descriptions of *The Heat of the Day*, for instance, which express her intentions, but are of interest to the specialist rather than the general reader. Several weaker essays, such as "For the Feminine Shopper," a 1956 guide to London shops, have also been omitted.

Apparently Bowen did not clip and save published copies of her articles, for none appears among the papers that she sold to the Harry Ransom Center at the University of Texas at Austin in 1964. She did keep carbon copies, often with handwritten emendations that can be compared to the published text. Between the typescript and published text, she sometimes, but not always, made further revisions. Whenever possible, I use the published version of an essay as a base text and compare it against the draft.

When drafts differ fundamentally from published texts, I offer both. I include the initial draft text of impressions at the Paris Peace Conference along with the three newspaper articles because content changes significantly between unpublished and published versions. Similarly, "Britain in Autumn," although clearly part of the stemma for "London, 1940," possesses important information excised from the later version. In a similar case, "Disappointment," rejected by *Reader's Digest*, was reworked for publication in two magazines, one in the US and one in the UK. Although the subject matter remains consistent, the two texts are quite unlike each other.

Using the printed text as a base has many advantages, such as stability and clarity, but this procedure also has liabilities. Preparing texts for publication, magazine editors trim words to fit into column inches or add space breaks, often in the middle of an idea. An editor's house style can interfere with Bowen's prose. In some cases, I have eliminated inappropriate space breaks because they do not conform to Bowen's intentions, such as I can discern them. Titles and pull-quotes in the middle of text have likewise been excised on the grounds that they are editorial interventions, not authorial decisions. Most editors respected Bowen's prose enough not to tamper with it too much. One notable exception to this principle occurs in "By the Unapproachable Sea," which was severely chopped by an editor at the *Christian Science Monitor Magazine*. In this case, I have created a hybrid reading text that combines material from Bowen's draft with the published text. In all instances, I aim to create a sound reading text, rather than a definitive text with an exhaustive list of variants. To this end, notes at the end of the volume fall into one of two kinds: textual emendations and brief annotations. If a significant change occurs between draft and published text, I have added a note to that effect. I do not annotate familiar names, such as Virginia Woolf, James Joyce, Cyril Connolly, Graham Greene, or Aldous Huxley. If a name or French word comes up several times, I annotate it only once.

The greatest challenge in editing Bowen's prose is spelling and punctuation. Editors at various magazines routinely altered her dashes to semi-colons or full stops. Some of her commas should be full stops to avoid comma splices. I flag idiosyncratic or erroneous punctuation. Some editors deploy the Oxford, or serial, comma; others do not. Following Bowen's example, I accept both and have not imposed uniformity in this regard. Certain spellings are unorthodox. To maximise profits, Bowen published essays in the US and the UK. Publishing in both places, her spelling sometimes has a transatlantic nowhereness about it. Editors inevitably altered spelling to conform to American or British standards. To create a degree of uniformity, I have adopted British spelling; hence "realise" instead of "realize" and "labour" instead of "labor." Other spellings have been regularised, such as "halfway," which appears in different essays as "half way," "half-way," and "halfway." Maintaining a measure of consistency requires minor alterations to orthography. Hyphens vanish from "to-day" and "week-end" to become "today" and "weekend." Russian names, such as Chekhov, Turgenev, Tolstoy, and Gorky, appear in any number of spellings in base texts, so I have standardised them. Such changes – adding or removing commas and hyphens, regularising spelling – have been made silently unless a change creates ambiguity. I do not, however, alter words without making a note of the change and stating a reason for doing so. I cannot claim that perfect consistency has been achieved across this volume; nor, ultimately, do I think it desirable. Each essay has its own context and flair.

J'nan M. Sellery and William O. Harris's *Elizabeth Bowen: A Bibliography* is an indispensable guide to Bowen's publications, with a comprehensive list of prefaces, essays, and pamphlets. I used this annotated bibliography to locate the majority of Bowen's uncollected essays. As I amassed articles, I discovered others by serendipity. In May 2007, a Maryland bookdealer advertised a sale of first editions, five manuscript letters, and books and pamphlets to which Bowen had contributed. The detailed catalogue, posted online, alerted me to unknown items, including Bowen's introduction to *The ABC of Millinery* by Eva Ritcher. On another occasion, the introduction to Rose Macaulay's *Staying with Relations* popped up in the British Library catalogue during a basic search of Bowen's works. Searching a database in February 2008, I stumbled upon the late essay, "Mirrors Are Magic," in *House and Garden*. In March 2008, when I thought my labours more or less finished, I spent a day scanning *Homes and Gardens* at the Library and Archives Canada in Ottawa. I was searching for "Outrageous Ladies," which, I conjectured, had been published in that magazine. Torn between curiosity and frustration at not finding that essay, I paged through wartime issues of *Homes and Gardens*. My efforts paid off, for I haphazardly found "The Christmas Toast is 'Home!'" None of these pieces is listed in Sellery and Harris's thorough bibliography. Similar cases are mentioned in the endnotes. I point out omissions from that bibliography in the spirit of collaboration, as an extension of Sellery and Harris's exemplary work.

If serendipity has its benefits, so does sleuthing. Bowen's business correspondence at the Harry Ransom Center provides details about the dates that articles were written and the magazines or newspapers in which Bowen placed essays. For instance, Sellery and Harris note that the typescripts for three essays about the Paris Peace Conference in 1946 are in the archives, but they do not give publication information for those articles. Bowen's business correspondence furnished me with clues about the venue of publication. In a letter dated 6 August 1946, Alan Cameron, answering a letter on his wife's behalf, mentions that she was "in Paris writing on the Peace Conference" (HRC 10.5). Tantalising as such a clue might be, it does not specify where she published her articles. In a BBC radio broadcast on 11 September 1959, she divulged that information under persistent questioning from a querulous interviewer: "I was writing in this case these three articles for the *Cork Examiner* for the readers in the South of Ireland who take in this far-reaching and important and fair-minded magazine. I wrote for it, since it stood for a certain standard of integrity and accuracy" (HRC 2.3). Knowing the name of the newspaper, deducing that the articles appeared in late 1946, I ultimately tracked down the three essays in the paper copy of the *Cork Examiner* at the British Library newspaper depository at Colindale.

Not all clues in the business correspondence led to success. For example, letters between Bowen and the Curtis Brown offices in 1952 indicate that she accepted a commission from Mr. Connell, an editor at the *News Chronicle*, for an article "on the position, opportunities and place of women in the new reign that has just started" (HRC 11.3). She submitted the article under the title "THE QUEEN AND WOMEN TODAY" by 19 June 1952 (HRC 11.2). A secretary at Curtis Brown sent along the galleys for Bowen to correct on 17 July 1952: "I am enclosing herewith an uncorrected galley proof of the article you wrote for the News Chronicle Supplement. You will remember that you gave Mr. Connell permission to make a few alterations provided that you saw the article before it went to press" (HRC 11.2). Bowen returned the galleys the next day. Confident that I had pieced together a puzzle, I called up the microfilm of the *News Chronicle* at the Library of Congress in Washington, DC. I assumed Bowen's signed article was published in a July or August 1952 issue. It was not there. Widening my search, I paged through the *News Chronicle* for 1952 and 1953 – to no avail. It is possible that the article appeared, as the correspondence indicates, in a "supplement," rather than in the newspaper proper.

I remain optimistic that this article, along with others, will turn up in the course of time. I cannot in good faith pretend that this volume represents Bowen's "complete" uncollected essays. A work in progress, this volume enhances understanding of later British modernism, as well as Bowen's versatility as an essayist. As vital documents about the state of literary and world affairs in the middle of the twentieth century, these essays capture a moment – the 1940s and 1950s – that only now is coming into critical view.

LIGHT

Modern Lighting

All day – speaking for these islands – our tone of living is conditioned for us: rain-light, sunlight, penetrating fogginess, or a metallic sunlessness that lets nothing through. Windows admit these facts, mirrors record them; we modify them the little that we may. But past twilight, we can create circumstance. In the smaller visible world we enlarge personally. Living is less that affair of function we were forced to suspect, more an affair of aesthetics. Coming in, going out, sitting still, looking – all our little tentative touches upon the actual gain in deliberation. We can arrange our lighting. We work like sculptors upon these blocks of pregnant darkness rooms have become. We can control shadow: place, check, and tone light.[1] The response from a light-switch, the bringing in of a candle is acute, personal as a perception.

It comes, of course, from yet another of those literary recognitions. We have travelled – been carried – some way since "she lit all the lamps to give the room a festive appearance" and "the firelight had a cheerful glow." All the time, we permit those writers to sharpen perception for us to the foremost, most brittle pencil-point, upon which at the ever-expected, supreme personal crisis we should not dare to press. In this case, we have uncovered for exploitation that most profound, implicit sensitiveness of our childhood – to the *idea* of light. Light as a sinister energy, not the universal mild exposure of day. There was the lamp-lighter mystery, the taboo on matches, that response – with dread – to poetry: "Lead Kindly Light,"[2] "The Dong with the Luminous Nose";[3] that excitement, before the most homely approach, of light coming up through bannisters on a staircase wall, the L of a door widening.

Who – since Da Vinci's notebooks first made the thing explicit – first carried on to literature this exploitation of a particular sensitive-ness? It was in *Madame Bovary* with its recurrent *crépuscule* that I had my first literary sense of the Vinci-esque chiaroscuro. The peculiar horror of Emma Bovary's fight for emotional survival is that it seems to be carried on in a succession of cold Norman half-lights:

her domestic interior, woods, riverside, muffled hotel bedroom; the death-panic in those darkening fields. Conrad's chiaroscuro is remarkable: his chief power. In *Victory*, man and woman talk in a room "like a cage" from the shadows cast on the wall from a lantern set on the floor. The old merchant with his candle precedes Lord Jim down a chain of dark rooms stacked with polished furniture. Stevenson mastered the method: particularly, a moving candle tightens the mood of "Markheim."[4] Throughout the "Tales," Poe flourishes the method: those red window-panes, the moon grinning suddenly *through* the splitting house-walls. Proust's pressure upon one's nerves of his super-reality – first pleasurable, then almost agonising – works this way: that intolerable high-up Balbec[5] bed-room is glazed with sea-reflections. St. Loup's favoured restaurant casts out into the fog its squares of light. Swann has to explain to the Duchesse, with embarrassment, how his death may prevent him from going with her to Italy – in social summer half-light, before a ball. In just how deep a tone of dusk Albertine[6] played the pianola, we shall not forget . . . In *Wuthering Heights* firelight is demoniacal, like nursery firelight through a fevered night.

But genius and even very high talent transcend method, manner, to blunder, almost, upon these felicities. The best in writing today is its fine, rather humble craftsmanship, of which manner is at once the tool and the enemy. Writers need an intense guardedness, a *flair* for the first breath of decline or exhaustion equal only to the modiste's. Already, perhaps, the "usual" manner is beginning to be discarded. There may be a return to sheer narrative, the: "And then . . . and then . . ." the suspense-element, no pause to say: "And picture . . ." The appeal will be chiefly to the ear. Responses will become elementary. Firelight will, once more, signalise only the momentous return of the traveller out of the dark and rain.

Perhaps then we shall stage our lives less carefully . . . But meanwhile, this affectability of ours has been recognized commercially. The shops will nurse this fad, like other fads, with a certain tenderness. Electric candlesticks are delicate with shields, to turn light back against the panelling. Impenetrably ornate pendant bowls toss light up to the ceiling, away from the eyes. Quite out of date is the diffused mild rosiness in which the Edwardian ladies bared, to drawing-rooms, their unscorched shoulders, but the shops are now bright with secretive, pleated shades which can space a whole room out into coloured islands. And in these, or under, we appear as we would wish to appear and have our friends all "placed" to perfection. Only in the remoter English provinces, in Irish cities where we are naïve with dignity, does incandescence still blare unchecked and electricity frown boldly. And in the villa drawing-rooms of North Oxford light comes down steep, distending intellectual eyeballs, outraging a sense kept delicate for the faint relief of façades and silver outlines on the Cherwell trees. Powerful minds interlock, and meanwhile light drifts and trickles down on the moiré wallpaper.

The 1938 Academy: An Unprofessional View

The first impression received, on entering Burlington House at the end of this or of any other April, is one of vastness – or sheer extension – and polish. At no other time of year does the building seem either so large or so overbearingly full. Acres of glossy canvas wall the visitor in and stare him out at the same time. The magnitude of the exhibition, and a sense of the ant-like industry that has gone to supply it are for the first few minutes quite stupefying: they keep the visitor vacantly turning on one heel, thumbing his shut catalogue, wondering where and wondering how to start. (Either numbers are hypnotic or we are born obedient: almost everyone works round the rooms clockwise.) Given the bulk and prestige of its contents, a visit to the Academy must be more than a visit: it must be something in the nature of an attack – method is wanted for it, and reserves of vitality. To visit the Academy belligerently is sheer waste of moral force – it has kept going on, and it will continue – while to mount the Burlington House staircase in an state of enrageable sensibility is simply to martyrise oneself. If one wants to jeer, one might just as well jeer at home. One cannot get past the fact that the Royal Academy is an institution, a topic, a tradition, and that it still exercises some sort of power – four reasons why one should approach it with, at least, curiosity. What is all this *about*? "Real art"? This will have stood for art for those thousands of people who, before the hundred-and-seventieth exhibition closes, will have struggled through the congested rooms, glued to their catalogues, casting hopeful glances at the canvases that glitter above the crowds.

From the Private View on, the galleries will be fairly solidly packed with people from all over our country. This almost religious attendance at the Academy constitutes, one must feel, the nation's homage to art. It is the middle and upper-middle classes who have leisure to represent the nation, and there is no doubt that the prevailing level of the Academy is middle to upper-middle class. Not a picture is to be found on these walls that is either gross or sophisticated, that is not in some sense "kind," that does not either idealise middle-class life or show some sort of little implied joke. No picture is in any way disconcerting. The Academy represents the *rentier* point of view – that the purpose of art is to inspire, to elevate, to console, and to titivate leisured fancy. A picture should (apparently) either set up pleasant sensation or tell a story – ideally, do both. It should, also, flatter the private fantasies or nostalgias of the person who believes himself to be normal, either by reinforcing his own view of himself or by crystallising the moments he remembers with most pleasure and least guilt – sunset (at the end of a satisfactory day), bathing parties, childhood, or the innocent and romantic phases of love. The successful picture should feature objects or scenes with which the greatest number of people have happy associations (vases of flowers, bridges across rivers, lawns, horses, picturesque peasants, ladies in evening dress, Cornwall, Paris, Chelsea, children, agreeable weather, boats) or else direct the fancy down unambiguous paths.

"Fashion always had and always will have its day, but truth in all things only will last, and can only have just claims on posterity," is the text for this year's Academy, on the catalogue title-page.

Constable,[1] who had a right to, said this. Used, however, in this particular context, the statement becomes cryptic. Must we drag truth up? Or does the Academy, boldly, stand for fashion? It does, it is true, seem to make up in fashion – a rather peculiar, prinking, cautious fashion, like English dressing – for what it lacks in style. Almost all the more showy pictures have an *approved* look: they show a manner of vision which is acquired, and acquired because it seemed correct. Manner, manner of seeing, has been borrowed from the Dutch masters, the French impressionists, young negroes, punctilious Germans, even from English painters whose work is not seen here. Immense capability – for hardly a single picture in the Academy is not "well painted" – has been able to put this learnt, unoriginal vision to almost fatally good use: fatal because there is so little naïveté left. Only the naïve picture, the picture naïve in the great sense, gives one the feeling that something new has happened. Or that something important, however slightly important, has been added to life. It is saddening, it brings one within reach of insanity, to look at hundreds of repetitive pictures, pictures palpably painted by formula. It is this brand of educated pretentiousness that does most to bring the Academy into disrepute. While April after April brings its fresh crop of old stuff, of brightly painted clichés, less should be said about "true" or "the truth." The English, like all plain people, fall peculiarly easy prey to affectation in forms they do not recognize.

1938 does not look like a bumper year. There are no problem pictures – except, possibly, Mr. Russell Flint's "In Their Own Home" (*Spain's Agony of Civil War*, 1936–1938), No. 117. This picture seems callous because it is not more callous: it does not evoke more than a mild sigh. Mr. Flint is much more at home with his pretty "Cynthia's Reflection," No. 132. The portraits have it, decidedly. All Mr. Eve's portraits stand out well: they are fresh and vigorous and look honest; they do at least magnetise the wandering eye. Quite insincere portraits are many, and negligible. Portrait painters, to live, must advertise, and one has got to see the necessity. Pictures in which fancy plays a more overt part are the other feature of the Academy, and here we enter a boggy tract. In this year's exhibition, there are from thirty to forty plain, decent landscapes which stand on their own feet, and which do at least command a feeble, fatigued respect. There are some detailed interiors of the sub-Dutch school, and vases of flowers that you can almost smell. (Miss Beatrice Bland's flowerpiece, No. 537, stands out as having more than verisimilitude.) But plain statement, which has its worth, is rare. In the greater part of the landscapes, the painters aim at the light that never was, and the effect is bogus. Only the major vision, the major imagination, ought to take liberties with tone and colour, the natural relation between light and things. The major imagination is lacking here, and the result is a long series of landscapes, of city scenes, of whirlpools, which should make drop-scenes for arty marionettes. Fancifulness without the force of imagination behind it is deadly: it seems to me that no one could leave the Academy for whatever destination, rural or urban, and not see the English scene for at least some hours with a perverted eye. Individually, few of these pictures are guilty of more than insipidity, but the cumulative effect of much falseness is bad.

The Royal Academy is, after all, an English institution: could not these fallals of foreign manner be dropped? A few pictures, not all of them prominent, relieve the eye with their matter-of-fact simplicity. Two of the old hands, Sir George Clausen[2] and Mr. A. J. Munnings,[3] continue to make felt an integrity of their own. And there is the Wilson Steer,[4] No. 38, just bought under the Chantrey Bequest.[5]

The picture of the year? This is a quite false, and alarming position, which only the Academy's puzzled and at the same time *arriviste* standard of values makes it possible for any picture to occupy. As it is, each year, one painter has his little day, like a May Queen. The most dignified, simple and urgent picture in this year's Academy is, probably, Mr. A. R. Thomson's "The Pilgrim Fathers Embarking at Plymouth," No. 751 – one of a series of four decorative panels for the Essex County Hall, on view in the Central Hall of Burlington House. Mr. Thomson's design, for design it is, has plainness, force and a proper sense of its function – one cannot say more. No. 751 may, however, have the disqualifications of its very qualities. The Academy picture of the year must make a bold but subtle bid for the passing eye, entice the fancy, hold the memory later and make stuff for discussion throughout the summer. Miss Louisa Hodgson's "The Birth of Venus," facing the door in one of the South Rooms dedicated to watercolours and tempera, has a quiet, almost stodgy ingeniousness – one could not call it audacity – and, less as a painting than as a successful flight of the fancy, commands an attention better pictures may miss. The South Rooms are retired: "The Birth of Venus" is likely to be discovered by those who are near the end of a weary round. This far from great picture has a kind of pretty triteness, a small assured smile which make it very refreshing after the convolutions of fancy witnessed elsewhere. It is a joke picture, but not facetious: it should reproduce well in a magazine. The smile it calls up, and gratitude for its simplicity, may make it the picture of the year. As far as I know, it has little technical interest, it is an Academy-goer's, not a painter's, picture, but it is nice and carried out with no fuss: at any rate look at it.

Christmas at Bowen's Court

My home in County Cork is lonely, even as places in Ireland go. In midwinter, it stands in a tract of silence – the hum of summer, the furious gales of autumn have subsided; through the stripped woods may be seen the empty distances and the mountains. No other season, here, might ever have been. Around Christmas, the sun rises late behind a group of elms some way up the lawn in front of the house, casting the shadows of the tree trunks in spokes, fanwise, toward the door. Seldom does snow fall: everything is shining and moist and still – as day goes on, the grasslands grazed by sheep take on a blond colour. The darkness of the mornings is atoned for by those long whitish glimmering evenings of the West.

The bald square light grey house is backed by a semi-circle of shallow woods; behind rise the Ballyhoura mountains. The outlook in front is clear, and on fine days sunny. The limestone of which the house is built was quarried nearby; high up under the roof is incised the date, 1775. Here, since then, my family in unbroken succession have celebrated their Christmases: settlers turned farming squires, they seldom went from home. They made life here, living what they had made. Now it comes to my own day, without anything having greatly changed – some trees have grown to majestic height, others have fallen; indoors the rooms have weathered under the force of daylight coming in for so many years through so many windows. This keeping of everything as it was is due neither to piety nor to taste: the Bowens have never been rich enough to be drastic: any new things brought in have so quickly faded as to be indistinguishable from what was there before.

It is at Christmas that the place looks oldest: its bony understructure stands out. The accumulated character of the house seems as inevitable as the lie of the land. All who have ever lived here are to be felt.

It is not, however, in order to spend Christmas with my ancestors that I return here each year from London. A journey through the cold winter skies needs a warmer motive: instinct, not sentiment, brings me home.

Bowen's Court is fifty-five miles from Shannon Airport. The first of Ireland on which I set foot, each time, is that glaring no-place of runways, hut buildings, transatlantic airliners refuelling – alongside those, our small Aer Lingus car taxis with confidence into place. All airports are so alike that, at the minute of landing, one might be anywhere – then, the eyes turn to the Clare hills in the distance; the lungs draw in the first soft breath of Irish winter air from the river flatlands. The track leading from Shannon into the country is a hard white ribbon, still too like a runway: my car races, as though to be clear of something. Not till one makes the junction with the ancient Limerick–Ennis road are the neutralising tensity of the journey, and, still more, the last of the nerve-gripping tentacles of London quite shaken off.

From now on reappear landmarks – the hogbacked bridge, the

spectacular ruined castle, the crossroads with the lemon-coloured inn. Afternoon is mirrored in the glassy curves of the river Fergus; other glints of water thread through the landscape; blue-brown horizons melt off into the sky. Hedges, cutting all this from sight, rise: I wind down the window to smell the fern-rot. Skeleton leaves have gummed themselves to the tarmac; split beech-husks crackle under the tires. A sheepdog leaps over a gate, attempting to head the car. Yes, this is Ireland, though not yet County Cork.

My route home crosses Limerick city. Christmas, now close at hand, has intoxicated, congested the lengthy streets. Autos nose their way on a sustained note from the horn; carts abruptly back out of alleys; buses slither and grind. Country people for miles around have surged into town. The tallness of the shabby Georgian houses, which have known grand days, sets up premature dusk, into which blazes the incoherent splendour of shop displays. Few are Limerick shops which do not stock everything: at this season, all things burst into view, with an overlay of attractive "novelties."

Onward from Kilmallock, my road home runs through the Ballyhoura mountains. Evening slips up their flanks as they unfold: a moon may be seen in the still translucent sky. A ridge of rock in the road announces, by an unavoidable bump, that one is crossing the boundary into County Cork. At the hour when I drive up to Bowen's Court, glimmers are still caught in the bare trees and reflected in the panes of the windows. A few rooks circle.

To speak of the house as awaiting one would be untrue – by coming back, one no more than rejoins oneself to an existence which is absolutely, tranquilly and timelessly independent of any one person. The effect of this is balm – the sense of fret, of crisis which one has come to associate with one's own identity slips away. In that moment, one becomes simply another wanderer back for Christmas. As for Christmas, it has already fully taken possession. To this, the Festival, the house does defer, as it does to no individual son or daughter. An august, additional presence is to be felt as I walk from one to another of the firelit rooms.

In London I look on Christmas as an ordeal. Some have called it a racket. In town we live on our nerves, dissect our feelings, know too much – and, at the same time, nothing. Here the mood waits, with its priority over all other feeling. Nor can it be called a mood, for it is outside oneself and thereby commands one. It has authority; it is racial, primal, mysterious and compelling. In so far as Bowen's Court like a vessel contains Christmas, it does so by virtue of being part of Ireland: the natural pulse of the country beats in its rooms, surrounding influences flow through it. One is aware, for one thing, of the ancient Christianity inherent in her very rocks and earth. Small ruined ivy-bound chapels alone in fields or on lake islands, destroyed but still sacred abbeys beside the rivers, continue to send out something.

From Bowen's Court, I hear the dogs in the distance barking. I hear the countryfolk who live "out behind" making their late way home through my woods – and sometimes a plane above the clouds droning its way in or out of Shannon. But I am to hear this only when I open a window and lean out, alone for a moment, to breathe the night air. For by now my house is also crowded and full of voices.

My grandfather had ten children and kept much company. He read prayers, on Sundays and feasts of the Church, at the billiard table which was in his day the principal feature of the hall, with the portraits of his (and my) more rakish and scatty Georgian forebears looking down quizzically. He wore a fine Victorian beard and was so masterful in his carving of the turkey, or possibly pair of turkeys, that all around the rest of the Christmas table there was an awe-struck hush. The diningroom, deeply curtained, was massive with sideboards, dotted with decanters, ornate with silver. The table could be extended to any length and had an equipment of twenty-four chairs – few of which, at Christmas, my grandfather expected to see unoccupied. Subsidiary relatives were bidden; respectful neighbours also could claim a place. Before his time the Bowens were more carelessly arrogant and more nonchalant, certainly gayer, perhaps happier: he inherited from them many acres in the counties of Tipperary and Cork.

Shorn of aunts and uncles, myself childless, and with my few Bowen cousins living across the sea, I am happy in my inherited neighbours. These, in default of other ties, have become my family. We have the same traditions, come of the same stock. At Christmas, the sociable pattern of the countryside repeats itself in my intercourse with their houses. In the late afternoon, we keep up a to-and-fro along white high-hedged damply glimmering roads. At nights, my car's headlights rake the dark of their avenues, or their cars' headlights rake the dark of mine. Together we are not casual: Christmas stylises everything with a light, sure touch of the ceremonial. In Ireland, however, ceremony, together with the magic of an occasion, exalts good spirits rather than constrains them. We are by bread rhetorical. We drink to the season, each other and the regretted dead. We drink – in fire-tinged rooms, strewn with dogs and jammed with obsolete furniture – out of hilarity, not in pursuit of it: tongues are unleashed before the glass is set to the lips.

Christmas Eve also brings more quiet, preparatory ceremonies to Bowen's Court. Some are generic to all homes, some special to here. The decoration, with holly and other foliage, of the pale blue inside of our Protestant church occupies the morning, the parcelling and delivery of presents to children and very old friends the afternoon. Beggars, whose status with us is almost sacred, come one by one up the steps to stand at the door. Many but not all of them are women: stately, draped in their rusty black shawls they bless the house before and after receiving alms. The Holy Saints, we hope, do indeed not fail to look down. The crux, toward the close of the day, is the installation by me of the Christmas candle – of scarlet, jade green, yellow or pink wax. Designed to burn from tonight until the Feast of the Kings, the candle is some twenty-four inches high and moreover of a circumference which forbids it to fit into the socket of any candlestick. I can only wedge it upright into an alabaster vase brought back by my grandfather from his Italian honeymoon.

The candle, having been lit, burns in a book-darkened corner of the library, consecrating into a nameless altar the card table upon which it stands. Its fellows are in every home at my gate. Slowly, with the coming and passing of Christmas Day, it diminishes, shedding coloured grease over the whorls of the alabaster – sometimes its flame swerves, as though caught by a breath. This ever-burning, ever-sinking candle becomes a timepiece: the dear season is not after all what it seems to be, an eternity.

Outdoors, however, time seems to have come to a shining standstill. The moss on the trees brightens to emerald; no shadow lengthens. This is the noon of winter – the fields smile, the mountains are pink in the sun. The bell from the hill has ceased; for minutes together there is no sound, no sound. The postman comes slowly up the avenue.

The Light in the Dark

The idea of Christmas is like a note struck on glass – long ago and forever. For each of us, this is the earliest memory of the soul. Day-to-day existence, as it goes on, drowns so much in its clamour, deadens so many echoes – but never this. Behind our busy thoughts and distracted senses remains a silence in which, again each year, the sweet resounding ring of the note is heard. We have expected Christmas, almost without knowing – wherever we are, wherever we turn, it claims us. The Holy Night links up all childhoods; we return to our own – to the first music, the first pictures, the first innocent and mysterious thrill and stir. Within the folds of the darkness, something has happened; even the cities know it, and the winter country seems to hold its breath. Once more we have the vision of wide night snow, of the shepherds listening and looking up into air rustling with wings of singing angels, and the Star in the blue of the frosty firmament. This is a time when magic joins hands with holiness. The dear, silly, gaudy symbolism of Christmas cards stems from race-myths and ancient midwinter rites. We inherit this feast from out of the dark of time before Christ was born – mankind sought it, from some primitive need.

There is the necessity to keep something burning – yes, and to make it shine afar. December is the year's midnight;[1] only the little flames of the votive candles show man to man. This reaching out, this signalling through the dark, is for something more than the communication of fears and loneliness; man joins man so that, together, they may lift up their hearts. Never has being human – that is, human only – been quite enough; from the first there has been our need for the miracle. As creatures, we are formed to adore, and marvel. In answer we have been given Christmas.

A ray falls on the crèche – on the bowed head of the Madonna, the white locks of St. Joseph, the upraised hands of the Child. Celestially lighted, the group of three is at the same time softly lapped by shadows; they are on earth. Among the straw of the manger, legend says, last summer's little wild flowers flower again. Half in the reflection of this glow, half in warm tawny gloom stand the ox and ass; we feel the rude strength of the stable roof-beams, over which brood angels. Mary's mantle, having gleamed so blue, also spreads its hems on the humble floor. Such is the scene of the miracle – is it not, also, the miracle of the scene that supernatural and natural should so sublimely merge? What is illuminated as we gaze, is the whole of the tender solemnity of life.

From the crèche light travels, resting on all familiar, domestic things; this is one gift of Christmas – a sort of vision. Now, we perceive the especial dearness of what is dear to us – home, faces, belongings, memories, ties. It is as though mists, of fatigue, of habit, cleared from between ourselves and that which we have and love. "On Christmas Eve," I thought, as a child, "even the furniture looks different!" The chests and cupboards, tables and chairs of my nursery shed on me, possibly, no more than the good nature which was in them always; I simply was more open to it that night. Something truer than fancy, less false than sentiment, makes us find rooms and people, around Christmastime, enchantedly kind – flowers smell sweeter; fires burn brighter; harmony appears in the pattern around us; the very taste-nerves quicken; there is a particular spontaneity about laughter. All this is blessed – has been so since the Star first halted over a roof.

Here is a season which sets a time of its own, finds its own language – the imagery of the calendar and the card.

Each of us, probably, has in mind one ideal and absolute of the Christmas card, as received in childhood. My own taste (date around 1910) is this – I behold a cottage gable in deep, dusky silhouette against an expiring gleam of sunset, one window lit; smoke goes up from the chimney. To this, a woodman returning, footprint by footprint, across the foreground snow; all around stretch white wastes, the bare trees are dark. How it glows and glows through that one small window – core of the world, magnet to man, the home! Towards it, the coach lurches among the drifts, the cravatted rider whips up his horse, the red-mittened children drag their laden sledge, the spotted dog lollops, the cat leads her train of kittens, the crinolined lady picks her delicate way. All Christmas-card-land creatures have the same destination. My woodman's cottage, crouched in smouldering evening, remains for me forever the symbol-scene – no better picture, before or since, has so fixed for me that light in the falling dark; or, by contrast, the elemental and daunting loneliness of the Elsewhere.

That sense of the Elsewhere, and of those straying in it, can but encircle Christmas, if one has any heart.

There are those whom Christmas touches only by its bitter meaninglessness to them – for this is a season to which natural indifference is impossible; those who dread or hate it shrink from its power. And – multiplied by the catastrophes of the world there are the derelict, the placeless; those who are where they are under duress, or who are where they find themselves by sheer bleak fortuity, without ties or love. Of these many, how few can be comforted – at least concretely; the practical reach and scope of our giving, in view of this trouble, can but seem poor and small. We *can*, only, humbly, keep these unknown in mind – which is to say, in imagination. The Child was born of his travel-wearied Mother, in a stable because there was no room at the inn. Is not this a time to remember the crowded-out ones? Now is it, at Christmas, when we feel to the full the happiest implication of being human, that the sense of all other humanity most insistently presses against our doors and windows. To meet it, we send out into the dark some thought – however groping, vague, and unformulated. Who is to say, at this season, what mystic circuit may set itself up between man and man?

At Christmas, no house is childless. Up to the surface wells a forgotten capacity for simplicity, an aptitude and eagerness for delight. The most elderly fingers tremble with expectation as they pluck at knots of tinsel ribbon; wrappings disclose "surprises" which send a flush up cheeks. The real children wake earlier – that is the only difference! Otherwise, as the day goes on, we old and young find ourselves all made equal, elated and solemn by ceremonial; this, in the home, it is which serves to lift the day up and shape its unique course. We celebrate, dazzled and drawn together; somehow more than ourselves. Who, what has joined our company? Today, tonight, the hours are deep and sounding, charged with the whole of time – with eternity. For indeed the truth of the Story appears most in that it has no end.

Ecstasy of the Eye

A dazzle of candles – a breath caught. The heart misses a beat: a moment, yet, too, an overflow into eternity. Rapture: what brought this rapture about? *What* has met the eye? What has leaped into view or, maybe, swum into sight slowly? A flamingo Venetian evening melting the lonely, glassy lagoons . . . Rainbow mist cast off into sunshine by playing fountains . . . The lofty and dusky light-lanced distances of the aisle within a cathedral or through a forest . . . "The moon," says the poem, "doth with delight look round her when the heavens are bare"[1] – so do we look round, moonlike, our landmarks nowhere, our small identities lost. First we are wholly startled, then wholly calm.

The eye's joy, and that joy's power. Denounced by the puritan. "Walk," *he* advocated, "with eyes cast down. See not; be not tempted to see!"[2] in his frightened soul lay his error, and his tragedy. Heaven draws near us, in this visual universe. Beauty burns clean.

Delight in seeing may have an inverse: anguish. I remember how, one summer, a hedge of roses, sky-high almost, all in bloom all at once, faced out on to a village street – and more, faced flame-on into the sunset. Cars drew to a stop, wandering passersby halted. There was stillness, a sense of satisfied glory. But also this: on the hedge hung an offertory box, with a placard above, which said, "Remember the Blind." . . . In through the slot tumbled our futile coins. The roses burned unbearably brighter, larger, as we turned away. *How* to make restitution? No means – on earth! . . . And, the beholding moment may bite with loneliness: lovers should be its sharers, but lovers (it may happen) may be apart. Instead, a stranger is namelessly at your side. Stranger? – no longer, though not a word may have passed: a bond has been sealed, though in this wide, anonymous, crowded world your two paths are never to cross again.

Ecstasy means being swept upward: airborne. But one cannot invoke that moment; it lies in wait, its arrivals are without reason. (One *can* stand stone-cold before a "beautiful" object.) Our travels are pilgrimages of hope; and, "Who knows?" we say, making ready for a party. Ecstasy's sources are *not* always ethereal: light, air, fire, and water. It takes off from chance revelations of human come-liness, human mystery – the turn of a head, a smile reflected fleetingly in a mirror, still more in water, a gesture at random, a figure's unknowing grace.

Most of all, there can be something visionary about happiness. In that instant nothing remains "ordinary." What had been everyday, familiar, stands out as though painted on glass with the sun behind. Then, therefore, wherever the eye lights there is delight. We have come to be like children at Christmas, and more than candles illuminates the tree.

New Waves of the Future

The beginning. Before that, what? Nothingness: earth "without form and void." The mighty Genesis story of the Creation, allegoric though science shows it to be, retains the hold that it had in infancy – it rings true to us, it has basic meaning. Light was what first broke on our newborn awareness; from then on, it stood for living and being. In itself a benevolence, it is as essential to us as the air we breathe – and as freely granted! We are light's children, expanding within it as plants do.

How light affects us, primitively sometimes, and sometimes subtly, we are beginning to learn. Our century is light-conscious, as was no other. We react more knowingly than our forefathers to light's dramas, variations, and possibilities. True, far back goes the association with Nature, with poetry, with romance – where would generations of lovers have been without the moon or the sunset, or children without the miracle of the rainbow? But we moderns love light with an extra ardour, seeking it out. We like best to go, to be, where it shines to the full. We construct our homes, so far as may be, of glass. And when, day ended, darkness blackens our windows, we make play with *lighting*: twentieth-century art which transforms rooms.

Yes, *let* there be light! For city-dwellers, the need approaches a thirst. The higher buildings soar, crowding the sky, the more closely they overhang and encompass us, the more precious becomes the bright element. There is a market for it, it costs money: penthouses, top-floor apartments are at a premium – many of us make do with reflected daylight, blue noon or the pinkness of sunset at one remove. Even so, the joy of it! Refracted downwards into our streets, light has something saving about it, like pure water. And it *does* enter; nothing can keep it out – slithering its way through venetian blinds, catching shop-front mirrors, striking through awnings, painting multicoloured traffic a shade more dazzlingly. And not least lovely, be it in city or country, is light's other gift to us: shadows.

Ever changing, shadows are light's language. It delights to cast them. Sharp, shapely, they accentuate light by contrast – the darker and clearer they are, the more burning the day. How dramatic their morning-to-evening movement, like the hands of a clock (before there were clocks man could measure time by them). Without them, light could be meaningless, overpowering! *Could* one inhabit, for long, a shadowless world? Unthinkable; as could be a quite soundless one . . . Valuing light, we instinctively learn how to live on terms with it. Designing our rooms, planning our gardens, we deal not in blank spaces and bald surfaces but in ornaments, objects, on which it may most effectively dwell, setting *them* off and enhancing itself. Scenically, we deliberately break light up, using columns, archways, screens of greenery, balustrades, pools. And may not light like us better for those devices? Outside cities, we seek as ideal sites for our homes those edging on woods: is not their demure half-dusk right background for a sun-soaked façade? Light, supreme in its contrasts, teaches a lesson. Playing tricks with it, we meet it at its own game. We have achieved a relationship. No fears . . .

Yet there were considerable fears, not so long ago. Dread of full daytime was prevalent with our great-grandparents. Primitive in origin, handed down to them, it was reinforced by Victorian genteelism. In refined homes, sun was Enemy No. 1. It ruined complexions, faded hangings and carpets, blistered enamel, and wilted plants. No lady exposed herself to its rays, and she took morbid precautions as to her parlour – shades lived almost permanently drawn down. Overclad gentlemen suffered like stranded fish, gasping; never did one abandon collar and tie! No child was let out of the house, for so much as a minute, without a sun hat. "Sunstroke" was the general, gripping obsession, even in quite temperate climes . . . Some of the safeguards against it were, one must say, pretty: instance, the parasol – ivory-handled, bedight with fringes or frills. Carried atilt by coquettish maidens or solemnly in the vertical by their chaperones, those little pagodas of taut silk shed a beguiling, colourful glow onto the delicate skins they sheltered. There were also arbors, entwined in jasmine or eglantine (and alas, also, running with earwigs) in whose fragrant if stuffy insides one could repose. Garden "walks," tunnels of darkest evergreen, cut out the peril of crossing an open lawn. Under shadiest trees one *might* sit out . . . Oh those timid summers!

Our boldness would seem revolutionary, and our sun-worship impious, to our forbears. We extend, hour-long, semi-naked, under that very orb from whose slightest glance they, muffled to the chin, fled. Are we (these newcomers) barbarians, they might wonder, or do they fancy themselves to be demigods? So entire has been the change in physical temperament that we of today might be another race, not merely another generation. We owe it to the Victorians to admit that science, by evolving the use of oils, art, by provisioning us with cosmetics, and fashion, by outlawing pink-and-whiteness in favour of olive-bronze, have aided, and eased the course of our "revolution." Not necessarily more daring, we are more fortunate: revelling, as we do, in the unabated glare of a day in summer, we enjoy an impunity undreamed of. Great-grandmother dared not, certainly.

This truth holds good with regard to homes, built for light, afloat in it when we wish. Gone are the drawn-down shades, the closed frowsty curtains. Yet, *her* frenzied solicitude for her parlour, her preservation of it by tomblike darkness, does merit less laughter and more sympathy. Costly crimsons could drain out to anaemic apricot, and huge roses on Brussels carpets be rendered ghostly. "Fadelessness" was a benefit unknown to her. Contemporary interiors suffer nothing. Day moves in and lives in them; they reflect it, colour it with their colours – fabrics, with all the glamour of the synthetic, some translucent as the glass of which they were spun, some sleek as the velvets they simulate, lose not an iota of their glow: it is imperishable. Underfoot, everlastingly vivid are the rugs . . . *She* dared not risk what she loved; we are risking nothing.

Physically, we of today *are* no less resistant to light than are belongings. But are we the more susceptible to it nervously? And does that sensitivity take toll, from time to time, of our psychic being? I think that possible. See how light conditions our moods, affects our energies, scores a zigzag across the charts of our temperaments. Good or bad light can make or unmake a day. Our obsession with "weather" is, fundamentally, concern as to weather's resulting light. Heavy rain is a manifest nuisance, but what depresses us is the miserable, dank extinction of everything, the unbroken gloom of lowering clouds. Certain dull days, heavily ominous, sky clamped down over the earth like a leaden lid, can be yet more demoralising than rainy ones. Snow at least sends up an uncanny glare of its own; and the moments before an electric storm, when black-purple, piling up on horizons, sets off trees, buildings, caught in last stabs of sunshine, have a kind of operatic excitement . . . Yes, our extreme light-consciousness cuts both ways – placing us at the mercy of meteorological changes and chances. For happiness, even for equanimity, we depend on Nature's caprices. That is, in the outdoor world.

The indoor, however, is in our power: home, our domain – and *its* lighting we do control. What resources we have, what alternatives. "Artificial light" once was the forbidding name for any amenity turned on after dark: today, evident "artificiality" is no more; subtle, artful naturalism has superseded it. Gaslight, or the earlier electricity, used to impact harshly on the rooms they revealed: now, soft, tidelike brightness laps on carpets and walls. Contemporary lighting is sympathetic: it can deepen calmness or heighten the party spirit. It does not dictate our moods; it expresses them, eloquently. It serves, it lends itself to, the domestic spirit: the lit lamp waiting by the waiting armchair – what a symbol of homecoming. The bent-down ray falling cleanly onto the page: what a reader's paradise. The tilted lampshade, letting glow gently lie on the smooth pillow: what invitation . . . Light chisels out for us[1] immortal and haunting images of our dearest moments.

And is creative in other ways – being able, for instance, to clothe a day-wearied room in evening illusion. It re-architects, adding further dimensions, new definitions. Here a diffused or there a directed brilliance kindles the atmosphere, adding a touch of "theatre," dramatising figures, flattering faces. Areas of shadow are gauzy veilings. Fleeting fingers of light move around: a bowlful of roses floats into ethereal view, then is lost again. Or a ceiling turns into a starry firmament. For a whole spectrum of wonders, thank electricity!

Yet . . . can anything better candles? Back they have come again, overflowing from the few there used to be on the dinner table into groves, groups, dozens that look like hundreds: triumphant, slender, twice as tall as they were (as though they had made growth since the last century), burning as though in their own honour. Without rival. So ever-living are they, and so timeless, they restore beauty to faces that knew it long ago. Now and then, a quiver of their pointed flames causes a vibration in the air round them – eagerness, the genius of all festivity . . . I quarrel with candles for one thing only; they set up a yearning in me for, also, firelight. Ah, *let* there be firelight, where there can be! Where there cannot, let me not think of it . . . And look, yet another talisman from the past: we reinstate the Victorian oil lamp. Amber and mellow, its radiance comes blandly forth from its frosted glass globe. This *is* domesticity: such a lamp is the occupant, by nature, of a circular central table, round which are gathered, sketching or stitching, a rosy, respectful family, while Papa reads aloud. May it steady us? Who knows? Welcome it back.

Light, light. Light, from whatever source! One great indoor playmate of light is the wall mirror, with its doubling trickery, its extensive power. Outdoors, the fit mate *and* playmate for light is water. Light likes pools, ponds, lakes, but is in love with rivers – their intricate skeiny currents, their falls and rapids, their dawdling pauses. But above all, fountains: impetuously springing up, up, up into light's embrace, casting inexhaustible plumes of dissolving spray . . . At Tivoli, above the Roman *campagna*, I watched an assembly of fountains in noon sunshine. That is the one time I have wept for joy.

PLACES

Britain in Autumn

It is an early October morning in Oxford Street, London. There is still the charred smell, the smell of dust, on what should be crystalline pure air. Sun, only just up, floods the now innocent sky, strikes the silver balloons and the intact building-tops. The whole stretch of Oxford Street, west to east, is empty, gleams like a floor and glitters with powdered glass. Down its distances, and away down its intersections, mists are unnaturally dense with a brown dust. And, along there, smoke is rising and melting from the shell of a store. At this corner where the burst gas main, flaring floors high, made a scene like hell in the night, you still think you feel heat. It is the silence that is the enormous thing – it appears to amaze the streets themselves. Oxford Street and some blocks of its intersections are roped off; there is no traffic; the men in the helmets say not a person may pass (but some do). Besides the high explosives that did the work we see, this quarter was, last night, seeded with time-bombs. So we are cleared, and wait for these to go off. This is the top of Oxford Street, near where it joins the corner of Hyde Park – like where Fifth Avenue joins the corner of Central Park.[1]

We people have come up out of the ground, or from the smashed blocks or places with time-bombs. We now see what we heard happen all through the night. In this corded-off silence we find ourselves on an island, which feels comic – please, when may we move? Standing, like risen dead unsure of their destination, in the mouths of shelters or doors of the smashed shops, we have nothing to do but smile or glance at each other, or at the sky, or yawn down the void streets . . . It has been a dirty night. The side has been ripped off one near block – the great sore gash is dusty, colourless, pale. (As bodies shed blood, buildings shed mousy dust.) Up there you see mirrors over the mantlepieces, shreds of carpet over the void. An A.R.P.[2] man, like a chamois, already scales the debris; we dirty-faced nomads look up at him. The charred taint is on everyone's lips and tongues. What we want is breakfast – bacon and eggs, coffee. We attempt little sorties – "Keep BACK, please! Keep OFF the street!" The hungry attempt smoking. "PLEASE – put that cigarette out! Main gone – gas everywhere – might send the whole place up!" Cigarettes are quickly trodden into the trodden glass. We continue to slouch in our cave-mouths; the sun goes steadily up. Some of us are dressed, others are not: pyjama-legs appear below overcoats. There are some Poles, who have lost everything all over again: in token of this they sit down, wherever they can. They are our elders in this, and we cannot help watching them. There are patently several pairs of disturbed lovers, making one think, "Oh yes how odd – love." There are squads of ageless "residents" from the tank-like[3] private hotels just off Oxford Street. There are the nomads of two or three nights ago who, having[4] been bombed out of somewhere else, pitched round here, to be bombed out again. There is the very old gentleman wrapped up in the blanket, who said two or three times, humbly, between the blasts in the night, "The thing is, I have outlived my generation" . . . We are none of us (except the Poles?) the very very poor: our predicament is not a great predicament. The lady otherwise dressed, in a fur coat, has hair in two stiff little grey plaits. She appeals round for hair pins: most of us have short hair – the pins are drawn for her from the Poles' heads. Girls step further into the light and look in pocket mirrors. "Gosh," they say. Two or three people have, somehow, begun walking when one time-bomb goes off at Marble Arch. The street puffs empty – more glass falls. Nobody got that – everyone laughs.

The effect of this is an unuttered morning hymn. It is a fine morning; we are alive.

This is the buoyant view of it – sane morning, the theatrical sense of safety, the let up.[5] We shall be due, at tonight's sirens, to feel our hearts tighten and sink again. Soon after black-out we keep that date with fear. The howling rambling over the darkness, the lurch of the barrage opening, the vile throb in the air. We *can* go underground – but for this to be any good you have to go very deep, and a number of us, for nervous or practical reasons, prefer not to. Our own "things," tables and chairs and lamps, give one kind of confidence to us who choose to stay in our paper rooms. But when the throb checks and deepens over the roof we must not think of what we looked at this morning – fuming glissades of rubble. No, these nights in October nowhere is nice. Where you stay is your own choice. How you feel is your own fight.

However many people have got together, each has, while the air whistles and things rock, his own deadly accesses of solitude. We can do much for each other, but not all. But between bombs we are all back where we were: the sense of community heightens; we all know, more or less, what has been happening to the others. The small-talk – absurd bubbles up from the deep – continues or people slump sideways and half asleep.[6] The thing learned about this kind of fear is that it is *not* cumulative; fear starts from scratch every time. Whereas, resistance is not only cumulative but more; it builds up a general fund. Before the end of one of these long raids you have felt something solid growing up in the room. That is why people get together. This is how we are getting to *like* each other. Once, if we "approved" of each other, it was enough.[7]

Autumn is a funny time to be bombed. It is the hopeful start of the home year. It is not a time when exalted feeling runs high. Autumn used to stop you sighing after the *Ewigkeit*[8] and make you feel how much you liked just *now*. You felt rooted deeply – and loved your roots. Even in Britain it was Thanksgiving time. Autumn used to be a protracted feast of Saint Cosy: the hearth meant a great deal, the moth-balls were shaken out of the fur coats, the children went back to school, the blue misty evenings drew in. In the country, in the city squares was the tang of weedfires, the brisk rustle of leaves being swept up. This year, leaves are swept up with a tinkle of glass in them. In autumn, wherever you live most touches the heart – and it is the worst time not to live anywhere. No, autumn is very anti-heroic. It is a time when you like your own place too well. Home *looks* so safe, you cannot believe it is not.

London feels all this this year, as she contracts round her wounds. Transport-stops, roped-off quarters and "dirty" nights, and the intensified love we each feel for our own place, have made her, these last weeks, a city of villages – almost of village communes.

Marylebone is my village. Friends who live outside it I think of but seldom see. They are sunk as deep as I am in their own new village life. We all have new friends: our neighbours. In Marylebone, shopping just before the black-out or hurrying home to batten down our hatches before the bombers begin to cross the sky, we wish each other Good Luck for the night. On one more of those mornings after the storm, we are out on our streets to find how everyone is. These mornings after the storm are great mornings for talk. Then, news comes filtering through from the rest of the villages. They say St. John's Wood took it harder than we . . . Camden Town is standing up to it well . . . Chelsea was hot again, they say . . . They say they brought "one" down on Paddington Green . . . Has anyone been lately to Piccadilly? . . . A Hampstead man was in here a minute ago, he said . . . A stop-press from Bloomsbury . . . God help Stepney, Bow . . . She's a Pimlico woman, her people are all there . . . How are they over in Battersea? . . . Somebody had a letter from Finsbury Park.

[excision][9] they turned us all out. This whole quarter was desolate, corded off because of time-bombs.[10] Dispersed, we Marylebone people camped about London in other villages that were kind but strange. It was then I made my bad move to Oxford Street, to be, after two nights, bombed out of there. When our time-bombs had been dealt with, they let us back. You can take it we were glad to be home again – and to find homes. How we talked in the shops! The fishmonger said he had seen me buying milk in Paddington. "Oh, were you there too?" (I had moved to a square in Paddington after they bombed us out of Oxford Street.) "No," he said, "I've got Finchley people. I was over in Paddington that day looking after a friend." The fishmonger, I and all Marylebone had detested our week of unwilling holiday. I had thought of my typewriter, he of dust gathering on his marble slabs – and of his fish in the "fridge," with the power off.

Regent's Park, in which I live, backs on Marylebone. [excision][11] Just inside the outer gates, a few yards from my door, an unexploded bomb makes a boil in the tarmac road. Round three sides of the Park stand cream-coloured Regency terraces of pillared theatrical beauty, built by Nash. Mine is the first to the left, just inside the outer gates – and no one else has come back to this terrace yet. (Perhaps they were not so homesick as we felt.) The terrace is E-shaped, set back behind a garden: in the silence under the rows of shutters a week's drift of dead leaves flitters up and down. Once a day, intrepid, the postman runs the barrier. (He is collecting shrapnel to make new shells: we give him any shrapnel we pick up.) The old iron outer gates, unused to shutting, stand so loose on their hinges that one can squeeze through. [excision][12] So, the deserted terraces ring round the shut park. Through the railings I see dahlias blazing their colour, rows of empty deck-chairs silting up with the dead leaves and water fowl, used to so much attention, moping along the long kerb to the lake. Once, one of those boys on bicycles got through and bicycled down the silence, whistling *It's a Hap, Hap, Happy Day*. The motif was taken up by the six soldiers inside the crater, digging out one bomb. [excision][13] We feel strongly about these men, who saved St. Paul's Cathedral. We feel far less strongly about St. Paul's.[14]

One change in Britain is that almost no one pities himself. The more that happens to you, the less you pity yourself. The reason for this is, we have no feeling to spare. The pity you spare for neighbours is terse, active, economic and gaunt. One thing absorbs us – anger. This anger varies over the face of Britain: I suppose you could make a chart of it. There is no acre on which it does not exist: in London and round the Dover coast its pressure is at the highest. This anger has lost us our native fat; the moral muscles stand out in everyone. And this anger acts like a weight in the base: it keeps us upright. Also, it keeps us calm. There is no question of your controlling such anger; such anger controls you. You do not spend anger like this in small change. It is the complete corrective for "big" talk. What I notice about the British now is that superficially we are more articulate. (Observe this new free flow of chattiness.) Fundamentally, we are more silent. Our talk is smaller than it has ever been; it acts as a cheerful nervous release; it does not attempt to connect with deep-down things. ("There now," you hear the lady say between two bomb-blasts in the pit of the night, "I left my coat and skirt at the cleaners: I wonder if I shall ever get it back.") By day, we neighbours discuss our own little angles on the nuisance – but its implications we store up. There occur some flare-ups of irritability, but as a general rule we are less *cross*. You notice this in queues, on buses, in shops. There is, on the whole, an unusual[15] nonchalance – what is the use of fussing about *that*? We need all we have: save everything, most of all nerves. There is, too, the factor of liking everyone better: everybody is *somebody*, for the first time. And you can't help feeling detachment. Those of us who have not yet lost stand to lose every time the siren howls. Collectively, the outcome of all this is a complete slump in the feeling of competition. In brief, since this Britain became a garrison she ceased to be a competitive society.

The implications of this disappearance of competition are going to be big – too big to discuss here. I am content to note its action on small things – dress, social habit, talk, etc. We must have been more motivated by competition than we had any idea. It worked in every one of our choices, from the choice of our leaders to the choice of our loves. Competition was the root of our snobbery – class-snobbery, beauty-snobbery, success-snobbery. In the last six months our British class-consciousness took a severe challenge, and has not stood up to it. The spell of the Old School Tie doesn't act any more. In leaders, as in neighbours, we look for only the one man – the man who has what it takes. Mr. Bevin (Minister of Labour), for instance, has first command of the air with his non-Etonian voice. The Etonian voice hasn't said what we had to hear . . . Meanwhile, we walk the streets shabby. Dress, for women, starts with the effort to clean the chardust from our faces and hair. We vary our turbans (cheap, slick and keeping the hair clean) and use double-strength lipstick to draw the eye from the smuts. Our get-up is no longer *at* anyone; it is a private flag. You must look as gay as you feel, which is remarkably gay. Those who don't like scratchy stockings go bare-legged. You see everywhere the trouser that comforts the ankle, the flat-heeled shoe for long pavement walks. You still see the flower worn in the buttonhole. If the lady in the fox cape and shadow stockings looks odd, you have to remember that may be all she has got. Yes, on the streets we do still look hard at each other, but the look has a different object. You look at eyes. You measure the guts and go. You look for the *someone* – how do *you* feel today? This exchange of searching, speechless, intimate looks between strangers goes on all over the place. But virtually, there are no strangers now. We all touch on the fundamentals we are not speaking about.

Small groups of people halt in front of a ruin. Maybe it is the new gash in your own village, maybe the gash you pass on your way to work. No, we do not take trips to look at damage; you see what you can see on your own route. Nothing is said because there is nothing to say. For the electric deep-down feeling the group makes a circuit, for a minute or two. But the people look at each other before moving apart. One day, when I was in front of a ruin, a French friend of mine, long living in London and in her A.R.P. warden's helmet now, came up to me. She said: "I am only afraid that the English may soon forget this; they are so good-natured." (She knew I was Irish: her race and mine are noted for the tenacious energy of bitter memories.) I looked round at the faces near us and said: "I think not." Her eyes followed mine and she said: "No. Perhaps not . . ."

We have almost stopped talking about Democracy because, for the first time, *we are* a democracy.[16] We are more, we are almost a commune. It is true that what we see, from day to day, acts as a leveller. All destructions make the same grey mess; rich homes, poor homes, the big store, the one-man shop make the same slipping rubble; the Louis Seize furniture, the installment suite raise the same dust from their splinters and rags. But the thing goes deeper than this: we could not see what we see as we do see it without feeling the force of a revolution in Britain that has already started and must accomplish itself. Bombs only mark the material end of things. Their psychological end will be much more lastingly felt. War sheds the blood, while our revolution goes on. Week after week this war-hidden revolution passes its sentences. Its discards, its no-goods, go to a limbo as unreturnable-from as the guillotine. Enemies of the people – leaders who could not lead, expensive idols who could not work their place – let them get out! They got out. Where are they? Nobody cares.

Undoubtedly bombing does something to you. But these few weeks of the *Blitzkrieg*, few and tense, could not have given us time to change as much as we have. The change in Britain dates (and this is important) from some months before the bombing began. Six months ago, we might have endured the bombing but we could not have *met* it. The change in us – we feel its effect now – began in spring, with Narvik;[17] it was on its course when we felt the blast of the crash of France. God or Hitler allowed us that long bright ghastly summer in which we find ourselves – just in time. The finding hurt. The cutting away of our dead wood could not have been more painful. September of 1939 had found us prepared to die but not to think. Perhaps (unconsciously) we would rather *have* died than thought. As things turned out, thought was asked of us first. We hated to – but we thought. You may say that, about the middle of summer, Britain woke up to find herself alone. As truly alone, she woke up to find herself. From then on, our spirits steadily rose – because we *were* alone, or because we had found ourselves? At any rate, what we found last summer we are using now that autumn is here.

Something bomb-proof was there in time for the bombs. We always might have patched up the *how* of sticking it. Now, which is far-reaching, we have the *why*. It is: THIS WAY TO LIFE. When you stand by to die every night you see, if only in moments, what life was meant to be. You ask, what stopped life being like that? You grow enemy-conscious. Nazis make a name and front for the Enemy, but we have bred our own, and deadlier, enemies. These are waiting, these may try to come back: *laissez faire*, subservience, smugness, habit-of-mind. Peace must only mark a new phase in our big fight. Then, God help those who in the name of Britain try to stand between Britain and life again . . . As they dug the bodies out of the too-shallow public shelter an onlooker said: "Well, they called this the people's war." It *is* the people's war, for the people's land, and what we save we rule. And we have it in us. It is this stir of big power in little people, the wide-awake look in the eyes, the nerve in the step, that makes this autumn in Britain a sort of spring.

By the Unapproachable Sea

Almost every small English town that I know has character: here and there one meets one that has personality – something hard to define, mysterious and important, in which present and past, the seen and the unseen, mix.

Hythe, Kent, is an instance of what I mean. The little town lies west of the heights of Folkestone, at the edge of the grey-green spaces of Romney Marsh. Its High Street runs along the base of a steep hill; all the way up the hill climb houses and gardens, and from its flank rises the great church. On the south side, a canal, then about half a mile of flat grassland, now separates the town from the sea front.

I say "now," because Hythe was not always separate from the sea – tides used to cover that flat stretch. She is a Cinque Port – and one must know something of England's history to realise how much that means. Hastings, Sandwich, Dover, Romney, Hythe: each held a Royal Charter from early Norman years. By the terms of the charter, Hythe and her sister Cinque Ports (so called from the Norman-French "cinq," five) became the givers to England of her first navy – fifty-seven hardy, small ships, manned by the men of Kent and East Sussex. Is it a wonder you feel this ancient pride in the air?[1]

Hythe, alone of the Cinque Ports, still has in her museum the charter dated 1278, bearing the seal of Edward I: in this the King confirms, upon his accession, liberties dating from the time of Edward the Confessor.[2]

Of the five, only Dover is still a port today: there have been changes in the bed of the Channel. But the names of the Cinque Ports stay written large; their time-honoured ceremonials are unchanged – and is it not in her ceremonials that you see, in flower, Britain's consciousness of herself? – and to be their Warden is a supreme honour. That their Warden now should be Winston Churchill is in tune with the Cinque Ports' spirit of these years.

The retreat, by a little way, of the sea has in no sense made Hythe an inland town. The sea-tradition is in the people's blood; there is a seaside brightness about the sunshine, and a salty freshness comes down the wide roads from the water front. The fisherman are still busy; among their number are those who used to man the Hythe life-boat – that capped its record by its heroic end in 1940 at Dunkirk.

How much had happened since then, and how much I wanted to hear! Hythe, I knew, had been suffering the tallest rigours of war. For only twenty-six miles or so of Channel divides this part of the coast from German-occupied France.

The closing of the area, at the fall of France, had led me to wonder how Hythe fared. I had no close friends left in the place; and happened to meet no one who could give me first-hand reports.[3]

It was, therefore, rather tensely that I entered Hythe, on the bus from Folkestone, on a July day of 1943. The coast was sunny, empty and seemed unnaturally quiet; a heat haze veiled the sea horizon, and France . . . Arriving thus, I was struck, as never before, by Hythe's smiling air of aliveness. At no time, I must say, did Hythe fall into the class of those picturesque, "semi-dead" towns, content to live on their past.

But this morning, after nearly four years of peril, the vitality of the place seemed intensified. There was, it was true, little traffic. As the bus stopped to put me down I heard, first, the loud singing of birds in the uphill gardens. I stood at one end of the narrow High Street – that, with its low shop-fronts and high-pitched roofs, looked to me, for that glad moment, just the same. This was the peak of the morning shopping hour; housewives[4] with baskets, in summer dresses, were in busy though placid movement. I saw no lines. I glanced up over the roofs and saw the embowered villas, and the great church soaring, intact.

But the street, I found, had suffered. Some stores were shuttered, clearly "for the duration," others completely gone. Hythe, with its eye for order and cheerfulness, has been[5] extra quick to clear away bomb damage:[6] today, grass and wild flowers clothed several gaps. It was often in high daytime, sometimes without warning, that bombs fell. (Almost before you can name him, the sneak raider comes flashing over the town, from the sea haze.) He is barely gone again, the Mayor told me, when all hands fly to work: an hour or two later, not a splinter of glass is left to litter the street, and the town has meanwhile, undaunted, continued its working day.

Exploring, again, the footways that run uphill, and the bye-streets that turn towards the canal and sea, I saw how blast had played its incalculable tricks with the old buildings.[7] The rustic movie theatre near the canal had been hit (mercifully it was empty) but was rebuilt, and is now open again. In daylight, the church windows were shattered. I talked with a woman who, with two other people, had from inside the church heard the bomb come tearing down. Their thoughts, for those awe-inspiring seconds, were for the building – for this very ancient church, with is soaring arches, is both the civil and religious centre of Hythe's life. Walking round it, I marked the Mayor's pew, with its book and cushion, and re-read human history from tablets all round the walls. After Sunday service, in the days I first remember, we children used to group under the church ilex trees to watch the soldiers from the School of Musketry fall into rank smartly for their return march.[8]

I thought of the absent, of Hythe's many sons and daughters who, perhaps, at this very moment, saw in their hearts this scene that I now beheld. I thought, what a lovely place to come home to! When the boys and girls do come home, they will not do all the talking: stories will have to be swapped – front-line Hythe has had a war of her own. She stands now, as ever, alert, in the forefront of England. But, now, ready not to be struck – to strike![9]

The equanimity of the Hythe people can be read from their sun-burned faces and cheerful eyes. They are now welded together into what seems one family – by dangers in common, by efforts shared. The Mayor – to whose leadership Hythe at once has responded so readily and owes so much – is proud of the people. "They just would not leave," he said. The very smallness of the community – a few thousand – helps to make Hythe the fine single working unit it is. People can be easily got together.

"And, finally," the Mayor said, "If you want to know how we are, have a look at our babies!"

Foreword to The Cinque Ports, by Ronald and Frank Jessup

This book on the Cinque Ports is a blend of portraiture with history, a picture of yesterday in the frame of today. The past of these places is of a length out of all proportion with their visible size; a particular glory has not so much departed as contracted into what for many people is little more than a legend, the rumour or ghost of a memory. Hastings, Dover, Sandwich, Romney and Hythe enshrine and honour their joint histories; yet it appears that outside the region these have remained, so far, little known. The names of the actual Cinque Ports are sometimes wrongly given; corporate or non-corporate members under their Charters are incorrectly promoted into their ranks, or confusion exists as to their relation with Winchelsea and Rye, the two Ancient Towns. As to fact, it has been the undertaking of this book's authors to enlighten us. But they do, as they have intended to do, more: they have evoked the atmosphere, revivified the excitement of centuries in which England first, as a power, began to be.

Today only Dover is a functioning port; only Dover and Hastings, with her sea front, either show growth or claim any forward position in contemporary life. Sandwich, Romney and Hythe, together with Winchelsea and Rye, conduct, with varying vigour, their own existences, attracting the visitor and attaching the resident who finds himself subject to their peculiar charm. Behind the rise then decline, as ports, of four of the five, and the recession from maritime prominence of the Ancient Towns, is to be traced the slow drama of a changing coastline. The determining factor has been physical. Indeed, as the authors demonstrate, few parts of the coast of England could offer a more ideal study for the historical geographer than does this, of Sussex and Kent, with its layer upon layer of extinct, eroded or shrunken civilisations.

Roman then Norman enterprise had as its footing a conformation so much altered now that one reconstructs it only by an effort of mind – nor had there not been change between those two epochs.

Stability, in Plantagenet times, was a fiction which study could have exposed; to that fiction the Cinque Ports owed their instatement, and to it their fast-growing importance and likely future were pinned, as it seemed, once for all.

The majestic, relentless war conducted by Nature against the Cinque Ports, and their defeat in it, could make melancholy reading, did there not stand out their triumphant human survival as institutions. As such, they were more than a local force; the extent of their dominance over sea and land was significant in the time which saw its height, has left its mark on all time, and, moreover, preserves itself in rights, ceremonies, procedures, and exercises of jurisdiction which have not, and will never, become unmeaning, nominal, or purely archaic. The joint history and individual stories of the Cinque Ports, with those of the Ancient Towns, are set out in pages now to come; it is not for a Foreword to either resume or anticipate. Ronald and Frank Jessup detail for us the constitutional framework within which the Cinque Ports, the Ancient Towns, and their subsidiaries, under their Charters, in and by virtue of their association, continue to act today. On the corporate and non-corporate members there has not, in this present volume, been room to more than touch: sensing unused material in abundance one is left hoping for further from these pens. Of the whole, the present-day setting is territorial – far away are the years when the Cinque Ports, by fulfilling their undertaking to man and send to sea all ships needful for the king's service, founded the Royal Navy. It was in return for this that reciprocal privileges were granted.

The authors, as topographers and archaeologists, could have kept to being no more than informative. It is a gain, however, that they do also address themselves to feeling (though never to sentiment) and to the visual imagination. By nature we enter more deeply into the stories of places we either know well or have been caused to see. As it stands, this book is equally fit to go to those familiar with Hastings, Dover, Romney, Sandwich, Hythe, Winchelsea and Rye, and to those who know them only by name. By the former, the evocation will be approved; for the latter it cannot, I imagine, fail to project pictures. The somnolent beauty of landlocked Romney;

Sandwich's steep-roofed streets lit by estuarial gleams; the changing light over Hythe, with its great Marsh vista, on its forehead of hill – all these are conjured up; and not less so Dover's strange blend of the utilitarian, military, and romantic. Old Hastings, still in essence aloof from the flourishing resort which shares its name, stands out in words, if still more in the photographs. Winchelsea, Rye reveal, to instructed vision, something more than their almost too evident picturesqueness. In all cases, there is direction of the eye to architecture and (more easily overlooked) the original plans and surviving structural features of towns once bound and now lost to the sea.

The Cinque Ports, and the whole belt of coastal country in which they stand, have an endemic temperament: something salt and sturdy about the very set of the bricks and stones, something vital about the surrounding contours – whether stretching flats, sweeping slopes, jutting heights. The people – race inside the English race – have, too, a character bred of their unique heritage, forged all the more perhaps by change and necessity. Of the many who care for this region, who seek or are haunted by it, few know it so thoroughly as these brother-authors – who are in fact authorities. Sons of Kent, out of a long heredity, these two are also linked in research. This adds unusual range and palpable substance to what is above all a labour of love.

The Idea of France

When I was a child I hardly travelled at all. The life of my parents divided itself between the town house in Dublin and the lonely old mansion in County Cork. We were – as I am still – Irish, and for Irish people the journey as far as England was, in itself, a sufficient undertaking.[1] Two seas divided us from the Continent.

My mother was content with this narrow life; partly, perhaps, because she was happy, but also because she had already travelled.[2]

Sensuous and imaginative, she had the power of attaching herself for always to places that she had, perhaps, visited only once – for a day, for an hour. Such places still existed as vividly for her as did the scenes of her everyday life in Ireland. She loved to make them known to me by her talk; she loved still better, I think, to enjoy them in silence, all by herself. I came to understand that when her eyes wore an entranced, vague look, she was far away – walking down an avenue, contemplating a castle on the top of a hill, gliding between the banks of a wide river, driving in a little carriage along the edge of a very blue sea, or standing, in such strong sunshine as we never saw in Ireland, in a square outside the great door of a church. – No, I cannot believe she had ceased to wish to travel: let us say that she had, somehow, reconciled her contentment with this desire.

In children there exists already that desire for the supreme experience that stays with the man or woman all through life. For me, everything centred round the idea of "another country" – which should be greater, brighter, more exciting, more interesting, in every way superior to my own. Its inhabitants, whom I should come to know, should be braver, more accomplished, more elegant, than anybody whom I had already met. (This did not imply disloyalty to my own home: it was a perfectionism that I could not resist.) Some children, in such a mood, map out for themselves imaginary countries – as did the little Brontës, children of genius. The simpler ones accept stories of Fairyland; the pious ones form ardent pictures of Heaven. My desires had a less ethereal trend: Europe would be enough.

I do not know how I came to form the idea that France was the centre of Europe. Traditionally, of course, the idea of France has always had a strong hold over Irish people. France was the friend, the hope, of those who for centuries had struggled for Irish freedom – at the same time, my own family, Protestant, landowning, Unionist, had never lent themselves to that struggle. My own people did not hope to see the French land, in arms, on the Irish shore: loyalty at least to the English king was inbred in them. No, *their* feeling for France was a sort of *culte*. It was a deep part of their culture; it was part, in an innocent way, of their snobbishness; it was part, perhaps, of their subtle and un-political anti-Englishness – for in fact they did not always admire the England that they did not fail to support. In short, I was brought up in, and did not react against, an atmosphere in which, virtually, all that France did, or could ever do, was ideal.

Physically, I do not think that my mother ever described France to me. I doubt, in fact, that she had been there as much as she had been in other countries. She had made me see the Rhineland castles and black forests of Germany, the peaks and cataracts of Switzerland, the olives and ruins of Italy. But when, at first, I had asked her: "But what is France like?" her face assumed an expression of mystic, reflective puzzlement. Therefore, France remained for me immaterial – and, perhaps oddly, this ceased to trouble me. The power remained in the name – which in itself seemed to me at once strong and elegant: there was a sheer sufficiency about the monosyllable. And the name, from remaining a name only, concentrated about itself ideality.

Looking back, I could wonder I did not come to hate France, so often was she invoked for the discipline necessary for a girl child. This second, secular religion of my mother's permeated each phrase of my upbringing. I was told: "A Frenchwoman never goes out without her gloves . . . A Frenchwoman, once she has left her mirror, never fidgets about with her hair or dress; she forgets herself; she has a perfect repose . . . A Frenchwoman dresses simply, but is impeccable as to her shoes and gloves." And to speak French was a necessity, as I began to realise with more and more pain. It is true that in insisting that I should learn French my mother and her sisters, who were so often with her, deprived themselves of[3] a favourite retreat – whenever their conversation became too interesting to be suitable for my infant ears, they were accustomed to change over into the superior language. They had been brought up, as children, by a French-Swiss governess, and they spoke French with fluency, charm and confidence; if not, perhaps, altogether correctly. Directly my mother and aunts began their French conversation, their faces would animate and their voices quicken; mystery, exclusiveness and elation were in the air. – And I? I suffered: as only the vain and inquisitive child can.

I am a bad linguist, and my French lessons, with my governess and later at school, were accompanied, chiefly, by mortification. I was most nearly faultless in the matter of irregular verbs,[4] which, at one school, I was made to learn as a punishment. I left my last school shy of speaking a word. When my ambition to be a novelist declared itself – and this happened early – an intellectual and emancipated London woman advised me to read *Madame Bovary* – "which," she said, "is the greatest novel in the world." She gave me the yellow volume. "But," I exclaimed in horror, "it's in *French*; I cannot possibly read French!" She replied: "You will find you can if you want to." This proved true – I, who had baulked at La Bibliothèque Rose,[5] found myself, almost without knowing, deep in the sorrows of Emma Bovary. I was staying, at the time, in the country, with my mother's favourite sister, who was unmarried. Now and then I would ask her what words meant. "What is your novel?" she asked kindly. I showed it to her: she looked kind as ever, but blank. "I have never heard of it: what is it about?" she said. I replied: "It is about a French doctor's wife living in the country."

Nothing but the convenience of my aunt's ignorance, at the moment, struck me. Looking back, it is interesting that a lady so francophile should have remained so ignorant of the French classics. I doubt, now, that my aunts or my mother had ever *read* French: any test to which their delicacy might have been put – and Irish ladies are delicate to the point of prudishness – was spared them. Nothing had ever ruffled the calm lake of their belief of the impeccability, in all and every direction, of any son or daughter of their beloved France.

Madame Bovary was the start, with me, of a long career of French novel reading. I read indiscriminately; always with one ulterior object – that of trying to know what France was *like*. I pieced word-pictures together, inside my own mind, into what must have formed a more fantastic *collage* than any Surrealist has as yet achieved. For, I had reached the age of twenty-one without having ever once been to France. Why? A variety of reasons, as impassable[6] as they were, most of them, negative: there was, of course the war of 1914–18, during which I grew up, due to which I missed my "finishing" year. Behind all this, I think, I had, and I was resigned to, the restraining idea that actually to *go* to France was an experience for which I was not yet ripe; towards which I must, patiently, graduate. It was a "some day" that existed in order to tempt me towards maturity.

No, I could not say: "I have been to France." But I *could* say: "I have seen her."

Yes, I saw France when I was seven years old. My mother, my governess and I, while visiting England, had arrived to stay with relatives at Folkestone. Along the Leas, that promenade at the top of the cliffs, I was taken for my walk, that first morning. It was a diamond-clear, almost colourless March day; I was so newly keyed up by the sea air, the unfamiliarity of the scene, that I was almost giddy. Suddenly my governess pointed across the Channel. "Look – !" she said, in a solemn and strained voice.

I looked. I saw a long violet shape along the horizon – more sharp, more shapely than any line. And at the moment, towards that violet shape, the packet steamer from Folkestone harbour below us slowly cut in the water a slanting furrow.

"That's not – ?" I said.

"Yes. That's France."

I had always believed *in* France; that was one thing. But had I believed, till this moment, that she *existed*?

Was it more or less poignant when, fourteen years later,[7] the façades and pier of Dieppe seemed slowly to move towards me, like arms already open for an embrace? The pure violet form that had ruled my imagination was dissolving, flowering into a mass of detail. I, long ago, had *seen* France. Now I was going to know what she was *like*.

Paris Peace Conference: 1946. An Impression

It is hard to separate the Peace Conference, 1946, from its setting, Paris. For me it would be, even, hopeless to try. The power to purge facts from one's own impressions belongs to the seasoned journalist that I am not. I am here as a free-lance, an onlooker, granted the entrée to the Luxembourg by the goodwill of those who hold that novelists should be let picture history, in its actual making, though they may not record it. Showing my pass, I entered the Palace courtyard, on the day of the Opening, with a sensation of awe – and that has not worn off since. Many things that the diplomat or the journalist proper would take for granted were new to me: from that hour, I have remained absorbed and impressed. At the same time I cannot leave behind me, when I enter the Luxembourg, my continuous consciousness of Paris at its gates – a Paris I had not seen since spring 1939, and which therefore invaded me with a renewed magic and a renewed force.

Or, should I say a quarter of Paris? The city, after years in which so much has happened, is still too much for me to take in as a whole. Perhaps deliberately, though also because the Conference ties me here, I have kept – except for a few excursions across the river – to this uphill world of the Luxembourg (Gardens as well as Palace), the Odéon, the fringes of the Sorbonne. Up here, it is very quiet, almost provincial; and one may see – as perhaps in no other quarter of any other great city – the pattern of everyday life. The narrow streets run deep between high, old, mysterious, dust-pale houses. There are intermittent, small, brave, rather empty provision shops; modest restaurants; hand-laundries from which comes the warm smell of ironing. At the top are the railings of the Luxembourg Gardens, with, between the clipped chestnuts, enchanting glimpses of pools, statues, the purple and rose and crimson of flowerbeds. The Gardens drain into themselves all the child-life of the quarter – and, they surround the Conference on three sides. It is very quiet – at the height of the day you hear a canary singing, a child practising the piano, dishes being washed up after a meal. And, every quarter-hour,

the soft, toneless striking of the Luxembourg clock. It is a neighbourhood of old people, their faces inscrutable with memories and
thoughts, and of sleek cats. Housewives come and go, with their
high-spirited faces and flat-heeled walk. This is the quarter, the
silence through which[1] go roaring, a long urgent file, the Delegates'
cars – on their way to the Conference, from the Right Bank. This is
the plan of small lives – lives which have lost much, and have
desperately much to hope for – which reaches up to the very walls
of the Palace in which the world's future is being planned.

In my consciousness, I feel a connecting thread between the
men, in there, sitting round the green tables, and the children, out
there, playing among the green lawns.

Certainly, the Conference has not been set on a drab stage. About
the Luxembourg Palace, for all its strength, there is something
feminine: one does not forget that it was built by a Queen.[2] In the
brilliant blue weather, heatwave, of early August, the Palace gave
out all it had of dignified theatricality. For renascent[3] Paris, as
well as for the visiting Delegates, the opening, July 29th, was
an emotional as well as a spectacular day. People pressed up to
the barriers as the cars streamed under the beflagged archway.
Followed, inevitably, an anticlimax: lessening interest outside,
threatening boredom within – for, indeed, the initial Plenary
Sessions, inescapable, time-losing tribute to formality and to the
amour propre of the Delegations, not only did not cut very much
ice but made one doubt whether ice ever could *be* cut. Resounding
phrases, irreproachable testaments to ideals, rolled, one after
another, up to the dome of baking, chocolate-and-gold Hemicycle,[4]
through afternoon after afternoon[5] of the heatwave. Tier upon tier
sat the impassive diplomats, the distinguished visitors, the saturated
journalists at the top. Nothing, one learned, would begin; nothing
that was anything could be expected to begin, till the Plenary
Sessions had run their course. Gloves were due to come off; and
gloves came off, pretty promptly, with the opening of the Debates
on Procedure – which were to put Conference nerves to their first
test by being held at night, and running on, at the worst, into the
small hours of the morning.

For the present, the Hemicycle plays no more part. All matters the Conference has in hand are concentrated in the different Commission rooms, behind sound-proof, heavily moulded doors. From the courtyard, the original bustle has subsided – the hands of the clock above the archway move round; the gendarmes half in a dream maintain their official stance – occasionally, the mid-morning or mid-afternoon hush is broken by an amplified voice calling for the car of a Delegate who has decided to leave early. Yes, everything happens indoors: from ten in the morning on through to a late lunch-hour, from three or four in the afternoon till around eight o'clock, the interior Luxembourg, on three sides of the courtyard, hums with the muted steadiness of a dynamo. Through the downstairs hall and stone passages of the centre block reverberate, with oddly ghostly effect, amplified voices of speakers at the Commissions. From the Press Room, Reception Bureau, and honeycomb-like offices of the secretariat comes the rustling stutter of typewriters, small and great. Piercingly, and irregularly, an electric bell rings. The dim electricity of the passages lights announcement-boards to which stencils are being always repinned. Packages of documents, weighty, are unloaded from vans, carried up steps. The come-and-go of messengers, on the stairs, in the anterooms, through the long enfilades of gold-and-white doors, is by now methodical and unhurried. On the grand entrance staircase used by the Delegates the cherry-pink carpet, since August, has worn perceptibly thinner.

The tempo, temperature, temper of the Peace Conference has, manifestly, varied from week to week. Press and radio have, in a broad way, registered its variations. Of course, as news must be news, there can but be a tendency to headline crises, or "duels," and to understress the no less trying effect of long dragging, nagging sessions which lead nowhere. Inside the Luxembourg, it is late August that remains on record as the worst bad patch, so far. Blotting-out rain, the strain of over-much work on small staffs, claustrophobia, and the rawness of feeling on subjects not to be got past set up a mood of discouragement, which, plus some verbal fireworks, could but have its effect on the outside world. On August 10th I had to go home to Ireland for three weeks: thus, I was to have for that period the singularly depressing long-distance view. "What," they said, "you've been at the Peace Conference? Doesn't come to much, does it? There they sit and sit . . . How it drags on . . . Can't well get up from their tables till they've accomplished *something* . . . No doubt the Delegates are in no hurry to leave Paris? . . . One hears they go to parties the whole time?"[6]

Cheerful falsehood embedded in a certain amount of melancholy truth makes one smile. There has been little of the Congress of Vienna[7] about the Paris Conference 1946. Receptions on the part of the Delegations have been reciprocal, functional and demure. No ladies, others than those in the secretariat, have accompanied any of the parties; and the Russians and some of the[8] Central Europeans have not burdened their luggage with evening dress. Among those who prefer to make the concession, *"le smoking"*[9] rather than the white tie is the rule. At the same time – and, surely, happily? – things cannot but be kept at a particular psychic-social pitch by this enveloping element of *la ville lumière* – the floodlit Place de la Concorde, in which cars move like dark fish in a sea of gold. Most telling of all, as host to the Conference the French Government brings to its hospitality an inspired sense of the romantic, the nostalgic and the spectacular. Instance – among many – the gala night at the Opera (when the façade became, to the eye, a cut-out of crimson cellophane and staircase and foyer challenged a Lubitsch[10] *mise-en-scène*) and the Versailles sunset party – where, as the last reflections died in the *Galerie des Glaces*, bugles called from the terrace over the darkening trees and more and more lights blazed on the indoor flowers. Versailles was, for that evening, called from the past to play her part of glory. And, surely these voices France can call on speak? The undying Old World seems to salute the New.

My return to Paris early in September synchronised, by chance, with yet one more of those changes in the interior climate of the Luxembourg. (Outwardly, too, there was movement, acceleration –

brighter, alternately clouding and sunny skies; the chestnut trees in the Gardens now crisp with autumn.) Some of the smaller Commissions had in sight, already, the accomplishment of their work; all had, in their different rooms of the[11] Palace, moved clear of the fulvous zone. In an atmosphere of, if anything, colourless equability, business was moving forward, points were being decided – things (though the world might not know it) were getting done. In August, I had been content to hover about the Conference in general – aware of its currents, interested by its rumours. This time, in September, this new, stimulating concentration in the Conference air made me wish to attach myself to one Commission only, and to follow it steadily through its work. The Political and Territorial Commission, Italy, was – and remains – the core and nerve-centre of Luxembourg. At it, all Delegations are represented. Its extensive agenda holds two combustible items: the Italo-Yugoslav frontier, and Trieste.

The Italian Commission (to give it its brief name) sits in the *Grande Salle*, upstairs in the centre block. The *salle*, of immense length, is of an over-gilded, tasteless magnificence that comes, with time, to have a hypnotic charm. Six high windows open, north, on the courtyard; a vast chandelier, above the conference table, with bunches of crystal wall-lamps, light up on darker mornings. Smoking is permitted: a blue haze hangs in the air above the Delegates' heads. This Commission, surprising as it may seem, has, so far, set up a record of amiability: the good feeling has, by now, been going on long enough to become a matter of comment by the Chairman. Actually, the Chairman (the South African Mr. Lief Egeland[12]) is himself to be congratulated, and one may hope will be – he combines a close executive grip with a sort of smiling, social control; not unlike that of a host's over his table. There may also be the factor (Harold Nicolson suggests this elsewhere) that a number of men cannot sit around the same table, in the same places, day after day without striking up some sort of physical-neighbourly good accord. Here, in the *Grande Salle* of the Luxembourg, one is in[13] the presence of men whose features, traits, intonations, gestures, and casts of mind have become, to each other, familiar;

one might say, sympathetic. M. Vishinsky's[14] shovelling gestures and pachydermatous, seeking turns of the head; the ironical smile and quizzical, heavy-lidded sidelong glance of M. Bebler[15] (on whom devolved the long exposition of the Yugoslav claims); the youthful, clear-cut frown of concentration on the brow of the South African Mr. Jordaan[16]; the doglike attentive attitude (hands, like paws, on the table) of Australia's Colonel Hodgson[17] – these are looked for, in turn. No less does a rustle of expectation precede the rising of Senator Connally[18] – to turn impressively, to make a pause no less so, to state, adjure, invoke. Only one personality, M. Molotov's,[19] gives off, when present, an absolute and inhuman greyness. Speech, with him, seems a calculated emission: it comes out in an atmosphere that is cold, dead.

In spite – or is it because? – of the *Grande Salle*'s calmness, widening divisions of purpose are to be strongly felt; and still more, in the case of the Russian *bloc*, the functioning of the iron directive. It could but be obvious to a child, to a savage, that Poles, Czechs, Ukrainians, Yugoslavs are attached to the USSR as are the fingers to the palm of a hand. Charges of pro-Italianism, of reactionary sympathies, against the other (or, "Western") Delegations are not for long allowed to remain absent from the lips of any of that *bloc*. For the onlooker, there is the sinister fascination of watching Russia create, by her own suspicions, a psycho-political situation that, actually, not only has not existed so far but need not, in spite of Russia, ever exist at all.

Paris Peace Conference – Some Impressions 1

General Smuts's[1] tribute to French recovery has been well timed. It had been felt to be owing. One honours the General for this *amende honorable*.[2] But also, apart from the speaker's wish to withdraw former hurting remarks, he has given voice to a very general impression. Whatever the achievement of the Peace

Conference, nobody who has attended it has anything but praise for its setting, and for the smoothness with which the machinery of the Luxembourg has run. Paris, indeed, has thrown herself heart and soul into her role as host of the delegations. Civility and consideration have appeared at all points; and, still better, there has been a heart-warming atmosphere of goodwill. For my own part, I remember, before the war, a certain crossness on the part of the French[3] functionaries: one hesitated to address oneself to a gendarme or present oneself at an official desk. The Parisian temper once seemed, to the visitor, overbearing and often short.

This has corrected itself in a striking way. Not merely politeness but real good nature reigns in the Paris air – nor is it confined to the surround of the Luxembourg. This seems worth remarking because, surely, good temper is a sign of good morale. The Paris gendarmes of 1946 are young and keen; they enter with smiling zest into the extra duties imposed on them by the Conference. At the outset, until a routine had established itself, those duties were sufficiently arduous; nor, in the weeks since the Conference has had time to settle into its course, has there been any marked relaxation. The scrutiny of entrance cards to the Palace has, though conducted politely, remained inexorably close. Before a major session, the business of getting an apparently endless stream of official cars in under one narrow archway into the Palace courtyard, directing their movements in that constricted space, parking the more important cars round the walls and getting the others out again through another arch, is no small one. At the close of the session the same process must be gone through in reverse. Cars the courtyard cannot contain are parked in neighbouring streets; and are expected to present themselves within a few seconds of being summoned by the loud-speaker. Any delay in a delegate's car arriving could cause endless umbrage – for national vanity, it must be said, among the twenty-one nations lies pretty near the surface.[4]

The days of the opening, July 29th, and the days immediately after it did, it is true, just verge on confusion. Paris, for that first fortnight or so, was in the[5] grip of a radiant heatwave. Cloudless blue skies and brilliant sunshine – in which the flags of the nations gave out their full effect – could not but be seen as a good omen: none the less, the heat for many meant extra strain. The Peace Conference formally opened at 3 o'clock, but since early morning the Palace had been a Babel. The world's Press, presenting credentials and queuing up for their cards, were vociferous and not always easy-tempered: here, again, national *amour propre* came in. It transpired that while the issue of blue cards (admitting journalists to the Palace itself) could, with discretion, be fairly liberal, the supply of pink cards must be severely cut. Pink cards gave admission to the Hemicycle, where the inaugural Plenary Sessions were to be held. The Hemicycle is considerably less roomy than the Dáil in Dublin; and accommodation for the Press, in the top gallery, was found to be hopelessly insufficient. All and more of the tact of the French staff at the reception bureau was required. Disappointed news-hawks clamoured and milled around. Many, resigned, took up a more or less permanent position in the Press bar. The serving of refreshments was not the only function of the bar – a large, pleasant, white-and-gold room with French windows opening on to a garden. Adjoining the Press room – in which a table was allotted to the Press of each of the nations – the bar assumed the nature of a club. There was no better place for taking, from day to day, the temperature of the Conference. Soon, an amicable (if quite unofficial) system of lending out the pink tickets was arranged: there was no journalist who, as far as I know, did not at one time or another mount the stairs to the Hemicycle. Many, to be frank, were soon driven down again by the pompousness of some of the delegates' opening speeches and by the grilling heat. It was agreed that the Conference would not get down to brass tacks till it had entered upon the committee stage. There was an immediate rise of tension and interest once those early Plenary Sessions were declared over. "Fireworks" began with the Debates on Procedure, which continued late into the hot nights. It was known, any gap or loophole left in rules for procedure might, sooner or later, cause a breakdown. It was during those Procedure debates that Russia first showed her determination to pull things her way.

Yes, it was then that raised, tense and suspicious voices first travelled over the amplifiers into the outlying rooms and stone passages of the Luxembourg. To myself, the effect of this amplification was uncanny. After the Plenary Sessions, one or another commission was "laid on" (for the benefit of the Press and general personnel of the Conference) at all hours of the Luxembourg's working days – and nights.

About the character and position of the Luxembourg Palace there is something propitious to the idea of peace. The Luxembourg, as many will remember, stands uphill, on the left bank of the river. It is surrounded on three sides by public gardens as lovely as any in the world – where children play, fountains plash, flowerbeds send up their mosaic of colour, old people potter serenely along the shady alleys of clipped chestnuts, and statues, gleaming against the foliage, embody the happiest memories of France. In my own mind, as the Conference proceeded, I never ceased to feel a vital connection between the unconscious children playing around the green lawns, outdoors, and the intent men, indoors, seated around the green tables. A French mother, by whom I sat for a moment in the shade of a flowering oleander tree, raised her head from her sewing and gave a glance at the Palace. "Peace for our children," she said. "That is what we are praying for; that is what we want."

These, now as the Conference nears its close, are a few of my memories of its opening. I shall write, next, of my glimpses of it at work.

Paris Peace Conference – Some Impressions 2

M y time at the Peace Conference, in the capacity of freelance journalist, divided itself into two visits. I was in Paris and daily at the Luxembourg, from July 28th (the day before the opening) up to August 10th; then, again, from September 3rd to 25th. In the interval I was at my house in Co. Cork. When I left Paris the first time, towards the middle of August, the Conference was just getting down to brass tacks – and some of these, as we[1] know, were to prove uncomfortably sharp. While in Co. Cork I received – as we all did – the impression conveyed by Press and radio that things in the Luxembourg were going slowly, badly, in an atmosphere of acrimony and frustration. None of the friends with whom I talked here seemed to regard the future of the Conference with anything but pessimism. In a sense it was interesting to obtain, halfway through my time at the Luxembourg, this outside view. The Luxembourg, with its close concentration and esoteric talk, tends, inevitably, to become a world in itself: one loses the sense of what is going on outside. While in Ireland, I could endeavour to see things in perspective; also, to gather the repercussions of what was happening, from day to day in Paris, on the public – the ordinary man and woman. It might have been well had some of the delegates and their over-worked staffs been able to take this kind of "breather" too.[2]

For, when I returned to Paris, early in September, I found that discouraging reports had not been exaggerated. The Conference *had* been going through a bad patch – though this bad patch, it turned out, was towards its[3] end. There had been stormy weather outdoors and in. The narrow, monotonous, taxing life of the delegations had been beginning to tell on the nerves of many – and that, unexpectedly early on. The average day of a member of a delegation is spent either in the Right Bank hotel which is his headquarters, or in a committee room of the Luxembourg. Transit between one and the other is hurriedly made in a glassed-in car. Evenings and the great parts of nights are spent either over papers or in informal but none the less exacting conference with members of other delegations. Official entertainments remain official, merely providing an ironically festive background for the further talking of Conference "shop." The delegation member seldom meets outside people – except sometimes on Sunday when he may take a short tour through the surrounding country, he has no opportunity to relax or let up. It is not to be wondered at that, in his tired mind, in which the affairs of his particular committee go round and round, irritations should tend to loom over-large and difficulties to take on a false proportion.

Such conditions are, I suppose, unavoidable. The delegations are in Paris to work;[4] their work has been, from the earliest, planned to schedule; extreme concentration, at whatever cost, is necessary. But these men, who have undertaken the almost superhuman task of building up world peace, are, it must be remembered, only human. In this particular, the East would appear to have the advantage of the West; the Russians, with their adherents,[5] the Slav *bloc*, would seem not to have a nerve in their stocky frames. Eating largely, presumably sleeping deep, the Slavs (at least, those in evidence at the Conference) seem rubber-tyred against fatigue. Their irritability arises from quite another source: their by now palpable persecution-mania – which, I was told, even takes the form of a touchy childishness on the subject of seating accommodation, etc.[6] It cannot be doubted that, in the late-August "bad patch," the Russians were calculating upon, and exploiting, the temporary nerviness of their Western colleagues (or, as they preferred to see them, antagonists). It was the ideal moment to adopt a policy of obstruction for obstruction's sake. The effect of a Russian voice going unintelligibly on and on in an already jaded committee room can be that, exactly, of an electric drill.[7]

I speak of "temporary" nerviness, because, with the start of September, the Conference entered upon a better phase. It might be described as getting its second wind. Conditions, as above described, did not change; but somehow the delegations surmounted them. Myself being back in Paris by this time, I no longer saw any home newspapers or heard broadcasts; therefore I do not know whether Press and radio registered, as they should have done, this indoor climatic improvement in the Luxembourg. There was nothing spectacular in this psychological change; possibly one could only feel it inside the palace. "We are all now as amiable as lambs," a friend[8] said to me. "You might almost think that nothing could be happening. But quite a lot is happening – we are, I believe, beginning to get things done."

I noticed other changes, on my September return. For one thing, the Press Bar and Press Room were comparatively empty. The Conference, as a discouraging topic, had, on the whole, been faded out of the news; the news-hawks had taken wing to more likely fields. Then, in the chains of secretarial rooms, up and down the stairs and along the passages, the original hectic clatter of the opening fortnight had given place to a steady workmanlike hum, to an orderly and methodical come and go. Returning, I felt an unexpected confidence in the Luxembourg as a factory of peace. Outside in the gardens, autumn gave crispness to the rustle of the trees.

During my August visit I had been content – like many other journalists, free-lance and otherwise – to hover about the Conference in general – picking up rumours, observing types and personalities, making flying entrances to the Hemicycle on a borrowed pink ticket, listening to snatches of radio-transfusion. That first fortnight of the Conference – my first Peace Conference – had been a deep and exciting draught in itself. But this second time on my September return, the increasing purposefulness of the Luxembourg atmosphere infected me. I wished to attach myself strictly to one commission and, during my time in Paris, follow its work through. I was fortunate in being able to obtain a ticket for the proceedings which were my immediate aim – the Territorial and Political Commission, Italy. This, one did not need telling, was now the core of the Conference. It was large, being attended by at least two or three members of each of the delegations. It was work of vast, one might say dangerous, importance; it had to deal with the combustible question of Trieste and also of the Italo-Yugoslav frontier – the proposed "French Line." That Commission has now, as you know, concluded its work. It is of some impressions gleaned from my three weeks' attendance at it that I am proposing next time to write.

Paris Peace Conference – Some Impressions 3

The Political and Territorial Commission, Italy, was, for briefness, known in the Luxembourg as the "Italian Commission," though there was, in fact, another (the Economic) dealing[1] with Italian affairs. The Commission, during the early September weeks when business could still be taken at normal speed, sat daily from 10 a.m. to a late lunch-hour. Its setting was the *Grande Salle* of the Luxembourg – a vast room, long as a cathedral, on the first floor of the Palace, with a row of windows overlooking the courtyard. The aspect was north, but the somewhat overheated colouring of the interior – tomato carpet, crimson velvet furniture, much gilding, walls and ceilings painted with sprawling nymphs and goddesses – took away any effect of coldness. Indeed, the *Grande Salle*, though far too ornate (it had been redecorated during a nineteenth-century period of bad taste), had something genial about it. This geniality somehow communicated itself to the Commission which – as one could not forget – was handling the dynamite of the Conference: the Trieste and the Italo-Yugoslav frontier questions.

Smoking was permitted; a blue haze hung over the conference table, mounting up to the glittering chandelier overhead. (The prohibition to smoke in the Hemicycle, where the more formal Plenary Sessions are held, adds much, I am told, to the wearisomeness of any proceedings there.) The very long, round-ended table of the *Grande Salle* is hollow in the middle, containing a smaller table at which interpreters sit. Journalists, comfortably sprawled on the velvet sofas, were grouped at one end of the room, and a few absent-minded gendarmes stood with folded arms. Through a series of mirrored doors, in the wall opposite the windows, the *Salle* opens into a long corridor, ending in a tea room and bar. Round those white-clothed tables and along the buffet a good deal of private, and obviously important, confabulation went on; the tea room was the rendezvous of Commission members during the tedious translations of longer speeches. This translation business was a hold-up involving considerable loss of time; repeatedly the

Chairman urged that Delegates who had prepared their speeches should send in copies in advance, so that translations could be made, typed, and circulated round the conference table. Though the speed-up would have been welcome to all, this was regrettably seldom done. The speech originally delivered in French, English, or Russian had to be spoken through in the two alternative tongues.[2]

M. Vishinsky's tribute to the Chairman, just before the Italian Commission drew to its close, may well have seemed, to the outside world, to have come from most unexpected lips. Actually, I think the Russians, to whose own touchiness I have drawn attention, were (to give them their due) the first to realise the absence of that tiresome quality in the Chairman – the South African, Mr. Lief Egeland. Mr. Egeland's impartiality, grip, clear-headedness, good temper and good manners stood out a mile. He appeared to have established long-distance friendly contact with every individual round the table; and to control, as he never ceased to do, the proceedings without giving offence. At the same time, his unremittingly businesslike attitude was appreciated. By general consent the Commission's having run so smoothly its dangerous course was due to him.

The delegations were seated around the table in alphabetical order according to French spelling – America, Australia, Belgium, Brazil, Canada, China, and so on. This, by a freak of chance, placed the USSR and the Yugoslavs near together, with only the South Africans (*Union de l'Afrique du Sud*) in the unfortunate position of being between them. The control exercised by Russia over her Yugoslav satellite was very obvious; personally I could hardly take my eyes off that group. One could be conscious from time to time of the Yugoslavs glancing sideways for their directive. The exposition of the Yugoslav frontier claims devolved upon a young speaker, M. Bebler; with a map of the territory in question hanging behind him on the marble fireplace he spoke (taking the frontier line in four sections) almost continuously for several mornings. To a pleasing personality he could add the advantage of speaking excellent French, so that the impact of what he said reached the greater part of his hearers directly. On their own merits his speeches, based on what he set out to be human[3] survival necessities of his country, and seldom unreasonable in tone, produced considerable effect; M. Bebler himself – undoubtedly one of the "personalities" of the Commission – seemed to be well enough liked by those round the table. But any sympathy he might gain was undone by the consciousness that Yugoslavia was being manipulated by the Russians.

The entire Slav bloc in its speeches levelled charges of pro-Italianism against the other members of the Commission. "You are," the rest of the delegations constantly heard themselves being told, "supporting a former enemy against a former ally." "In that case," was the inevitable riposte: "What about Russia's support of Bulgaria's claims against Greece?" Ironically, I believe that, as the Commission went on, the Russians and Yugoslavs succeeded in manufacturing in others a pro-Italianism which had not, necessarily, existed at the start. Russia and Ethiopia, as we know, have little reason to love Italy, and the Dominions[4] are, in the main, not pro-Latin. But by the sheer aggravation of the Slav charges, one could feel many of the other members of the Commission slipping more and more, and perhaps unwillingly, to the Italian side. The East-West split, which General Smuts has deplored, was inexorably being wrought in the *Grande Salle*.

But for these bad (if deliberately bad) tactics, the cleverness of M. Vishinsky is not to be doubted. Outwardly, M. Vishinsky has a warm, vital, bonhomous personality. Clumsy in his movements as a bear, he has a quick twinkling play of expression; in all this, and with his reddish face, he is in striking contrast to M. Molotov. Molotov's absolute greyness of speech and person sent out a sort of fume whenever he was present and rose to speak. He seems to be the one hundred per cent bureaucrat, sub-acid in mind and person, incapable of any impulse of the heart, even anger. One could feel him strongly antipathetic to the majority of the persons there. It is an extraordinary experience to have sat in a room with those two men.

Prague and the Crisis

"Best of all," everyone said to me, "you should have come to Prague at the blossom time." Driving in from the airport, I saw February afternoon light fall on a winter-worn, phantasmagoric city. This was the light of no February I had ever seen: light at once subtle and staring – Central European, to myself I called it, and there were days before its effect on my senses quite wore off. It heightened the impact Prague must make on any newcomer, and, still more, my sensation, as a Britisher, of having come from the periphery of Europe into its very heart. This was no city in Technicolor – but at every turn, as it opened and closed round me, it had the ghostly hyper-reality of a photograph: a grey-brown print cunningly tinted in.

But a photograph is two-dimensional; and it was the impossibly many-seeing dimensions of Prague that hit me. Half a dozen cities, each with not only its own architecture but its own psychology, seemed, here, to be superimposed upon one another. The effect of density could have been unbearable – and, frankly, for hours together to me was. Throughout my ten days' visit there were times when nothing was possible but the nullity of my hotel room: I became prey not, I believe, to any nervosity of my own but to a nervosity weighing in on me from the outside. From no single individual whom I met – and how many, many I did meet! – did this come to me: good heart as well as stalwart nature beamed from every face turned to me in talk. For the Czech is (I can think of no other word) collected. Unlike the more loose-knit Anglo-Saxon he cannot afford to indulge in nervous play: everything matters too much. His unremitting internal excitement is to be felt: it is never exhibited. So, the oppressive excitement I felt in Prague must have come to me from something collective.

In reality, of course, the city, heaped up and down its hills each side of the Vltava River, divides itself into quarters whose age-characters are distinctly marked. The effect of confusion, contusion, rises from the inevitable carry-over of one's own sensations as one moves about. The ear, having at one instant been stunned by a naked and unabated racket of twentieth-century noise, is at the next daunted by ancient silence. Prague silences, when they *are* suddenly met, have something of the quality of deep, static water – and, like water, seem to reflect themselves on to the buildings that shut them in. Prague's Old Town is full of such creeks and pockets; and silence (unlike water) runs uphill, across the statued Charles Bridge – through arcaded squares, cobbled footways, and hanging gardens – to the Cathedral. But, does silence at any point reign completely – did it this fatal February? Never quite. Nowhere, at the most spectacular city height or deep-sunk little corner of an ancient building, did I find myself quite out of range of an open window emitting a voice; and, posted outside that window always at least one figure, listening. The voice of radio, carrying yet one more political speech.

In Prague one feels the youth of Kafka, as in Dublin one feels the youth of Joyce. There is, about the whole range of architecture, from the crabbed, arcaded medieval to the soaring, pastel-tinted steel-and-concrete, a sort of visionary, still incoherent power. Shadows fall oddly; the bone-and-soul formation under a passing face stands out by some trick of chiaroscuro. There is a touch of obsession, an unaccountable quickening of the step, in the most ordinary gait of the Prague citizen about his business. The Bohemian Czech, man or woman, is in the main thick-set; as though an inherited density of personality formed round it one type of physical build. In men, this physique is expressive: in women it seems more negative – a sign (or so I read it) of as yet imperfect development *as* women.

For decidedly this is a man's city. Brilliant and memorable women whom I met were the more memorable in being rare. Eager, vital, and sensitive young girls with whom I talked seemed to be opening their eyes on a future hazy and undeclared. All, or almost all, girls, I was given to understand, now pass through college – but after that, what? There may be, must be, officially many answers: *I* drew my own from the faces about the streets. In Prague, I felt, you might be something in *spite* of being a woman, but you would be unlikely to be anything *because* of being a woman. The majority, in

Prague, of my own sex did not either dress or comport themselves as though they hoped to be anything more than useful; their faces wore acquiescence to a point which almost attained sublimity. *Was it sublimity?* My own Western fretfulness, many times, felt rebuked. This majority of the women I was judging were peasant-type; not at grips with, not so much as aware of, the multiple finesses of city life; unnatural, still, in their styleless city clothes. Our idea of woman as the practitioner of the art of life would make nonsense to them. At the same time, even if one surrenders the idea of life as an art, one must see it – all the more see it, surely? – as movement in *some* direction. This passivity looking out of the eyes and faces of the women I saw in Prague awed me. There was about it a sort of piety, something at once inherited and espoused. It was not weariness – psychically as well as physically they were untried-out, still full of silent potentialities, strong. Not holding back; more, not having yet come forward. All the same, I thought, what next – what next? When will these women feel it is time to ask in what direction, towards what destiny, they and the children they are bearing are being carried?

This was, however, only one of the points on which I felt I brought to Prague an extraneous judgement. I felt my foreignness most, and with most humility, among a people so clement to foreigners. It could have been uncanny to be in the heart of a city of whose language one understood not a single word – in which street-signs said nothing, and newspapers were so much black and white.

It was I, in this land-locked capital, who was the outlander; I was as separate from the articulate life of Prague, this Prague full-set for its crisis of February, 1948, as a dog running about among people's feet. I therefore *felt* a kindness not to be worded – the hand stretched out to swing one onto the overcrowded footboard of the overloaded tram; the street-directions given in voluble sign-language; the patience with which my desires were reasoned out, and, on streets or in public places, the decent, candid staring which could give no offence because it intended none.

Yes, I was in early-February Prague as a cat or dog might be in a house where something is going on – uneasy, but never uneasy for myself. The city was interpreted for me by many Czech friends who could speak English. But past the point where their outlook or their experience stopped, there was silence.

It was to be wondered at that Prague was not more deeply stultified by its years of the Nazi reign of terror. As things were, I could see what my friends there meant when they said: "We are not fully awake from that nightmare yet; we have not fully recovered." I was in flats where any unexpected ringing of the doorbell had – and how lately! – been heard with terror; where any footstep on the stone staircase outside might be carrying doom.

Story after story, of kinds not to be written down, entered not only my ears but my spirit – and these were stories carried in the personal memory of hardy, ardent people with whom I daily talked. Perhaps, at fleeting moments, some part of what had happened was to be guessed from behind the eyes; but it was never, in any one case, told me by the man or woman to whom it *had* happened . . .

Late-winter sunshine struck through the flowering plants in the double windows; beyond which rose, cut out, a mellow, yellow gable, or hung, as though on glass painted, an aerial view. What I was being told could have seemed incredible – but, no: nothing is incredible in Prague. Suspense tightened the air all the time I was there. Was this no more than climatic? Was this a residual suspense, left behind by the Occupation, unable, so far, to have dissolved because there had been so much of it? It was open to me to think so – I could not think so, quite. We were still in the middle of something; destiny was not finished.

No Britisher, these days, travels for no reason. I had come to Prague to be a lecturing author. This, however, was something better than an onus; it was a key. I was met by, and shall remember always, the city's intense, whole-souled, quivering receptivity to art. (If, indeed, as I have suggested, the Czechs do not reckon life as an art, that is because they put art on the higher plane – life is for hard work; art has the rank of religion.)

To talk about literature to a Prague audience was to have a sense of almost mystical contact – it mattered so much. These were people who had risen at five in the morning, worked all day, and now, next, would be fighting their way home on the insufficient trams to outlying quarters of the city . . . The Opera House, theatres, concert halls, lecture rooms – everywhere from which, as Prague feels it, eternal life emanates, is in Prague packed. Among the depleted shops stand out the bookstores – colourful, tempting, and (at least when *I* last saw them) cosmopolitan.

In the theatres, there was being bold experimentation with Shakespeare and Shaw. Most of all, however, the Czech capital struck me as having an impassioned wish to enlarge and forward Czech art, to make it a vehicle for the whole force of national self-expression – and, as such, to make it worthily known abroad.

Leaving Prague, in February, I felt that I left behind me a people awed by consciousness of their destiny, as one might be awed by an elemental force. What next turn that destiny was to take, or how soon, how many of those I left knew? There were questions one instinctively does not ask; I had not asked them. A country, like a person, must travel its own path – that path may, at times, be lost to a friend's view.

Hungary

I was in Hungary from the 16th to the 23rd of this October, 1948 – lecturing on literary subjects for the British Council. Or rather, under the auspices of the British Council – actually, two of my three lectures in Budapest were delivered to the Hungarian-British Society. The H.-B. Society is run by Hungarians, with official approval: it is sponsored by the Cultural Department of the Hungarian Ministry of Education.

At Debrecen,[1] I delivered a lecture on Sunday morning in a hall of the town Museum. I understand that this, though arranged by the professor of English at Debrecen University, was a public lecture – the hall's being packed and the audience's being both attentive and enthusiastic was[2] therefore not only encouraging but interesting.

I allow, of course, for the fact that Debrecen's having been a Protestant stronghold makes the cultural tie with England of long standing, and still, one could feel, vestigially fairly strong.

The attendance at the Budapest lectures was equally good, the reception friendly. These Budapest lectures were by invitation: there was in Budapest no equivalent to the "open" lectures in municipal buildings such as I delivered in Prague (in early February of this year, just before the Communist *coup*) and in Vienna later in that same month.

It was clear to me that, if only for commercial reasons, the present Hungarian government is anxious that knowledge of the English language should not lapse. I gather that, therefore, little intimidation against attendance at English lectures exists – provided that the lecturer be ideologically harmless. As against that, it obviously required courage for any Hungarian to have *social* contact with any British person. It was surprising, considering the system of espionage and notation of every individual's movements, how many Hungarians did take the initiative where I was concerned – or, at least, accept invitations to meet me. Apart from journalists seeking interviews, I had several callers at my hotel, who sat talking to me in the public rooms. My callers were obviously nervous and self-conscious, but mastered their nervousness well. Conversation during such visits was always of a guarded and superficial kind: the main intention seemed to be to convey goodwill and to be, at least for a few minutes, in the presence of somebody from the West.

Two of the factors in my good reception were, I could see, nostalgia and curiosity. Reasons for the nostalgia were obvious – the British are associated with "the good days." Curiosity came from the fact that there had not been a British novelist-lecturer in Budapest for some time: the Hungarians are enthusiastic readers of fiction. Also a British woman visiting lecturer was a novelty.

I think that as a novelist-lecturer I had certain advantages in my brief view of Hungary. The *general* nature of my subject attracted a more mixed audience, and got me contact with a wider variety of people, than I should have had if I had been a specialist. The (right or wrong) idea which prevails in England that the novelist is socially entertaining exists – to a very marked degree – in Hungary. The sociability, desire for pleasure, and conversation for its own sake of the Budapest people were outstanding – walking about Budapest by myself, as an observer, I saw evidence of this everywhere; in the streets, the cafés. That streak in the temperament of the people seemed in itself to constitute an *unformulated* resistance to the regime.

All through my stay in Hungary I received the impression of being in an occupied country, in which any genuine life was being lived surreptitiously. The effects of fear and mistrust were to be felt at every turn. In public places, conversations, though animated, were always conducted in lowered voices. In a large café, for instance, one had the impression of being in a hall of whispers: café orchestras seemed to serve the double purpose of suggesting gaiety and providing a screen for talk.

I was interested to note that, so far, the Communist authorities have done nothing to restrict the pleasure-life of Budapest. Music and lights continue late. Like (I imagine) all foreign visitors to Budapest under the present regime, I was surprised by the survival[3] and apparent prosperity of streets of luxury shops. *Who* patronises those shops – which, apart from their expensiveness, cater for sophisticated taste – is a mystery. I am told that a *new* "new rich" class has sprung up since the Communists came in. In general, people who *can* still retain or obtain money may still, apparently, spend it how they like. Possibly a clean-up is still to come. This would, however, obviously be so very much against the grain of the national temperament that one wonders whether even the present government might not hesitate to undertake it.

The Budapest "workers," like the reduced middle classes, are obviously pleasure-seekers. Standard in looks and style of dress in all classes (or ex-classes) is high. It would, I felt, be difficult to extirpate from the Hungarians the (now denounced as "bourgeois") romantic idea. Among city women, the stocky "comrade" type idealised by the USSR does not seem to exist. Time and money are spent on personal appearance – with good results.

It was impossible – and would have been foolish – to ignore the warping and distorting effects of the present regime on both personal and general life. I was told, and could believe, that in these days, no one Hungarian totally trusts another; and I could feel that it would have been both unfair and rash to repose entire confidence in any one Hungarian. Incalculable pressure could be applied to any person at any minute; nerves in many people seemed to be near breaking-point and under pressure anybody might do anything. A proportion of people have joined "the Party" for expediency reasons: the struggle for existence is severe, and any political handicap might be fatal.

At the same time, I was made conscious at every turn of how powerful the submerged "Western" idea is in Hungary – the more powerful, perhaps, for *being* submerged. It is the perpetual alternative to present miseries. The whole Hungarian *amour-propre* (and I have never been in contact with a race in which *amour-propre* was more powerful) seems to be bound up in the idea of the Hungarians being a civilised people. Both as to culture and way of life, one feels the constant derivative from France and England. In the case of many Hungarians, I feel it would be fairer to speak of self-respect than of *amour-propre*.

Sensitiveness to Western opinion – even, I found, among some of the Communist officials – is immeasurably strong. I was made aware that, for a variety of reasons – perhaps an almost grotesque variety of reasons – a maintenance of contact with the West is desired. I got the feeling that the British were being anxiously watched, and that the continued presence of British people in Budapest, and the occasional arrival of British visitors there, was of morale value. I may be pardoned for speaking intuitively, even sentimentally, when I say that I felt that "Do not let us go!" was the prevailing Hungarian attitude. It was conveyed to me not only in my direct contacts with people but in small ways, by strangers. Those guarded and wary demonstrations *were* small, were barely perceptible, but cumulatively they became important. I feel certain that in our relations with Hungary there is a potential to be kept in mind.

(I except from my generalisations about Hungarians any few

survivors from the *ancien régime*: such persons are, ruthlessly speaking, negligible.)

The association, in the Hungarian mind, of British with the Liberal idea is striking. The 1848 Centenary Exhibition had just opened while I was in Budapest: it had in prominent view a number of pictures and documents which were reminders of British support for (a) Hungarian Liberalism (b) the Hungarian national struggle. This exhibition had been projected, and conceived in its general lay-out and detail, two years ago, prior to the coming of the Communists[4] into power. It now stands (as far as I could see) more or less as it was at first conceived: its whole trend is patriotic rather than political. The more we can "play" 1848 the better, it seemed to me. The sending of a British historical lecturer to Budapest at this juncture could be excellent. I myself felt that not too much stress could be laid on one's interest in and sympathy for Hungarian national (as opposed to present political) life.

The "Officina" Press in Budapest puts out magazines (of a literary nature) in English, for English readers; and a booklet on historical relations between Britain and Hungary was given me. The stuff I was handed, I noticed, dated from 1946, or earlier: there was, therefore, no line-up with present ideology. Those booklets, etc., have not yet, however, been either cancelled or re-edited – possibly because they may be taken to be acceptable; possibly merely because there has not yet been time to replace them. The idea, therefore, of a continued courtship by Hungary of British opinion is still being conveyed.[5]

The Party's hold seemed strongest on the student age-group. Most of the technique of propaganda seemed to be on that age-level. Apart from the nightmare aspects of enforced Communist government, I thought that the majority of adults were bored and exasperated by its noisy side: perpetual student demonstrations, amplified voices of noisy speakers travelling down the streets. The contempt of the adult for the adolescent was evident. In the main, the Budapest Hungarians seemed to me adult – intelligent (rather than intellectual), ironical, self-mocking, self-critical. They seemed to me embarrassed – as apart from being, also, tormented – by their present position. I had a conversation of some length with the Dean of the Arts faculty of Budapest University: he reported that his new batch of students show interest in practically nothing but politics: they have no cultural background, read little, and find concentration difficult. The nationalisation of the universities has entailed enormous reorganisation on the administrative side: during this, education in any real sense has been halted. The Dean so ordered his conversation as to allow me to infer more than he actually said: with him, as with other persons of integrity with whom I talked in Hungary, I had the sense of communication with a gagged person speaking by the eyes.

I was made aware with him, also, as with others of his calibre, of the enormous good faith still vested, however,[6] desperately, in the democracies of the West, and particularly in Britain. The lessening of any cultural ties that we *can* maintain with Hungary would be, I am convinced, not only a blunder but a betrayal.

The existence of a branch of the British Council in Budapest is of importance to a number of people who – either from ignorance of the English language, inertia, or timidity – do not take direct advantage of what the Council offers. If the Council in Budapest were to shut up shop, I believe that the moral effect would be more widespread, *and* more unfortunate, than it is possible for people in Britain to compute. The British Council people in Budapest are, personally, not only liked for their friendliness, they are admired for their nerve – and, perhaps most important of all in that atmosphere of universal mistrust, trusted for their discretion.

The pipeline (book supplies, etc.) to provincial centres is obviously of value. The shortage of scientific and technical books in Hungary is, just now, considerable: research students owe much to British supplies – which the Hungarian government, whatever may be its attitude, could not (I gathered) afford to see suspended.

It struck me, also, that the British Council people have, through their cultural activities, very much wider and more free contacts in Hungary than could be possible for the personnel of the Legation. To put the matter crudely, I was surprised at how far, in all senses, a

British[7] person *could* travel on the cultural ticket. I myself could wish to see a greater import of general modern British literature – fiction, biography, criticism, poetry, and *belles lettres* – into Hungary: a further grant for this purpose could not be better spent. Under present circumstances, attractive books would be ideal carriers of the Western idea. At present (I suppose inevitably) there is a time-lag of about twenty years in Hungarian knowledge of English writing: few of our more mobile and genuinely contemporary writers seem to be known. English writers of the "Twenties," who *are* read, convey the idea that we are still bogged down in a stylish but intensely upper-bourgeois mood of cynicism and iconoclasm.

I do not know how best to word my conviction that the Hungarians are not only susceptible to contact but worth contacting. I felt them to be a race formed psychologically – as they are physically – for health, and capable of supporting (though *not*, it seems, of instating) a good government. At present they are unnerved, demoralised, and, in the main, supine. Axiomatically, a people is supposed to get the government it deserves – but, when a government has been imposed by an outside power,[8] *does* the above hold good? Hungarian faults seem negative – lack of single-mindedness, lack of stamina, lack of drive. All the same, it seemed to me that the Hungarians are to be admired for having conserved what they have: their evasiveness works both ways.

Granted all that, the Hungarians have, all the same, certain temperamental as well as physical affinities with us – I, for one, have never felt myself to be in a less "foreign" country.

My view of Budapest was, owing to the shortness of my stay, incomplete and patchy. On the drives to and from Debrecen (which were by different routes) I had a memorable but of course purely transient view of the countryside – suburbs, villages, industrial towns, agricultural land, vine-growing areas, and the Hortobad.[9] Backwardness and beauty were the chief impressions I got. The peasants looked impermeable, and as though they would be passively obstinate. In spite of talk of mechanised farming, I saw only three tractors in the course of our crossing of immense spaces of land. Cattle and horses few: a heavy toll was taken by the Russians. The effect of emptiness was, I realised, due to the concentration of *all* dwelling-houses in villages: it has, I learned, been established that the average distance to be travelled by the village-dwelling peasant to work on his own land-strip is five miles. Ten miles of walking, or wagon-travel, has thus to be computed in with the working day. I do not know whether this distance-factor is to be used by the government as an argument against peasant ownership and in favour of the proposed communal farms.

The size and good upkeep of village churches, and the number of shrines and Calvaries along the roadsides suggested that religion keeps its hold on the peasant mind. I was in Budapest one Sunday, in Debrecen the next: in both cities there was, throughout the morning, a tremendous ringing of church bells – Catholic and Protestant. I was told that, within the last year, there has been more church-going by both denominations. Apart from a deepening of the spiritual need in time of trouble, church-going is one of the few "opposition" acts not yet punishable by law.

Without Coffee, Cigarettes, or Feeling

When first, in 1954, I entered a German city, with its spectral buildings and tattered skylines, I asked myself: How can it feel to be young among these ruins? I had come here to Germany to speak in some of the universities about the present state and the future hopes of the novel in English, and the technique of writing.

The discussion of imaginative writing raises, I had so far found, almost every question under the sun, from the most vividly personal to the most coolly abstract and theoretic. But my experience had, when I came to Germany, been confined to Britain and America – the fact was that I had up to now spoken and (which was more important for me) listened to the fortunate children of the democracies. First, therefore, in being the most my business, of the postwar German enigmas which confronted me was that of the outlook, intellectual interests, psychological background, plans, hopes and intentions of present-day German youth. To which was added my own personal, human, I suppose essentially feminine query, "How does it feel?"

"To feel is fine," said somebody, "if one can afford it." I received the impression, as I kept moving from place to place and from group to group, that though German shops are stacked with attractive goods, paint bright, flowers almost everywhere, feeling remains one of the luxuries Germany still feels she dare not afford. It delays, it sidetracks, it is uneconomic – and, within recent memory, it betrayed. Stoicism, with which goes an intent concentration upon purpose, is the prevailing note, no less among the young than among the older, no less with student girls than with student men. Questions as to pleasure – "What do you like to do? What most amuses you or pleases you? What seems to you most worth doing for its own sake?" – are met, though never with hostility, with a kind of puzzlement and dumbfoundedness. Self-expression, that aim we democracies are working so hard to inculcate, is a fascinating, increasingly tempting, but none the less still somewhat foreign idea.

I was in Hamburg, Göttingen, along the Rhineland and in Berlin. From what I saw and heard, it seemed that the cost of university living was being kept down to as low as possible – at the cost, inevitably, of some amenities which the American student would associate with college days. Mainly, the students came from the region, and for the sake of economy lived at home or with friends; others in hostels sponsored or owned by the universities and necessarily run on austere lines. Canteens, equivalents of the coffee shop, cater for midday dinners but close when the academic day is over. Tightness of schedule, pressure of work allow few breaks (a pity, I thought) for sociable coffee-drinking; and coffee, still a commodity at high price, is beyond the reach of the average student's purse. The students, girls in particular, wanted to know about extracurricular activities – in fact, few aspects of college life in America and Britain interested them more. They were kindled and charmed by the possibilities. Themselves, they seemed to be up against two primal difficulties: time and place – "But how can there be *time* for all this?" they continued enviously to marvel.

Some of the hostels have downstairs public rooms, available for authorised student meetings; and approved societies did, I found, exist. International affairs, home economics are, not surprisingly, two outstanding interests: speakers are brought in, discussions follow – or should, but here again time may intervene. The rooms in which the societies meet are granted for a rigidly fixed period only – "and often," as someone dolefully said, "just when the thing is reaching its peak it is necessary for us to break up and go home." In the past, in pre-Hitler Germany, the student society or *Bund* exercised considerable power; to the point, sometimes, of revolutionary force. When students met, it could be taken that there was something cooking. Nazism, as we know, was quick to take over the student bodies as power centres: it may be because of this that student clubs or societies now seem suspect (or so *I* thought) by the students themselves. German girls and boys of today dread wouldbe "operators" among their numbers – "the danger of a club or society," one boy sombrely said to me, "is that it may come to be dominated by one or two persons wishing to gain position or to exercise power over the rest of us."

However, in spite of these deprivations, "life" as one understands it does spring up – how can it not, when one is young? In each place, the students *could* be felt to be a community, within which existed sympathies and attractions, shared points of view and exchanged secrets. One lack – and lack it is felt to be – is the chance to contact, as student-to-student, young travelling Americans and British. "They come," it was explained to me, "naturally, always in their vacations, which are at the same time as ours. All of us are therefore at that time scattered, away, at work elsewhere, or else at home. We see them; we watch them with great interest – there is so much we should like to discuss. Sometimes one is lucky enough to make a contact; but on the whole we are a little shy." They wish, and one wishes on their behalf, that there could be some extension of student interchange. Sometimes I felt bad questioning them, when there was so much they wanted to know from me – they have a lust, a passion for "other countries." Some few that I met were to attend, in the coming summer vacation, student or generally cultural conferences in England; the means for this had presumably been found. But without "business" one must remain where one is: France, Spain, the ever beloved Italy, and the vitally interesting America are closed to most of the students whom I met, who desired no more than to go there, be there, see. No, no law, so far as I know, operates against what they desire; there merely is the everlasting constraint of the slender budget; plus, still more, the necessity to work, work, *work*.

University standards are exacting. To obtain a degree must take four years. The entrance standard is high; and to emerge with a degree (without which the whole of life would be disempowered) entails the unremitting exercise, the single-minded, almost fanatical concentration of all that one has of brain, nerve and energy. To this end, one must be content – and they *are* content, in the main – to forgo or at least impoverish all other variants of life. There is no soft option, no easy way. The German university differs from what would otherwise be its counterpart in America and Britain in that it is not to be regarded as a social-cultural preparation for general life: it is a factory for efficiency, an intellectual-professional forcing house. No one goes there who is not thought likely to stay the course in an out-and-out cerebral career. And this seemed to me to be bearing hard, in particular, upon the young women. For a woman in her young days, life should be opening up, not narrowing down. Many I met looked, for all their good appearance and high spirit, decidedly anxious and taxed and tense. There was something nun-like about their devotion to their future career: when I asked them (outright) whether, surely, they did not intend to marry, they looked not so much embarrassed as at a loss. For if they married, if they gave themselves over to the superabundance of German domesticity, all this they were doing would have been "wasted." Higher education in Germany, I was forced to realise, aims not so much to widen and enrich life (that is, process of living) as to reduce it to one functional purpose.

All universities to which women go are co-educational; there are no colleges for women only. Most of the young women I met were to be teachers; a smaller group were to be civil servants, and a still smaller one physicians, chemists or technicians. Germany's present vast recovery need seems to have finally broken down the traditional and Nazi-enforced idea that woman should keep to children, kitchen, and church[1] – should she show herself able to make good in other fields, she is welcome in them: all hands are wanted! Which is excellent – though, one inclines to feel, German womanhood comes to emancipation the hard way.

It was hard to elicit, from any talk, how far or how high ambitions soared. The future profession had been chosen, already, when the student entered the university – among the students admitted there are, apparently, few whose decisions are yet to make. The possibilities of the profession chosen necessarily limit the horizon and qualify the ambitions of the student – few I met could, therefore, permit themselves flights of fancy. At the moment, freedom counts for less than security. "Did you ever think," I asked successions of students, "of adopting one of the 'free' professions – such as, for instance, being a writer? Did you ever wish to 'explore' in any way, or to take risks on the chance of fame, unique success, or perhaps rewards greater than you might reach by the beaten path?" The answer, after a pause for thought, was in almost every case a shaken head. But remember, this is a special, conditioned age group. Germany's students may be answering differently ten years hence.

When I say that ambition seemed to be national more than personal, I in no way mean that these girls and boys struck me as tinged by a dangerous nationalism. Their concern is for their country and its recovery – hence, I think, the stress they lay on security: the greater number of secure persons Germany contains, the more secure as a country she will be. Also, they witness the ruin left by the excessiveness of the Nazi daydream: do all dreams, perhaps, seem to them dangerous things? Their imaginations are for the time being kept battened down; nor, I think, is much done to arouse them. University classes, for instance, take the form of lectures; classroom discussions are almost unknown – thus, intellectual initiative, a querying attitude or individual thought, though not forbidden, cannot be stimulated. Classes are large, individual contact with the professor or instructor is not possible during a session, nor is he accessible betweentimes. There can be only brief comment on written work. "We feel we do not get as much from our professors as they could give us, and might possibly like to give us," said one student. I felt that the very build, the ground plan of the average German university, tended to cut off the faculty from the students – there is no equivalent of the campus. I felt, too, that most of the students would be shy of asking a professor to clarify a point, or of stating any intellectual difficulty of their own.

"We are taught," said one girl, "more than we need to know." "But isn't that better," I asked, "than to be taught *less* than you need to know?" She pondered, then said: "I'm not so sure. Maybe if I were taught less, I'd think more."

And another stimulant to imagination, the reading habit, is also missing. Hard study, several of them told me, excludes or severely cuts down reading for pleasure. Books, new books, are very expensive. University libraries and the public libraries (which are excellent) lay in only a small stock of contemporary fiction, biography or poetry. It is hard for the student to get anything like a comprehensive picture of the present-day literary scene – contemporary European and American writing is unheard of, apparently, as a classroom subject. (The American-sponsored Free University[2] in Berlin was, I discovered, a fine exception; and I should like to think that there may be others.) The creative wish of the student therefore cannot be stimulated and led on by evidences of creative achievement elsewhere. "Where are *your* writers coming from?" I asked them. The wise reply was: "We shall need time." And time will, one may be certain, show – one can feel the German imagination germinating under the present rather hard, bare surface. One longs to give these young people the gift of leisure, time to reflect and idle, space within which what is lyrical in their temperaments may expand.

Think, however, they do. Have they, then, as an age group for themselves evolved any special philosophy? They are interested, they tell me, in the Time-spirit[2] – it fascinates them, to affiliate art with history. They believe there to be a special importance in being alive *now*; and, in so far as they can, they study the effect of the Time-spirit on their contemporaries. They believe that one feels, thinks and acts according to the spirit of the time into which one is born; to them, a generation is (or almost is) in itself a race. They do not, I think, feel that the Time-spirit exerts compulsions; but they do feel it develops within its children certain awarenesses, tendencies and capacities: in fact, that each epoch has its hallmark. They feel that people living within the same time, though in different countries, have more in common than people who, though they have lived in the same country, have done so in different times. Thus national boundaries don't mean much to them. It might be said that this vital stress on the present is the young people's manner of shaking off the blame and misery of the past – what might be *their* views as to German war guilt I naturally did not care to ask them. But myself I thought it meant something better: an eager wish for community with the rest of the world.

How they feel about the present separation of eastern from western Germany also went – or at least so I felt – rather too deep for direct questioning. Many had missing relatives, some lost whole families. In speaking of the future, they often speak of "the time when Germany shall again be whole." They did not strike me as politically minded; and they were averse (though always courteously so) to discussing politics. Their outlook, their hopes had liberal colour, though they were conservative as to institutions, and, as to customs and ways of life, wished for improvement, enlightened progress but nothing in the way of basic change.

There is something like a devoutness in the students' attitude to the task of life. College age is much what it is in America, eighteen to twenty-two, but many of them seem older. Though cheerful, or willing to be cheerful, they are (I felt) fundamentally grave. The singing beer garden days are over: junior groups can neither afford to drink nor afford the time to recover from "thick" evenings; and cigarette-smoking also costs too much. Existence, in fact, is stripped of many small, supernumerary pleasures; and yet in some indefinable way one felt that it *was* being enjoyed. They are tired, sometimes; yet a renewing zest keeps them at their nonstop activity. Almost all of them work their way through college, though not on the American plan – the intensive pressure of the curriculum, the amount of home study required make it impossible to do outside work while the university is in session; it is during vacation time that most of the students disappear into factories or offices; or, in the case of the men, do heavy manual work at road-repairing or reconstruction building – factories keep short-term openings for students, and extra hands for any speeded-up enterprise are to be counted on during vacation periods. This (for the student must continue to study during vacation evenings) puts an extra tax upon him or her.

The answer to my original question, as to how it feels to be young among these ruins, was not to be found in so many words – nor in so many words can I give it here. I can see, now, the wisdom of the remark made to me, as a provisional answer, by a non-German friend who had been in the country since 1946. "*You* see the ruin and the destruction," he said, "all in a blow, because you are coming new to it. What you cannot see is how far more dreadful it was, and what a triumph is represented by the restoration of even this much order. Where you see destruction only, the German beholds the marvel of reconstruction, the re-emergence of form from chaos – he is more than steadied by this, he is elated." Of the young people, this is particularly true – and best of all, they need not only look on what is being done: they can have a part in it. Young Germany, and most of all its students, has what maybe the young of the democracies lack just now – a vast, commanding and to them noble incentive. Everything that they do counts; everything they give themselves to matters. True, one is only young once, and some of what should be youth's pleasures are passing by them. But is it not one's ideals which make life worthwhile and, by doing so, keep one happy? *Their* ideal is single – it is Recovery.

Regent's Park and St. John's Wood

Regent's Park is something more than an enclosed space; it has the character of a terrain on its own – almost, one might feel, a peculiar climate. The impression, on entering by any one of the gates for the first time, is of dreamlike improbability and a certain rawness; as though one were looking upon a masterly but abandoned sketch. The first thought is, "Can I be, still, in London?" – for, in this enclave as nowhere else in London, British unostentatiousness drops away, to be succeeded by something stagey, bragging, foreign; none the less drenched in and tempered by northern light. "The Park," be it understood, comprehends the Nash[1] architecture with the scenic layout: the two form, as they were intended to do, a whole. At no point, however bosky, in the interior is one to forget the Regency terraces, upon three sides overtopping the trees.

Regent's Park backs upon, and has as its southern base, Marylebone Road (formerly the New Road) and stretches northward towards the heights of Hampstead and Highgate. That the beauty of those – as they then were – green hills might not be lost to view, the top of the Park was at first left open: along this top runs the cutting of the Regent's Canal. That, later, Albert Road should come into being – on the far side of and open on the canal – was, one must suppose, inevitable: the ideality of south-facing building sites, looking down over gladed acres, was not to be ignored. The Albert Road Victorian houses were to be short-lived: almost all have, now, given place to high blocks of twentieth-century flats. Thus, if one were to tip the present-day Park map into the vertical, one would see it as a flat-bottomed Regency cup, filled to the brim with green, with a modern lid.

Regent's Park in its north-east corner harbours the Zoo: when the wind blows one way, roaring of lions or shrieks of monkeys are wafted down. Seen at sunset across the Park playing-fields, the Mappin Terraces take on the queerness of Dali rocks. Albany Street and Park Road, both now considerable thoroughfares, run, respectively, up the Park's east and west flanks; the air here inside, however, just as it breeds mist, seems to have the property of consuming sound – over lawns, walks, flowerbeds, groves, mounds, and artificial water there hangs what is in the main silence. On summer evenings, silence inside the Inner Circle (now Queen Mary's Garden) is pleasantly torn across by amplified scraps of Shakespeare from the Open Air Theatre.

In 1811, a year felicitous in view of the projects of the Prince Regent and John Nash, the lease of land then known as Marylebone Park – which was, in fact, a rough space of fields and market-gardens along the still raw New Road – reverted to the Crown. Mr. John Summerson,[2] in whose *John Nash* and *The Building of Georgian London* the history of our area is set out, and by whose research I profit, traces the growth of politer London northwards throughout the eighteenth century. But, he remarks, Fashion had brought itself to a halt at the New Road – thus far, no farther! Socially, therefore, Regent's Park was the most daring feature of the "Metropolitan Improvements" town-planning project, rational if spectacular, that the Prince and his architect undertook. The new Regent Street, cut through from south to north, was to terminate in something newer still: "a private garden city for the aristocracy." Of the great gated enclosure to be called Regent's Park, the terraces, with their theatrical palace-like painted façades facing in on the green, were to be, as it were, palisades – and, about the terraces' dun brick backs, turned upon all the rest of London, there is still something daunting and palisade-like. Inside the Park – and, indeed, its proclaimed attraction – there were, by the original Nash plan, to have been twenty-six villas (in the Italian sense), each artfully set in the landscape of grass, water and trees.

Unhappily, Nash's imagination overshot that of the patrons for whom he bid. Though by 1816 the roads, fences and plantations had been completed, and the bed of ornamental water dug, Nash had already received a set-back. Of this he wrote: *The numerous applications I had from men of rank and fortune, when the design was in agitation, to set down their names for Sites for Villas within the Pale of the Park, justified the expectation of that part of the improvement commencing immediately; but before the roads were completed and the park inclosed, the disposition to build-ing suddenly became paralysed.* There had, furthermore, been advanced an opinion that too many villas would spoil the scenery – as Nash saw the villas *as* scenery, this was the more annoying. Of the twenty-six envisaged, eight only were built (four, and a lodge of the fifth, today survive). Nash, however, did not lose confidence: *As the Park increases in beauty, it will increase in value . . . the first occupiers will stamp the character of the neighbourhood.*

Nash's voice is the swan-song of an age in which culture was linked with wealth, taste with breeding. He conceived Regent's Park for a *beau monde* which was in fact already on the decline – which possibly had never existed, really – and Regent's Park was finished just in time to be an anachronism. Between 1821 and 1826 almost all the terraces were built or building; and, if there had been shyness as to the projected villas, the terrace houses filled up as soon as their roofs were on.

The Park ground-plan is true to the design – the Outer Circle contains the Inner Circle; which is to say, one road describes the circumference of the verdant Park; another, in the Park's centre, loops round an inner garden – today, Queen Mary's. The Outer and Inner Circles are connected by a subsidiary road emerging opposite York Gate. At this point starts the lake; which, at first no broader than a canal, bends at the Park's south-west corner, widens out opposite the west-side terraces into a sheet of water with wooded islands, then, to the north, splits widely into two prongs. Here, the whole disposition of water and trees round it could not be more lovely: there is an infinitely romantic mystery about the distances – I believe London holds no landscape to challenge this . . . On the east side, the layout, though pleasing, is more conventional. As the Park sweeps north, design expires completely: somewhat unmeaning stretches of grass, with goal-posts, vanish towards the Zoo . . . There are four gateways – Hanover, Clarence, York, and Gloucester – though the Park can be entered at other points.

Regent's Park was thrown open to the public in 1838; today, it contains attractions Nash did not foresee – a boathouse, a children's paddling pool, a tea garden; and, inside the Inner Circle, the famous rose-beds and the aforesaid Open Air Theatre. With spring, blue-green deck chairs come out under the yellow-green, flickering trees. In spring tulips, in autumn dahlias form a brilliant ribbon along one reach of the lake.

At present, after years of damage and vacancy, the terraces (some still undergoing repair) are in all-day occupation by civil servants: in the early dusk of winter, before the Ministries go home, entire façades are lit up – row upon row, the windows between the pillars shed blazing gold. One might take it that the *élite* had returned to earth and were embracing the whole Park in one enormous party. Ironically, these houses, built for festive illusion, never can have achieved it so completely as at this closing hour of an official day.

All the same, they have known festivity, good wine, reflection, talk. In the main, Regent's Park has attracted, as residents, solidify-ing bohemians. Actors, painters, singers, sport and theatrical promoters, editors, critics, poets in these large-roomed, large-windowed terraces lived their more mellow years. Professional people, barristers, doctors, in whose careers temperament as well as intellect played a part, sought these houses out; aristocrats deviating towards imagination joined them. To such, Nash's vision spoke; virtuosity summoned the virtuoso. The naïveté, the swag-gering, lyrical imperfection of Regent's Park may correspond with something in the creative nature. One must have worked, perhaps, one must both have succeeded and failed, before one can enjoy Nash. Sweet, specious, spacious, the scene he set has the character not of an inheritance, rather of an award.

St. John's Wood is uphill neighbour to Regent's Park – its south-east corner (which is Lord's Cricket Ground) and the Park's north-west just do not touch: St. John's Church, a landmark, stands between them. One enters St. John's Wood between the tan-talisingly high wall of the cricket ground and the railings of the church's long, pleasant graveyard – here, only trees weep now, melancholy hangs lightly over the antique headstones: Joanna Southcott,[3] of the famous Box, and John Sell Cotman[4] lie among others here.

Region of hills and declivities, ridgy skylines, quietly rising and falling roads, St. John's Wood starts with romance from this conformation, and has the further charm of the earliest villa-architecture, of one kind, known in London. This is the Eyre Estate: yet another experiment, Mr. Summerson shows, in planning – here, on a doll's-house scale. An existing map for the project, dated 1794, features one, at that time, absolute innovation: semi-detached villas. In favour of these, a pioneer break was made with the ruling London tradition of terrace-houses. That is not to say that St. John's Wood is without terraces – some, e.g. St. John's Wood Terrace itself, are of stucco, nice in ironwork detail and mouldings of the very narrow front doors. But the predominating impression is of villas, in whose styles the late classic and early romantic alternate. These seem to have come straight from Ackermann's[5] pages: their time colour is early nineteenth century. Laburnum, lilac, acacia appear indigenous.

The spine of the region is Wellington (which becomes Finchley) Road; the approximate boundaries are as follows – on the north, Boundary Road; on the south, St. John's Wood Road; on the east, Avenue Road; on the west, Maida Vale. Characteristic of St. John's Wood, however, is a very quiet network between the thoroughfares. Altogether, the concept would seem romantic privacy – just as Regent's Park expresses august showiness. Here is the extreme of the individual, as opposed to the extreme of the social, idea – though fancy is tempered by sense, taste, order, and wit. Retirement, with tenderness as its base, is suggested at each of the many turns; most of all by those high garden walls with doors in them. Creeper-draped verandas, gardens in which birds sing, add enchantment – so much so that, at the time of my girlhood, the idea of the entire St. John's Wood being an abode of love had not yet evaporated; it was only respectable to live there, I was told, if one were an R. A.[6] . . . St. John's Wood's name drifts across the pages of many novels;[7] alas, here as elsewhere daylight grows greyer now. Actually, those few secluded ladies were neighboured by a strapping proportion of highly respected families of successful artists: this was, and is, an ideal place to bring up children, think, paint, write, sing, enjoy *villegiatura* inside London. Studios ran into the gardens. In *Tempestuous Petticoat*, story of her own childhood, Miss Clare Leighton[8] pictures it all for us. Landseer,[9] George Eliot, Bradlaugh,[10] Thomas Huxley, and Herbert Spencer also lived in St. John's Wood. Stephen Spender lives there now.

Into no part of London can blocks of flats have intruded more inappropriately, with less grace. Monster-high, and giving an impression of sheer dull bulk, to the extent of seeming of beef-red brick right through, these blocks in St. John's Wood statically trample upon the neighbourhood. There are not yet many, but there are more than enough: we are given to understand there will be more. Below and between them, the fragile be-villaed landscape exists with a nonchalance which one has to honour: this out-faced war; can it survive stupidity? Ominously, lines of bomb-damaged villas are being left to rot, trees of their gardens growing in at their windows; someone is waiting, greedy, for their ideal sites. Over these little cadavers it is impossible not to shed a tear – they were so smiling, gay, neat, compact, warm; so much what so many people want, above all, today.

New York Waiting in My Memory

"Seventeen years," I told myself, "since I was here last." With the friends who had met me at Idlewild, here I was driving into New York. Seventeen years – a young lifetime. Children born since I left were now thinking, reflecting human beings. As for me, perhaps I am no longer objective about time. My years of absence reckoned up sounded many: but somehow time is only real to me as a personal sensation rather than as a fact – therefore according to feeling it shrinks or stretches. Now, as the Manhattan skyline once more rose around me, I could not *feel* that I had been so long away. I had been away, yes – indeed since I was last here had not the world convulsed itself, did we not all now, as a generation, carry the mark of new, ageing[1] knowledge? "So much has happened," I heard my thoughts reiterate, "so much has happened since."

But somehow on this pale, bright, wintry, early morning, at the end of a transatlantic journey by air, thoughts only seemed like a speaker in the far distance. Sensation was the immediate, engulfing thing. That whole orchestration which is New York beat upon my strung up senses and nerves. Are not most travellers after a long journey in a slightly hallucinogenic[2] state? The tense, soaring, spectacular, squeezed up, vibrant city seemed to merge into that. Most of all exciting was the familiarity. Yes, I had the illusion of not having been away. All those years, when so often I had not known I thought of it, New York must have been powerfully waiting in my memory: now, as though there had not been more than a minute of interruption, it resumed its hold.

One thing I had forgotten: the uncanny daylight glare, and the mutedness of a hotel bedroom, which though right in a city's heart, faces out on nothing but sky, soars high above traffic sound.[3] To arrive by day in a London or Paris room, I recollected, was to enter semi-darkness, to grope one's way to a window opening on other windows, to shut oneself in with a resonance from the roar of streets.[4] By contrast, for these first few minutes, this New York altitude seemed naked, lonely, intimidating, a shade inhuman. My defensive reflex was to jerk down the blind. I retreated from this first overwhelming morning into a no time, no place, a dark-blue[5] calico nighttime, through which I drowsed or slept. Through the opened top of the window, wind which raced round the skies kept the blind in a gentle state of tapping or rippling. This seemed part of the elemental restlessness of New York, belonging with what I had felt before – awareness of something striking up through the tapered, civilised buildings, out of the primal rock.

Daylight splashed in whitely around the blind, and, likewise, my blur of drowsiness was shot through by close-up memories of rooms, faces, street scenes, snatches of talk. Fragments of the New York of seventeen years ago had been conjured back by this 1950 morning onrush of sounds and sights. Association – what a projector it is. Around me in the half-dark, my hotel bedroom, with its chintzes and lamps, was as pretty as a guest room in a friend's house. My bed was soft. Today must wait till tomorrow.

It did. Actuality opened up with the earliest ringing of the telephone. Here I was, myself such as I am at the start of the third of my visits to New York. I could hardly wait to be out and about the streets. I had an hour before my first appointment: would I have been human if I had not headed for the shops?

These comprehended more to me than the wish, or indeed power, to buy. New York shops, for the Britisher, are something better than marts: they are revelations – yes, and symbols, too. Do we not see America as nurse, promoter, cherisher, and custodian of the amenities on behalf of all of us till the better days come? To think of nice things, even, heartens one up – who would postpone the chance of seeing them on display? Not, surely, the least of life's good graces expresses itself in objects shaped for pleasure – in smiling, stylish, modish, capricious, witty, above all *pretty* things.

Windows and showcases speak a particular language to the newcomer. Is this, alas, the song the sirens sang? No: thanks to some happy adjustment of the heart, the effect is less tantalising than reassuring. After all, the world seems less gritty and bleak and harsh. What the eye most feasts on is not mere luxury; it's luxuriance. Desire is sunk in joy that such things should be. I gazed till a visual delirium set in. Colours swam together as though I had become hypnotised by an aquarium, or crushed upon one another like many orchids. I saluted pretty devices to make life simple, simple devices to make life pretty. Workaday objects, even, carried small gleams of art. Best of all, in the little avenue shops, I loved the exuberant toys and fantasies not to be eaten or used or worn. (At home, almost everything is *for* something.)

This was one way to ease in. If I seem in this first addiction to have slighted the more "real" New York, remember that a peculiar focus must be allowed for. This same need for allowance, I felt, in a different context, later when I embarked on talk. Might not some of my comments, or questions, or answers to questions put, sound either frivolous or crazy? They asked me, for instance: "Do you find New York changed? Does it seem different to you – this time?" This posing of fundamental queries – lightly, as it were in parentheses –

must be a characteristic of New York talk. How glad I was to be back again, deep again, in its charms and perils. Nowhere else that I know is the conversational atmosphere so taut, pungent. Oh, to me this was heady, congenial air – the tempo, the range, the flavour, the intimacy, renewed their magic. In this city, interiors, whether of restaurants, bars, or friends' apartments, seem to be framed, and above all lit, for talking. In the matter of room lighting, New York compared to London is not so much prodigal as clever: diffusion, obliqueness, under-watery shadows give a touch of drama, an expressive intensity to faces, figures, and hands. The indigenous talker may take this asset for granted: the visitor – how can he, or she, not? – reacts. It's impossible not to come across.

Back, though, to the leading question – did I find New York changed? How could there not be change in my own view of it? This time, I looked at and looked for different things. So, accents shifted, proportions altered – perhaps. We all, these old or new friends of mine and I, have had to subject our personal values to a white-heat test. We have either grown up, or become conscious of the imperative necessity to do so. The searches and challenges in talk are no longer intimately idle: they have behind them the major searches and challenges of life. I was startled by the acumen, the psychological nearness to the mark, of the questions put to me about Britain: and, for my part, I never had the sensation of trying to answer across a gulf. I felt nearer people, I think, than I ever had – either in the New York of before, or elsewhere.

It occurred to me to wonder, from time to time, whether psychological difficulties might not be greater here (or at least more felt here) from the very fact that *outward* life runs more smoothly. Or, more apparently smoothly. I don't discount ubiquitous economic pressure, career anxieties, and so on. At no time, whether in the Old World or New, can it ever have been less simple to be a person. But there's this: in Britain our powers of apprehension are kept banked down by minutiae;[6] our faculties for worry are to an extent drawn off, or sidetracked, by hitches, stoppages, shortages, nagging little frustrations in the should-be ordinary conduct of a day. We exist by makeshift, which is preoccupying. Perhaps, accordingly, we envisage less, analyse less, ask less – in short, think less? Also, in thought as in speech, we are less articulate.

New York, as a city, seems in itself articulate – more so to me than others. Non-stop, it sends out messages, intimations, in its own tongue: the visitor sometimes can, sometimes cannot, interpret these. The vivid shifting daylight, the changing waves of expression carried by faces on all the streets, the alternating mutedness and hysteria of the traffic sounds, all say something. The way height is forced up, up, up by sheer lack of space gives – gave me, the stranger – a momentous, violent impression of nervous urgency. I never woke, any morning, without the sense that something terrific was going to happen shortly. This eased off during the days: exaltation came to its peak in the liquid glittering beauty of the evenings. (My visit was during a fine spell.) How can I say whether the city's voltage is higher now than it was? Europe, battered and weary, is temporarily in a low-pressure belt: the "lift," *here*, could but affect me strongly. Is velocity greater than it was? I reacted well to the high pedestrian speed – in all other cities *I'm* the impatient one. Less happy – in common, I gathered, with most New Yorkers – was I in taxis: to be locked for what felt like eternity in a traffic block set a stiff test to my nervous control. Happily, New York keeps on recharging one with the amount of energy that it uses up: it returns what it takes, often throwing in something more. On the count, on this score, I found myself up, rather than down.

Visually, had the scene changed – in those seventeen years? They told me it had: it must have. *My* eye could keep no check of the altered skylines: buildings torn down and replaced, landmarks gone. I could realise how, for the adult New Yorker, the city must teem with architectural ghosts, also what many, painful rents there must be in the individual map of association. I could, to an extent, compute the rate of change by what I, in the weeks of my visit, saw – the eruptions, the chasms, the drillings, the hammerings, the titanic rhythm in which steel frames of tomorrow, blocks were being swung up and bolted up, floor by floor. Out round New York's rawer edges, the effect, to me, was as though bombs had ploughed their way: construction and destruction, at one phase, operate much the same. Startling, by contradistinction, were old corners, into which silence dropped like a big stone in a pool. Nothing in Europe looks older, smaller, or kinder than what, in New York, survives from another age.

Everywhere, there seemed to be much more colour – but, again, was this the susceptibility of my own eye? Streets were not only architectural but chromatic riots, with a deep glowing reiteration of plum-crimson. I was dazzled by awnings, yellow cabs, flowers – and, this year's hats made the streets bobbing flower-beds. Chalk-white glints kept flashing at me, like a semaphore, from the women's spring suits. The mass effect of women along the streets was of verve, individuality, suppleness, due, I guessed, both to fostered dress-sense and the tremendous ranges of style, size, shade, and, above all, price, in shops. The inspired cut of the clothes – I once or twice thought – deserved better stuffs. As against that, the London woman's passion for "lastingness" chains her, for too many seasons, to outmoded styles. If New York frocks are for today only, ephemeral, they have the petal-freshness which goes with that. Sartorially, New York has no yesterdays.

New York, I know – and they tell me – is not America. She is unique, phenomenal. But, to this speaking phenomenon could any other country have given birth? For the European, New York translates at least some part of America's message. Her vocabulary can but have its limitations: there is much, much more to be said than New York can say. All the same, for us – for me, certainly – something crystallises, during however brief a stay on the Manhattan rock. My brain and nerves quickened: but the communication went on through my heart, where its meaning stays. First and last, I perceive, the communication's medium was forthcoming kindness. Contacts – in talk, in the clasp of hands, in sympathies, in unspoken mutual reassurance – are not such fleeting things. They have a virtue; they leave one freshened, stabilised, and enlarged. I should not dare to say that I found New York – what a glancing surface view of it I have given here. But New York found me – again. Can one speak of a city as having genius? Whether one can or not, I do.

PEOPLE

Miss Willis

I was at Downe House for the last three years of my school life, 1914–17. Miss Willis's school, when I went there, was still young; it had been started in 1909.[1] Looking back now, I can realise what an intensive character it had taken on in that short time, and also how unique that character was. Though one or two of the "original" girls, who could remember the first term of all, were at school with me, it still was hard to imagine that Downe had not been there always. In my time, there were never many of us (seventy, perhaps, at the very most) for our numbers were limited by the capacity of the old building, the Downe House, Downe, Kent, from which we took our name. Yet somehow Downe never felt like a small school: for one thing, it was untainted by amateurishness, and its ruling ideas gave one a sense of size. Outwardly, little may have differentiated it from those many other pleasant establishments, girls' private boarding-schools, dotted over England in country houses. Of such places, parents all say the same – "Girls are so happy there . . . such a nice atmosphere."

Decidedly Downe had an atmosphere, but the word "nice" was particularly satirised by Miss Willis – she regarded it as a witless adjective, whose use implied a retreat from discrimination. There was a sort of astringency in the air, which came from a mistrust of the *faux bon*.[2] Also, Miss Willis made it clear that happiness was to be incidental: we were there to work – actually, a peculiar happiness did distil itself from our routine. We were never bored; nor did we ever feel (in which we were right) that there was anything unreal or sequestered about our existence. Miss Willis's wish, which expressed itself in all her dealings with us, was that we should grow up; she would say, drastically, "Don't be *girlish*." She had a way of confronting us with our immaturity which made us not like it, made us recoil from it without need of further comment from her. But this was subtly and above all never unkindly done; she never humiliated us – her[3] attitude, more, was: "Come, come, *you* can do better than this!" She gave us an idea of ourselves.

Her ideas did not thin out into theories; they merged themselves into the being of the school. Her genius showed itself in two ways: as a teacher she was evocative, as a headmistress she was creative. What I seem to remember about my Downe House education is, my own discoveries. I imagine she intended this to be so. One was aware of being gazed upon, not from a too great distance and with discernment,[4] while one arrived at things of one's own accord. Her almost impassioned dislike of waste (given point to be the tragedy of those war years) made one feel that idleness was uncouth and dingy – though that one was never idle I cannot say. We were convinced that Miss Willis knew all about us, and I do not believe that we were wrong. Her physical serenity, her calm air of semi-abstractedness, the fact that she seemed to have time for everything, made her our ideal of control. She did not, however, tolerate hero-worship. My most constant image of her, in those days, is someone moving about in blue-grey tweed, with two large dogs. I do not think I had ever realised how spoken English could sound, or what an instrument speech could be, till I heard Miss Willis – teaching, in chapel, or at the beginnings and ends of terms. I have also never heard anyone less rhetorical. There were also interviews of another kind, alone with her; and then she was in another vein, con-centrated, searching and analytical. When she went round the bedrooms saying goodnight to us she sometimes could be persuaded to stay and talk, and then she would be very, very funny – laughter could be heard by the envious and impatient ones next door.

Her room, in which she saw us one by one, was narrow and white-panelled, with a window away at the far end. While she considered one, opposite her in a chair, she would twirl and spin the pencil hanging from a cord or chain round her neck.

Paul Morand

A pallid and heavy Mongolian face, like a mask put on once, for effect, that has grown into the flesh. A face like a buffer, from which curiosity – as it is intended to – rebounds. An uncommunicativeness unlike the nervous *noli mi tangere* the English put up. It remains impossible to believe in such impassivity: no one could be as phlegmatic as all that. When an Englishman is phlegmatic one always feels he is being phlegmatic at somebody: apparently M. Morand is not being phlegmatic at anyone. All the same – what goes on? On this fleshy mask expressions – the lifted eyebrows or broadening of the face by half its width again in a smile – are from time to time registered, sharply as exclamations.

There is a determination about M. Morand – perhaps unconscious – never to be observed observing, a pronounced uneagerness to express himself. His eyes, like slits cut into the inner darkness, with hardly a glint, move – or are moved – decisively from figure to figure, person to person, with an incuriosity so placid as to be inimical. In repose, the look comes to rest a few feet from the ground, fixing space with an intensity, an air of communication that it denied to objects, and immediately crystallising above the carpet, between the legs of the furniture, a small dark very concrete world. Or, he sits knees apart, kneading the fingers together softly and loosely, looking into the segment of darkness between the palms of the hands with a half-smile that is, upon the slightest sign of attention, instantly and politely effaced.

His presence makes itself felt immediately and increasingly, like a cat's, in the room. He can make himself felt, in flashes, as *very* nice. Flashes of high vitality, like sparks struck off by a planet, from an intensive well-being. Flashes of sheer goodwill from someone, perhaps too sure of himself, who has no more to acquire. Evidently he regards some part of himself as an instrument, whose power is in its edge, which he keeps guarded. Apart from this, fearless; having no capacity for pain.

Having advertised, explored, and recorded sensuality to the final

degree, his personality remains an enigma. Possibly he has none –
beyond the physical.

His politeness – meticulous – is like a series of bills being
promptly paid. His silences – discordant in general talk – are remarkable. The English, nervously over-communicative, have learnt
to invest their silences with a nervous and personal quality. But the
silence of M. Morand is as unpersonal as the silence of a street
down which no motorcar happens to be passing.

Mainie Jellett

I first knew Mainie Jellett when we were both little girls:
her mother and mine were friends, and neighbours in Dublin, and
Mainie and I must have[1] first met and looked at each other solemnly
before we were either of us able to speak. The little Jelletts and I
used to meet on our schoolroom walks through the streets and
squares, and were often in and out of each other's homes. And I was
one of the children who went to the painting classes which, held by
Miss Elizabeth Yeats[2] in the Jelletts' Fitzwilliam Square diningroom,
saw the opening of Mainie's life as an artist. I remember the
excitement of that free brushwork, the children's heads bent, all
round the big table, over crocuses springing alive, with each stroke,
on the different pieces of white paper. If she and I shared, as
children, the same burning wish, it was in those days an inarticulate
one. My wish has taken me down the path of another art. During
our working lives, we worked in different places, and met, where I
am concerned, too seldom. But I have never lost the proud sense of
being at least a contemporary of Mainie's, and a friend in the sense
that distance and separation do not damage. To have worked *with*
her must surely have been a great thing.

I saw her last, last October, in the quiet back room of the Leeson
Street nursing home, where she lay with her bed pulled out under
the window. A fire burned in the grate, and brick buildings in

115

October sunshine reflected brightness into the room. The eager, generous little girl of my first memories was now a thin woman, in whom the fatigue[3] of illness, mingling with that unlost generosity and eagerness, translated itself into a beauty I cannot forget. The greatness of Mainie Jellett was to be felt in many ways; but not least in her simplicity. She was not only easy but, which is rarer, easing to be with: she not only calmed one but re-lit lamps which seemed to be going out. I felt very much her junior, in vision, in virtue, in experience of what is truly life. Among other things, we talked about the book she had been reading, which had been in her hands when I came in, and about its author, Dorothy Richardson,[4] a woman unknown personally to both of us, whose strain of genius has not yet been enough recognized by the world. Mainie recognized it: she talked to me about writing with a pure comprehension of which, I think, few actual writers are capable. I know, now, that for her all the arts converged: they are different manifestations of something single. For a long time, Mainie studied the piano, which, up to the time of her last illness, she played often and beautifully. Her music is palpable[5] in her painting . . . In that October hour, we talked about many things, and discovered (where I was concerned) so many new things, that this for me was almost like a first meeting. It had certainly none of the character of a last one. And it was not a last one. Mainie's death has been a deprivation for so many people that I only can with humility speak of my own sense of it. But for her it can have been only another step on. The immortality of what she did and was remains.

I have begun this memoir in a simple and personal way because I cannot write about Mainie Jellett in any other. Her affections were vivid, and I think it would seem to her natural to be spoken of first in terms of ordinary human memory. There was something about her that would discountenance "sought" phrases and carefully chosen words. But also, I have her own authority – the authority of her essay, "An Approach to Painting," published in *The Irish Art Handbook* of two years ago – for my idea that an artist's natural place is in the heart of human society.

I believe (she says) in the necessity of a sense of craftsmanship being highly developed in every professional artist; they should be capable of executing whatever job they are commissioned to do adequately. An artist should be a competent worker as in the periods when the Guild system operated, have an honest standard of workmanship like any competent worker in other walks of life. The idea of an artist being a special person, an exotic flower set apart from other people, is one of the errors resulting from the industrial revolution, and the fact of artists being pushed out of their lawful position in the life and society of the present day.

Artists as a whole are people with certain gifts more highly developed than the general majority, but for this very reason their gifts are vitally important to the mental and spiritual life of that majority. Their present enforced isolation from the majority is a very serious situation and I believe it is one of the many causes which has resulted in the present chaos we live in.

The art of a nation is one of the ultimate facts by which its spiritual health is judged and appraised by posterity . . .

Mainie Jellett's place in the art of Ireland is beyond discussion: what is not less striking is the advance she has given to Ireland's art's place in the art of the world. Could one say that, her nationality being part of her temperament, internationalism was part of her discipline? One of her pupils, Stella Frost, writes: – "Her gift to Ireland was a rare one. Being national in her outlook, no small accomplishment in the circles in which she was born, she was at the same time international. By her specialised knowledge of the art of other nations, both ancient and modern, she was able to link up the best in all art and to weld it into the living expression of her own work and into that of her pupils. Her vision knew no bounds whether of art or religion, the only necessary passport to her sympathy was sincerity of spirit."

First, her life as a pupil. In Dublin, after Miss Yeats' classes, she worked with Miss Celia Harrison, then with Miss Manning, in the Merrion Row studio; then, about 1915, went to the Orpen class in the Metropolitan School of Art in Kildare Street, to study from the life. Early in 1917, she went to London, to work under Walter Sickert,[6] at the Westminster School. (At the same time, during those London years, she was a piano pupil of Miss Lander's – herself a pupil of Leschetitzky:[7] it was not until Mainie Jellett was twenty-two that she decided that she must, wholly, concentrate upon painting.) In 1919 she left London, to go, in 1920, with her friend Miss Hone to Paris, where they both worked in André Lhote's[8] studio. It was in 1923 that both Irishwomen became pupils of Albert Gleizes;[9] and after Mainie Jellett returned to live, to paint and to teach in Dublin, yearly visits to France for study with Gleizes, in Paris or at his house in the Rhône valley, continued up to 1933. During those years, she exhibited paintings in Dublin, London and Paris . . . In 1922, on a visit to Spain with Miss Hone, she was profoundly impressed by El Greco's work, as seen in its natural ground of the Spanish landscape. Months in Lithuania, in 1931, gave a fresh wave of impetus, mingled with her delight in what she called, to her sister, "Hansel and Gretel" surroundings. Her last visit to France was in 1939. War clanged a gate shut between her and the Continent. But she had reached her maturity. Learning days would never be over; but now she learned from herself – learned, perhaps, even in teaching, for is there not in teaching, at the height to which she brought it, some blessed endless reciprocity and exchange?

Teaching took time, drew steadily on her psychic powers as on her physical strength, and made less, if in the quantitative sense purely, the body of her own directly creative work. Her selflessness with regard to art showed itself in her selflessness with regard to younger artists, who might (from the outside) have been felt to stand between art and her. I think, too, that what might be called her family sense – the most sweet and human, surely, of Irish traits? – appeared in her attitude to her pupils, these younger brothers and sisters of the brush. Talking, before she died, to her friend Miss Hone, about her teaching, she said: "I suppose I had a desire to impart the little I had to give. I felt it was not given to me just for myself."

Mainie Jellett's essay on her own painting (already quoted) is startling in its objectivity. It is at once an analysis and the statement of a creed. "In recent years," she says, writing two years ago, "my work roughly tends to divide itself into three different categories: –

(i) Non-representational painting based on some emotional contact received from nature or experience, but first born in the mind.
(ii) Non-representational work based on Christian religious subjects treated symbolically without realism.
(iii) Realistic landscape treated in a manner inspired by Chinese Art, and direct realistic studies for exercises and reference."

She speaks of having gone through three major revolutions in her work, style, and ideas, and of, after each of these, starting more or less afresh. The first came with study with Walter Sickert – revolution in composition and use of line, realism, new understanding of the Old Masters. Sickert, being in the direct line of French impressionist painting, was the stepping stone towards the next revolution – Paris and Lhote's studio, with its work on modified cubist theories. "With Lhote I learnt how to use natural forms as a starting point towards the pure creation of form for its own sake . . . and to produce work based on a knowledge of rhythmical form and organic colour, grouping towards a conception of a picture being a creative organic whole, but still based on realistic form." Lhote was, in his turn, to be a stepping stone to the third revolution: as a student of Albert Gleizes. With him: "I went right back to the beginning, and was put to the severest type of exercises in pure form and colour . . . I now felt I had come to essentials, and though the type of work I had embarked upon would mean years of misunderstanding and walls of prejudice to break through, yet I felt I was on the right track."

So it happened that Mainie Jellett brought back to her native city a dynamism[10] that at first, as she had expected, was found unfriendly, destructive, even repellent. She had gone so far as to go, it seemed, out of view. A mystique without the familiar softness, expressing itself in the ice of abstract terms, and the apparent subjugation of the soul to the intellect, took some accepting. A whole force of opinion clings strongly to the idea (or superstition) of art's *spontaneity*, and believes that in theory and discipline, past an accepted point, the artist can do himself nothing but injury. Such opinion she was very slowly and very quietly to confound. (Humanly she was of the type that obeys Christ's injunction to offend none of these little ones.) It became apparent that her spirit had only gained in fullness through its recognition of intellect. Her poetic spontaneity, her human apprehension of life round her, had been strong enough to "take" the cold discipline. This spirit, which knew its own needs, had had nothing to fear – and, more, it could allay fear in others. Always, her attitude to her art had been a religious one – as, indeed, in the human part of her life appeared self-abnegation and humility. The most profound element in her painting was – from the very fact of its *being* the most profound – the slowest to emerge; many of the pictures painted in the last three or four years of her life were religious in feeling as well as subject. We have *The Ninth Hour* and *The Madonna of Eire*. And not from a less deep, in fact from the same source, came the vision that gave us her Irish pictures – for instance, the *Achill Horses*, whose growth I had seen in her studio, from sketch to sketch.

Mainie Jellett expressed in her talk to friends, states in her essay and made felt in her painting, her consciousness of her own, and our own, time, with its death throes and birth pangs, its agonising transitions. She ignored nothing. Art to her was not an ivory tower but a fortress. We could have wished her beside us, on into the growing days. But she leaves with us a spirit fortified, and fortifying, by its belief.

Foreword to Olive Willis and Downe House, by Anne Ridler

There was an Olive Willis before she was known to her many pupils; in these pages she is seen for the first time on her way to becoming the headmistress known by so many. Childhood and family background, the Roedean schooldays, her time at Somerville, teaching experience after Oxford before the founding of Downe House, all play a vital part in the story.

Personality – physical personality with all that it holds of mind, spirit and temperament – is hard to express in words. For those who knew Olive Willis this is not necessary – for ever she is to be called the eye; but for those who did not know her or for those who met her only in later years, the youthful, adventurous foundress of Downe House cannot be easily pictured.

I first learned with surprise from these pages that Olive Willis had at one time been "an ugly duckling" for she had a peculiar and formidable beauty – the beauty of fruition: I think of her in the days of the original Downe House, when the school was young enough to be in a way a miracle; an idea realised, a dear achievement. There was something about the face that would now be "contemporary" and as I see her, Holbein should have depicted her. I speak of her beauty as formidable; it was so unwittingly, in its open calmness. It was far from, and indeed alien to, *prettiness* of any possible kind – the beauty was of a spacious mouldedness with which went the Holbein-like setting in of the eyes (later alas, changed by glandular illness). There was a formidability, too, in being confronted – though often smilingly – without any equivocation.

I do not remember Olive Willis in terms of colouring, other than the colouring of her clothes; which, subduedly vivid, seemed a living part of her person, and, as such, made good anything Nature had not given her. She used no make-up – that being less unusual then than now. I speak of this attribute of hers, her looks – one rather would say, her *look* – not because she was aware of it, but because

I think it may have accounted, to a degree at least, for her equilibrium. It had come late to her (apparently); she had grown up learning to do without it. She was none the worse for it.

It was the equilibrium which affected us. I may say that, given the particular years I was at Downe House, there can seldom have been a time when equilibrium meant more. Death and destruction and, what children find most demoralising, disruption encompassed the outer world. I cannot, however, see Miss Willis's equilibrium as called forth by the patriotic demands of the First World War. She and Downe were what they were in spite of the war, not because of it. The maintenance of everything that there was seemed natural. The sedateness of our surroundings, rooms and garden, the intellectual tautness of lesson hours, the directedness, by a sort of remote control, of our indoor and outdoor hours of leisure, made juvenile hysteria stand out sharply, by contrast, and appear, by contrast, the more deplorable. I recall, for instance, few or no cases of *schwärmerei*[1] – though I learn that there was, at some time, the threat of an epidemic, swiftly remedied by a satirical play in which Miss Willis herself took part. There were, of course, romances – which, innocently being no more than that, could well go under the heading of education, of a kind which is, after all, extremely important. We were constantly, if much of the time subconsciously or at least indirectly or even hazily, aware of Miss Willis. We were convinced that she Knew All. *How* she knew appeared to be somewhat occult. Not only, it goes without saying, were we not spied upon, we seldom had the sense of being observed. By chance, by blunder, we might cross her line of vision. To attract her gaze, actually, was rare and memorable.

I went to Downe in September 1914. Olive Willis then was (I only now know) thirty-seven years old, and the school seven. My own age[2] is exactly that of my century; and at that time the early 'teens were, I think, the ideal age to start at Downe – then, the existences of the younger children, though satisfactory and diligent, seemed a trifle shadowy. The dire word "adolescence"[3] had not, then, entered normal vocabulary, and frenetic concentration on that age's "problems" played no part in the Downe House ideology. One was the age that one was – and hoped for the best. Being addressed as "children," hearing ourselves spoken of as "the children," made for democracy with regard to age. The effect was unsentimental – indeed, anti-sentimental – brisk and astringent. *Girls*, one associated with the fiction of Miss Angela Brazil;[4] "girlishness" was at the best a lapse; were it chronic, it could have been a malady. Among the greatest of Olive Willis's creative powers, as they affected the school and us, was her gift for fitly applied derision. It cleared the air. There was an incentive not only not to *be* foolish but to be the reverse. On faults or blunders due to passion or obstinacy, I do not recall that derision was ever turned.

She was not, I think, always just. Who can be? Only the paragon; and there was too much humanity, too much vehemence, in Olive Willis's nature for her ever to have been that. She detested greed, for instance, and did not always distinguish that from ravening youthful hunger. Outbreaks of nocturnal sweet-eating disgusted her to a degree I can never forget. Other trivial, idle or sluttish offences could spring up into an enormity that shook her, and in consequence us. But always, proportion returned. The crises, when they were over, became salutary. Best of all, one could speak up. One did so, and would be listened to. Downe would have been no place, I fancy, for a spiritless girl. There were few of them – was spirit injected into us?

The educational aspect of Downe House, the method, manner and standard of the teaching, has been so well covered in this book that I cannot see that I can add anything. There must have been (in fact, here we learn that there was) a close interaction between the staff. Of the different subjects we studied at different hours, each seemed to have bearing upon the others: learning was composite. Miss Willis's own teaching – literature and history – does not stand out for me as a distinct memory, perhaps because it sank so deep into my experience that I hardly know how far, at the outset, I was aware, and how far she made me so. It was incisive teaching. It was also an invitation to perception. Beyond that, it begat the wish that, having perceived, one should convey. Should one say, she instigated? And as teaching, it fulfilled in its own way what by Shelley's definition is a function of poetry: to cause us "to imagine that which we know."⁵ These were, perhaps, modern methods before their day. There was the further dimension – religion. For many of her pupils, those were foundation years. The school then had, and for some time longer was to have, no chaplain. Weekly confirmation classes taken by a visiting clergyman were *pro forma*; actually and effectively we were prepared for our confirmations by Miss Willis. This book outlines her own religious history. Her spiritual genius, or genius for things of the spirit, drew, one may take it, something, but cannot have drawn everything, from her pilgrimage as an individual: it seemed transcendental. Yet her teaching of candidates in the classes and her Sunday evening addresses to us in chapel were boned, too, by sturdiness, by a regard for the concrete. She left little out of account. She weighed, she deliberated, while she spoke. Her irony was not banished from chapel talks, which were often disturbing, sometimes iconoclastic. No two were alike. "O Strength and Stay upholding all creation" was the recurrent Downe House Sunday evening hymn.

This book, with its great record, fills me with wonder. I don't think that I and my schoolfellows and our many successors were crass enough to take Miss Willis for granted; we had at least some conception of what she was; but how many of us realised how much she did, how incessant were the demands on her, how various and far-reaching her activities, how very many the outlets found for her sympathies, which were inexhaustible? How could she be – as she, indeed, was – so much to so many people? She lived her life as she saw that life should be lived. That says much, when one thinks how large was her vision. Being and doing became inseparable. Yet, was she not a contemplative by nature? – the cast of her countenance, her abstractedness, the quality of her thoughts when they came out, always did to me suggest that she was. She was almost never alone – that is *my* memory, and this book confirms it – almost never alone; did she never wish to be? At the old Downe, her room was midway along the passage that was the spine of the upper floor: within that room, it seemed to us, there were for ever murmuring voices. Outside, frequently, there was somebody wait-ing for somebody else to come out. I and my contemporaries, now living under no greater pressure than she did, rely immensely on saving solitude, on silence, on going off the air. Such interims were denied to her – or, she perhaps forwent them. How taxing, how exacting were the relationships in which work involved her, or in which she involved herself? Some at least, it is known now, were far from easy ones. In what for another woman would have been hideouts, the cottage at Aishold, the *villino* at Lerici,[6] there were always guests. (Her impossible, handsome Samoyed dogs at least did not speak!) And all through the Downe House years, in Kent, in Berkshire, unceasingly, children, children, children . . . us.

How we came back; how unfailingly near she was to "ex-children" whose lives were lonely or stormy. Pure refreshment and happiness, one is happy to think, came to her through generations of her family and a legion of friends of all ages. Yet Olive Willis remains a mystery and a miracle. God with her, with grace and strength she did what she did, was as she was.

HOUSES

The Christmas Toast is "Home!"

"Are you going home for Christmas?"

My friend shook her head briefly. "Not this year – no."

I felt half sorry that I had asked the question – I saw such a world of homesickness in her eyes. And yet, I saw in her eyes, at the same time, an illumination of memories. There is a magic about the word "home."

What is this love of home that runs through all human nature – the most abiding, unchanging love that we know? To feel estranged from home is a disaster: we feel we have lost the better part of ourselves. I suppose that our love for home is unchanging because, in its essence, *home* itself does not change. Home stands for kindness and safety and understanding. It stands for tradition.

In peace-time we love the tradition behind our lives without, perhaps, being clearly aware of it. We take it for granted. However far we may travel, however much we adventure, there lies at the back of our mind the thought, "Home will always be there." And most of us, in those unthreatened days of peace-time, could identify home with the house itself – the front door opening on to the street or garden, the windows letting in early or late sun, the firelight reddening the winter dusks and dancing on familiar tables and chairs, that, from having lived so long in the rooms together, seem to share some secret among themselves. We saw these things in a happy haze of associations. We could take it that, whatever happened to us, *their* untroubled existence would go on.

War makes us more conscious, anxiously conscious, of the value of everything that is dear and old. Now we are fighting for those very traditions we took for granted in years before. In so far as home is a material thing – a house – we must face it that this may be demolished at any time. For some of us, this has already happened. And some homes that have not been hit by bombs have had, all the same, to be given up (at any rate for the time being) because of the war. In those cases, have we been left with nothing? Is "home" gone? No, assuredly no. Homes are much more than rooms and tables and chairs. Homes wait in our hearts till we can make them again.

Above all, the home means people – their trust in each other, their happy habits of living, the calendar, year by year, of family life – returning seasons, anniversaries, birthdays and, above all, Christmas, the greatest home festival. At Christmas, how strong the pull of the home is! There comes a call that our hearts cannot deny. At Christmas, we turn to our own people: we go home. And, when the Christmas journey cannot be made in real life, it is made with all the more longing, in the imagination. The Christmas letter or telegram from the exile to the people at home, saying, "I am with you today," speaks a real truth. At Christmas, wherever we find ourselves, our hearts are back in the beloved place.

This wartime Christmas, many, too many, home-going journeys will have to be made only in the imagination, made by the heart. Lack of transport (cars off the roads and these pressing requests, for our country's sake, not to travel by train) or the demands of war work must make breaks in the customs of years. And this wartime Christmas, when home stands for more than ever, when we feel its tug as never before – it will not be easy to stay away!

To put the matter the other way round – you or I may happen to be the stay-at-homes, to whom the others cannot, this Christmas, return. Those empty chairs by the fire, those empty places at dinner will need facing with a high, cheerful spirit. Our thoughts can keep the Christmas circle unbroken – even though sons and daughters, brothers and sisters, husbands and fathers may, by the war, have been scattered all over the world. Yes, there will be absences; there may even be silences – hardest of all to bear. Where is he? Where is she? It would help if one only knew. Of one thing, however, we may be certain: wherever "they" are, they are thinking of us – and home. From wherever "they" are – in the snows, in the desert, on the high seas – their thoughts will be constantly winging back. The thought of home at Christmas, a light that cannot be blacked out, sends its reflection to every part of the world. The darkness of war only makes this light stronger by contrast: it is a steady and constant beam.

I speak of empty places – but need there be empty places? If the home's own children must be absent this Christmas, may it not welcome the children of other homes? This war has filled England with strangers, with men and women from far away, who may not for years have seen the faces they love. We may ask ourselves, what must Christmas be like for *them*? Are they homesick? How can they not be homesick – the soldiers from the Dominions, the soldiers of the Free Forces, the refugees whose homes, so tragically left behind them, are, this Christmas, under the Nazi heel? We, whose English homes mean so much to us – let us make it the rule that, this Christmas, there shall be no strangers. We cannot, perhaps, do much, but a little could go so far. For each chair of ours that we fill, for every Christmas greeting, there will be one lonely person less in the world . . . And perhaps, hundreds or thousands of miles away, one of our own absent ones may be finding just such a welcome at some unexpectedly opening door.

What *is* home? Must it be a narrow place, from which the family bars out the world's troubles, ignoring these in a happiness all its own? Surely not. If home were selfish, our loyalty to it would make us not better but worse. It is true that we turn to home for its quiet, its privacy, its uniqueness. All the same, we go wrong if we do not realise that home – each home – is a living, organic part of the world. The happiness and strength that home generates were not meant to be confined within four walls.

I like to think of my home as a thing of windows, not as a thing of doors. Doors, I mean, are meant to be shut, and when shut they are impenetrable. Windows, on the other hand, are there to admit light and refreshing air; I look out through them; they frame for me pictures of the outside, ever-changing world. I want my home, above all, to have an intense aliveness, to hold many books, to have room alike for old and for new friends. At the same time, it must not be restless: at the heart of all its aliveness it must keep a magnetic centre of stillness and peace. And to this let others have access, as well as me.

One's home is one's castle – yes. But must this mean a castle defensively guarded, with drawbridge always raised? The castle (however tiny this may be) should show above all a confident graciousness. And the first of the graces is hospitality.

War has taken away, for the time being, what we *used* to regard as the three essentials – safety, privacy, independence. But were these essentials really? For without them home still goes on; it triumphs; we can feel its undying value as never before. Outer changes, temporary deprivations, have left the core intact. Home, through these dark years, shows its unrivalled power to refresh and to rest us, to reassure and to cheer.

Peace will see many homecomings. It will see old homes re-opened, new homes built. The memories on which we must live, this Christmas, will become, for a later Christmas, happy realities. New homes, with their faces turned to the sunshine, will embody dreams that have had to wait. Meanwhile, Christmas bids us take heart from our memories and be strong in our dreams. In heart we are close together. Christmas speaks the message of an eternal kindness. The Christmas toast is – "Home!"

Opening up the House

"And they returned again into their own place."[1] . . . All over Europe, people are going home. I am thinking of those who have homes to go to, who find what was there before, there still. Gates, or doors in walls, are being pushed back on their rusty[2] hinges, paths hacked through overgrown courts or gardens. Boards are torn away from in front of windows, or shutters clatter open: rooms breathe again. Fires are lit, and smoke twists its way again up the damp chimneys. Tiled floors, hallways, and shafts of staircases give out the echoes once so familiar. Rusty water – first drop by drop, then in more certain gushes – trickles out of the taps. Switches, stiff from disuse, are flicked up and down – sometimes light comes, sometimes it does not. As an organism, the house comes back to life slowly: like the people returning to it, it seems dazed.

I began with Europe, but there are too many implications; the picture is too big. So I find myself narrowing down to England. Here, there are the houses that have been left behind – boarded up, standing still, waiting – and the houses that have gone on, occupied by strangers, put to uses one could not have foreseen, mounting up, all the time, bewildered lives of their own, stories that will be guessed at but never told.

Those that stood still, empty, were mostly the little houses, holiday places, homes of retired people, in the coastal areas closed in 1940. They were too small or remote to be used as billets for soldiers; and not so placed as to offer concealment for guns. In winter, damp made maps on their walls; in summer the window-sills, on which cats used to bask or bathing suits used to hang out to dry, warped and blistered. All the year round, through those lost seasons, their structures shook with reverberations: tiles flew from the roofs and the windows cracked. The more sheltered gardens, under shoulders of hills or in folds of downs, grew into forests; porches and balconies became knotted across with liana-like creepers, and tall grass grew up above the lost penknife or the forgotten toy. The rhythmical leisure of the aged or the sharply accented holiday happiness of the young remained sealed up in the uninhabited rooms. Those houses had an acute existence in the thoughts of those who were banished from them. And, for their parts, they wore for the passer-by an air of puzzled loneliness and desertions.

Houses that had to be left when war came, and which were thereupon occupied by unknown people, will confront their returning owners with their own complex mystery. Like the members of the family, scattered and parted and ignorant of one another's whereabouts, the homes have had experiences of their own. Major damage or drastic rearrangement is in itself a story, too long and too well-known to tell: I am thinking only of the more subtle traces of "other" occupations.

Those unnumbered human beings who came and went – kept it in motion by the clockwork of wartime, using the furniture, opening and shutting doors, neglecting or at random cultivating the gardens to which their tenancy gave them a passing right – have left something behind them, something that will not evaporate so quickly as the smell of unfamiliar cigarettes. These now departed dwellers in one's house cannot fail to be seen as either enigmas or enemies; one must try to dwell on them as enigmas. Rings left by glasses or burns left by cigarettes may mark those parts of the rooms in which they preferred to encamp. Dinges in the springs of armchairs and sofas record their characteristic ways of sitting; and books displaced or upside down in the shelves indicate what they read – if they read! They preferred, apparently, to sleep in the diningroom, dine in the sleeping porch? Blotters remain crisscrossed with their different writings; it is to be guessed from the ink on the mantlepiece that someone wrote his letters standing up; and ghostly indentations of someone's doodling are found on the left-behind telephone pad.

Did "they" like it, here? Were they homesick, the whole time, for that place of their own that they had, in their turn, left? Did they, in their turn, speculate about "us"? The house knows, but cannot tell us. One cannot say.

So much for those war sent to live in the homes from which war took us away. But what about us – about the sensations and problems involved in our coming back? The return, however calmly one tries to take it, cannot but be in the nature of ordeal. How can it not drag things up? It may have been looked forward to; it may have been dreaded. For some, it may mean the entry alone, into rooms that someone beloved will not see again. Opening the door of this house left years ago – and was it really only four, five, or six years ago – maybe to be made conscious, all in that one moment, of what seems to be an eternity of loss and change. Or perhaps, on the other hand, as we cross the threshold, all those intervening years, those years away, will suddenly, magically contract. Five, six years ago will seem "only yesterday."

Whether the homecoming be wholly happy or troubling and overcast, it must be disturbing. It must be accompanied by a whole rush of sensations against which we have no armour, by the breaking upon us of a great wave of memories we did not expect. The smell of the waxed floor, the tapping of the blind-cord of the staircase window in the draught as the front door opens, the green garden reflection cast into the glass front of the bookcase, the sound of the bus from the village changing gear on the hill, the just perceptible hiccup or syncopation in the tick of the kitchen passage clock – all these have been lying in wait for us all these years. Today they command us. Are they a little altered, a little strange? Or have we changed? Or is there no change at all? Dare one hope that? Can one pick up, now, here, from the point at which one left off? The marker waits in the half-read book – a blade of grass of the summer of 1939.

Nothing undoes the years. The children who were in the nursery are at school; the children who were at school have grown up. And, strangest of all, the grown-up who plucked the blade of grass knows that he or she did not yet realise, *that* summer, what more growing-up was to come, what that would mean. To the children born somewhere else, during the war, this is going to be an unknown house. They sniff about for its history, like little dogs for scents. "What used this to be?" they will say. "What used you to do with that?"

Mrs. X, from the village, has been already: she has lit the fire, her husband has filled the log box. As the first evening goes on and the log box empties you will find, tucked away at the bottom, a 1938 evening paper. A Saturday paper – somebody coming for the weekend must have brought it down from London. What a lot of pages there used to be, and how did they fill the papers in those days? What is in the Chinese bowl on the top of the tallboy? The same one brass curtain ring, three beads, and two stumps of pencil. *Have* they been there all the time, or has Mrs. X piously put them back? The picture postcard of Lake Garda has, naturally, gone from behind the clock . . . What a good thing there is so much to do – that one cannot simply stand here remembering, feeling, thinking! A house is a practical mechanism, after all – a job, a premises to be re-opened.

Quickly, as briskly as possible, you go up and down stairs and in and out of the rooms. You find yourself humming a tune you had quite forgotten – it must have been waiting here, on the air. Two or three of the curtains show dropped folds; a stain has begun to creep down the landing wall (is a gutter blocked?), and why did "they" never tack down that edge of carpet? You had always intended to tack it down yourself . . . That smell of warm linen seeps out of the airing cupboard. In the downstairs cloakroom, there is still the smell of old mackintoshes, but no mackintoshes – now, where have the mackintoshes been put away? Somebody has removed the two china dogs, out of harm's way, from the top of the bureau – but you prefer them *in* harm's way: you put them back there.[3]

You may or may not have come back alone. If more of the family have come back with you, they will be excitedly calling from all parts of the house. Gratification, indignation, or surprise will be in their voices. On the whole, it is better *not* to come back alone. Better quickly call the family council – agree, there is so much to do, one does not know where to begin! There will be, none the less, enthusiastic beginnings in all directions. Note by note, the different instruments in the family orchestra strike up. Someone sits on the stairs; someone races through the attics; someone begins to punt furniture back to its old places; someone makes a discovery; someone laments a loss. And someone, having wandered away to stand for a long time on a carpet at the end of the garden, comes back to announce: "I felt for a moment, just now, as though I had never been away!"

Home for Christmas

This is meeting-again time. Home is the magnet. The winter land roars and hums with the eager speed of return journeys. The dark is noisy and bright with late-night arrivals – doors thrown open, running shadows on snow, open arms, kisses, voices and laughter, laughter at everything and nothing. Inarticulate, giddying, and confused are those original minutes of being back again. The very familiarity of everything acts like shock. Contentment has to be drawn in slowly, steadyingly, in deep breaths – there is so much of it. We rely on home not to change, and it does not, wherefore we give thanks. Again Christmas: abiding point of return. Set apart by its mystery, mood and magic, the season seems in a way to stand outside time. All that is dear, that is lasting, renews its hold on us: we are home again.

Talk comes out in rushes, all inconsequence; questions crowd on each other, too many to answer – but what matter? There will be tomorrow. Tonight, beatific lassitude sifts down on us: we shall sleep deep in a remembered room. Home, for the head a pillow – simple as that!

Not quite so simple. Humanity is a complex thing. Home during our absence, we must remember, has settled into a rhythm of its own, and on this (however joyously) our return impacts.

Since last we hung up holly wreaths, lit candles, saw the glittering tree, time has not stood still – and not only that but both we and Christmas would be the poorer if it had. As it is, we bring to the season, each time, an awareness deepened by more experience. The atmosphere, the air in which candles burn, the margin of shadow around the tree are intensified, for we perceive more, know more, feel more. The genius of Christmas is, we do not outgrow it. We do not outgrow it because it grows up with us.

Also it is a milestone. Happy pause in existence, like no other, Christmas none the less invites us to measure time, to look back, forward. The happenings, possibly the changes, inward or outward, of the past year – what have they amounted to?

In our growing years, nothing goes for nothing. We are keyed up by a sense of emerging pattern. Each and every experience, bad or good, matters: never quite are we left where we were before. There will have been steps taken, revelations, gains of ground, finding of powers. Equally there may be losses to be cut, mistakes to be lived down, heartbreaks either to be defied or healed by being forgotten, if forget we can. We have not stood still. Inevitably, everything constant about Christmas causes us to realise, by contrast, the forward moving fluidity of our own lives.

In families reunited, among old friends, Christmas touches what is beneath the surface. Memories are active. Till-now-forgotten hopes, lingering expectations are given voice to. Older people close to whom we are, are disturbed by the poignancy of Christmas, and their disturbance affects us – long-standing ties are stressed, former days recalled, the absent are present in talk and the dead return. Sometimes for the young this is too much. "Something happens at Christmas I rather dread," I once heard a girl say. And I think she had also in mind this – loyalties, fidelities become all-important, and it is expected that we respond to them. *Do* we, as fully as once we did? In growing up are we also growing away? Even if we are not, may others think so?

These Christmas days, so ideal, must be so short – do we compute what infinite care has gone to the making of them ideal? More may attach to our homecoming than we wot of: how far can we envisage its other side – the viewpoint of those who are returned to? These are the people who have been learning to do without us, without loving us less: absent, we have lived for them in those vivid pictures formed by the mind's eye. Constantly, maybe anxiously, we have been held in thought; our existences, busy and far away, thronged with fresh interests, peopled with unknown friends, have had to be pieced together from letters. At home they have tried to envisage all – but how can they? Home, in the main, tends to dwell with its own ideas of us.

Basically, home is right. Family intuitions, instinctive judgements are seldom wholly out of the true. At the same time there *have* been changes in us for which our elders cannot account, or for which they find it hard to allow. Sometimes, it may seem, love is too blind to change, sometimes too quick to apprehend or suspect it. Days back home again, even Christmas Days, may be clouded – however fleetingly and faintly – by unspoken dissonances or disappointments. We no longer quite fit the picture which had been formed of us; we perceive, or fancy that we perceive, momentary dismay or puzzlement in loving eyes. Are we not puzzling even to ourselves?

Unconsciously, family love exerts a pressure to which, at a stage in our youth, we react uneasily: we may feel surrounded by expectations we cannot satisfy. And on our side – had *we* expected too much of home? No, surely. Only one must remember that home-coming is preceded, on both sides, by anticipations keyed to a high pitch. The glowing first hours, first evening, are at that tenor. In the days to follow there must be a keying down, an easing into things as they really are. For us too, in absence, memory may have over-gilded a few pictures. And this, also, should be taken into account – each return has in it, in spite of the carry-over, some element of a fresh start. The mistake, and it may be a mistake on both sides, is to imagine that one can pick up a life again – any life at all, even home life – at exactly the point where one left it off. The marker is in the book, one opens at the same page, reads the page again, but some-thing more has entered into the meaning.

Home was our first world – it was at one time *the* world: we knew no other. Now we do know others and we partake in them. Those other worlds' existence, our share in them and most of all their share in us will be sensed by those for whom horizons have stayed more narrow. There need not be conflicts but there must be adjustments: the new asks to be reconciled with the old. Let us, in so far as we can, bring home our "away" experiences like gifts, in our talk unpack them, freely show them around. Boast, even. Let us be ourselves.

Christmas magic lends itself to a harmony. At Christmas, bridges are cast between one generation and another. Also, we meet again our contemporaries. We ourselves are by no means the only home-comers. Back to the old focus, the former setting, will be coming our intimates of the former years. Groups, scattered lately, will re-form. Once again we are to be in the presence of those from whom – how short a time ago? – we could not have pictured ourselves apart. Hardly a day, once, went by without a meeting, hardly an experience or experiment was unshared, not a plan was made without consultation. We more or less had the same thoughts – or at least so it seems, looking back. We measured ourselves, very largely, by one another; sometimes there was the stimulus of rivalry. Childhood, school days: many of the friendships date back to then. Together we launched into adolescence. And in most cases nothing came to an end – simply paths divided. Simply a matter of going to different colleges, of careers in cities far apart, or now, perhaps, marriages. So much packs into so few years when we are young. Throughout all that has happened – *have* we kept contact?

It does matter. In the crowd among whom we grew to an age, one or two personalities stand out. We invested love in them – love as we knew it then. Imaginatively kindling one another, we sent off sparks; also, how we laughed! Knit by the same curiosities, how we speculated! . . . Such young friendships, first friendships, are indissociable from our own identities; they colour life for us, and the colour stays. Then, for some outside reason, comes separation; circumstances and settings change – no longer are there the days in common. There occur gaps, silences, dislocations and, most trying of all, ignorance as to what one or the other may be doing. Is one forgetting, is one forgotten? No. But possibly there could be loss of touch. It becomes essential to meet again.

Christmas presents the scene, offers the reason. Now to catch up with time, fill in the gaps, repair the losses! The friend is coming on a visit; or the friend is coming from far away back to her family, our neighbours. Do we perhaps feel just a shade of apprehension? So much, it may be almost too much, has come to attach to the meeting, so long planned. Face to face, how shall we both feel? Shall we not know where, how, to begin again? Have we been left behind by our friend, outdistanced? If you or I am[1] the one to whom less has happened, we shall be the one most prone to suspect change. We dread, perhaps, the loss of some common ground. "*Will* she be different? How, after all this, if I begin to feel that I hardly know her?"

Miraculous how, in an instant, such fears disperse! Actual sight of the face, sound of the voice, feel of the touch – and the mists are gone. It *is* as though one never had been apart. Estrangement – how could we have thought it possible? The fact is, when a friendship is a reality it is comprehensive. It can take into itself, and draw increase from, anything and everything that happens. Achievement, fulfilment are not its enemies; other loves and discoveries do not steal from it. We are not sundered from the friend who may happen to move ahead of us into fields unknown – is not his or her experience in part ours? It is through one another, often, that we make growth . . . Is to meet again an ordeal? Beforehand only. To *have* met again is sheer reassurance. And each time, after the first time, more so. No two meetings, like no two Christmases, are ever quite the same. Something is added.

Yes, more always. This glow of Christmas, has it not in it also the gold of a harvest? – "They shall return with joy, bringing their sheaves with them."[2] To the Festival, to each other, we bring in wealth. More to tell, more to understand, more to share. Each, we have garnered in yet another; to be glad, to celebrate to the full, we are come together. How akin we are to each other, how speechlessly dear and one in the fundamentals of being, Christmas shows us. No other time grants us, quite, this vision – round the tree or gathered before the fire we perceive anew, with joy, one another's faces. And each time faces come to mean more.

Is it not one of the mysteries of life that life should, after all, be so simple? Yes, as simple as Christmas, simple as this. Journeys through the dark to a lighted door, arms open. Laughter-smothered kisses, kiss-smothered laughter. And blessedness in the heart of all. Here are the verities, all made gay with tinsel! Dear, silly Christmas-card sayings and cracker mottoes – let them speak! Or, since still we cannot speak, let us sing! Dearer than memory, brighter than expectation is the ever returning *now* of Christmas. Why else, each time we greet its return, should happiness ring out in us like a peal of bells?

Bowen's Court

The house stands in lonely country. From its windows nothing but trees, grassland and, at the back, mountains are to be seen – no road, no other habitation. It is square, high and set in a shallow hollow, screened by plantations from the winds blowing over heather and bog behind it. Fair for tillage, better for grazing, the acres are watered by springs and streams, and here and there gashed by limestone cuttings – the stone the house is built of was quarried locally. White-grey, the classic façade stares out from its leafy background – still somewhat a foreigner to the landscape. Such is the home envisaged and brought to being in County Cork, some two miles from the Limerick border, by my ancestor Henry Bowen III, who in the year 1775 saw the roof on and moved in with his family. His descendants have lived here ever since.

The house faces south, on to a vast open field known as the lawn. Woods reach out and partly enclose the sides; at the back are the stables and stable yard; with, beyond them, the farm enclosures and buildings, and the walled three-acre vegetable garden. Everything functional is hidden: the Bowen's Court frontage is social. The main door gives on a terrace, from which steps descend to a gravel sweep – destined for the turning and drawing up of carriages yesterday, motorcars today. Henry Bowen III, high-spirited Georgian, could not have conceived of life without hospitality: the arrival of visitors from a distance continues to feature our days and nights. So great is the silence around the place that one can hear anything coming miles away. The horse age lasted a long time in County Cork: clearly do I remember the spanking trotting, sound of whirling wheels, creak of leather and shafts. Motors turn in more stealthily at the far-off gateways, yet never take me totally by surprise.

Ireland, small as it is, can give the effect of being a stretching continent. Tract after tract of emptiness seems unbounded. Our distances reckoned in terms of miles work out to be tiny, all but laughable – but what counts here is distance as a *sensation*. Bowen's Court, today, is in fact, by no means out of the current world, yet its first isolation forever stamps it. The green illusion remains unbroken. But what I do not see is, all the same, there. Sunk between stone walls and belts of woodland, a main road runs glossily past my gates – the Dublin–Killarney through route. The diesels of the Cork–Dublin railway stop at Mallow, within half an hour's reach. Shannon airport is fifty-two miles from me – in some weathers a big plane, off its course, thrums its way over Bowen's

Court roof and treetops, far up over the cloud ceiling. The beat of the engines sounds lost, labourious, anxious – anachronistic. Not more so than the hum of the tractor in the next valley or, at harvest, the shuttling roar of the combine. Mechanisation no more than scratches the surface of that timeless enormous hush which is our norm.

The disturbers are what they have been always: wind, rain, thunder. The elements play cat-and-mouse with my innovations – I listen to radio, the reception crackles; I have a telephone, but the service is subject to inexhaustible "acts of God." All dwellers far out in the[1] country, I know, are hit by crises and dislocations. What is peculiar to Bowen's Court seems to be that it takes practically nothing to make one feel that the twentieth century is, after all, a fiction.

Henry Bowen III, in choosing his site, was not aiming at loneliness for its own sake. He built where seemed to him best, within limits set by the boundaries of his bare inherited land – hollow for shelter, aspect for sunshine. Nevertheless, his ambitious mansion islanded itself in a wide sea of country. He was neighbour to none.

In his correspondence, during the building years, I find no mention of any architect: I am told it is possible he did not employ one, but, instead, had Bowen's Court copied from a plate in one of those albums of classical architectural engravings much in circulation, then, among country gentry. It says much for Henry and his contemporaries that they let their fancies be fired in such a way. Crude as may have been their personal habits, brutish the noisier of their pleasures, they at least respected a culture they could not claim. The same spark appeared in Henry when he stocked his library with many noble classics, Latin, French, English. He had each binding stamped in gold with his wife's initials.

Alas, the Bowen's Court bookshelves suffered a furious later purge at the hands of a Mrs. Eliza Bowen, wife of Henry III's second son Robert I. This took place *circa* 1820. Eliza, a vigorous Plymouth Sister, threw out all novels and many dramatic works, including the greater part of Shakespeare – how she overlooked Dryden I never know. She also banished card tables – slender circular models, folding into half moons, with which all livingrooms were provided.

(The delinquents, no worse for eighty years of disuse, were retrieved by my mother from a Bowen's Court cellar – their tops still caked with tallow from the candles of all-night players.)

Poor Robert I was a victim, and not the last, of the depletion of the family coffers caused by the over-expenditure on Bowen's Court. Henry III had called a halt, though not soon enough, when he had furnished and decorated the main rooms – contenting himself, when it came to the outdoor scene, with planting trees (now grown to great size) and throwing out one long avenue to the west. Thus the surround of Bowen's Court remained in more or less its untamed romantic state. My Victorian grandfather Robert II laid down a second long avenue, to the east, and levelled a croquet lawn under the drawing-room windows, ornamenting the slope above with exotic shrubs. Two water closets, encased in a sort of tower, were gummed by him on to the back of the house; he also added offices and a butler's pantry.

Henry VI, my father, kept Bowen's Court much as his father left it. As my father left it, it came to me.

From outside, the house looks larger than it is. Many are the windows: on front and flanks there is a polished expanse of glass. Inside, the rooms are spacious, elatingly high, surprisingly few. Bowen's Court is three floors high – four if you count the basement. The ground floor proper contains four livingrooms, all of the same size, and the capacious shaft of the main staircase. The entrance hall (to be numbered among the livingrooms) has on one side the library, on the other the drawing-room, behind which the diningroom is set.

Between room and room there are high mahogany doors; another, at the end of the hall, leads to the foot of the staircase. Two wide flights, massive with carved banisters, terminate in a gallery: the second floor. Opposite the head of the stairway opens "the lobby," an upper hall having on either side a square corner bedroom with narrow dressing room – a third, similar bedroom is approached from the gallery.

The *grand escalier* goes no further: due to economy it has shot its bolt! So to the third (and top) floor you must ascend by the "back" stairs, more humbly zigzagging up from the service quarters. By this means you are landed into Bowen's Court's one startling feature: the Long Room. Long indeed, intended to be a ballroom, this runs right through the heart of the house, front to back, south–north. Each end holds three crouching windows – and each end seems unbelievably distant from the other. Along each side, spaced far apart, are doors: in all, six bedrooms give on the Long Room. Above this? Nothing. Bat-haunted rafters, the Alpine slated formation of the roof. That is all. Our living space is contained in this one upright block: nothing straggles beyond it.

My purpose in keeping Bowen's Court going differs from that of my forebears, and more widely than difference in generation can account for. It is more specific. They were landowning gentry who administered property, farmed some hundreds of acres, drew rents from the rest. I am a writer, living by my pen. The house today is maintained as a place to write in: as such it happily is ideal – were it not, I could and would not maintain it.

Everything during the working day subordinates itself to the study table. As though on another planet the wind hums, a garden cart creaks, dishes clink on a tray. At all other times insistent, Bowen's Court *has* the power to disconnect itself from my consciousness. Yet not quite: something filters in from the green environment, feeding imagination, generating thought. Out of the timeless atmosphere comes, like a bright new moment, an idea. Yes, the place *is* crowded, not by phantoms but by images; other-than-physical inhabitants it has – the urgent characters in my growing stories. And this I find: at Bowen's Court, unlike elsewhere, there is no sharp break or disharmony between writing and life. To live is to be in company, to share. Of the friends who join me, many are writers.

The big livingrooms, asking for sociability, never are disappointed for long. Writers on the rebound from their exacting solitude are the gayest mortals: toward evening there is a banging-open of doors, a haste to look for each other, talk, exclamations, laughter. Bowen's Court then becomes what artists must have, an extensive playroom, and what friends like best, a nondesert island. It can be gone away from, then come back to – in the car we slip through a landscape liquid with sunset; or we walk in file through the woods in sight of the mountains, beating back brambles, talking over our shoulders. For a pause it is also a great thing to be sitting in twos or threes on the terrace steps, gazing at the lawn in front of the house as though it were the sea, we birds on a rock. Indoors we fool with invented games by the phantasmagoric light of a wood fire, or play cards at the original tables. Meals, now, we eat in the entrance hall (the former diningroom, at the back, having been abandoned: it was too cavernous).

The last act of any Bowen's Court day plays itself out in the library or drawing-room . . . Pink curtains drawn, lamp-lit, with a fire in a wreathed Victorian grate, my grandmother's drawing-room has the effect of keying us up to its mild grandeur. It was decorated, and has not been changed since, when that Elizabeth came here as a bride: 1859. She loved its grey-and-gold scrolled wallpaper, and plaster frieze swagged with roses – and I don't wonder. I and my friends crowd stylishly, if not formally, on the central outsize vermilion sofa. In here, the only cerebral touch is the ebony bookcase she gave her eldest son, my father, for his mounting number of school-prize volumes. The shelves were gentle to them, being velvet lined.

The library, family livingroom (for we are a family) looks slap-dash, weathered and workaday by day: book-lined walls, book-loaded tables, capacious shabby honey-corduroy chairs. But it takes on a majesty with nightfall. Deep in their ranks sunk between the windows, books seem, while receding into the dark, to exhale their being into our talk; their intellectual wealth mellows the air into curls of our cigarette smoke. In here, conversation sweeps, swoops, takes an unforeseeable course – by now the ribbed velvet arms of the chairs are rubbed to a gloss by the hands of excited talkers. ("Your intellectual friends," said one of my aunts, "seem to be exceedingly hard on furniture!") Book-housing space has become a problem: by now my own bright-jacketed newcomers are wedged alongside calf-bound classics of the age of the house, or crushed between stout Victorians in maroon or olive. Each season's hatch out, from New York or London, must find for itself a footing, where it can – and each year, some author bids for permanent place. Do we need a second Eliza, a thrower-out?

It is in the library that I remember Eudora Welty,[2] in the first hour of her first visit, turning her head, remarking, "I've just realised, I don't think I've ever been so far north before." (We checked on an atlas later: she was right.) Eudora, gracing the drawing-room both in her own way and as a Southerner can, played the plaintive, long-neglected piano; one June midnight, too, she emerged from the kitchen having conjured into existence an onion pie. In the library I recollect Evelyn Waugh,[3] scooping desultorily, a little crossly, at a bat which had shattered the evening for me by flying in – I cannot stay in a room with a bat: I cannot endure them! David Cecil,[4] having retired for the night, was heard by his floor neighbours in a spooky monologue. It transpired next morning that a white owl had stood unblinking at the end of his bed; in vain had he reasoned with the intruder. Nor are bats and owls the only nocturnals. Oxford talkers take little count of the clock: David, again, and his colleague Isaiah Berlin[5] are known to have started a conversation at the foot of the stairs, around midnight, and to have finished it close on two hours later, not more than six steps up.

Cyril Connolly's visit, one sunny April, coincided with that of Virginia Woolf.[6] By mischance nothing was recorded, for Cyril's diary, otherwise ever ready, was of the kind which has a lock: at Bowen's Court locked it had to remain, for no sooner had he arrived than he lost the key. Cyril, a themic[7] creative talker, developed at least one theory in this house: he traced the low ebb of Irish romantic passion to the anaphrodisiac effects of the constant potato. Virginia, serenely standing out on the steps, watched her spaniel racing over the grass in front. Dynamic, speedy and graceful country walker, she outdistanced the rest of us on our pilgrimage across the fields to the Bowen's Court wishing well. (Few leave this house without having "had a wish.") What she wished, as she cupped the spring water in her hands, I shall never know . . . When Virginia'd gone, I told my matriarch cook, "That was the greatest living woman writer." Old Sarah, who disliked any connection between ink and the should-be elegant sex, sniffed, "I'd have known she was a *lady* by the stately go of her!"

Seán O'Faoláin,[8] helping me lock up – a nightly ritual involving heaving an iron bar into place, then fastening the hall door on the inside with massive chains – remarked that *here* was a Big House ready for a siege! Complex race memories, conflicts, the raids and burning of The Troubles of his young days and mine simultaneously stirred in us two Irish – I whose first Irish ancestor had come from Wales, he descended from the ancient inhabitants of the land.

Frank O'Connor,[9] chanting in the library, dropping his head back as did Yeats, recalled the magnificence of the Midnight Court, poetry and bawdry of an Ireland before the potato had struck root. New Ireland tore to my doors in the form of my cousin Dudley Colley, a racing ace: his glorious Frazer-Nash enraptured Carson McCullers.[10] In a flash, long-legged Carson was in the driver's seat. "I'm off," she cried. So strong is visionary force, the stationary car seemed to roar and devour space: Carson's face grew tense with the thought of speed, veritably her hair streamed back from her forehead.

Bernard Shaw has denounced one fatal cleft in society: Heartbreak House on one side, Horseback Hall on the other. Yet by happy accident, Bowen's Court is a merger. Yes, I live right in horse country: fox hunting, racing and stud farming occupy the majority of my neighbours. Of these neighbours many are, also, my friends – there is a to and fro, when the day's work's over, between their and my far-apart houses. In the main my neighbours still live much as my forebears used to: farming, thinking concretely, cultivating their gardens (in a manner for which the reward is lovely). Do I feel a dissonance, or a dislocation, when they and writers meet round my dinner table? None being there to *be* felt, I do not. On the one hand, Cork native sociability is omnivorous, unsuspicious, eager, quick to be charmed and won. On the other, nothing is like the life from creative people at play: poets, novelists, philosophers, even critics effervesce like uncorked champagne. There is laughter sparked by new contacts; there is the spell of the card game. Wildly assorted Bowen's Court parties may be – country folk, visiting aunts and cousins, house guests literary or academic, plus transients on the road for business or pleasure. However, people take to each other.

*

"How does it feel," I find myself asked, "living with ancestors right on top of you?" Or more simply: "Don't you ever feel crowded?" At a glance, the question is sound enough: it could be oppressive, were this place no more than a pocket of ancient sentiment. But you cannot discount the force with which life renews itself: what chance has the past against the vividness of the living moment? Family continuity has the interest of *any* continuity: just that – it in no way acts as a spell. My predecessors in Bowen's Court were my kin: this makes for my knowing more about them than I should had they been of some other stock. Letters, personal papers and legal documents, birth, marriage and death dates entered in the family Bible give me the objective facts with regard to them; the factual outline is coloured in by intuition, hearsay, maybe legend. Moreover I can see what most of them looked like – many of the Bowens and their spouses had their portraits painted; the pictures in tarnished gilded frames hang in a crowd round the hall walls; elsewhere, cabinet drawers are stuffed with daguerreotypes and photographs. All this serves to fix my ancestors for me as four-square persons who, though unknown to history, become in their way historic through having lived. While I in my turn live, they are not forgotten. But on top of me? No.

Traces of themselves they have left behind them are concrete – broken musical instruments, signatures diamond-scratched on window panes, curios brought home from foreign travel, a silent gold heavy half-hunter watch, a riding crop with the thong gone, a compass with needle forever still. A big shell from Naples cameo-carved, a bracket on the wings of a tiny eagle. Such trifles are eloquent; they speak of foibles, tastes or tenderness.

There are, in addition, relics of broken-off activities: grandfather Robert II's close-kept estate ledgers, now musty, or a milking stool half-painted with water lilies. And between those who were here and me there is a physical link, forged of touch and sight – a matter of handling the same door knobs, mounting the same stairs, looking out at the same scene through the same windows. But most of all they and I are akin in one thing: the business of keeping going.

The keeping going of Bowen's Court has from the first preoccupied its owners. Good years, bad years have but slightly varied the weight of the undertaking. To an extent I profit by my ancestors' forethought, to an extent I am hampered by their misjudgements. The place is rich in outdated innovations. *I* face a paradox: by today's notions Bowen's Court is an anachronism; none the less, by the light of today I can solve some of yesterday's problems. Once this house was operated by hosts of servants: wages were low, labour never scarce – chains of hands slung the dishes, piping hot, from dusky kitchen to shining diningroom table. Rainwater, steaming in monster jugs, was levitated upstairs to many bathtubs. Now electrification and plumbing do most of that, plus the ingenuity of my cook and maid, a modicum of my energies, aid from guests.

One thing makes the house contemporary: its straightforward plan – no passages, whimsical complications or murky corners. (The Georgian living pattern fits today's better than the Victorian.) I use just over half the number of rooms, on each floor the sunniest; those withdrawn from, are kept sweet by the air coming in at their large windows; there is something placid and seemly about their emptiness. Bowen's Court has lent itself to this compromise – had it not, indeed, it could not survive: a saving pact has been reached between past and present. My standards of comfort, habitability, are far from those of my ancestors, which is well. I suspect sometimes that I am better off, thanks to concentration of heat, lighting, colour into a smaller living space, here, now, in my own way, than they in theirs. Yet I don't doubt they had their own satisfactions: this is a house constructed to be enjoyed, by whatever stratagems, in whatever manner.

At the outset I spoke of this house as social, with hospitality as its inbuilt ideal. Now I think again, there is something more to it. This house was built for a family – so it makes one.

Bowen's Court seems to me like a ship that has steadily, forwardly voyaged through time. Almost two hundred years, today, since the launching. From having forged through storms, sheered its way past reefs and pulled clear of whirlpools, it has accumulated organic confidence. Yet also it *is* a house, founded very deep. From its daylit big rooms and green surrounding lands a succession of sorrows, deaths, trials, debts, disappointments have somehow evaporated like mists in sunshine. Hopeful as to its being, in spite of all, it begets hope; serenity is the constant.

Like Bowens before me, when grey rain sheets County Cork and gales rattle windows and buffet the house corners, I take exercise indoors – I walk the Long Room. This has been play deck since it first began: violent tennis and hockey and roller skating have taken place here; and generations of children have pounded or slid, yelling, from end to end. Circuses have been staged, melodramas improvised; talent ran, also, to whistle concerts and shadow shows.

Only one thing has this commodious ballroom never once been the scene of – dancing. Any ball is held, by tradition, down in the drawing-room. Why? *The Long Room floor will not stand up to vibration.* So I was told by my father, he by his, his by his father, whom his father had told. No one of us, in consequence, ever tried. This anomaly, typical of my family, strikes my closing note. Acceptances, do they not make up life? I wonder, looking out of the Long Room windows at the mountains behind, at the lawns in front and the lights through the veil of rain sifting softly, slowly over the lonely country.

IRELAND

Letter from Ireland

Cork city has been very gay of late. Summer weather persisted, just lightly chilled, and on long gay glassy evenings the Lee estuary looked like the scene set for a regatta. Galway oysters reappeared at the Oyster Tavern, off Patrick Street: this is a long cavern of dusky mirrors with a grill fire (which grills really superbly) glittering at the end. The Opera House on the quayside reopened, and Jimmy O'Dea[1] packed it for two weeks. Ireland's great little comedian is a tragi-comedian. He is a pool of temperament. There is a touch of Stan Laurel, a touch of Chaplin: any affinities he has belong to the screen, not the stage, because he has such a very *exposed* nature. He is ultimately and first of all himself. He is a Dublin man, but Cork thinks the world of him.

Cork left Cork for Killarney when the All Ireland Hurley Finals were played there. Tipperary won. This was a great day for the whole of the South of Ireland; special trains were run and the roads for a hundred miles round streamed with cars and bicycles, most of them flying flags. The Tipperary contingent passed my way. Those who unluckily could not get to Killarney stood on banks for hours to watch the traffic. This is, in the literal sense, a very quiet country: the Troubles and civil war were fought out in an almost unbroken hush, punctuated by a few explosions or shots. Voices are seldom raised, and you can (so to speak) hear a dog bark or a milk-cart rattle or a funeral bell toll two counties away. But these great Sundays of sport galvanise everything; from the moment you wake you know that something is going on. This last year or two, the town of Killarney has begun to cash in on sport. Last year they had a Big Fight there. Hurley is the fastest game, short of ice hockey, that I have ever watched. It is a sort of high-speed overhead hockey, played with sticks with flat wooden blades, and it looks even more dangerous than it apparently is. Though a game that would melt you in the Antarctic, it is, for some reason, played only in summer. I do not think nearly so much of Gaelic football. But I have only seen this game played in a sea mist, which, milkily shrouding goals and players, added to an effect of aimless mystery: there seemed to be effort but no fun, and sea birds – this was in the flats behind Waterville, County Kerry – circled rather drearily overhead.

Yes, certainly in early autumn the Cork social season is at its height. And English visitors constantly overlook this. English people apparently come to Ireland for reasons – such as scenery pure and simple – that would get me nowhere. (I except, of course, fishermen.) They disembark their cars from SS *Innisfallen* on to the Cork quay, and rattle at high speed, with minds set on the sublime, out of one of Europe's strangest and most beautiful cities. They go in droves to stay at boring hotels on lakes or bays. These hotels seem to me boring because they have no local life; they are built for strangers who want to look at scenery. Their lounges, though often lofty, are claustrophobic, and often smell of milk pudding. Their social atmosphere seems to be subnormal. I should add that these are very good hotels for those who like to stay in hotels of this kind. The surrounding scenery is handsome and undisappointing – if this were not so, the hotels would not be there.

But so much fun is to be had in the small towns. The small town hotels in Ireland are brightening up, and are now perfectly possible to stay in. They have a great *va et vient*,² and their saloons in the evening are full of excellent talk. In the town, there is nearly always something going on – a fair, a funeral or a politician's visit. Or if something is not going on while you are there, something has gone on just before you arrived, and everybody is willing to tell you all about it. All summer and autumn, circuses or strolling players are on the roads: these pitch their tents nightly and give their shows at the edge of one or another town. The remoter cinemas show where good films go when they die. South Irish small towns are beautiful in an abstract manner, with painted houses, wide streets, big dusty squares, knolls of bronze beeches and dark, quick rivers. They are full of shoe-shops, china shops and "medical halls." Dogs lie asleep in mid-street in the hub of the town, only dislodged now and then by big red Great Southern buses. When a bus pulls up in a town a surprising number of people come out of shops and pubs and stand round the bus in a ring, as though a whale had been landed.

153

Anybody who gets into the bus or gets out does so in a glare of gratifying publicity. When the bus has been looked at for about twenty minutes it gets up, as it were, and dashes out of the town. To those who are set on scenery, and must have it, I would explain that most small towns in the coast-counties of Ireland are set in as much beauty as anybody could wish, that most streets have a backdrop of dark blue mountain, whether close or distant, and that on fine days they are drenched in dazzling light. The official grandeurs of Ireland are generally, too, within quite possible reach.

For two or three weeks after Horse Show, Dublin sits back and looks rather desultory. That gala week in August involves the whole south of the city, which becomes a sort of annexe of Ballsbridge. Dublin goes all out, and becomes very European. It seems such a pity that Horse Show should coincide with the height of the Salzburg Festival. When we become the United States of Europe, one may hope that something may be better arranged – though it will have to be made perfectly clear, from the outset, that nothing can alter the date of Horse Show. In September, Dublin stops being anti-climatic. Early autumn brightness polishes the façades of Georgian streets and squares; russet edges the trees in the park and along the canal. This autumn the city looks very brisk. One set of traffic-lights has been installed at a lower corner of Merrion Square: the tempo of progress is setting in. Car-parking regulations are being tightened: another sign of how prosperous we all are. There is a boom in civic pride – a fine exhibition of prints and maps, depicting the past of the city, has been opened and ought not to be missed. The Irish Academy of Letters has just elected three new members. The Abbey Theatre has started its winter season. The Grafton Street shops are full of the autumn modes. Trouble was caused at the trials before the motor races in Phoenix Park by a party of peacocks that escaped from the Zoo and, in the gloom of a very early morning, filed slowly across the racing track. This is said to have happened twice. But by the crucial Saturday, the surviving peacocks were under lock and key. Ireland becomes safer, though never obvious.

Ireland Makes Irish

Ireland makes Irish, there is no doubt. It is impossible, for any length of time, to be *in* this small vivid country and not *of* her. For centuries she has been drawing strangers to her, absorbing them, kindling something in them, and moulding them into replicas of her own stock. Look back at the past, at history – how first Strongbows,[1] Anglo-Normans, then the Elizabethans, then the Cromwellians came to conquer and seize, and stayed to possess and love. In about two generations, we reckon here, the non-indigenous family has begun to show all the native traits. No country, probably, has taken a sweeter or by the end more gentle revenge upon its invaders.

What has proved so winning, so holding, is, I think, the manner of life here – life infused with a tempo and temperament bred of the magic Irish light and the soft air. Inevitably, I speak of the manner of Irish life I know best: that of the country houses. Many of these were built by former invaders who struck roots: the blending of their stone faces into the green surround, so that the houses look like a natural part of the landscape, seems to symbolise the acclimatisation of their owners' spirits to the adopted land. Indoors, something at once grandiose and nonchalant seems at once to lull and to animate the rooms. Inherited from the old native lords of Ireland, who kept open house, there is a high tradition of sociability – here, there is no halfway: you must either enjoy this flux of people coming and going or adopt the other extreme and announce yourself a recluse. Neighbourliness – unchecked by the sometimes extreme isolation of country houses – is a habit. Then, there is the enormous, encircling element of the out-of-doors, which begins to beckon you from the moment you open your eyes in the morning. What a great part of this life is spent in the open air! All the year round – if you stay all the year round – sport, the farm, the garden, a dozen other calls and duties and pleasures set up a hardy indifference to the capricious weather.

And even indoors, the rooms themselves never have a totally

indoor feeling: all day, through their many big windows, they are pervaded by the sky's light and the rustle of trees. In their grates, log fires blaze with their pale flame most of the year round – for in Ireland really hot spells are few – and these fires are magnetic during brief indoor interludes of the day. As evening approaches, more logs are piled on; the warm light flickers through the dusk of the room. And these ever-burning hearths symbolise, too, I think, a genuine intensity of home life, a centring of interests, a democracy of the old and the young – a sharing of whatever may be afoot by the children and the many dogs. Children ride hard and, given their heads, run wild: the schoolroom is an unwelcome alternative to the river, the woods and the stable yard. Above all, as part of this scheme of things, the Irish servant is not to be overlooked: from the patriarchal butler, with his Old Testament vocabulary, down to the young "mountainy" kitchenmaid with her bog-water eyes, there extends a benevolent attitude to "the Family" tempered, I ought to say, by an extreme shrewdness. Less numerous, it is true, than they used to be, Irish country house servants, indoor and outdoor, remain a host in themselves. What they do not know about what is going on is, you will soon discover, not worth knowing. In trouble they are allies, in an emergency fellow clansmen; and nobody enters more thoroughly into the spirit of a party.

Much in this way of life is unique Irish, a carrying on of self-sufficiency and feudalism from the long-ago days when the Irish lord's castle was a little state or court in itself. But much, also, is unique chiefly in its survival: there are, or used to be, affinities everywhere. I have heard Irish country houses likened to those in Poland and pre-Revolutionary Russia – and indeed, the life on country estates described in nineteenth-century Russian novels, Tolstoy's and Turgenev's, has always seemed more than half familiar to me. Also, I have been given to understand that these Irish houses – or rather, perhaps, the way of life that they stand for – are not unlike some in the deep South of the United States.

Few of these Irish houses are, by European reckoning, very old – the mullioned, quadrangled Elizabethan pile of England and the peach-pink brick manor are equally unknown here. The majority of our houses are Georgian, and are anything from modestly to magnificently Italianate, according to their owner's rank and wealth and their own size. Very often the settings are of a dreamlike beauty: there was always a tendency to build overlooking rivers and in rivers this country is rich. Gleaming curves of water, clifflike rocks, the varying tapestry of woods and supple outline of mountains are to be seen from windows.

Our ancestors' love of the scenic had, however, to be kept in check by their desire for shelter and dread of gales – in some cases, caution won, and we then have mansions sunk deep in lush green saucers of park and wood. I should make clear that the "park" of the English big house is here, in Ireland, known as the "demesne." Demesnes are, usually, encircled by mile upon mile of grey stone wall; these having been built, in many cases, to give employment during the distress of the famine times. The appearance of such a wall along the roadside indicates to the traveller that he is approaching a house: were the wall not enough, he could note the planting of trees – the screens, knolls, groves and, running in from the gateways, the apparently endless avenues of beech, chestnut, or lime. If our ancestors' *folie de grandeur*[2] embarrassed us, their descendants, with mansions of sometimes preposterous size, we owe to their large view and foresight these lordly trees.

Yes, the time-colour of this way of Irish country living *is*, decidedly, eighteenth-century. Each country gentleman, no less than his neighbour the duke, was an authoritarian and, to the last inch, a character. On the single, square block of the gentleman's seat, inhabited by himself and his family all the year round, as on the colonnaded, salooned, and terraced mansions of the peer of the United Kingdom, visited for only a few months in each year, one finds reflected the influence of the Grand Tour, the classic engraving and the liberal days when Europeans of culture were one great family.

Humanism stocked little or large libraries with books which their owners, drunk with the open air (and not, I fear, always, with that only) respected but were too drowsy to read. Cellars and stables, extensive, were built to be kept stocked. Now coach-houses have become garages, but the yard trees still cast their shadows over mounting-blocks, and the old rich smell comes from harness rooms. Courtyards of out-buildings – dairies, meat and game larders, "wool rooms," storerooms of all kinds, carpenters' sheds – show how each of these houses used to function as the self-supporting unit it once was – when the nearest town lay at the end of a day's journey and roads were not lightly set out upon. The walled garden, large enough to provision a small army, lies often some distance from the house.

All our architecture is not Italian-square: in the decades around 1800 Gothic romanticism, also, invaded Ireland, giving us our sense of famous castles. Some (as, for instance, Lismore, County Waterford) were raised on old Anglo-Norman fortified sites – the "modern" castle incorporating ancient wells, deep-sunk networks of rock passages, battlements, and keeps with walls eight foot thick. And inevitably, many inherit ghosts. With the theatricality of the nineteenth-century crenellations, turrets, pointed windows and polished, dusky galleries and corridors, only the purist would quarrel. It should be said, at the same time, that not every self-styled "castle" in Ireland *is* a castle: the possession, anywhere in its grounds, of a darkling old Norman fortress-tower (and of these there are many) entitles to this dignified appellation the more modern, unassuming and sunny house.

Gardening, in this country, rapidly becomes an infatuation – and, indeed, what gardens there are to show! The alluvial soil round the river houses, the steamy, moist, sheltered heat of the valleys, produce a luxuriance that is almost frightening. The conformation of the ground, so often, above rivers, in natural terraces, tempts the gardener on and on into further landscape effects. Ruined towers are niched and draped with bloom. The walls and yew or beech hedges of the enclosed gardens make ideal backgrounds for deep herbaceous borders. From peaty soil, azaleas and rhododendrons blaze through the early summers. Tropic speed and richness of growth, here, of course, cut both ways – allow a few months to elapse, and Nature, with her own inordinate beauty, has obliterated all marks of man's, or of woman's, hand.

Land of bogs and rivers and woods and banks and wide fields, how can Ireland be anything but a sporting country? Deep in the tradition, inseparable from the idea of life here, are the horse, the rod, and the gun. Of the Irish hunts, it is not necessary that I should sing the fame: they have great histories and propitious futures. And our trout streams and salmon rivers, equally, hold their place in the memories of great men all over the world. I think it one virtue of Ireland that sport and sportsmen are not isolated; they enjoy the goodwill, approval and interest of the countryside as a whole. Not here are hunting, shooting, and fishing regarded as the preserve of a special class: no particular snobbery, for instance, surrounds hunting: anybody who possibly can turn out does so, and everyone else is glad to see him do so. Households, great or small, down tools and rush to the windows to watch the hunt cross the land: rare, even in cities, is the black-coated worker who does not from time to time handle a gun or rod. Sport, here, is the mighty equaliser, the great solvent – in it, any difficulties or differences of race, politics or religion are forgotten, merged. There is no what one would call "attitude" towards sport in Ireland; it is in the very air, as natural as love or death.

This way of life has its documentation and its literature. Arthur Young, for instance, that eminent and sociable eighteenth-century agriculturist, leaves us, in *A Tour in Ireland*, the record of a round of visits he paid to Irish country houses in the summer of 1776. Much that he had to say is still to the point. Young's *Tour* has lately been edited by Dr. Constantia Maxwell, to whose own pen we owe the contemporary but not less interesting *Country and Town in Ireland under the Georges*.[3] Then, we have the vivacious *Retrospections of Dorothea Herbert* – a late eighteenth-century young lady whom nonstop party-going, throughout the south of Ireland, coupled with love trouble, sent mad. These three books picture the past – things have sobered down since the days when Miss Herbert danced, Arthur Young took coach, and the four first Georges reigned over their Irish kingdom. None the less, a thread of psychological truth knits up Ireland's yesterday with her today. Equally, the mirror which Irish fiction has held up to Irish life does not tarnish: the novels of

Maria Edgeworth and the stories of Somerville and Ross show us an Ireland that still, in essentials, lives.

Are we, then, in Ireland, unchanged – perhaps too wonderfully unchanged – in a changing world? Are these houses, with all that they stand for, anachronisms? Fairy-tale retreats from the harsher realities of the twentieth century? Play-houses? No, surely, I, who love these houses, would rather see the last of them razed to the ground than believe that true; and I do not believe it true. Inherent in this way of life, as in all others, is responsibility; the sense of one's debt to society. Ireland, so free with her good times, is none the less no place for the professional good-timer; she has a salutary, rigorous, harsh streak. Her very weather – those gales from the sea or mountains, those foggy dripping silences of mid-winter, those days upon days, at all seasons, of binding and blinding rain – searches out the weak places in your morale.

And her weather is only one of the tests which Ireland applies to character. Her people, themselves, are great summers-up: they soon know what you or I am[4] worth – and by that, I do *not* mean, worth in money. Money, here as elsewhere, can buy much, but not everything – and in Ireland, it is just what money cannot buy that is most worth having: affection, fidelity, respect. The good feeling that has kept Irish houses going has been, always, a matter of reciprocity: "the Family" in the big house has its part to play; and that part may call for everything that one has. Courage, dignity, fair-mindedness, and a willingness to understand and help in other people's troubles are expected. And, what is due to one's employees and neighbours is no less due to the country in which these houses stand.

These Twenty-six Counties[5] of which I write are not merely romantic old Ireland; they are young Eire – and Eire working out her destiny, grappling with her problems, hoping to take her place worthily in the world of today. She has a right to ask for the understanding – and, should she need it, also the help – of those who by birth or choice live within her shores. Domestically, we are managing to adapt these great rambling houses to both the needs and restrictions of modern living – simplifying and cutting at every turn, using electricity to save man-power. In the same sense, I believe it is possible to bring these beautiful legacies of the old world into line with the more arduous ideals of the new.

How They Live in Ireland: Conquest by Cheque-Book

Ireland – the Twenty-six Counties, Eire – is again in the throes of invasion.

"How many times, let me see, did they conquer us with the sword?" says my friend, rhetorical in a bar in Dublin. "This time, they come to conquer us with the cheque-book."

I hope it may not come to conquest: there is bound, however, to be a stiff battle between indigenous old values and imported new. The Ireland of peasants has always moved slowly: the climate has made for fatalism, the Catholic religion for a mystique. A time lag is to be felt in the atmosphere: for the first few hours after the arrival from England (such a short journey!) one experiences a dizzying sense of strangeness.

The Irish standard of living has been, up to now, low. Look at Mick Mac's wages: in the towns his people would not do much better. The secure class, but in a small way, are the civil servants. The teachers have, with reason, been agitating for higher pay. There *is* big money in the country, but it does not travel out of the middle class: the "strong" farmers, the shopkeepers in the towns, the merchants and the professional people have it. The gentry are, in relation to their liabilities, as poor as the peasants and as behind the times.

Money having all run into one deep narrow pocket, its effect on the general Irish idea of living has on the whole been small. That is what I mean by a low standard – "simple" would, perhaps, be a better word. A very much smaller percentage of people keep motorcars. Taste – in dress, furnishings, food, entertainment – is unsophisticated. England and the United States, between them, have succeeded in dumping their cast-off fashions there: jazz upholstery, orange taffeta, imitation Sheraton[1] interspersed with chromium tubular experiments still dominate the average middle-class home. Farmers' daughters, with moony-milky faces of the 1840 album type, go to Mass or to town in crenellated veil-hung hats. Rich manufacturers copy the *Tatler*[2] photographs, enlarging the check of the tweeds by half again. Not much wine is drunk – after the fall of France, when imports stopped, supplies lasted much longer in Ireland. Gala food is at the twelve-year-old level: much mayonnaise and cream.

The expenditure of the rich middle classes is, in short, childish, resulting in an effect of innocent vulgarity. There is one inhibition, a lurking fear of any ostentation that could be jumped upon. Why? Because in Ireland it is fatal, the beginning of the end, to expose oneself to ridicule. And nothing is found more ridiculous, nothing is visited more cruelly, than the attempt to hoist oneself out of one's own class.

This must be true of the bourgeoisie of any country still haunted by the romantic-reactionary idea. That idea makes for a far greater austerity than is now thought. It denies moral prestige to the possession of money. (Land is another thing.) Class, in itself, as a principle, is not attacked in Ireland: it is part of the *status quo* that the Church supports. The landed gentry and aristocracy were denounced in so far as they were British *protégés*, collaborators from the national point of view, and in possession of forcibly seized land: now the land has gone back to the people, they are innocuous. And more, they have gained a place, if a shadowy one, in the Irish moral-mystical plan. Their obligations have outlived their wealth: so long as they live up to their obligations they are welcome to stay. Those who were not wanted had their houses burned by the people between 1919 and 1922. Those who stayed farm the acres of their remaining land, and are linked with their employees and neighbours in the struggle for life. They are the Protestant minority, decimated by several wars; their sons always fight in the British army – though the attitude of the Irish gentry towards England is by now equivocal.

This is true of the Ireland of up to now. I should say, of up to 1939 – for the war's effect on neutral Ireland was that of cold storage. The isolation of Eire (after the suspension of travel in 1940) acted as a preservative: if anything, traits and habits became more set and more marked. At the same time, independent ideas of some value began to germinate. *Now,* those are being threatened – as everything else in Ireland is being threatened – from the outside: by the postwar invasion.

Now, not in spite of but because of being old-fashioned, Ireland has become very desirable. Not only her food but her mood is being suddenly bid for and bought up. The boom, the inrush shows a reaction against the fatigues and horrors of the mid-1940s. Normal travel facilities from England (though not yet *to* England) having been restored, summer holidaymakers came over in thousands to eat, rest and look at places which have not known war. Tourists are no part of the menace of which I speak; they were expected, and prepared for.

No; the menace (which we may exaggerate) is the exploitation of Eire as a residential playground for the non-indigenous rich. Just now, Irish country houses are fetching fabulous prices. In Eire, sport – hunting, shooting, fishing – remains unthreatened; comparatively speaking, their cost is low. The lower income tax is an inducement to naturalise. Drink and food plentiful; a pretty steady supply of domestic servants. Wages (as above stated) still, as compared to England, fantastically low. A climatic blend of ease and hilarity. In short, in fact, apparently, the good-timers' paradise.

And, of course, the multiplying and speeding up of air services is a great factor. Eire finds herself suddenly in the heart of the map. The Shannon airport links her with America on the one hand, the European continent on the other. Collinstown airport (Dublin) connects with London.

Eire doesn't want her rates of living sent up by people who can afford to pay any prices, and her morals sent down by sophisticates who imagine that in Ireland anything goes. The country, actually, *is* making its own slow but dogged way towards progress, to an enlightened concept of living. Her government has the problems of housing, town-planning, health, and education under closer consideration than might appear. Eire, at this juncture, vitally does not want her apparent backwardness patronised and exploited. Above all, she does not want "passenger" residents, a new wave of settlers whose object is to bypass responsibility. The country has a strong, inbred sense of propriety – woe, in the long run, to those who offend. Six years of isolated neutrality, with its problems, have gone far to help Eire to grow up. She does not feel like a playground and does not want to be one. Against this new weapon, the cheque-book, what defences is she going to put up?

Ireland

Ireland is a little country with a long legend: many associations go with her name. She has a subtle hold upon the imagination; she haunts the memory – never, perhaps, growing quite familiar even to those who know her all their lives; for she is perpetually showing some unexpected aspect of her face. Weather, notably capricious, makes for the variations in her mood, and her landscape dramatically changes; within less than an hour along the road one may have left a rocky gorge for the suavest pasture-land, a verdant and humid river valley for a stark upland, or a towering promontory of cliffs, wave-beaten, haunted by mewing gulls, for the most serene golden-sanded bay. To visit Ireland means to carry away a strange and sometimes disturbing blend of impressions; can so much, the visitor asks himself, really have been contained in so small a space?

To travel in Ireland, it has been said, is to travel some way back in time. The pressures of the modern world seem to lighten; tensions relax. A sense of the past pervades the visitor, stealing over his senses with the tang of turf-smoke, the half-awake look of low-roofed grey or white houses, the sleepy hum of the wind through trees. Horse and ass carts still set the paces of the highways;

ironshod wheels rattle along the lanes; the swish and glitter of automobiles still seem something of an anachronism. Farms and mansions, sheltered by belts of woodland, have the air of being remote from change; the tiny and undulating fields, crisscrossed by unmortared stone walls or bosky hedgerows, look like a patchwork counterpane in a nursery. Life goes on, but beneath the spell of monotony Ireland *does* progress; she is shaking off the reproach of being a "backward" country. New schools and hospitals go up, creameries thrive, industries revivify small communities, highroads acquire surface, and housing projects extend villages and add new outer zones to cities and towns. It will be long, however, before this strikes the visitor's eye; predominatingly, Ireland looks as she always has: wayward, unregulated and picturesque. The factory flanks upon the ruin; dusky dark-windowed stucco or stone façades soar over the up-to-date little shop-fronts. Modernity still seems an uncertain overlay, an experiment which does not go far – whole stretches of Ireland remain untouched by it.

Tourist organisation does much for Ireland; sometimes I fear, however, that it may confine the visitor somewhat too rigidly to the beaten tracks. Those who can spare us not more than three or four days must make do (and will do far from badly) with the motor coach, the planned route, the prescribed hotel and the more famous highpoints of our scenery – seacoast, mountain and lake. Wholly to shun the tourist areas would be to miss what has made Ireland famous in song and story: the drip of the waterfall in the lush woods of embowered Killarney, water-threaded Kenmare, Glengariffe's tree-reflecting tides, the purple of Connemara, the blue of Donegal, the song-haunted glens and sculptured coastline of Antrim. These are among Ireland's jewels, and she is proud of them. But we have more than these numbered beauty-spots. This is not simply a country to be viewed, it is a country to be explored and savoured. Something here, in the air, is the foe of hurry. Spirit, like beauty, is elusive; mystery is lying ever ahead, beyond those still further ranges of hills, round valley's corner and the turn of the river. Ireland calls for individual voyages of discovery.

Our official scenery is on the grandiose side; in some lights it has almost a painted look, and it has perhaps been pictured rather too often. But we have also countrysides in a subtler vein: small mountains swell gently out of the cornfields; white roads twist and wander to destinations whose names have seldom been heard. The southwest coast is fretted with estuaries, up whose wooded silence creep lonely entering tides. Rivers trace a course which is worth pursuing: castles, abbeys and small towns, each with its history, are strung along them; one watches the salmon leap and the heron skim. Spanned by many arched bridges, overhung by crags, mounting meadows or terraced gardens, the rivers of Ireland are not less noble than the rivers of France; known to the fisherman, they are not enough (*I* think) sought out for their own sakes, for their romance and beauty. One hears less (and I always wonder why) of the Irish rivers than of the Irish lakes. Out of the western midlands, the heart of Ireland, the great Shannon sweeps onward past Clonmacnoise (with its grouped Celtic churches, crosses and towers) through the panorama of Limerick and Clare, widening out into sheets of water dotted with islands, narrowing in again between folding hills, till its banks fade with distance: it has come to the sea. But I think, too, of our Blackwater of the south, welling up away in the mists of Kerry, curving west-to-east through the counties of Cork and Waterford, under the bridges of Mallow, Fermoy, Lismore, till at Cappoquin it takes a right-angle turn, proceeding southward to the Atlantic between ranks of Ireland's mightiest trees. Youghal, small fortress city with crumbling battlements, keeps watch at the Blackwater's mouth. In its final reach, between Cappoquin and Youghal, the river is navigable by motor launch; elsewhere, good roads follow its course.

Youghal is an example of something else I count among Ireland's charms: historic and beautiful little towns. It, like the not far distant Kinsale (which, still more unspoiled, is also in County Cork), is built on an estuary; both have been thriving ports and are the holders of ancient charters. Both have been battlegrounds; both are now images of tranquillity – fishing boats bob on the tide by the sleepy wharves. Towns such as these were built when culture still stamped prosperity. There are Venetian windows and fanlit doorways and after dusk, when the lamps are lit, one looks into high-ceilinged, moulded-and-marbled rooms. Here merchants dwelled, and sea-going captains knew the pleasures of home. Steep silent streets and still steeper footways mount between garden walls; archways give on courtyards. In Kinsale, you see women in hooded black cloaks, fashioned a hundred years ago. Ireland's seaports of the southwest and west, set back in their sheltering bays and estuaries, have about them a touch of Latin Europe: from here there was trade with France and Spain. And on them (with the exception, perhaps, of Galway) sophistication has not yet laid its hand: the visitor is welcome but not exploited. Youghal boasts a *plage*,[1] but this extends at a distance from the narrow traditional main street.

Inland, there are towns of no less character, small enough to be sweet with country air, but none the less sedate with a civic dignity: courthouses, clock-towers, fine façades, tree-planted walks on the river frontages. Indeed, these are cities in miniature; they contain a flavour of living – for generations they have been centres, social no less than commercial, for the outlying regions in which they stand. Having been at their height in the eighteenth century (when bad roads and difficult transport sundered most Irish countryfolk from Dublin) these tiny cities are august-provincial[2] capitals, each with its ghost-grey spell. Clonmel, in County Tipperary – which owes its wealth of classical architecture to the richness of the surrounding country, some of Ireland's finest pastoral land – and Westport, in County Mayo – whose town-plan was the work, I have always heard, of a Frenchman – are fair examples. These, and others, are not places to hasten through: at the first glance they are apt to reveal little, but it is repaying to linger and gaze in them.

Where to stay in Ireland is a matter, clearly, for individual taste, plus the factors of time and cost. Against the larger, "recommended" hotels, absolutely nothing is to be said except that they essentially *are* for tourists and, consequently, are lacking in local character. Conveniently placed in the famous beauty-spots, they cater for sightseers in a hurry; their cuisine, like their décor, is international. Those wishing to savour Ireland at more leisure would do well to try the hotels in the smaller towns, many of which have been brought, if not up-to-date, at least within reach of that objective; quite a number are good in a simple way. Former coaching inns keep their big bedrooms, mysterious corridors and (if you care for it) local colour: in the bars and coffee-rooms you hear racy talk. If you prefer to shun towns, seek out the guest-houses into which many family mansions have been converted: here, at the end of your day, you may fall asleep near a whispering river, the sheen of a lake or the natural somnolence of trees.

Irish cooking has not a promising name: it is fair to say it *is* bad when it is pretentious. Keep, if you can, to the simpler "food of the country" (yet another reason to seek out the smaller inns). It has been remarked that the best of our specialities, as a drink and food, are characterised by a slightly smoky flavour: certainly that holds good of Irish whisky, tea, ham and bacon, eggs fried over an open fire, soda-bread (baked atop of a pot lid and strewn with ashes) and grilled or fried lamb or mutton chops. And the fluffiness of the Irish boiled potato, often cooked in its jacket, has not been overpraised. The deep-yellow "farmers' butter" is deliciously salty. As against that, we are bad at pastry, poor at sauces; and our coffee-making notably is abominable (travellers would do well to import with them some "instant" brand of coffee, and make their own).

At no season, I am compelled to say, should one come to Ireland without at least *some* warm clothing. Prepare for the worst as to weather: if you have done so it is likely our contrary climate may shower upon you bland golden days. Your most memorable, your sublimest moments in Ireland may be when ethereal light and transparent colour break through, the minute the rain has stopped. Bring with you, however, provision for indoor days or otherwise undiverted hotel evenings: playing-cards, games, puzzles, mystery stories (those last, in the British "Penguin" edition,[3] you are likely also to pick up along your way). And above all, get the most from your Irish travel by providing yourself with maps and the better guidebooks. I would recommend, too, a selection of "background reading," i.e. books not in the guidebook class, such as Frank O'Connor's *Irish Miles*, Seán O'Faoláin's *Irish Journey*, Dr. Praeger's *The Way That I Went*, and (if you care for the still fairly recent past)

Dr. Constantia Maxwell's *Country and Town in Ireland Under the Georges*.[4] A beforehand reading of any or all of these should help you plan your individual route. And why not a pocket-size volume of Irish history? More than one of such is, admirably, now on sale.

Introduction to The House by the Church-yard, *by Sheridan Le Fanu*

*T*he House by the Church-yard was first published in 1863, one year before Joseph Sheridan Le Fanu's other great novel, *Uncle Silas*. Of the two, *Uncle Silas*, with its small cast and highly concentrated psychological interest, may accommodate itself better to readers today: it being just over a century since both books were written, *Uncle Silas* may seem the more "modern." Those whose addiction to Le Fanu derived from the fascinations of *Uncle Silas* may (I do not say must) experience a set-back when first they embark on *The House by the Church-yard* – less taut, less apparently sure in "tone," disconcerting in its oscillations between sinister grimness and full-blooded jocosity and, here and there, threatened by diffuseness. Such, frankly, was, at the outset, the reaction of the writer of this introduction. It took time for the excellences, chief among which are the almost uncanny force and total originality of *The House by the Church-yard*, to seep through. That having happened, the novel obtained a grip nothing can dislodge.

Le Fanu, one may take it to be known, was an Irishman. When I had the privilege of writing an introduction to *Uncle Silas*, I spoke of its being an essentially Irish novel in an English setting. Something profoundly, temperamentally, differentiates it from the English-Victorian novel of mystery and suspense – such as Wilkie Collins' *The Woman in White*. The oblique and more than semi-mistrustful view of character (or characters), the unopposed great part played by obsession, the acceptance of more or less permanent insecurity as a basis for life, all belong to, all emanate from, the further side of the Irish sea. Le Fanu's Irishness, it could be argued, stood out the more strongly when, for the purposes of a story, he set himself to treating with English characters in England. *The House by the Church-yard*, I have now to admit, contradicts that. That the *mise-en-scène* is, and the entire cast, with one exception, are Irish doubles the author's own native characteristics. Le Fanu, here, is steeping his story in what was to him a prenatal atmosphere, an atmosphere so normal, so natural to him that he can – one might feel – for at any rate the duration of the story, conceive of no other as being possible. The point of view, the evaluations, the mood, the dilemmas are all Hibernian – what one does wonder is, how far they were comprehensible to his English readers? For Le Fanu's Ireland is far from being "stage-Ireland"; it is Ireland as he knew her to be, for better or worse.

The happenings in the action of *The House by the Church-yard* pre-date by just less than a hundred years the time of the telling of the tale: 1767 is the date specified. The narrator is an anonymous old man, whose curiosity as to a by-gone drama was, he explains to us, originally stirred, during his boyhood, by the coming to light in a village church-yard of a skull with two deep clefts, plus a round hole in the back of it. This old man (or rather, the Le Fanu behind him) cheats liberally – albeit with an effectiveness by which the cheating is twenty times justified – in the matter of what goes into his narrative: no amount of burning[1] into the letters and diaries to which he purports to have had access could account for the authenticity, the sometimes fearful vividness, down to the last detail, he gives to what took place before he was born – or indeed, thought of – or for his omniscience as to not only the doings but feelings and thoughts of people on whom he had not, and never could have, set eyes. Not one scene in the book seems at-one-remove; on the contrary, the action of *The House by the Church-yard* unfolds itself directly, immediately, close-up to you and me. This good old man, with his singsong expressions of nostalgia for an epoch he fancies – perhaps rightly? – to have been more *simpatico*, more agreeable, than his own, early on is faded out of *The House by the Church-yard.* This I feel entitled to promise you – lest he put you off. (Why, incidentally, *did* Victorian writers burden themselves and their novels with "intermediaries"? Why does Emily Brontë use them in *Wuthering Heights?*)

The House by the Church-yard is set in what since has come to be known to James Joyce devotees as the *Anna Livia* country: Chapelizod, in the Liffey valley. Few making a Joyce tour, as now organised, will omit Chapelizod from their itinerary. Its name is now the poor place's remaining glory; apart from that it has come to be little more than a lustreless over-run from Dublin. Even by the 1860s it had, according to our narrator, lapsed, being dominated if not by satanic mills by frowsty, smoke-engendering factories. Bearable in his boyhood, it had been at its heyday in the 1760s: that is, when the events related in *The House by the Church-yard* were taking place. "In those days, Chapelizod was about the gayest and prettiest of the outpost villages in which old Dublin took a complacent pride. The poplars which stood, in military rows, here and there, just showed a glimpse of formality among the orchards and old timber that lined the banks of the river and the valley with a lively sort of richness. The broad old streets looked hospitable and merry, with steep roofs and many coloured hall-doors . . . Then there was the village church, with its tower dark and rustling, from base to summit, with thick piled, bowering ivy." Equivalents of the vanished prettiness and propriety of Chapelizod still are to be found – long may this be so! – in up-river Lucan and, still more, in the more-intact, further up-river Leixlip (Co. Kildare).

Poplars were not the only military feature: the Chapelizod of the time of *The House by the Church-yard* had the prestige and enjoyed the panache of being the headquarters of the Royal Irish Artillery, or R.I.A. – not, pray, to be confused by English readers with the I.R.A.! The barracks, the parade ground with its great gate, were along the riverside. The officers lodged on the drawing-room floors of sedate little houses on the aforesaid streets. The commander, "fat, short, radiant General Chattesworth," abode, with his lively spinster sister and pretty young daughter, in a nearby mansion, Belmont, over-looking the river from the heights – many such are, I am glad to

171

say, still to be found in this neighbourhood. General Chattesworth is, we find, overshadowed socially only by the local peer, Lord Castlemallard, a dreamy bore.

The cast of *The House by the Church-yard*, in the main male, is largely though not wholly military. Civilians are represented by Dr. Walsingham, the Protestant rector, his genial Catholic opposite number Father Roach, the physician Toole (whose relations with Sturk, the army surgeon attached to the R.I.A. are not so ideal as they should be), Irons, the lantern-jawed parish clerk, and, not by any means least, the dark-avised Nutter, miller, whose chief income is derived from his agency of the surrounding Castlemallard properties. To these are added two men of mystery: haunted young Mr. Mervyn, who arrives with a coffin and stays on, in a perpetual brooding frenzy which leads ladies to think he may be an *âme damnée*,[2] and suave, sophisticated, middle-aged Mr. Dangerfield, Englishman, who moves in for no declared purpose, renting a riverside villa delightfully known as The Brass Castle. Dangerfield is Lord Castlemallard's agent in England, where – Irish peers enjoyed the best of both worlds! – properties are yet more extensive, and more valuable. A second putative *âme damnée* is handsome Captain Devereux, of the R.I.A. The R.I.A. contribute to our story also, most notably, corsetted, on-the-make Captain Cluffe, Lieutenant Fireworker O'Flaherty (one of the "ferocious O'Flaherty's" from Galway) and dear, ingenuous, generous, fat little First Lieutenant Puddock . . . In spite of this bevy of males, if one may so call it, *The House by the Church-yard* could have been subtitled, "a novel without a hero." There is, actually, no one central character of either sex. As "heroines," Lilias Walsingham and Gertrude Chattesworth amicably divide the honours; yet, neither girl plays a major part in the plot – one of them is to be made momentous, and deeply moving, by her illness and death. Gertrude's Aunt Rebecca is more in the forefront – handsome, something of a volcano. Miss Magnolia Macnamara and her mother are comics (something in the splenetic Thackeray manner). It is two at the first glance inconspicuous matrons, Mrs. Nutter and Mrs. Sturk, who are to become most drastically involved, in whirlpools of menace, terror, piteous anxiety, darkling mystery. And there is an evil-precipitating adventuress out from Dublin, Mary Matchwell.

With near-genius, with which goes a friendly equalitarianism in regard to them, Le Fanu keeps this host of characters in play. Never for long does any one of them leave the story. His hero-less plot is kept spinning by a diversity of crisscrossing passions. He *does*, one has to admit, introduce a villain, though so subtly, and with so many light and deluding touches, that this creature's enormities hardly are to be suspected until the end. Rivalries and antagonism are at work, pressures exerted. A criminal drama, set in another land, proves unfinished; it continues to operate in and round Chapelizod . . . All this sounds like, and indeed is, the stock material of one kind of fiction. What, then, causes *The House by the Church-yard* to soar above endless other novels of what might otherwise be its kind? I would suggest, Le Fanu's curious, near-visionary manner of seeing and way of writing, his what one might call depth-charge perceptions into feeling and motive, his sympathy with the off-beat, with deviation, his none the less uncompromising sense of what *is* ethical, and, most of all, the acute, sometimes almost unbearable emotion, always too astringent to be emotionality or sentiment, with which he suffuses his key scenes. He is aware of the monstrous, and makes a not wholly ironical bow to it: his Black Dillon, that perverse young surgeon of genius cynically weltering in the stews of Dublin, plays but a brief part but is unforgettable.

This novel has rare, few, lovely and on the whole heartbreaking lyrical episodes. It is also roared through by an intense sociability. Bravura rates high, and "gaieties" – in the full and enthusiastic connotation those have in Ireland – are dear to his pen. We have the shooting match, with its merry onlooking troops of ladies, the fair at Palmerstown, the military ball, the *al fresco* entertainment given by the R.I.A. to the neighbourhood, fifes, bugles and other supporting instruments joyously loudening the air of the lady-adorned, tree-shaded riverside. The dinner party at Belmont, at which interesting Mr. Dangerfield first appears, is rendered with every shade of social precision.

Note three particularly Irish attributes of Le Fanu's, all of them to the fore in this novel. (1) His feeling for, acceptance of, and matter-of-fact though none the less terrifying treatment of the supernatural, as exemplified by the hauntings of The Tiled House, young Mr. Mervyn's dwelling. (2) His depiction of servants, together with more irregular hirelings who surround households, such as "the Widow Macann . . . who carried the ten pailfuls of water up from the river to fill the butt in the backyard every Tuesday and Friday for a shilling a week and 'a cup o' tay with the girls in the kitchen.'" The intimacy, the complicity, the often-shared desperations of the employer–employed relationship, as it is in Ireland, can seldom have been, and may never be, better drawn. (3) His sense of the illimitable majesty of death, and its train of incurable desolations. We see a young student, agonised by sympathy, trying to tender comfort to an old clergyman bereft of his dear daughter: –

"Oh, Dan – Dan – she's gone – little Lily."
"You'll see her again, sir – oh, you'll see her again."
"Oh, Dan! Dan! Till the heavens be no more they shall not awake, nor be raised out of their sleep. Oh, Dan, a day's so long – how am I to get over the time?"

In *The House by the Church-yard*, some enchanting lyrics, such as the one beginning: –

> The river ran between them,
> And she looked upon the stream,
> And the soldier looked upon her,
> As a dreamer on a dream.

– are sung or recalled. And a long moralistic ballad is intoned in a pub, taking off thus: –

> There was a man near Ballymooney,
> Was guilty of a deed o' blood,
> For thravellin' alongside wiv ould Tim Rooney,
> He kilt him in a lonesome wood.

Where did Le Fanu get these from, I wonder – did he write them? They stand, in their ways, for what might be called the opposite poles of the book – whose first event is a torchlit midnight burial, surrounded by secrecy, odour of disgrace and unspoken horror, and whose last is a sunlit, splendid young-aristocratic wedding. A damaged skull, we recall, set the story going. By the end, we have learned whose the skull was – yes, we *have* learned, but without greatly caring. That this should be so is, I feel, a tribute to and not a reflection upon *The House by the Church-yard*. So much has been stirred up, such an orchestrated variety of sensations has been lived through, so much that was unexpected has teased our nerves and so much that is tender and beautiful touched our senses and delighted our spirits, since the story began, that the original mystery has been swept away – on the much water that has, by now, flowed under the bridges.

THINGS

Toys

"TOY," says the Dictionary, " – a plaything for children or others." Among the *others*, you and I, I hope, may be counted in. Sad indeed is the man or woman whom, at this or any season, toys' magic leaves cold, who is exiled from the interior world of play. In that world, all centuries and all races meet – for indeed, since there have been people we may take it that there have always been toys; they are inseparable from our humanity. In caves, in tombs, in long-buried cities they have been found. We know that the young brides of history took their playthings, along with their wedding chests, into their husbands' families;[1] and that the East has child-mothers whom the living baby does not soon console for the banished doll. The toy is the first possession; it has the power to concentrate all the imagination and every feeling. How we envy in children this concentration, and how we share it, however momentarily, when, as grown-ups, we become givers of toys! Left to itself, it is true, the child finds or makes its own toy – the bone, the queer-shaped pebble or bit of wood, the bunch of grass (doll-shaped), the empty box or spool – for resourceful is the imagination, forceful are the imperatives of play. But to be ideal the toy should have something added. *Is* it too much to say that it should have magic – an outside magic, something not known before? Invention, and high invention, should have gone to its making – for, to give absolute joy the toy should open another epoch, as being something the child has not known before.

Actual ownership of a new toy is dizzying. Before this, perhaps, the toy has been known by desire – through the plate-glass window, from the other side of the counter it has been gazed upon, with an ardour no other unliving object will again arouse. (But then, a toy is not an unliving object.) The small misty patch left by breath fades from the toyshop window; the child unwillingly turns away – to think of, to dream of and to desire nothing in the world but that particular thing. To set one's heart on something – oh, how consuming the process is! Children, like other shop-gazers, do deliberately court this mixture of anguish and ecstasy: in the windows, along the counters, they are in search of that without which life must, from the moment of seeing, become unlivable. If they do not find it, they feel flat, let-down, cheated: the shop, for today at least, seems a poor affair. So great, indeed, are the joys of this envisaged possession that the toy desired but never actually owned does not count, by the end, as a total loss. Highest of all, in fact, in the Valhalla[2] of my toy-memory stand those that I wanted but never had – most notably, a toy theatre, with several changes of scenery, lit by electric light.

Should a toy as a present, I wonder, be a complete surprise, or should it be the realisation of a long-formulated wish? There is much to be said on both sides: chiefly, the answer lies in your child's temperament. There are those for whom "the surprise" in itself is the major thing: the very shape of the parcel should give nothing away. But the greatest mystery-lover cannot abstain from guessing; and, so often, out of the string of guesses one rather definite hope takes form – such form that its disappointment may threaten tragedy. But the situation, after a moment, saves itself: after all, the surprise-glamour is strong . . . One thing I should never do is, lead a child round a toyshop, without warning, to make an immediate choice. "Whatever you like; anything in the shop!" This is too much – how can he but lose his head? In the same way, a too sudden present makes for dumbfoundedness: it is stared at, walked around, considered from every angle, with the air of judgement being reserved. The donor feels disappointed – is this, then, not what was wanted? No, it is not that – exactly. But, as one must remember, a fancy takes time to grow.

Toys for today must be the toys *of* today. One can see that with each generation of children the formula for the enchantment differs. Toy psychology changes, from age to age. The doll from the tomb, the miniature chariot dug up from some lost city would, though touching enough to the grown-up person, do little to your or my girl or boy. Even the toys of our own childhoods would hardly "take" now, I fancy; while those of our grandparents', reverently preserved, would have little more than museum interest. I, for instance, knew of my mother's dolls by reputation: they sounded entrancing creatures – for she talked of them vividly. But when she returned from a visit to her old home with, in triumph, one of these dolls to *show* me, the spell broke. The pallid smeared waxen features, the limp limbs shocked me so much that I did not know what to say; and my mother's childhood, which I had almost shared, shot away from me into the cold remoteness of time. Much more happy was my relationship with my Aunt Laura's Japanese doll, Thomas; but for this there were several reasons: – he was my contemporary (for she had acquired him since she became my aunt); he was a highly dramatised character, whose misdoings and sayings never came to an end; and he was a distinguished foreigner, an exotic. If not to all foreign toys, to the Japanese certainly fascination clung. What was it – their oddness of colour, their sheer perishability? Those oiled-paper butterflies on their frail bamboo frames; those "mystery" flowers that, in a glass of water, uncoiled from confetti-sized discs into blossoming trees; those miniature lanterns, fans, parasols; those ferocious but strangely un-weighty tigers of what appeared to be frozen cotton wool – they are unforgettable. Out, now, upon Japan and her machinations – but how well she knew how to speak to the childish heart!

As to peasant art-and-craft toys from outlying parts of Europe, I was as a child, and remain as a grown-up, doubtful. These are, or were till the outbreak of this war, timeless: always about, and registering little change. Colourful, animated they are, certainly – but is not the fantasy element in them too self-conscious; at any rate, for the British child? Their place seems to be more the mantlepiece than the table or floor. And then, as a rule, they are no more than two-dimensional; and can one hope to play, with anything like conviction, with a cow or a peasant that, however gaily painted, remains perpetually in profile?

Convincingness – ah that, surely, is the pre-requisite of the good toy. One must remember, play is a serious thing, and what is designed to be played with must not be a grown-up joke. I should doubt whether a facetious toy has ever drawn from a child a more than polite smile. Unfortunately, while children's stern humour protects them against facetiousness, they have less effective armour against vulgarity – in the matter of this, they are at our mercy. I declared war years ago (not that it did much good) against the "googoo-eyed" doll and all her company. "Googoo's" progenitor was, I fear, the apparently innocent "Kewpie,"[3] who reigned, briefly, circa 1913.

That year saw, too, a great jump forward in naturalism in dolls' faces. The angel simper started to disappear. (Had it once, I wonder, been hoped that this would provide a model for dolly's young mistress? If little girls were not angels, they ought to want to be.) For some time before this, *mechanical* realism had been aimed at; the really "good" doll, on being tilted backwards, had for years been able to shut her eyes with a resigned click; dolls already had jointed wrists (I used to pray for a doll with jointed fingers); beauties had sweeping eyelashes; and "real" hair, which could be curled with irons, was, at a price, superseding the fluffy wig. But *psychological* realism was new – in fact, it was revolutionary. Dolls stopped looking sweet-tempered and looked sulky. Their unbreakable "composition" (rather than china) faces recorded cryptic frowns. If the morality was for the worse, the realism was for the better. For only one out of five little girls wants her doll to be a mock baby, just to dandle and croon over; the other four want their dolls to be characters. And these newcomers were, I remember, first called "character dolls."

Do we want in toys, then, absolute realism? Is the toy to be a scrupulously correct miniature reproduction of something the child already knows in real life? This – until toy-production was brought to a halt by the war – would appear to have been the most recent trend. One class of toy, at least, advanced in "life-likeness" as it advanced in finish. The other class started away from life at a right-angle, into sheer, one[4] hundred per cent fantasy. Of course, the one and final test of the toy is the degree of pleasure it gives your child. This accepted, I – from the outside – should still have said that either extreme was a mistake. Can an out-and-out "model" rank as a toy proper? Smallness, a fairy-like quality, will always be fascinating;

but about mere correctness, in toys, there must always be something null. Must (for instance) we, whose lives are telephone-ridden, find no other gift for our child than a miniature telephone? Nature has endowed most of our children with something more valuable than any present from us – a magnificent surplus fund of imagination. At the same time, she balances this with common sense. Without revolting this common sense – as the purely fantasy object may easily do – should not all toys leave *something* to the imagination? Are we in danger of toys that forbid play?

Let me speak of a few more classics. There are mechanical toys – champion breakers-down; but fun, after that point, to take to pieces. There are educational toys – which, for all their forbidding name, sound a delightful challenge to ingenuity: they speak straight to the brain and the fingertips in their language of pure, hard form and primary colour. These last, indeed, head the third and important class: the non-representative. They are not copies; they are not concrete fairy tales; they are "things that one does other things with." Do these, perhaps, give most pleasure – the most diversified, lasting pleasure – of all? The doll sheds its limbs; the pistol ceases to fire; the plastic farmyard submerges into disorder; one after another the wheels come off the lorry. But, while Nature encourages us to meddle – while there are sands to dig in, undergrowths in which to make tunnels, and streams to dam – shall we not always love, above what is made already, that which we can make into something else?

Calico Windows

Calico windows[1] are something new – in a summer bare of fashions, "crazes," or toys. They pitch home life in a hitherto unknown mood. In the theatrical sense, they rank as "effects" of the first order. They cast on your ceiling, if you have a ceiling left, a blind white light, at once dull and dazzling, so that your waking thought every morning continues to be, "Why, it must have snowed!" They lighten and darken slowly: inside calico windows it might be any time of year, any time of day. Through their panes you hear, with unexpected distinctness, steps, voices and the orchestration of traffic from the unseen outside world. (Talkers outside a calico window should be discreet.) Glass lets in light and keeps out sound; calico keeps out (most) light and lets sound in. The inside of your house, stripped of rugs, cushions and curtains, reverberates.

Few of these new-fashion windows are made to open: you cannot have everything. However, the sashes of those that do, fly up with ghostly lightness, almost before you touch, showing you summer still outside.

This cotton and cardboard 1944 summer home, inside the shell of the old home, is fascinating. With what magic rapidity was it improvised and tacked together by the kind workman. The blast of the buzz bomb marked the end of the former phase. The dreamlike next phase began with the arrival of workmen. As though just hatched, or dropped from the skies, these swarmed in their dozens in your street. Soon they had disappeared, without trouble, inside the blasted-open front doors – yours having its share. So many and so alike were the workmen that, still dazed, you failed to distinguish one from the other, and only attempted to guess their number when it came to finding cups for their tea. They were at it almost before you knew they were there – smashing out what was left of glass, smashing down what was left of plaster, wrenching out sagging frames and disjointed doors. The noise they made at their beginning, if just less, was more protracted than that of the explosion. But nothing makes you feel calmer than being taken in hand.

Coughing in the fog of dust they had raised, scrunching over chips of glass on the floors, the workmen, godlike, proceeded towards their next stage, that of sweeping, hauling, measuring, hammering. Only just pausing, they listened patronisingly to other buzz bombs passing across the sky: you knew nothing more could happen while they were with you. To watch them filled your post-blast blankness; to watch them made you feel you were doing something yourself; and to know that *you* were not paying them was most heartening.

The calico for the windows arrived in bales, along with the felt and boarding. Workmen carrying these in wove their way between workmen carrying rubble out. The rubble was tipped from baskets on to a mounting mountain outside your doors; and the mountain was bypassed by still more workmen with tarpaulins with which to drape your roof – these last disappeared upstairs and, for all you knew, never came down again.

The whole scene was one of rhythm and, soon, of order. Watching the bold creation shape itself, you exclaimed, "Of course, of course!" The light new window-frames, primitive as a child's drawing, which have been constructed out on the pavement, are now fitted into the old windows. The outside world disappears. The workmen's are the first faces you see in this to-be-familiar calico light. You have now been tied up, sealed up, inside a tense white parcel. The workmen see it is good. They go.

You are left alone with your new sensations. The extraordinary is only at the beginning of its long reign. So many footprints are in the dust that you lose track of your own; you lose track of yourself, and you do not care. The peace of absolute dislocation from everything you have been and done settles down. The old plan for living has been erased, and you do not miss it. Solicitous for the safety of your belongings, the considerate workmen have hidden everything: the lamps are in the hat-cupboard; the telephone has been rolled up inside a mattress; your place in the book you were reading when the bomb went off has been religiously marked with a leg that blew off the sofa; more books are in the bath. And everything seems very well where it is. Especially does it seem good that the position of the telephone makes it impossible for you to tell anyone what has happened, or to reply if anyone asks you. Already you feel secretive about your pleasure at the dawn of this new, timeless era of calico.

And next door? For you are not the only one. You run in to ask how the next-doors sustained the blast, but how they feel inside their white box is a more intimate question. Next door – now that you come to listen – sounds remarkably silent: can they have gone to the country? If so, have they any notion how much they miss? Next-door-but-one, and next door to that, add their quota to the deserted silence.

No doubt, however, everyone else, like you, is standing still, taking stock, looking round. Now you think, you find you are making no noise yourself – they probably think you have gone away.

But perhaps as that first dusk falls your curiosity heightens, till you go out to make a reconnaissance. Your street, chequered over with black and white, looks somehow coquettish and self-conscious. Going farther, you are perhaps diminished by finding your entire neighbourhood endowed with this striking new thing in panes. Seen from the outside, all the way down a street, calico windows lose tone. You begin to wonder, inimically, how long these good people's windows will stay clean, and what they will look like when they no longer are. Now, in this hour before blackout, lights flower behind the crisscrossed frames. Do that young couple realise, or should you tell them, that they perform a shadow-play on a screen? No polite person stares in at a lighted window, but what is to stop you staring at calico?

Back home, you remember you have no blackout. You grope to bed in the calico-muffled dark.

Those first twenty-four hours are only the sharp-edged beginning of the mood. You must live, of course; you must pick up at least some of the pattern; you must at least play house. You discover that what turned on, turns on still – hot water, wireless, electric light. Whether willing or not, you disinter the telephone from the mattress, to explain you are quite safe, perfectly all right, happy; and to learn, from the pause on the wire, that you are disbelieved.

But everything comes from a distance; nothing disturbs you. Each time you return home, shutting the door behind you, you re-enter the mood. The hush of light, the transit of outdoor sounds, the bareness in here become familiar without losing their spell. Life here – life in a blasted, patched-up house – is *not* life, you have been indignantly told. What is it, then – a dream? We are, whatever else we may be, creatures of our senses, varying with their food. Is this different food for our senses making us different creatures?

This tense, mild, soporific indoor whiteness, with, outside, the thunder of world events, sets the note of the summer for Southern England. I say to myself, all my life when I see a calico window, I shall be back in summer 1944. Then I remember – when war is over, there will be no more of this nonsense; we shall look out through glass. May the world be fair!

Introduction to The ABC of Millinery, *by Eva Ritcher*

Millinery – who disputes the fact? – is an art. Like the other arts, it has flowered out of civilisation. For centuries, Woman has desired that her head-covering – be it cap, bonnet or hat – should in itself be a thing of beauty. A thing which shall at once express and flatter the wearer *and* be, gaily, in tune with her own time.

But also, because such intense importance attaches to it, millinery has appeared to some of us to be a sort of enchanted mystery. It has been taken for granted that the artist-milliner is either unwilling to give away his or her secrets; or, at any rate, would not be able to find the language in which to impart them. Now there is better news. Eva Ritcher, herself the possessor of the master-touch, one might say the magic touch, is about to open what has hitherto seemed a locked door. *The ABC of Millinery* is intended for the laywoman – for the woman who loves hats but who up to now, where the creation of hats is concerned, has considered herself an outsider.

This is the book for the reader whose fingers have itched to attempt millinery, but whose good sense has warned her against the blunders she can but make if she is not helped. A book for the reader who, having been offered inferior hats in shops, can but have thought: "I'm sure *I* could do better than *that*, if only, if only, I knew how . . ." A book for the reader with time and taste. Indeed, a number of reasons may have made us wish to be our own milliners – we may have difficulty with head-sizes, we may live in districts where good hats are difficult to buy; or, the hats of distinction, to which we aspire, may be at prices beyond our means.

Having in mind the public for whom her book is meant, Mrs. Ritcher writes in ideally simple language. There is nothing esoteric about her vocabulary. The various processes of millinery are described by her in plain terms, step by step, as in standard dressmaking instructions. She is – as indeed the hats which come from her own hands show – a woman of imagination: she shows her imagination, here in her book, by being able to put herself in the place of someone beginning at the very beginning. Equally, Mrs. Ritcher does not assume that the home-milliner will have at her disposal all the equipment of the professional milliner's trade – blocks, etc. Foreseeing this difficulty, she has helped you to meet it by suggesting substitutes, where possible.

The author of *The ABC of Millinery* brings to her work not only flair and experience, but an unusual cosmopolitanism. She has lived in Paris, New York and Hollywood. Those who have known her personally, those who have been so happy as to attend her shows or wander round her *salons* will be able to realise how all this reflects itself in the Eva Ritcher hats. To be the wearer of a Ritcher hat breeds a sort of unselfconscious happiness which I, for one, consider to be the ideal mood. And there is another aspect of Mrs. Ritcher (important, I think, with regard to this book): she is not only creator but teacher too. Herself a model milliner, she has for some time been running her own school. In this, she takes her pupils – as she will take her readers – direct to the up-to-date methods of model millinery.

These methods discard many of the cumbrous, lengthy, old-fashioned processes – through which you and I, if not warned by her, might have thought it necessary to labour, and to labour (as the sad "effect" might have proved!) in vain. Over-elaborations of wiring and stiffening are, for instance, we joyfully learn, no more – they are things of the unregretted past! To the new method, the essentially modern "plastic" sense enters in: it is based upon careful shaping, and upon skilful treatment of the materials themselves. Understanding love of the *nature* of the material, and sense of the possibilities for its best use, would appear, today, to be the ideal feature of all design – whether in architecture, interior decoration, fine cooking or (to return to our object) millinery. To see Mrs. Ritcher handling the stuff which will make a hat is to be conscious of inspiration passing up from her fingertips to her brain. Inspiration is an extreme form of awareness. She hopes, in writing this book, to impart at least her own awareness to you. Dear readers, seek and cultivate such awareness – from it, in time *your* inspiration may come!

From this plastic feeling for millinery (if I may call it so) come hats which are light, living, graceful in line; hats which will keep their shape – and, with that, their sympathy with the wearer – up to the very last.

And indeed – as this book importantly shows – the "very last" of a good hat is a long way ahead. Given good stuff to work on, the possibilities of remodelling seem endless. To remodelling a special chapter has been devoted. Need we be ashamed to admit that the sensation of going around in a last-year's hat does have a lowering effect on the morale, however one may attempt to brave it out? Mrs. Ritcher's demonstration that no hat *need* be a last-year's hat is as valuable as anything she has given us.

"If anyone," says a friend, "can make a woman hat-conscious, it is Mrs. Ritcher." Hat-consciousness in a vacuum – that is to say, without a good hat to wear – *could* be a frustrated, unhappy state. Mrs. Ritcher transmutes it into a happy one by making the creation, and the possessorship of a good hat possible for any woman with clever fingers.

Her aim is to bring out the sense of style latent in most of us. I do not, in fact, feel that the appeal of this book of hers need be restricted to would-be hat-makers. *The ABC of Millinery* should be read by every woman who would like to know, essentially, what a good hat *is*. This she may learn from Mrs. Ritcher, element by element, chapter by chapter. Nothing – which is worth noting – in this book is based upon any *immediate* fashion; therefore, you will find nothing likely to "date." You may study, here, the principles which underlie great millinery – that subtle blend of individuality and fashion. My advice to readers who cannot hope to embark upon the actual making of hats is this – take what you've learned from these pages to heart when you go shopping. No longer will you, in show rooms, find yourselves adrift, depressed and confused. Let this book be your guide to the Good Hat.

The Teakettle

When I begin to speak of the teakettle, all, but *all*, of my friends exclaim, "you mean teapot!" Thus is the noble, necessary kettle slighted. Virtually, it is unknown to history; poetry's tributes to it have been niggardly; seldom has it posed for its portrait. Sadly few kettles are in museums – to the kettle's past has gone (I find) but little research. Meanwhile the teapot, that famous beauty, revels in every kind of publicity. Skills of every kind have gone to adorn it – it has succeeded in being everything, from classical-type to romantic-pretty, from aristocratic-looking to good and cozy. At one time, the teapot aped the form of a wine vase; at the other extreme, Cubism took it over (not, it has been agreed, with the best results). Apart from favourite teapots in daily use, many are singled out to be sheer ornaments.

The background kettle goes into the pot-and-pan class.

Yet, where would the teapot be without the teakettle? Nowhere. What would the teapot be without the teakettle? In effect, nothing.

The sapient and civilised Chinese grasped those two verities fairly early – tea-making being among the arts they first pioneered in, then perfected. It was in the eighth century (A. D.) that the Chinese made their epoch-making discovery – i.e., that one does not boil tea; one infuses it. For that, what is necessary? Boiling water. Repeat, boiling – water right *at* the boil. How best should that reach the tea leaves without (on the way) exposure to cooling air? Down a spout. How was escape of heat (in the form of steam) through the open top of the vessel to be prevented? By the addition of a lid.

The ingenious eighth-century Chinese therefore at once designed, and put into use, a small tea-water kettle. On the chafing dish principle, this had beneath it a portable charcoal burner. This was (I have ascertained) the first known teakettle. The English were slow to profit by that particular wisdom of the Orient's; tea itself having reached them in the seventeenth century, they became from then on increasingly fervent addicts. They continued to boil tea-water in sloppy cauldrons – enterprise with regard to tea taking the form, chiefly, of heavy smuggling, to evade the sky-high tariffs.

More or less exactly 1,000 years after the teakettle notion had dawned on China, it at last found favour with English genius. The teakettle, once it began to be made in England, developed an English style of its own. Sturdy in outline, it had an ample base. Destined to be perched upon stoked-up coal fires, it needed to be resistant to their heat – accordingly, it was wrought of the stoutest metals: iron or copper. Smoke soon blackened, soot caked, its veteran surface. And, although it had a handle above its lid, near *that* dared venture no human hand! To shift or lift such a kettle, one used a pothook.

How unlike its dainty Chinese progenitor! Our teakettle, grimed by hard years, was rated accordingly. Thankless treatment rewarded it, often, for faithful service. None the less, this tribe maintained an *élite* – slenderer, shinier kettles – which fared better.

Delightful as may be the shape, glaze, porcelain florals, gilt swags, cameo profiles, bird or scenery motifs, or all or any decorative medallions upon the teapot, without the teakettle there can be no tea. The teapot, for all its charms, is a sheer dependent. The chubbiest, homiest-looking brown glazed earthenware teapot is – as to this – one with its ornate sister. The brown teapot, with its realist farmhouse ancestry, does not (be certain) kid itself as to that. The fragile porcelain teapot has learned humility. The antique silver variant is no fool, either – whether upright Queen Anne, curved

Georgian, fluted Regency or rotund Victorian. The teakettle, nominal servitor to the teapot, does, in actual fact, play the master role.

That axiom is instilled into all true tea-makers. Tea-making's whole, old lore concentrates in one saying: "You bring the Pot to the Kettle; you *don't* bring the Kettle to the Pot!" Why? Because, not more than a split second must elapse between the lifting of the now-at-the-boil kettle from the flame and the tilting of the still-at-the-boil water on to the tea leaves waiting (inside the waiting teapot) to be infused. Moreover, the teapot will have been scalded prior to the spooning in of the tea leaves, else the "bite" of the boilingness of the water might be reduced. The iniquity of bringing to the kettle a teapot with coldness in it is very great.

The teakettle summons the teapot at its psychic, own, imperative moment. That we should require the ear-splitting "whistling" kettle to blare forth that moment shows (*I* think) some decline – should the kettle-lover not recognize what is happening by means of some tuned and alert sense? The kettle first "sings" (that, poetry *has* allowed it!) then approaches the boil at noisy crescendo. Once at the boil, it changes its rhythm. The steam's fierce sibilance is what is chiefly, now, to be heard. Air vibrates, startled, at the mouth of the spout.

What a drama. What a dramatic contrast with the actual, timeless calmness of *drinking* tea.

Long gone, the formal tea-hour once spun its magic. There was an element, also, of ceremonial, Oriental-descended, not inappropriate. English country houses (of which the greater survive as viewable "stately homes") set up a special mystique with regard to "tea." That word stood for far, far more than the beverage. "Tea," in fact, was a high, a drawing-room occasion: some ladies dressed for it specially – hence, the "tea-gown." Observant (and imitative), the French preferred to call this occasion "*le five-o'clock*." And then it was that the teakettle, along with the teapot, enjoyed full limelight. In sailed the two heavenly twins, of silver, resplendent, borne on a silver tray. The tray came to rest on a low but abundant table – whereon "iced" cakes, ethereal pastries, "hot cakes" (liquid with butter), delicate sandwiches, petal-thin bread-and-butter waited, set out on a lacy cloth. Flocks of teacups looked like a *corps de ballet*. Any hostess of worth insisted (although there were servitors) on going through with "making the tea" herself – as audience, her guests. The kettle and teapot were, it must be stated, non-identical twins, for the former was elevated some 3 to 4 inches on its silver tripod, within which pulsed a spirit-blue flame. An essential attendant, naturally, was the tea caddy, silver as they come, with its little scoop. The kettle, it need hardly be said, required not more than a lick from the small blue flame. The drawing-room-entering kettle contained water already brought to the boil, off-stage. A caked old black kitchen kettle had, very probably, done the work.

For all their grand style, all their polished paraphernalia, those long vanished drawing-room tea hours were far from freezing ones. "The cup that cheers, but not inebriates," is – *I* feel, always – a line written with more than an impish smile. The drinking of tea sets up an inebriation of its own. It was, in fact, denounced by furious puritans, than which a greater tribute could hardly be. Talk around those glittering tea tables (one may gather, from the reading of any period memoirs) had a peculiar, relaxed but racy, above all intimate flavour. Gossip, glancing confidences and charming if perilous innuendo flourished no less when un-heated by alcohol. From those rosy or turquoise cups, with their frilled gilt lips, *what* insidious aroma came floating up?

It floats up still – changed though the scene is. Endlessly, now more casual, the set-out of tea engenders the ancient magic – to which are added fewer of the perils, more of the sweetnesses of intimacy. Here still, *still*, is an hour like no other! Gently social – when it is social at all: ideally an hour for two, for dear friends. An hour, even, for the solitary, who drawing her small tea-tray alongside her big chair, turns her lamp on her book, preparing to sip and read. But, does she read? May she not find herself musing on other tea hours? In the other big chair, opposite, has she not perhaps an imaginary companion – someone who was there yesterday, will be there tomorrow, or who through the very fact that he cannot be there again will be there always?

Tea can be drunk in the garden; that is lovely. It can be drunk in a big bay window outside which sweet-smelling spring rain is falling. But I think the ideal tea is drunk by the fire. And does not fire call up a rotund presence, singing, still-languidly steaming, upon the hob? (Hob, *yes*: though where are those hobs now?) Dear kettle, wherever you work, however you boil – circular gas flame, plugged-in electricity or the wavering spirit-stove – I love you.

Thank you for tea. Without you, there could be none.

On Giving a Present

The giving of a present can be surrounded by a glow. *Is*, indeed, so surrounded, for if it lack that, it is[1] not the act I mean. This is a joy which is not childish, yet is a child's foreknowledge of what joy can be. The infant tottering forward with the fistful of clover, the small embroiderer or constructor secretly, feverishly at work, the artist-to-be splurging round with crayon or paintbrush, dedicating his picture to its inspirer, all have culmination in mind: the ideal moment. The idea has had a miraculous conception. Not only to love is to give, to give is to love. The moment comes nearer. There is increasing rapture.

Outgrowing the age of inspired making, we enter upon the age of inspired chase. One may pursue the ideal present in either of two ways: by pre-envisagement, or with an open mind on which what *is* the answer is to burst like a vision. A present's "ideal," clearly, only when it can be seen in sublime relation to the particular person it's destined for. For days together, it may happen, what is being sought refuses to be tracked down. Or, confusion sets in: the seeker blunders his way through forests of other possibilities. The cherished, original image of the thing – formed in part consciously, though with a subconscious element – seems to correspond in no way with outer, concrete reality: the most recondite shop, the most (one might have imagined) inexhaustible gallery, fails to produce its like.

Does it not, in fact *can* it not, exist? "Exactly what is it that you are looking for?" one is asked, with professional sympathy, skilled patience. "I don't know. Yes, the trouble is, I do know – I can't say, exactly. If I could only see it . . ."

Then follows the poem day: the present is come on.

Such a present, found, is a trinity. It incorporates the giver, its magic self, and the man, woman or child to whom it must go. It is to be the language of a relationship, *the* relationship, sensitive and specific. It touches, possibly, on the harp-strings of particular memories, so subtle, one would underline them in no heavier way. It recollects, sometimes, a desire fleetingly, waywardly given voice to. The imperishable is somewhere within a present – perishable, fragile, destructible in a moment of mischance, tarnishable, subject to loss or robbery though it itself is. The thing is sought for its genius, not for its lastingness. There is a Valhalla where vanished presents remain.

Desire: in divination of that lies the essence, the secret, of present-giving. Mysterious is every human being – oneself, the other – and also boundless. We are surrounded by dreams, hopes, wishes we do not know of; or know of only when, in a flash, by chance or more than a chance, they are fulfilled. We have unavowed, innocent loves and likings: deep-down, personal, not to be dictated to by "taste" – and how those extend to the world of objects! The happy present is one which goes straight to its mark. The comeback: a delighted answering cry, "How did, how could you, know me so well? This, I have wanted all my life!" Such can giving be – the giving one dreams of . . . Such a giving has little to do with actual *need*: the conferring of "practical," useful presents goes altogether into another bracket. Many gifts can be thoughtful and meritorious – there they stop. They do not deserve to be sneezed at. The fancy cooking pot, the natty travel-accessory, the newly devised aid for the keen gardener are "outs" for the giver where vision is not. They are safe bids; they quite possibly meet felt wants. They bespeak knowledge of, and sympathy with, the recipient's addictions, interests or habits. The inspirational present is more daring – *it* charts unknown seas.

The present that satisfies desire, the present the giver desires to give, costs money. Why should it not? – is it not right it should? Why should what is lovely be had for nothing? Like it or not, there is no way round this. Felicitous descents on the local flea market, triumphant extraction of spoils from the junk shop backyard are so rare these days as to make no matter. No object gains virtue by being blemished; the charm of the once-was, in poor condition, is running out. Perfection in the thing-to-be-given is a *sine qua non*. The present you set your heart upon giving costs always more than you can (or should) afford: that's invariable, that is axiomatic. By that, the true, temperamental giver is stimulated, rather than deterred. Extravagance, in the glorious sense, adds zest – nay, and more, rhapsody – to the present-giving. With an equal recklessness, time is disbursed, in the search; to which may be added the toll taken of nervous concentration, physical energy, as the obsessed seeker zigzags from street to street, plumbs the depths of shop after shop . . . No iota of the expenditure goes for nothing. Found at last, placed at last in hands it was meant for, the present gives forth like an aroma, or sheds round it like light from an extra aura, its costliness: it is thereby enhanced. There is not vulgarity in this – why should there be? Simply, delight is heightened. Not only the insight of the giver but his persistency, his perfectionism, his disregard for any and all things other, are to be perceived: in *these* lies the value. Thus[2] is received such a present – the emotion is pure.

What, though, of the have-nots? Frustrated givers, like to frustrated artists? The needy and straitened, the almost wolfish haunter of shop windows is to be recognized. His is the hardship, if not of giving nothing, of giving limitedly and thriftily – as he can, not, oh, not as he *would*! He stares through glass at fantasies past his reach. Toyshop, florist, furrier, jeweller: he completes his round. Voluptuous hesitations, esoteric searches, dizzying choices cannot be his. Shorn of giving-power, in the world of the concrete, what else is a man or a woman shorn of? Not, perhaps, the entirety one might fear. There remains a domain in which wealth is: there can be in people a giftedness, of the heart, brain, spirit, which can endow moments, spark pleasure alight where there was none, turn water to wine. To love is to give. Thrown back on his own devices, *this* giver becomes a sort of illusionist, transmuting the gaudy card with its bells and reindeer, the packet from Woolworth's, the bedraggled chrysanthemums from the late-night flower stall, into the things of wonder that he would have them be. And to those to whom they are given they're things of wonder; they rejoice hearts, they are memorable years after. What makes a present a present is its accompaniment. For want of that, the costliest can fall flat; *with* that, the more shines out the intrinsic beauty. To have an empty pocket is, for the lover of giving, a hard fate. Yet, still more unfortunate is the ungifted giver – he, that is, who lacks gift for the art.

How greatly this is an art (though warmed, too, by love) one realises when the art is missing. Ironically, the deficiency is most marked, often, in those who can spend *ad lib*. There is what one might call the didactic giver, who donates what he feels ought to be wanted, whether it be or not: pompous aids to culture, massive costume jewellery to a slender woman, an over-loud striking clock. There is the do-as-you-would-be-done-by (in his own way touching, a perpetual juvenile) who gives you what he would crave himself – and far, far from your own can his cravings be. There's the obtuse, who simply cannot envisage into what surroundings the gift will go – the *châtelaine*, pressing a flagon of perfumed bath oil ("You'll so love to lie and soak in this") on the poor parson's wife, who habitually skips, after two minutes, out of tepid water into a draughty bathroom. There's the giver hypnotised by sales-talk into sending you what "they" tell him is *à la mode*. And the graceless one, who lets you feel he's conforming to a social custom *he* regards as extortion . . . Such unfortunates go through life with a dim sense of injury: have they ever been thanked sufficiently? – they suspect not. And they are probably right: thanks are more than lip-service.

"More blessed to give than to receive."[3] . . . Is it? Are not the two complementary? Is not the one high pleasure matched by the other? *I* sing the praise of those who know how to take. What is lovelier, or a dearer trait in a friend, or simpler, or more fulfilling, or more heart-warming, than an overflowing willingness to receive? There are few words, sometimes; the delight is a shock, making, rather, for an ecstatic silence. Incredulity, almost, that an object, that a moment, should be so perfect. Then, from the eyes raised to the giver's face, what is felt, all that is felt, brims over. Gratitude is a spontaneity, an emotion; the heart can almost be heard, momentously beating.

"*Look* at it; I mean, look at it! Only look at it."

And you look, as though you had not seen it before.

The dream has been realised, the present given. The consummation.

The Art of Giving

A gift is a sort of ideal object. A glow surrounds it – the feeling of friend for friend, the delight of both in the gift itself. With this goes a trace of the fairy tale – may not some benevolent spell, charm or power be embodied in what we give one another to touch or wear? The gift starting upon its journey has more than a destination, it has a destiny – to enter a life and to play a part.

There is such a thing as the gift which seems ideal in its own right. As such, it captivates our fancy; it cries aloud to be given – but to whom? "Yes, I bought that," (who has not heard it said?) "because I longed to give it to *somebody*; but now I can think of no one who would be right." Our speaker has looked on giving the wrong way round – can a gift be perfect, can it be a gift at all, out of relation to an existing person, the already known and envisaged friend? So, the "perfect" gift in the abstract is to be fought shy of: first of all, in the act and the art of giving, must come our sense of someone, and how to please him. Sometimes, by happy chance, the eye may light straightway on the ideal thing; more often it is to be a matter of patient, long, exacting search. The reward is, not seldom, a flash of insight. When *that* has happened, the gift we choose will be not merely "right," it will be the inspired one.

The inspired gift may be of a surprising kind – out of accord with the general, accepted view of what would be appropriate for So-and-So. Human nature is made up of contrarieties and oddnesses, submerged dreams and contradictory hopes. At heart, so few people correspond with their outward, conventional personalities. And is it not to the heart, to the hidden real life, that the gift may hope to address itself? The more we care for people, the more we perceive what they are, what they love or want. The grave adult, for instance, may cherish a childish wish for a toy or game, or the plain-living woman yearn for some spangled trifle; or the lazy beauty may be inwardly longing for something on which to use her hands or try her brain. Wonderful is the gift which, somehow, fulfils the secret desire. "How *could* you know this was what I wanted? Why, I don't think I even knew myself!"

We must not, however, too often dare too much or fly too high. Only real, and it may be rare, inspiration warrants taking a chance with the inappropriate; in the main, our support must be common sense. In the light of that, gifts may be found to fall into three groups – what a friend would want, could want or should want. The "would want's" may be considered the safe and obvious – the book for the reader, the stylish kitchenware for the artist cook, the scarf or costume-jewel for the girl who apparently cannot have too many. Of the "could want's," discovered by insight, we have already spoken. With the "should want's" we may enter dangerous ground: never let giving be dictatorial! There *are* gifts which convey a hint of reproof or well-meant suggestion towards reform. B's neglected room or apartment may need prettying up, but unasked contributions towards that, the over-exquisite lampshade or table linen, are more than likely to leave her sore. An infelicitous gift may heighten perversity, wound pride, set up a complex or, simply and worst of all, cause tears. Let the giver never appear to direct or moralise. Then, has "should want" giving no other, more sympathetic aspect? Surely – for have we not many friends who should want, and should moreover have, much that on principle they deny themselves – deny themselves, perhaps, even the thought of? Theatre tickets, flowers, new little dress accessories, magazine subscriptions, and a whole host of more or less costly not less delightful things are the "should want's" of those we deem too hard on themselves, or whose rigid unselfishness we deprecate. The major lacks, abstinences or losses are outside our power to repair, but smaller deprivations we *can* make good – imagination counts, often, for more than money.

The object of giving is to give pleasure. Much pleasure turns on memory – the fact of *being* remembered and, no less, those memories which the gift may evoke or speak. For are not gifts in themselves a language, sometimes more expressive than could be words, and quick to stir up associations? The glass ship speaks of the day spent sailing; the leaf-motif brooch or embroidered handkerchief recalls the walk in the forest; the little gilded Italian box evokes the golden, foreign days of a shared holiday. Gifts are, in short, friendship's symbology. And they may be tokens of memory in another way; that is, by at once reviving and meeting a long-ago expressed wish or aspiration – uttered maybe impulsively, half at random. "Oh, I should like to have one like that!" or "I've always wanted . . ." The moment occurred, perhaps, idling before the windows of an antique shop – a notions counter, a bookstore, a puppy display or a flower show are no less likely. From such do we gather, and hoard, our clues. Yes, look back again into yesterday – was not something uttered?

Pleasure does also lie in the sense of novelty – the possession of something not owned before, or the reaction to sheer and intrinsic newness. A gift, not original in itself, making no claim to be new on the market, may please through filling a gap in our friend's belongings, an either felt or half-realised want. But also, what about novelty in the other sense – the dazzlingness of the caprice, device or invention which each year sees conjured into existence? Glamour (face the word boldly!) surrounds the being of what has not been in being until today. "Novelties" – trifling, gay and ephemeral – have their place in the fairy-tale ambience of giving. Yes, by this time next year they will be out of date; but meanwhile, they sing the rhapsody of the moment. Is it not that rhapsodical moment we seek to give? Is fantasy ever to be despised? Fantasy *may* tinge the practical object – if we give a broom, let its handle be of a shining colour; if we give a casserole, let fascination be in its glaze.

Enlarging newness may, still more, be in[1] experience of an aesthetic kind. That we give with the picture, book or phonograph record. When we thus donate an experience, we should have in view not only our own taste but the friend's capacity – what will *this*, which we value, mean to him or her? On book or music choices so much hangs – for here we deal in communication. Ought one to send an unread book, guaranteed by fashion, praised by hearsay? Instinctively, one would rather feel not – "I have loved this; I hope you may love it too," should be, with this sort of gift, the implicit message. Yet affection prompts us to offer the very latest, newest. In that case, once hear the record on its way to the friend; or, despatching in its unthumbed freshness the copy of the book, add: "Lend this back to me when you're through: I should like to share it."

Ideally, we should be giving all the year round – the calendar is crowded with anniversaries; any day may bring forth an occasion to mark. But inevitably, as to practice and fact we do of course give most at the universal, traditional giving season, Christmas. Above all things giving should be spontaneous. Tradition need not, however, rob it of that. Christmas is not a compulsion, it's a great opportunity – in itself a feast, a gift to the giver. Now is the time for contacts: distances shrink, gulfs are bridged, silences melt, estrangements are mended. Now is the time for expression. And in so far as giving is, too, a language, is it not now widened in eloquence by the gaiety, the fantasy, the multiplicity of the things coming crowding into the Christmas market – things conceived and devised specially to speak, to please, to enhance a love or liking, to convey a sympathy or a gratitude? There is more now *to* give than at any other time: let us profit by this Christmas vocabulary . . . Even so, choice may waver, hesitate – we may commit ourselves to what, after all, seems just not ideal. But gifts, let us remember, gather grace on their journey, and receive grace from those to whom they go. Leaving our own hands they may seem imperfect: they are perfected by what comes out to meet them – the glad welcome, the answering memory. To its reception does every gift build up: each one awaits its fulfilling moment.

Mirrors Are Magic

Mirrors. We live in a world of them, a reflected world. What tricks they know to play, what a spell they cast – and have cast for how long?

Who first backed glass with quicksilver? From that came the mirror as we now know it. Before that, humanity made do. Ladies peered into small ovals of polished metal. The fair youth Narcissus leaned over a mirroring pool, with fatal effect – he fell in love with his own face, and died of love for it. A Roman emperor,[1] nervous for good reason, caused the principal corridor of his palace to be lined with specially shiny, reflecting marble, that he might see if assassins came creeping up on him. Yes, the mirror-*idea* was present, right back through time: accordingly, many were the mirror-substitutes, some ingenious (as you may see in museums), some natural (like poor Narcissus' pool). The desire to see oneself, or should need arise, keep watch on what went on behind one's back, was met by a variety of devices.

So far, the mirror was functional; it served purposes – the small metal hand mirror, although often pretty enough, did not claim to be an aesthetic object. A wider concept came in with quicksilvered glass. As size enlarged, so did the possibilities – decoration, refraction of light, the charm of illusion. How great could be a great mirror's intrinsic beauty as a thing-in-itself! Artists-craftsmen, incited by that discovery, wrought marvels, insetting the looking glass into gold and silver, intricate inlay or carvings, or precious stones.

Those early masterpiece mirrors must have dominated – for were they not semi-miracles? – the ducal or princely homes they came to adorn. Paintings, doubtless, crowded the walls around them, but the mirrors outdid their rivals in one particular – *they* were living pictures, their subject, the current moment. "Come, *be*!" they cried to their owners. "Move, act, love, hate, draw swords, snatch kisses – *we* will reflect you!" And so they did. Moreover, their limpid surface registered changes, onward from dawn to dusk, and by night redoubled the hundreds of festive candles. They dramatised life; they made theatre of human comings and goings. Mirrors' presences heightened, in men and women, that self-awareness which is civilisation. Those lofty and lengthy rooms on which mirrors gazed were already stage-like: grandiose, formal. Mirrors stylised them further. And well that suited the mood of the day's grandees, for whom life was, unceasingly, a performance.

If an ancient mirror could speak of its young days, if its memories could be photographed back to us – what stories! Is it haunted by what it reflected, a vanished world? Met within such a mirror, your face or mine takes on an air of transience, ghostliness almost – what is *this* face but one of the countless many which glimmered, here, for a moment, then went their ways? Look deeper into this mirror: the Past itself inhabits these watery purplish depths, made more mysterious still by a faint tarnish. Lovely, dimmed, this museum-piece holds secrets inviolate. Should you bring home such a mirror (at what a price!), your home must adjust itself to an alien element. You're exposed to a haughty, fateful, shadowy gaze, until you come to terms with your treasure, and make a friend of it.

Mirrors can be uncanny. That they figure so often in fairy and witchcraft stories is not surprising. Old lore attributed to them occult power, or inclined to denounce them as aids to magic. Malevolent queens have made them their confidantes – "Mirror, mirror on the wall, am I not fairest of them all?" – and spell-workers found in them their accomplices. Conjurers use them: "All done by mirrors," explains some sceptic, some knowing one in the audience – but why not, how not?

Mirrors themselves are magic. That superstition surrounds them, one cannot wonder. Dislike, if not actual fear, of breaking a mirror is embedded in most of us, nor can reason dislodge it. Although one may brave out the fear, or laugh it off, it stays potent in others, for which reason, a mishap with a mirror must be concealed, as instinctively, hurriedly, as one conceals the fragments. Otherwise, some good friend comes on to the scene, moaning, "You *are* going to be unlucky!" Most of us know of people whose dread of a mirror-breakage comes near neurosis. One such replied to a questionnaire as to what is the most bloodcurdling line in English poetry, "Oh, Tennyson's, '*The mirror crack'd from side to side.*'"[2] The same person, when watching a Western, closes her eyes when the boys storm in and shoot up the saloon; even on the screen, she cannot abide the sight of a splintered mirror. Most women dare not be ridden by such fears – were ill-luck so ready to jump on us, or so easily courted, our lives would be riskier, far, than men's. We resort to purse mirrors, and handle them, ten times daily. And, those slippery mirrors live pouched in glossy-lined purses. So . . . ?

Yet, mirror effects, and mirror associations, for us in our generation are mainly cheerful. Mirrors (with which go expanses of mirrored surfaces) enlarge life. They extend, or seem to extend, space; they increase light. They make less that sense of constriction, of claustrophobia, which could be a creeping threat upon modern living. Were they gone, we should find our world cut by half (what, for instance, more shrinks and darkens a room than the removal of an accustomed mirror?). But mirrors are far from going: they spread, they breed and increase. Never, as ornament, totally out of fashion, they promote themselves from a fashion to a necessity – social, humanistic, and psychological. Huge, bright vertical lakes of mirror now so obliterate walls that the walls seem built of them.

In our cities, mirror is used as lavishly as imperial Rome used gleaming veneers of marble, and with the same intent – to suggest opulence. Also, this heightens pleasure – in restaurants, cafeterias, ballrooms, dance halls – and kindles a sense of glamour and magic luxury. Prototype use of mirrors is the Versailles palace's Galerie des Glaces, with its blend of lost-looking reflections and gilded cobwebs – unique in history, more unreal than any fairy tale, this hall of illusion enthrals the tourist. Versailles in its heyday was for the *élite* only: our mirror-world, in continent after continent, is democratic, open to all and any. One makes free of mirrors outdoors as well as in; in shoals, we stream past the mirrors inside the shop fronts. Alongside us speed our images, merged with many. The intellectual, lonely one's lonely question, "What am I – *am* I? If so, what do I look like?" can be answered at any moment, at any turn. Do mirrors, possibly, mitigate city solitude? Does one not, in the crowded flow across mirrors, have a sense of the human tribe to which one belongs?

This other dimension, this reflected existence, is a gain, on the whole, but can be confusing. Can one always be certain where "reality" stops and its reflections begin? To enter a much-mirrored room can be disconcerting – most so, when the room at the same time is unfamiliar. To-and-fro bounce the reflections, extended endlessly. How many clocks, one may wonder, lamps, and vases of roses actually *are* there in here? And still more (and still more important) how many people? Actual persons jumble with what might appear, at the first glance, to be their twins: the same figure perceived at various angles multiplies into two, three, or four. The shy or near-sighted latecomer, on the threshold, has the daunting illusion of entering a large party: those present reduce, when greeted, to half-a-dozen.

Never is one quite alone in a mirrored room – and there can be times when solitude could be restful, still more times when one would not wish to be watched, least of all, by one's ever-critical self. I heard that objection applied to a sumptuous bathroom, by a faltering guest. "But I don't, I'm afraid," she sighed, "come out of my bath looking like Venus rising from the waters. I come out boiled like a lobster, completely crimson. On such occasions, one of me is enough." One may hope that merciful steam blurred the mirrored alcove.

Taking leave of the mirror, let us send it back to the role it had at the outset: that of accessory. A servant of vanity? What a bully it can be! What a morale affecter! It can make or unmake, by prognostic, one's day or evening. Ostensibly, one requires it to be "frank." Temperamentally, one prays that it may encourage. "Tell me something," one tells it, "but not too much, please." Clinical exactitude, and precision one does require for the applying of make-up or the shaping of hair, yet the finished work needs a nimbus of slight illusion. Your chosen day-to-day mirror should be at a halfway point between fair and cruel.

There can be unrelentingly adverse mirrors: one of those, I consider, could wreck a hat shop, or, by distortingly broadening the female figure, put an aspiring dress salon out of business. An unfavourable mirror, rightly disliked by you, should by no means (hostess!) find its place in your guest room.

Arguably, much of a mirror's verdict is conditioned by its situation and lighting – a truth which the British, that hardy island race, either scorn or strenuously ignore. A British dressing table, that institution to which the mirror is clamped, is placed in (across or under) a window, thereby compelling its victim's face to confront itself in the full blast of unsparing daylight. Better to know the worst. By night, an overhead light up near the ceiling, sheds down a disparaging, stern, and no-nonsense ray.

Yet no mirror dare one quite bypass, like it or not.

Do we act up to mirrors? Do we try out on them expressions, gestures, not yet released to the world? At the start of the morning or evening mirror session is our attitude pugnacious, or placatory? That assessing stare we level at our reflection may not be exactly inimical, but it is seldom tender. What would it be like, I do wonder, to be a beauty – one who only at long last turns away from her mirror, reluctant, yet with a satisfied sigh?

What I do not believe is that my mirror gives me any idea of *me*. Looking into a mirror deliberately, I see nothing but a person looking deliberately into a mirror. My few but for that reason notable self-encounters have been unsought, a matter of chance or accident. I'm waylaid by an image, as though by an ambushed bandit, in some unexpected mirror around a corner, in some shop window distant across the street, or coming my way, down some mirror-protracted corridor. Do I know myself when I meet myself? Yes, I find, I do.

WRITERS AND THEIR BOOKS

Jane Austen

Jane Austen, who died a hundred and eighteen years ago, brought the English novel to a point nearer perfection than it has reached since. As a form, the novel has several parts or aspects – social photography, charted emotion, dialogue, delineation of people. Each of these has been made, from time to time, by (in her sense) "respectable" novelists his or her main province. It is possible to give a fair, if flattish, picture of life by approaching one's subject ably on any one of these sides. But Jane Austen's ability was comprehensive: she did more than approach a subject, she surrounded it. Thus her novels are novels in the most classic sense.

Their Englishness is, moreover, their peculiar triumph. The English novel has, on the whole, suffered from having been written after writers' glory in being English had begun to decline. The most minor Elizabethan play has a quality – a kind of absoluteness or thoroughgoingness – that the most distinguished novel too often lacks. (*Wuthering Heights* is the best exception to this.) There is a great drop in pressure: greater, I think, than the change of medium – prose for verse – accounts for. In this field, the nineteenth-century Russians succeeded to what properly should have been the English heritage: heroicness, a kind of overbearing spirituality. Tolstoy is in the succession of Shakespeare, Dostoevsky of Webster. English novelists, whether consciously or unconsciously, wear their nationality as a shackle rather than as a decoration of honour. Moral strife is, largely, their subject: it is the greatest of subjects, but in approaching it they suffer from moral cramp. With the close of the eighteenth century, French classical influence with its restraints gone, fancy, let loose again, showed a good deal of weakness. Enforced form had bolstered this weakness up. But now columns gave place to arches and tracery: one no longer built to enclose light but to cast gothic shadows. Life is always impinged upon by a literary fashion, and Jane Austen saw round her a world in which, genteel and orderly as it was, the new sensibility began to luxuriate. On what promised to be a kind of garden jungle, a sinister dusk of ferns, she imposed her two twin orders, Elegance and Propriety. Qualities one would be prepared, in the last resort, to die for, that one would be prepared, at least, to sacrifice a life to, take on an ideality of their own. Her sense of values was more than positive; it would have been passionate once put to the proof. The unchangingness of her characters' moral colour, the unswervingness of their pursuit of an aim, would make them major, apart from anything else. Her people are so relentlessly thoroughgoing – Anne Elliott in her regret, Miss Bates in her power to bore, Fanny in her humility, Mr. Darcy in his pride, Elinor in her stability, Harriet in her goosishness, Mrs. Bennet in her desire to get her girls off, Emma in her determination to rule – that she creates, in the heart of the mannered Regency, a muted Elizabethan world of her own. On the polite plane, violence has its equivalent. Witty, detached, engaging and travelling lightly, her pen has been dipped in the purest English ink. *Persuasion* and *Emma* are as outstandingly English as *War and Peace* is Russian or *L'Éducation sentimentale* French. Her keen eye is for the manner, but sees the spirit behind.

She lived, it is true, in a small and very secure world, in which values were not questioned: nothing got dragged up. Her unperplexity – or the resentment it arouses – is perhaps at the root of many objections to her. The charge of tameness against her is in itself so wild, the charge of triviality so trivial, that there must be something rather deeper behind them. She has been more fairly, perhaps, disliked than patronised – her own ironic remark about the two inches of ivory[1] always pursuing her. No woman had ever less the provinciality of her sex, no lady less the provinciality of her sphere. It is all very well to talk grandiosely about the world in general: one's nearest hope of knowing the world in general is to synthesise one's knowledge of the particular. Accident – the accident of her birth – dictated the scene and scope of her novels but did not restrict their power. She was a very rare example – perhaps Proust was another – of intelligence articulating with the social personality; she was one of those happy natures whose very stuff is intelligence, with which nothing goes to waste, that everything aliments. Provinciality is a malady bred of being too much engaged with one's surroundings: the provinciality of Bohemia is well known. To be unprovincial is to know what is important, to see the exact importance of everything that you see. To underrate a deliberately quiet life is, absurdly, to confuse experience with knowledge. Every writer is born with something to find out, and Jane Austen, by dancing circumspectly at county balls, chatting with people in drawing-rooms, staying with her relations and visiting Bath and London, found out what it was necessary for her to know.

She enjoyed being a woman, and being a gentlewoman. Emulativeness and the succeeding antagonisms did not distort her view of the other sex. Her men characters appear in company only, and are present only in relation to women – as hosts (Sir John Middleton, Mr. Weston), fathers (Mr. Bennet, Mr. Woodhouse), uncles (Sir Thomas Bertram), suitors (Mr. Elton, Mr. Collins), flirts (Frank Churchill, Mr. Wickham), *partis*[2] (Mr. Bingley), husbands (Mr. John Knightley, Mr. John Dashwood), incalculable admirers (Mr. Darcy, Henry Crawford, Henry Tilney), or, though rarely, the magnetic beloved object upon whom happiness depends (Captain Wentworth and, passingly, Willoughby). Their appearance in any of these roles she describes with an unastounded, friendly exactitude. She had a keen cool amused ear for how gentlemen talked. Sport, business and manners in love were not her province, but she did know a little about the Navy and usefully brought that in. The Army remains an occupation for officers when not busy dancing or paying calls. With her respect for the Church, Henry Tilney's charming whimsical elegance was not out of colour. It is not because Edmund Bertram is an earnest young clergyman that he does not, as a hero, entirely come off. Their cloth does not protect Mr. Elton and Mr. Collins . . . In men, she honoured integrity (even stiffened at times by a touch of priggishness, as in Edmund Bertram and Mr. Knightley), expected and was amused by amiability and good address, and was agreeably susceptible to charm – no woman who was not could have brought Frank Churchill, Willoughby, Henry Crawford and Henry Tilney to life. She must have been one of those fortunate young women who can enjoy glamour without having illusions. She writes about men with a distant confidence that I believe to be justified. It is women who write about men with an awful matey knowingness who give one a saddening sense of the handicaps of their sex . . . Adultery occurred but was also outside her province: "Let other pens dwell on guilt and misery."[3] She was, however, not squeamish: the disgraceful affair of Willoughby and Miss Williams, though touched in fairly lightly, is not scamped. The thought of sexual misery both depressed and offended her: moreover it was socially inconvenient. It is true that her characters are preoccupied with marriage, and that the novels hinge on who is to marry whom. But the subject, with its ramifications, is absorbing still. And when one heard more about marriage one heard less about sex.

Her two most imposing men are Mr. Darcy in *Pride and Prejudice* and Henry Crawford in *Mansfield Park* . . . Mr. Darcy falls for Elizabeth Bennet, with her disconcerting charm and impossible family, against his will: he shows the extraordinary bends and twists a reluctant love takes. In a crisis – and his relations with Elizabeth, up to the end of the book, are a series of muffled crises – Mr. Darcy retreats on a violent formality. Compound of passion and snobbery, he is a Proustian figure. Humiliated by his own inconvenient love, he tries to put his friend Bingley off marrying Elizabeth's sister Jane: the Bennet family simply do not do. Encounters between Mrs. Bennet and Mr. Darcy, in Elizabeth's hearing, are studies in acute mortification. He was a man of the strongest family feeling; had he not been, his own aunt, Lady Catherine de Bourgh, would have distressed him more. Evidently he had the maximum power of embarrassing people: why else should the dauntless Elizabeth have minded so much when he came on her walking with her uncle and aunt in his park? The situation was, it is true, a little embarrassing, but something about Mr. Darcy made it a good deal worse. He is a good man, a man of integrity, with the sombre attractiveness of a wicked one. Returning again and again to Mr. Darcy, one pays Jane Austen the compliment of deciding that there was more to him than she knew. He has that cloudy outline important characters should have; does not seem to have been "created" in the limited brain-bound sense so much as observed fleetingly out of the corner of an eye, recollected uncertainly, speculated upon. One takes him to be a devious, constantly self-regarding and very passionate man – but he soars out of the picture – most of him happens off. In a woman writer's book, any man who is intended to be either important or magnetic ought to have this quality . . . Henry Crawford is more energetic, dashing and unscrupulous. He has a certain *beauté du diable*.[4] Though not, like Frank Churchill, a high-spirited, rather engagingly silly flirt, he is sardonically irresponsible where the Miss Bertrams are concerned. He is the most sophisticated of Jane Austen's men, and has also an excellent intellect: when he is at Mansfield Park they have good after-dinner talk (*vide* the conversation about Shakespeare). He had "moral taste" – a particular aesthetic sensibility to innocence – which is in keeping with his character. ("Moral taste" is interesting: only highly civilised and really rather morally neutral people have it: it is the stuff of James and Turgenev novels).

Henry Crawford watches the young shy Fanny – who already so much attracts him – and her sailor brother William together. He

> saw, with lively admiration, the glow of Fanny's cheek, the bright-ness of her eye, the deep interest, the absorbed attention, while her brother was describing any of the imminent hazards or terrific scenes, which such a period at sea must supply.
>
> It was a picture which Henry Crawford had moral taste enough to value. Fanny's attractions increased – increased twofold . . .

He enjoyed, in fact, and enjoyed morally also, this innocent kindling of her windflower beauty. But there is a kind of niceness about Henry Crawford; no hint of the jaded palate about his feeling for Fanny. His susceptibility is complex. Fanny's refusal to marry him twists him back on himself in a mood of destructive ugliness and ill-temper. His affair, then elopement, with Maria Rushworth (*née* Bertram) is the result. One can only suppose he turned to Maria Bertram as being the type of woman he really most disliked – neither gallant nor innocent. It was one more of his "freaks of cold-blooded vanity." Had he not, already, virtually, "lost the woman he rationally as well as passionately loved"? It is impossible not to be impatient with Fanny for her refusal (if one has not, indeed, become impatient with her already). Henry Crawford was her one chance of growing up. As it is, she remains with the colourless Edmund: loyal, jejune and prim. We are told Henry Crawford regretted the injury he did to Mansfield Park in ruining Maria. But this regret in itself may have been a bitter pleasure. There are times when one feels Henry Crawford an exile from a French novel. But he remains an Englishman. Jane Austen knew an amazing amount about him, and – involuntarily – liked him a good deal. Like Mr. Darcy, but more so, he towers outside the book in which he appears. Mr. Darcy is part of the structure of *Pride and Prejudice*, but Henry Crawford counters the moral rhythm of *Mansfield Park* – which is at once the most intellectual and the most nearly insincere novel she wrote.

Her women – even her quieter women – have an astounding vitality. Only Fanny Price is unvital, and Fanny does not, to my mind at least, come off. Elizabeth Bennet and Emma have a Shakespearean gallant calm uncoyness. These two heroines diffuse themselves through the pages with such extraordinary brilliance that it is difficult to believe they are not in the room. Anne Elliott's is a vitality of the heart: she has Fanny's delicacy and recessiveness, but is not at any moment insipid or dim; you would always know she was there. She is essentially grown-up. At a time when to be unmarried at twenty-seven tended to be either pitiable or ridiculous, she remains assured and graceful, playing the piano for the young people to dance . . . Marianne Dashwood, though her view of life is intended to be preposterous, is lovely and moving, with her great dark eyes. Elinor Dashwood is stodgy but has a nice humour and behaves really extraordinarily well.

Emma and Elizabeth only discover their own states of heart towards the close of the novels they animate. Elinor loves Edward and Fanny Edmund from the outset; Anne's regret for Captain Wentworth, then reawakened love for him, is the spring of her being. Emotion in Elinor, Fanny and Anne is pertinacious, patient and curiously clear-headed. Marianne, on the contrary, is not only swept off her feet by her love for Willoughby, but positively leaps into the wave. Elizabeth's and Emma's awakenings to love are excellently in character. Nothing dims Elizabeth's gallant wit: she goes on gently pulling Mr. Darcy's leg. With Emma "the dread of being awakened from the happiest dream was perhaps the most prominent feeling." All the same "while he spoke, her mind was busy."

Anne Elliott's feeling for Captain Wentworth is the only love in the novels which is poetic. Elinor Dashwood and Fanny both make one feel they feel the young men in question do not really know what is good for them. In not one of the novels does the simple upright worldliness of the setting (it would never do to marry any young man who would never do) invalidate any emotion felt. Antisocial love is not necessarily stronger or purer in quality than social love.

Jane Austen's attitude to each of her women is different. Emma is seen, and felt, as divinely unconsciously funny throughout. To see one's heroine through in a comic light, without buffooning her or devaluating her for the other characters, is an achievement. (Incidentally, Emma's feeling for Frank Churchill is an excellent study of vanity in the heart.) Fanny is not Jane Austen's type at all – she is projected, too palpably "created," a *tour de force* which does not come off. Jane Austen's love of goodness impregnates all the books, but it did not do to centre this round one character: she has rather a forced tenderness for Fanny. Elinor she liked but was not interested in; Elinor is a straight line of sanity ruled through the book, serves her purpose staunchly but remains rather abstract. Marianne she deplored, but Marianne remains moving; unforgettable is her scream of agony after getting Willoughby's fatal letter (and what a model of an unforgivable letter: "the lock of hair which you so obligingly bestowed on me") . . . Elizabeth Bennet was clearly a joy to write about, to share vicissitudes with: Elizabeth and Jane Austen were kindred spirits; when Elizabeth came into being they were the same age, both going to balls . . . Harriet was a sweet goose she had to like, Jane Fairfax intimidated her as much as she intimidated Emma, Mary Crawford's charm gained her in spite of herself, Lucy Steele's vulgarity and bogus emotion afflicted her as it did Elinor . . . Anne Elliott remains the beloved grown-up friend, whose sorrows are shared, whose patience is honoured, whose beauty is seen. Jane Austen envelops her, unconsciously, in the greatness she had herself as a woman, the poeticness, the submissiveness, the courage that the younger novels had not yet brought into play. In *Persuasion*, Nature is present, and tenderly felt: up to now it has been simply a social factor – weather.

And what weather – opportune sometimes, difficult others, a saver of situations, a precipitator of crises. Snow in Highbury, rain in Bath, the June heat of the strawberry party at Donwell, through which Jane Fairfax sets out, distracted, for home, which made Frank Churchill so cross. The gay blowy day at Lyme Regis. What a glow from the fine day fixed for an outing – "Wednesday was fine, and soon after breakfast the barouche arrived . . . Their road was through pleasant country." And, apart from the weather, what parties! Few writers' novels can hold so many, none so directly convey that (if the expression may be forgiven) a good time was had by all. She also transmits, with an extraordinary vivacity, the pleasure that people – in or out of love – take in each other's society: the charm of a new acquaintance, the surprise of a morning call, or the delight of looking at someone pretty. Here is Mary Crawford playing the harp in the rectory drawing-room:

> A young woman, pretty, lively, with a harp as elegant as herself, and both placed near a window cut down to the ground and opening on a little lawn, surrounded by shrubs in the rich foliage of summer, was enough to catch any man's heart.

Elizabeth Bennet, with her colour, her grace, her vitality, is the most palpably attractive of the heroines (did she not magnetise Darcy's unwilling eyes?), Mary Crawford the most glamorous of the women. Emma must have had a lovely complexion, Elinor Dashwood had a pretty figure. None of her heroines are paragons, but they are all successes. She has a woman's regard for women who are a success, as well as the author's semi-parental pride. She knows, too, how to make the onlooker's eye add quality to its object: Emma is seen as Highbury's most important young lady, Elizabeth as she so disturbed Mr. Darcy, Fanny kindling to brilliance with brother William, with Henry Crawford sitting watchfully by.

No possible shade of being bored, offended, mortified, non-plussed or flattered is overlooked by her, or not faithfully rendered. She was right: her people were young, vitally young, and when one is young these things are very important. A malaise, a regret, a reverse, what one thinks of somebody, what somebody seems to think of one, either muffle or decorate an entire day. The interaction of social and personal feeling was her subject, like Proust's, and her diagnosis was as correct.

The technique of the novels is beyond praise, and has been praised. Her mastery of the art she chose, or that chose her, is complete: how she achieved it no one will ever know. Though I suppose that none of her books are flawless, I cannot think of one clumsy blunder she made. Her intellect was so immediately applied, so closely related to what it fed on, so unabstract that it seems fitter to speak of it as intelligence: it was intelligence of a sublime kind. If she did speculate, this must have been in a series of photographs. She was as sensible about ideas as she was about men; she must have had a most uncloudy mind. Any wisps of reverie floating about in it got solidified into little touches in books. She was, in fact, the rightly adjusted person . . . The kind of novel generally *called* intellectual is thin in texture, so that the anxious operation of the intellect shows. Because as a story it does not quite come off, you feel more bound to honour the author's high intention. But Jane Austen's are the truly intellectual novels because her mind impregnates the whole of their matter, functioning in every comma, adding colour, force, light.

Any great book strikes one as having imposed itself on its author. The element of invention, of ingenuity, is palpable only in sec-ondary books. But no book imposes itself on a passive mind. Something other, outside, may command and mobilise the imagination, but the brain has to leap up to cope with this, like a swarm of post-office hands with an incoming mail. The greater the force and speed of what is happening imaginatively, the colder and closer scrutiny this must have from the brain. An artist, to be effective, has to be half critic. Fancy and reason ought to have equal strength: in Jane Austen they had, which is why she wrote what were almost perfect novels. Her wit worked well, allowing her fancy pleasure; her fancy, by not halting, brought her wit to no heavy and cold pause. Her style is balanced, like someone skating beautifully. Her exhilaration must have been tremendous: perhaps she only half knew what was going on. An artist can never be fully conscious. But neither can he cut ice if he is not an unremittingly conscious executant.

She wrote novels, and wished to write nothing else. "Yes, novels," she says in *Northanger Abbey*, ". . . performances which have only genius, wit and taste to recommend them." When she died she was not old, and might still have written more. She had been ill for some time before that, and *Sanditon*, which had been put away, was unfinished, which is too bad.

Introduction to Pride and Prejudice, *by Jane Austen*

P*ride and Prejudice* is, by the general vote, the most popular of Jane Austen's novels. Written when she was young, it seems to give a foretaste of her entire powers – powers which, in the range of her later work were to group and define themselves rather more. The all-round Jane Austen reader, invited to name his favourite among her books, may single out *Mansfield Park*, *Emma*, *Persuasion*, or, though more rarely, *Sense and Sensibility*; but will then, almost always, bracket: "And, of course, *Pride and Prejudice*." In the first case, the choice will have been according to individual temperament; but in the second the feeling has been generic. Which is to say, that no lover of the essential Jane Austen can fail to delight, fully, in *Pride and Prejudice*. Is it too much to say, those who cannot care for this book should not hope to see the point of her work at all?

In its original form, this novel was written before Jane Austen was twenty-one, and was by her entitled "First [or, False] Impressions." Her father, the Rev. Mr. Austen, offered a sight of the manuscript to the publisher Cadell in November 1797, recommending it as being "about the length of *Evelina*," but Cadell replied, one must hope courteously, that he was not interested. So the manuscript went into an abeyance of more than fifteen years: *Sense and Sensibility*, published in 1811, preceded it into public notice; and it was when encouraged by that success that Jane Austen revised and re-titled *Pride and Prejudice*. The novel was published, in three volumes, in January 1813; a second edition was issued in the September of the same year.

Pride and Prejudice does, I think, carry characteristics of the century within whose closing years it was first written – the eighteenth. The style shows classical influence; the feeling for "rationality" is strong; in the attitude to a good many matters there appears a Georgian realism. Gently born, child of a cultivated and sheltered home, the young Jane was not obstructed from reading widely: she was free, in this particular, of the taboos which were, later, to cramp the outlook and promote the insipidity of the Victorian "miss." Her admiration for Fielding, most masculine of novelists, was to leave its mark, admirably, on her own work – particularly, surely, on *Pride and Prejudice*? We find throughout this novel something racy, gallant and un-coy, a naturalness with regard to the other sex, a love of movement and of the open air. Elizabeth Bennet is (to the scandalisation of Miss Bingley) a great walker – ranging the Hertfordshire field-paths around Longbourn; forever afoot, alone, through the spinneys of Rosings park. She is all for travel, and sets out on journeys with an almost boyish zest. In fact Elizabeth, within her own range of life, is not less adventurous than Tom Jones. Unlike her sister Mary, Elizabeth is no bluestocking – at the same time, like her creator, she is well-read; she has wide terms of reference; her conversation is more than vivid, it is articulate, spirited and precise. She is, in short, a child at least of the sunset of the Age of Reason.

Most of all, however, *Pride and Prejudice* has about it an early-morning sparkle. It conveys, more than almost any other novel, the exhilarating sensation of being young. The Jane Austen of the original version was, we may remember, of an age with her heroine: both were girls of twenty. And whatever shaping or chastening the manuscript may have undergone in revision, none of its first freshness was lost. Technically, *Pride and Prejudice* shows no immaturities; the style has exactly that light strength to which few youthful writers attain; the very naïvetés show assurance. Examining the structure and development of the story, it is hard to believe that this is not the work of a long-experienced hand. Yet, throughout, the prevailing effect *is* youth. Everything is seen with a bright eye; both the actual and the emotional colouring have a clear-tinted brilliance; the shadows may not be many but they are sharp and long. If the youth in this novel be diamond-bright, it is also, from time to time, diamond-hard: one is reminded, in reading it, that young persons are remorseless in observation and not always kind in judgement. The young Jane Austen did not suffer fools gladly; and of pomposity, priggishness, pretentiousness or sheer silliness she was inexorably aware. *Pride and Prejudice* cannot be called a kind book. But not less there is this to be said – that there is not a touch of shrewishness in the comments or of vulgarity in any of the smiles; that the principal butts for ridicule in the novel, Lady Catherine de Bourgh, Mr. Collins and Miss Bingley, are prosperous persons, well able to take care of themselves (if necessary, at other people's expense); and that Jane Austen allows full play to the saving graces – Sir William Lucas's self-importance, for instance, being counterbalanced by his good nature and warm heart.

Another youthful feature of this novel is its rendering of mortifications – social, it is true, chiefly; but how, when one is young, those can get under the skin! The embarrassments, for a young lady of feeling, of having to enter society in the company of vulgar relations had already been treated, possibly over-treated, by Fanny Burney in *Evelina*. Jane Austen's touch on the subject is more restrained, more delicate and more deep. It was difficult for the two elder daughters of Mrs. Bennet, – who were at the same time elder sisters of that dreary show-off Mary and of the officer-chasing Lydia and Kitty – not often to squirm. Jane Bennet's golden charity does, to an extent, blind her; though she suffers tortures from her mother's tactlessness when Bingley, apparently, defaults. Nothing blinding Elizabeth, one must the more admire the rareness with which she does squirm, the poise and quickness with which she carries bad situations off. The high point, perhaps, comes early, with the Netherfield ball: we feel, at a moment, pass through us Elizabeth's burning blush – by the end: "To Elizabeth it appeared, that had her family made an agreement to expose themselves as much as they could during the evening, it would have been impossible for them to play their parts with more spirit, or finer success . . ." Later, at Rosings, she has to accept in part the justice of the indictment, in Mr. Darcy's letter, of every one of her relatives but Jane.

The social precariousness of the Bennets, as a family, is indeed essential to the plot of *Pride and Prejudice* – and what a plot it is! It moves with a steady speed; it never knots itself up; every incident in it develops or furthers something. There is a faultless life-likeness in the emergence of each successive event – goosey Lydia's elope-ment, for instance, comes as a thunderbolt to the reader no less than to the Longbourn household; but, upon second thoughts, it is sadly not impossible. Mrs. Bennet, for all her fatuity, is right: a dark future does lie ahead of the Bennet girls should they not find husbands, for the whole of their father's estate is entailed away – to the egregious Mr. Collins. Mr. Bennet, a landed gentleman in a small way, has married beneath him: on the maternal side the girls have a network of relatives – one uncle a small-town attorney, another a City merchant – who, by Bingley-Darcy standards do not make the grade at all. Only the honour due to the Rev. Mr. Collins' cloth shelters his fearsome unpresentability – yet, the undowered Elizabeth could be considered rash in refusing him. (She is to refuse the first proposal of the sought-after, eligible Mr. Darcy with as much determination, and in a blazing spirit: *that* proposal of marriage, couched in the terms it is, insults her, rightly, very much more deeply than could a "dishonourable" advance.) That Charlotte Lucas should, gratefully, accept the rejected clergyman, is likely: the Collins marriage serves to open up, as the next field of action, Rosings in Kent. (We are to have Pemberley, Derbyshire, also, before the end.) Mr. Darcy's aunt Lady Catherine's happening to be Mr. Collins' patron, so that Elizabeth, visiting the bridal Charlotte, has Mr. Darcy once more crossing her path, *is* a coincidence, but such do happen – polite England is small, and used to be smaller still. Darcy's proud reticence as to Wickham's past – that attempt to make off with Darcy's own young sister – is not only in character; it does, as he feels himself, make him in part responsible for Lydia Bennet's fate – hence the quick, energetic and all-out manner in which Darcy takes a hand in the Lydia-Wickham crisis, thereby revealing himself to Elizabeth in a new light. Hostile critics of Elizabeth – and there always are certain Miss Bingleys among Jane Austen readers – suggest that it was the glories of Pemberley which first made her falter in her resolution never to marry Darcy. Surely, rather, it was that seeing him of his best on his own ground, and his warmth and naturalness with her uncle and aunt, the Gardiners of Gracechurch Street, which began to change her views and soften her heart?

The plot and the characterisation of *Pride and Prejudice* are, really, inseparable: it is unsatisfactory to discuss the two apart. The subject, it must be remembered, of the entire story is the false, or misleading, nature of first impressions. One cannot follow the action without perpetual reference to the actors. Here is a novel of character in the perfect sense – in which no one acts out of character; and, still better, each person, *by* acting, provokes from some other person action that is no less characteristic. It is not hard to see why Darcy, reluctantly, fell in love with Elizabeth: she is enchanting – a Shakespearean creature, a Rosalind or a Beatrice in prose. She has her limitations – scant patience, imperfect tenderness (those two qualities with which Jane Austen, older, was to beautify Anne Elliott in *Persuasion*) but one feels, with Elizabeth's character, that there is more to ripen: she is a brilliant girl on her way to becoming a noble woman. Nor, I think, is it ever hard to see the secret of Darcy's impressiveness – stick, prig and snob though he shows himself up to near the end. There is a perverse charm about his frigidity, wariness and hauteur. For many women, Darcy remains the most fascinating of Jane Austen's men – his rival being a very different type, dashing Henry Crawford of *Mansfield Park*. In general it must be faced that Jane Austen is not successful with her straight "good" men. Darcy is, as we are to discover, good; but he is just enough salted with contrariety.

As for the other characters, they are a galaxy: here showed genius. It is hard to divide the personages of *Pride and Prejudice* into "major" and "minor": each one is three-dimensional; not one is ever to be forgotten. One can say, merely, that some are at further remove from the core of the plot, or front of the stage, than others. After Elizabeth and Darcy, Mr. and Mrs. Bennet are, by consent, the masterpieces. These two are exquisite comedy – though, as a married couple, there is submerged tragedy in them too. Infinite, in its time, must have been the disillusionment which drove Mr. Bennet to the solitude of his library, to his utterance of those superb, deadly sardonic remarks . . .

> Mr. Bennet raised his eyes from his book as she [Mrs. Bennet] entered, and fixed them on her face with a calm unconcern which was not in the least altered by her communication.
> "I have not the pleasure of understanding you," said he, when she had finished her speech. "Of what are you talking?"

Mr. Bennet's attitude to his family, its hopes, fears, alarums and vicissitudes, must be described as cynical: his second daughter Elizabeth is his sole kindred spirit – and even she is shocked, at that dreadful Netherfield party, by the publicity of his snub to Mary. Taste, tongue and turn of mind all affiliate Mr. Bennet to the eighteenth century: Jane Austen's later novels show no other later version of him . . . Mrs. Bennet is a too familiar figure: the once very pretty, still very silly woman – here is a portrait inspired by a naughty delight, unsoftened by charity. "She was a woman of mean understanding, little information and uncertain temper. When she was discontented she fancied herself nervous. The business of her life was to get her daughters married; its solace was visiting and news."

Condescending Lady Catherine de Bourgh and her minion the capering Mr. Collins are comics to be relished without a pang. Agreeable, unstable Mr. Bingley and well-mannered Colonel Fitzwilliam, of brief appearance, are perhaps the most nearly shadowy characters in the cast. The Netherfield house-party, the Meryton worthies, and the militia officers, down to Denny the subaltern, perfectly play, at their moments, supporting roles. Mr. and Mrs. Gardiner are admirable spokesmen of commonsense: indeed, Mrs. Gardiner helps to advance the plot by her power of summing up situations . . . From first to last, the quiet but utter effectiveness with which the characters, one by one, are made to enter the story is to be admired. The entire Longbourn family, for instance, has been introduced to us within the first two chapters; Mr. and Mrs. Bennet have revealed themselves, with everything that they are, in the dialogue of the very first page.

No, Jane Austen burdened none of her novels, and least of all burdened *Pride and Prejudice*, with paragraphs of introduction or explanation. As to this, and other forms of novel-technique, she was to advance a long way beyond her master Fielding; and that her Victorian successors did not choose to learn more from her is to be regretted. Only now, perhaps, are we returning to the idea that bulk of words, in a novel, is not a virtue – *her* novels do, it is true, attain to a certain length, but that is because much happens, not because much is said. Also, she showed in her youth, with *Pride and Prejudice*, a discretion from which she was not to deviate: the discretion, it must be felt, of a great artist – she recognized, and kept to, her own field. She wrote of the world she knew; world of the southern English counties; of parsonages, manors and occasional great houses in parks; of lawns and ballrooms and drawing-rooms; of country towns and villages. Her characters are drawn from the country gentry, sufficiently dignified but obscure – persons ruled by formality, circumscribed by convention, and conscious of living under close observation by one another. Such a world may be tame or dramatic, according to how you see it – or according rather, perhaps, to how much you see. Jane Austen, second of the two daughters of a well-connected Hampshire clergyman, saw everything. Giddier (by some accounts) than her own Elizabeth, and no less apt for flirtation, she would put down her pen and delightedly dress herself to go dancing; nor did she disdain the pleasures of "visiting and news." But, some part of her being belonged, and stayed, outside the bounds of her age, sex and class. She apprehended, one can only take it, more than she knew consciously: the soundness, the variety and the range of the psychology in her novels are astounding. Thackeray or Balzac might have made more of Darcy than she did – but she, having thought of him, brilliantly sketched him in: he may be left incomplete, he is never false. Her refusal to dwell on "scenes of guilt and misery" was, later, to be stated in *Mansfield Park*; but that, in her young days of *Pride and Prejudice*, she *was* conscious of gulfs and threats one can never doubt. Her regard for morality was in her later work to become pronounced; but from the start her sense of virtue, or sense of what was really virtue, was true. To be at its greatest, comedy must impose on its writer one kind of discrimination. For, as Darcy remarks –

"The wisest and best of men, nay, the wisest and best of their actions, may be rendered ridiculous by the person whose first object in life is a joke."

"Certainly," replied Elizabeth – "there are such people, but I hope I am not one of *them*. I hope I never ridicule what is wise or good. Follies and nonsense, whims and inconsistencies *do* divert me, I own, and I laugh at them whenever I can . . ."

Jane Austen, at those same follies, laughed whenever she could. She has left us her laughter, in *Pride and Prejudice*.

What Jane Austen Means to Me

My love for Jane Austen is a kind which, from time to time, brings me into head-on conflict with a number of her other admirers. Is this, perhaps, an aggressive statement, in regard to an author herself so calm, lucid, mannerly and detached? If so, may I be forgiven. But it appears to me that Jane Austen is, very often, praised (with a hint of patronage) for the wrong reasons.

"Such a delicious, dainty, *miniature* little world!" one hears excellent people say. "Such an escape from the violences of today. Her characters are as pretty to look upon as a group of Dresden figurines on a drawing-room chimney-piece – sheltered, a little unreal perhaps, but how soothingly remote from our harsh realities!" And so on . . .

Yes, there's a tendency to regard Jane Austen as a creature of lavender and lace – arch, whimsical and a trifle fluttery. Whereas in fact, beneath her smiling guise she is a formidable artist. Few English novelists have been more adult.

I did not read Jane Austen till I was twenty-two. That I had never done so before was – I am certain now, looking back – a form of resistance on my part against propaganda in her favour: I'd not only omitted to read her, I had refused to. For how many weary years had she not been urged on me as an ideal writer for teenage girls; with how many daintily bound and winsomely illustrated volumes of her works had I not been presented!

I had taken part in Barrie's *Quality Street*,[1] I had re-read, a number of times, *Cranford*,[2] and I revelled in the Louisa M. Alcott books – but at that point, or rather from that point on, my enthusiasm for anything "old-world" stopped short; young ladies with V-shaped feet, swan necks and sashes under the armpits seemed to me to be denizens of the insipid universe of Christmas cards, needleworked blotters or theatricals in the rectory garden.

Blood-and-thunder I read through my teens, and was none the worse – till, the stirring of a desire for something more set me ranging through fiction for what should be at once an emotional widening of myself and a fresh intellectual adventure.

Some, though not all, of the novels of Thomas Hardy, Meredith, Tolstoy, Henry James, Flaubert, Conrad, Dostoevsky, Balzac and Maupassant were already, accordingly, known by me when I took from a bookshelf my first Jane Austen.

The scene was the rain-darkened salon of a small Italian lakeside hotel; outdoors, Como was gloomily blotted out. There was nothing else to read, nothing else to do. The book I reluctantly opened was *Pride and Prejudice*.

Soberly, I cannot regret that I came to Jane Austen late on – that is, compared to most people – in my reading life. The early twenties may be the ideal time to receive the first of the impact from her genius – I say "first," because I so much consider that one's original reading of the novels is no more than the outset of a lifelong relationship.

She is a writer impossible to outgrow; at any age, she seems to be one's contemporary – not merely keeping pace with one's own experience but casting light ever ahead of it.

Having, as she so much has, a superb and evident readability, she *can* be read, on a certain level, by a reasonably intelligent child of ten – a child can laugh at her comedy, sense her drama. But one needs, I'm sure, at least a degree of maturity to grasp the problems she really poses, to feel the exciting rightness of her evaluations, to measure the emotions she keeps in play, or to suspect the depths under her bright surface.

I think of Jane Austen as a writer to come to when one's own personality is at least *some* way upon its long, slow path to being formed. I do not consider her to be a writer for adolescents (hence the stupidity of the propaganda which, in my young days, attempted to thrust her on me) because adolescents tend to despise control – life, in their view, should be subversive, stormy; they see a controlled existence as dim, poor, tame.

Only when one sees how much there *is* to control, sees how futile chaos is, sees what anti-climax succeeds overweening passion, does one begin to appreciate Jane Austen. Only then does one see what she writes *about*.

Not one of her major characters is timid – nor, when one comes to glance for a second time at them, is a single one of the characters un-adult. Elizabeth Bennet, twenty-two-year-old heroine of *Pride and Prejudice*, first glittered and glowed her way into the view of me, the twenty-two-year-old reader, as a creature who, though (like myself) liable to mistakes, was never not in command of a situation. She had dauntless physical energy, she had wit; there was something Shakespearean about her – she was, I consider, "modern," and modern in a sense in which no girl has quite achieved being modern yet.

Young Emma Woodhouse, in *Emma*, shows – for all her lovable absurdity, her deplorable wishes to interfere – much the same gallant, generous high spirit. Fanny Price, shy, delicate niece in proud *Mansfield Park*, and the subtler Anne Elliott of *Persuasion*, might seem to be creatures of less vitality – but how finely steely their fine-strung wills are!

Possibly Fanny is a prig; Anne wins our hearts from her fortress of lonely courage; ultimately, both triumph . . . In the world of Jane Austen, evil or fear is[3] seldom depicted *directly*; but she does show, in her representations of vanity, self-delusion, power-obsession, resentment, greed or deceit, the ever-present and threat of malignant forces. Her central characters seldom are out of danger – from within, if not from without. Hence, in each case, the suspense of the story!

It is said that Jane Austen cannot "draw" men. The fact is, surely, that she does not attempt to – in so far, that is, as drawing implies either anatomisation or diagnosis. Her central masculine characters (or heroes) are more in the nature of reflections, in mirrors, or striding shadows cast on carpets and lawns. But how revealing may a reflection be, and how significant are shadows! Jane Austen is more honest, and more timeless, in showing the place of Man in a woman's universe than any woman writer before or since.

Seen from the outside (never, note, from within) her heroes are august, moody and unpredictable. Emma, for instance, never knows when she may not next be censured by Mr. Knightley; Mr. Darcy's captiousness, tinged with hauteur, is not without effect on the bright

Elizabeth; Anne Elliott, though she tells herself love is dead, cannot but be conscious of some enigma behind the courteous coolness of Captain Wentworth – her girlhood's lover, re-met in later life.

In *Mansfield Park* it is Henry Crawford, nominally the villain, who masculinely dominates the scene – pallid beside him is the virtuous Edmund!

Hardbitten, intelligent, sensual, worldly, and with a fineness of taste which subjects him to Fanny's "moral charm," Henry Crawford is not only the most attractive but the most commanding of the Jane Austen men; Fanny's refusal of him, and that only, fatally tips the balance inside his character – his disgraceful elopement with Maria is a piece of only too good psychology.

No less sure is Jane Austen's touch on the light-weight charmer – Willoughby in *Sense and Sensibility*, Frank Churchill in *Emma*. Is she at her best – as is sometimes said – in her depiction of fathers, brothers-in-law and clergymen? And in one great particular, as to men, her realism is satisfying and faultless: her men have always something to *do*.

They are sailors, often away at sea, or landowners occupied in estate management; they are lawyers, or sportsmen, or hypochondriacs (like old Mr. Woodhouse) or sardonic recluses (like Mr. Bennet). They, in the main, being Englishmen, prefer each other's company to that of women. They are not only occupied but pre-occupied – they enter the arena of the drawing-room only passingly; in a minute or two they are up and off again. (One may recall Mr. John Knightley's contempt for the too-agreeable clergyman Mr. Elton – "When there are ladies to please, every feature works.")

One cannot but be reminded that Jane Austen, one of only two girls in a large and vigorous family of brothers, grew up in what was primarily a man's world. Also, the southern English county society in which she lived had not, though elegant and polite, lost its underlying primitive pattern. And a further reason for her realism in regard to men may have been that her literary master was Henry Fielding, that above-all masculine, eighteenth-century novelist. Nor was she the worse for any of this.

*

How far is it possible to be influenced by Jane Austen? How far have I been, and in what way? At the age when first I knew and was drawn to her, I myself was first beginning to write. I could not but analyse the technique of every writer whom I admired – and no doubt equally I absorbed something of the spirit of any book which impressed itself upon me.

To Jane Austen I claim no unique reactions: mine was that of most other people – sheer, pure, unmitigated enjoyment. I did, of course, naturally ask myself why and how a pleasure like this had been brought about; and, under analysis, there emerged for me what she essentially has – a faultless sense of and regard for proportion.

Without that, either her heights of comedy or her melodious undertones would have been impossible. Though proportion in her sense I have not achieved, I have not ceased to keep that ideal in mind. Also, she made manifest to me the wisdom (that is, for a novelist) of confining one's art in the bounds of a world one knows. In my day, that is more difficult than it was in hers – scenes now shift so fast; the once-fixed patterns break up; one knows more worlds than she did, but no single one so well.

Be that as it may, I remain convinced (I learned that from her) that a novel, like a play, requires a stage. Or, if not a stage should I say a frame? Strength – and what a strength had Jane! – comes from the acceptance of place, of time, and also of the certain rules of Society.

As is known, all her six novels hinge on the conflict between reason and emotion – or, to put it more simply, thought and feeling. Of such a conflict, all of us must be conscious within ourselves – to me, it has always been particularly fascinating as a subject, and the Jane Austen treatment makes it still more so.

How far *is* intuition to be trusted? How far should one yield to the pressure of law and order – or, are all pressures necessarily bad?

More and more, I dislike "theory" in novels (Jane Austen's express no theory of any kind) but also, more and more it appears to me that necessarily a novel must have morality, as hers have. Without recognition of right and wrong, there can be no tension, no interest, no colour. The alternative, the sense of the right or wrong may be on any scale: it may, as with her, be evident in minutiae. It may be that I learned from her what an art it is to make little things largely felt . . .

At the outset, I spoke of her as formidable – this, to me, seems a thing that an artist should be. If this quality in her is overlooked, that may be because of the very quality I would most gladly learn from her – restraint. She was aware of violence, be sure.

Persuasion

Jane Austen is, in the main, delighted in as a smiling satirist – a person most herself in the comic vein. Her art could seem drawn to the sparkling shallows rather than to the greater depths of emotion. Extreme grief, turbulence or despair are banished from her pages, where not shown as the penalties of excessive romanticism. All but one of her heroines are youthful, capable of feeling, but still untouched by the more searching experiences of life. We observe that, throughout most of her writing years, Jane Austen deliberately chose restraint – she had, it is true, a warning in the absurd contortions of sensibility to which some of her fellow-novelists could go, but we may be certain that for her choice there was also some compelling personal reason. Not till she came to write *Persuasion* did she break with her self-set limitations. Did something in her demand release, expression, before it was too late? This was, whether or not she knew it, the last book she was to live to complete.

Persuasion strikes a note unheard hitherto. It is a masterpiece of delicate strength, suggesting far more than is put on paper. For it was not that the author abandoned or turned against restraint: on the contrary, she made it her study – its hard cost and no less its painful causes are shown. *Persuasion*, whose lonely heroine, young no longer, seems committed to all but silence, is in fact a novel about restraint. It is, too, a novel about maturity.

Somebody, discussing fiction, remarked that whereas men write better about a first love, women write better about a second. For our sex, do the original raptures tend to evaporate from the later memory? One would hardly think so; it takes, at least, remarkably little to recall them – an ancient dance tune, a dessicated flower in a drawer, a scrap of all but forgotten handwriting can bring back the magic of a moment. Possibly women's first feelings are less articulate – for it *is* a fact that the heart's awakenings, young love, whether in boy or girl, have been more lyrically pictured by male novelists. For instance, does any young girl in fiction rival Tolstoy's enchanting, enchanted, unwise Natasha of *War and Peace*? In *Persuasion*, Jane Austen does not, admittedly, deal with a second love – but she is concerned with a young love which has grown up, which has steadied, lasted, felt the stress of reality, woven itself into the fabric of a life. Anne Elliott is not a girl but a woman – though a woman doomed, it would seem, to unfulfilment. Because of a mistake she cannot retrieve, the future is to be empty for her. In Jane Austen's day, a spinster of twenty-seven was to all intents and purposes a nobody – a seat in the background, an anxious place on the margin of other people's activities were the most such an unfortunate might aspire to. When we first meet Anne Elliott, this is her lot. And worse, it is her lot by her own fault.

Tormentedly yielding to persuasion on the part of a worldlier older friend, Anne, at nineteen, had broken off her engagement to Frederick Wentworth, the then young, penniless naval officer. Nor had the love affair ended only thus: Anne has the additional pain of knowing that her weakmindedness (as it seemed to him) aroused Frederick Wentworth's contempt and anger – utterly she had failed and disappointed him. Now, for eight years, intense self-reproach has mingled with her regret. For his sake, the best she feels she can hope is that Wentworth by now has forgotten her – she has spoiled her own life: is that not enough?

There is present, in that early history of Anne's everything that could have made a warped creature. Do we not all know women with poisoned temperaments, in whom some grievance or disappointment seems to fester like an embedded thorn? Today, with a hundred careers open, it is or should be easier to forget – but Anne, condemned to the idleness of her time and class, has not an interest or an ambition to distract her. Endlessly, if she so willed, she could fret and brood. But no: she shows an unbroken though gentle spirit and, with that, a calm which does not fail. From what inner source does her courage spring? Love, although lost to her, still inspires her. Her undying feeling for Frederick Wentworth, the unshadowed nobility of his image, still lights up for her the entire world. For Anne Elliott *to* love, to have loved, is a tremendous thing. Somehow, therefore, she is set apart from those whose easier longings have been satisfied.

Hence, I think, this reticent woman's hold on the reader – one is drawn to her as to no other more outwardly striking Jane Austen heroine; one feels honoured by being in her confidence; she is sympathetic rather than coldly "admirable." Her slender beauty is thrown into more relief by the bumptious, apple-cheeked charms of the young Miss Musgroves. Playing the piano while her juniors dance, listening to the long and imagined woes of a series of discontented matrons, Anne Elliott remains in her quiet way the mistress of any situation. Unlike the blameless Fanny of *Mansfield Park*, she never is over-meek, subservient or mousey. She never pities herself: who dare pity her? The dull young squire Charles Musgrove, now her brother-in-law, had been, we learn, Anne's unsuccessful suitor; in the course of the story she is to attract the eye of a jaded, roving man-of-the-world. If life *is* "over" for Anne, it is so by force of her own decision – she can contemplate no form of the second-best.

Persuasion's heroine, when we first meet her, owes her poise to a sort of sad inner peace, the peace which comes with the end of hope. She does not expect, and she cannot wish, ever again to see Frederick Wentworth.

Yet, she must. And we watch her through that ordeal.

Frederick, now Captain Wentworth, a naval hero enriched by prize-money, reappears in the Elliotts' West-country neighbour-hood. Here, in these same places, these rooms and gardens charged with so many associations, the former lovers are forced to meet face to face. Forced? – yes, for Anne it amounts to that. She hears the news of his coming with apprehension. He, by all signs, does not any more feel anything; she must conceal the fact that she feels so much. Nor is this all – she is to look on at Captain Wentworth's flirtation with and apparent courtship of her sprightly young neighbour Louisa Musgrove. For Frederick, Anne seems to be hardly there. Is it, for him, as though she had never been?

No. His formal good manners to her have a touch of ice: he has not forgotten, for he has not forgiven. Meet as they may as strangers, he and she cannot be strangers truly. Always, they are in the presence of crowds of people; there are walking-parties, dances, country house merry-makings, and there is the expedition to Lyme Regis which so nearly has a tragic end. One thing Anne *is* spared – prying or mocking eyes. For that eight-years-ago engagement had been kept secret: no outside person other than Lady Russell (whose advice had wrecked it) had ever known of it. Now, Lady Russell is elsewhere. Nobody, therefore, suspects either Anne's anguish or its cause.

All through *Persuasion*, the scenes in the country, at the seaside, the later episodes in Bath, we react to the tension of speechless feeling. Yet somehow the novel is not a thing of stress; it has the harmony of its autumnal setting. The landscape, the changing season, are part of the texture of the story. Here, as nowhere else in Jane Austen's work, brims over the poetry of Nature – uplands, woods and sea. We are tuned in to a mood, to a sensibility which (being at once Anne's and her creator's) rings beautifully true. And, as the plot of *Persuasion* unfolds itself, we follow each development through Anne's eyes. Or sometimes, we keep watch on her behalf. Is Frederick Wentworth relenting? – or, had his coldness, from the first, been a matter of self-protection? Has his indifference to this older Anne been less than she had imagined, or he had thought? So we suspect, some time before Anne herself has dared to envisage the possibility. We begin to be impatient for the *dénouement* – of its kind, the suspense set up by *Persuasion* is as keen as any I know in fiction.

Then it comes – that extraordinary scene in the Bath parlour when, while Anne is talking to other people, Frederick sits absorbed in writing a letter. Then, rising, he leaves the room hurriedly, "without so much as a look." But next:

> Footsteps were heard returning; the door opened; it was himself. He begged their pardon, but he had forgotten his gloves, and instantly crossing the room to the writing table, and standing with his back to Mrs. Musgrove, he drew out a letter from under the scattered paper, placed it before Anne with eyes of glowing entreaty fixed on her for a moment, and hastily collecting his gloves, was again out of the room, almost before Mrs. Musgrove was aware of his being in it – the work of an instant!
>
> The revolution which one instant had made in Anne was almost beyond expression . . . On the contents of that letter depended all which the world could do for her!

There are, I know, those who find in *Persuasion* one fundamental improbability. *Would* Anne, even when very young, have let herself be persuaded by Lady Russell into making a break with her true love? The weakness, the lack of faith – the cowardice, almost – seem out of accord with the heroine whom we later know. One must recollect that Lady Russell's argument had been a wily one – she had represented to Anne that a penniless youthful marriage would be a fatal drag on Frederick's career. Anne had given up Frederick for (as she thought) his sake – though mistaken, her decision had been selfless. Also, at nineteen, repressed and young for her age, she was unaccustomed to trusting her own judgement. Ignored by an arrogant father and elder sister, she had found in the worldly-wise Lady Russell her first friend – whose word, accordingly, carried undue weight. The time, moreover, was long ago: girls deferred, instinctively, to adult authority. But should we not, before either decrying Anne or declaring her weakness to be "impossible," think again about this question of influence? Dare we say that a friend's opinion, forcefully put, never has affected our own decisions? And is it not in regard to what matters most – for instance, some vital question of love – that we are most at the mercy of what is told us?

Caught in a tempest of feeling, we lose our bearings: it may not be easy to know what is right or wrong. The truth, we may only perceive later – not, it is to be hoped, too late.

Jane Austen's otherwise open life contains one mystery: her love affair. Nobody but her sister Cassandra knew of it; and Cassandra, who outlived Jane, kept silence – it is known that, before Cassandra's death, she destroyed revealing letters written by Jane. The probable scene and time of the love affair have been pieced together; no more can be established with any certainty. It is understood that the love was mutual, wholly happy, tender and full of promise, and that there would have been marriage had not the young man died. Had Jane Austen married, it seems likely that the world would never have had her greater later novels – fate, by dealing that blow to her, has enriched us. Balanced, wise and adorable are her comedies, but her true depth was not to be felt till this final book. This, I think, is her testimony to the valour, the enduringness of the human spirit. She believed, and she was to show, that love for another can be the light of a life – can rise above egotism, accept hardship, outlive hope of reward. Out of a hard-won knowledge she wrote *Persuasion*.

Introduction to No One to Blame, *by H. M. Taylor*

Mrs. Taylor calls this an autobiography: actually, it is a critical work. She falls in with the rules of autobiography by telling her life-story in the first person, but in doing this she has added a good deal more. Her conviction that she is not remarkable, her lack of concern with romantic aspects of "character," and her absence of any attitude towards herself, other than the assurance of quiet knowledge, give her book a sort of authority that, in autobiography, is exceedingly rare. I suppose that one cannot exercise such authority unless one is completely disinterested.

Too often, an autobiography is either a *tour de force* or a licensed lapse from the ordinary reticence. The unexpected stratum of soft silliness, the governing prejudice or fantasy, or some residual angriness left from early reverses is too often laid bare. Perhaps few autobiographies start from a healthy impulse: the autobiographer is the egoist on long-awaited promotion, the person distinguished enough, by now, in some other field to feel free to assume that his own life and his fancies should now be as important to other people as they have long been to himself. As Mrs. Taylor herself, correctly, has it: "Usually, no one has the courage or the will to write an autobiography unless he has played a successful role in social life, or has been in the public eye through some form of useful or artistic service, or has associated with great or eminent people. Sometimes, all these reasons for seeking literary publicity have been combined – a combination that has made the narrative more interesting and more appreciated."

Appreciated – but at the cost, almost always, of something of a step-down. The step-down is in integrity, if in nothing else. When the "important" person makes himself his own subject, the degree of candour has to be calculated. (Trollope,[1] who did not always keep this in mind, sent his own shares down for decades after his death.) The autobiographer who is already "important" is already part of the great public illusion, and must be careful how he handles himself. He may write himself up, but he must not write himself down. He may be apparently frank but he must be showy, and showiness does give frankness a sort of taint. Though he may not be guilty of one misrepresentation – that is, in the region of outside fact – his is compromised before he sits down to his table; he cannot command the entirely free pen.

Mrs. Taylor is different; she starts from scratch. She has lived in what we call complete obscurity. Having stated that she is "very ordinary," she does not bother to overstress even that. As far as I know, this is her first emergence in print, and, in the account she gives of her own life, she speaks of no wish to write for writing's sake. She has always been very busy, and she is not an artist; her autobiography is not intended to be, and is in no sense, a *work* of art – the touches of art in it are involuntary, struck out like sparks from her urgent sense of the truth. She has the stuff for art (in fact, life) here, but uses it for analysis. Her vision and her efficiency – there is no other word for it – could have made her a major artist; as it is, they have made her – against her repeated showing, throughout these pages – a major character.

In her generation, the woman of character was not quite so rare. But largely, women of character bloomed into notice out of the leisured class. Mrs. Taylor grew up in surroundings, in circumstances, in which character shows itself largely in opposition – to poverty, the threat of obliteration, sickness, fear – and in which even very vigorous natures, used up by the struggle, tend to stay inarticulate. She came of a poor family, mill-workers, in a North Country town, and she was born decades before the exceptional child was offered any hand up out of the rut. Her efforts to better herself were all frustrated – humiliatingly. As a little girl with a cough, plain, she says, and left half deaf by an illness, she had "big ideas." Her father was tubercular, mystically religious, unrealistic, a failure by the standards of his own world; her mother, another woman of character, was embittered by unwanted pregnancies and the struggle with life. The child worked in a cotton mill from the age of eleven, off and on till she was a woman of twenty-nine. She was constantly ill; her adolescence was wretched; her embryonic feelings of love were nipped; she had an odd relationship to religion (one could hardly call it religious experience) and she suffered social humiliations in her attempts to make a career for herself through the Evangelical movement. Her late marriage was overshadowed by her sick mother's presence in her home. In fact, everything happened that cripples or warps a nature – a woman's nature especially.

Not only was this nature not warped, but one does not read this book as the tale of a hard case or a "brave soul." The soul-sufferings of the "sensitive" bourgeois child are, as a rule, recorded with far less impassivity. Mrs. Taylor writes of her youth and childhood with a matter-of-factness that completely rules out pity. Courage and will – to fall back on her own words – are the two great elements here. She records conditions and facts with a sort of impatient bareness – it is her own deductions that interest her. And it is her own deductions that raise her book to its remarkable level. For she is one of those people to whom experience (whatever its nature) is intolerable only if it is meaningless. Such people can bear what they can assess. Feeling drives them to thought, and such minds come to maturity when they have found a method by which to re-read life. The method – or code – differs: the personal life may be re-read in terms of religious experience, of political conviction, of whatever the final illumination appears to be. Mrs. Taylor has chosen psychoanalysis.

Psychoanalysis has provided the method, as well as, perhaps, the impetus to the book. No "jargon," however, spatters these lucid pages; the writer makes use of no term from the new science to authorise or to short-circuit her own thought. She does not either challenge or dogmatise. By her showing, it is the Unconscious that spins the plot – the untoward, cunning Unconscious – once we called it the Devil. She shows how this evil agent hides at the root of the very virtues of poverty – self-sacrifice, family piety, religious exaltation, industry, bravely endured illness – and even, in some cases, prompts the manifestations of courage itself. Unregenerate pride – we are back in the old Evangelical terms. At its slightest, the Unconscious acts like a poltergeist . . . In this examination of life's generic evils, this moral-critical undertaking of Mrs. Taylor's, terms and names do not seem to matter much. Honesty can always make itself clear; it authorises any language it finds. Mrs. Taylor has continued to seek truth, continued to discard what she found untrue. Her book holds not a factitious or specious line. She writes in a calm-active daylight of mind, at an age when most women muster up fantasies.

I have spoken of her involuntary – one might almost say impatient – touches of art. And the story-interest appears from her first page. The balance between the story and the analysis seems to me to be quite faultlessly kept. There is clear, more than photographic, family portraiture – and there are some excellent upper-class Evangelicals – snobbish – and lower-class Evangelicals – on the make.

Throughout, not a touch of resentment or acrimony or desire to settle up old scores disfigures the narrative. Mrs. Taylor makes felt that understanding, that aristocratic kindness that one finds only in the mature great. Repose shows even in painful parts of her writing: she is a woman at peace with her own mind.

James Joyce

The death of James Joyce was felt by few in his own land as a personal tragedy. He died, as he lived the later part of his life, outside Ireland. Those of us who met him, met him in Paris, where he was almost an object of pilgrimage, or during his last shy, brief appearance in London. His Dublin days are so long ago, now, that his personal legend – idiosyncrasies, humours, habits, addictions, gestures, weaknesses – lives for very few people. His youth in Dublin remains for us inside the crystal of his art: to those of us who have read *Dubliners, A Portrait of the Artist as a Young Man* or *Ulysses*, he is forever walking the Dublin streets or looking with us along the wet sands of the Bay. But how many Dubliners still in Dublin actually remember the man passing, or look at a stretch of railing, a bridge parapet, a street corner, and say: "*That* is what I always connect with him?" It is surroundings that tie us closely to people, that are the earth of friendship. And that physical, associative tie with his countrymen Joyce broke when he went to live abroad.

Yet he was before all an Irishman. All the cerebral complexity of his later art went to reproduce the physical impressions that he had received in Ireland, in youth. These obsessed him – and all the more, perhaps, because he had withdrawn from them, as though in fear. Of his life abroad we have no record of his at all – it is as though that life no more than flowed over him. Ireland had entered him: it was the grit in his oyster shell. Great linguist, he explored and discarded language after language because of the, to him, final inefficacy of any language at all. Sensation was, above all, his subject, and the sensations that were his fever and pain are common – what remains extraordinary is the length he travelled in his efforts to put sensation into words.

Is it not Joyce's fundamental Irishness that has defeated, and in some cases antagonised, the critics forced into pronouncement by his death? The English can never know us – and are we ready to know ourselves? To challenge our view of ourselves, I should say that it is more academic than we realise. Our talk and writing, and most of all when it is about ourselves, is more full of conventions than we know. Joyce was unacademic, and by not a single convention did he save himself from his awareness of life. What he laid bare, or what he scorned to conceal, has been repugnant first of all to his countrymen. He was a great buffooner, a great scorner – in that, is he not like most of us? Only, his scorn and buffoonery admitted no stop. His early work is inundated with pity – and it is in our power to feel pity that we, as humans, are at our greatest. If there seems in the later work to be less pity, that came, I believe, in Joyce from the natural human refusal to suffer too much – to suffer, in fact, to that extent of which he was capable. (For the thing about pity is that it *does* make us suffer: it is much more than an imaginative act.) Pity for the frustrated dreams of the living, pity for the finished dreams of the dead – gradually, Joyce withdrew from pity, as he withdrew from Ireland.

This is part of the end of his longest short story, *The Dead*, from the collection *Dubliners*, published in 1914. Gabriel Conroy and his wife have been to a party, on a winter night: the evening stirs up strange emotions in them, and on their return she tells him about the young man, Michael Furey, who had loved her when she was a girl, and had died. She lies on her bed weeping, then falls asleep.

She was fast asleep.

Gabriel, leaning on his elbow, looked for a few minutes unresentfully on her tangled hair and half-open mouth, listening to her deep-drawn breath. So she had had that romance in her life: a man had died for her sake. It hardly pained him now to think how poor a part he, her husband, had played in her life. He watched her while she slept, as though he and she had never lived together as man and wife. His curious eyes rested upon her face and her hair: and, as he thought of what she must have been then, in that time of her girlish beauty, a strange, friendly pity for her entered his soul. He did not like to say even to himself that her face was no longer beautiful, but he knew it was no longer the face for which Michael Furey had braved death.

. . . The air of the room chilled his shoulders. He stretched himself cautiously along under the sheets and lay down beside his wife. One by one, they were all becoming shades. Better pass boldly into that other world, in the full glory of some passion, than fade and wither dismally with age. He thought of how she who lay beside him had locked in her heart for so many years that image of her lover's eyes when he had told her he did not wish to live.

Generous tears filled Gabriel's eyes. He had never felt like that towards any woman, but he knew that such a feeling must be love. The tears gathered more quickly in his eyes and in the partial darkness he imagined he saw the form of a young man standing under a dripping tree. Other forms were near. His soul had approached that region where dwell the vast hosts of the dead. He was conscious of, but could not apprehend, their wayward and flickering existence. His own identity was fading out into a grey impalpable world: the solid world itself, which these dead had one time reared and lived in, was dissolving and dwindling.

A few light taps upon the pane made him turn to the window. It had begun to snow again. He watched sleepily the flakes, silver and dark, falling obliquely against the lamplight . . . Yes, the newspapers were right: snow was general all over Ireland. It was falling on every part of the dark central plain, on the treeless hills, falling softly upon the Bog of Allen and, further westward, softly falling into the dark mutinous Shannon waves. It was falling, too, upon every part of the lonely churchyard on the hill where Michael Furey lay buried. It lay thickly drifted on the crooked crosses and headstones, on the spears of the little gate, on the barren thorns. His soul swooned slowly as he heard the snow falling faintly through the universe and faintly falling, like the descent of their last end, upon all the living and the dead.

This could not be gentler: there is the sound of snow in it. And Joyce the man kept, as I understand, this gentleness with the people he loved. In the foreign countries he was to live in, his home life was dear to him. But as a writer he was, too, to develop that wayward and jeering cruelty that is either the inverse of pity or a reaction against it – cruelty that is a rigid abstention from feeling of any kind. It is never brutality: it is too full of nerves. I do not say we are often cruel, but when we are, is it not like this? Joyce's portraits – some of the figures in *A Portrait of the Artist* and *Ulysses* – are drawn with a mercilessness more shocking to many people than any of his obscenities. At last he turned from character: in *Finnegans Wake* all human forms disappear.

Was Joyce irreverent? I think not. His apparent irreverence is a sort of despair – the outcry of a reverence that has thwarted itself. All through *A Portrait of the Artist* there is a man asking too much – an *attacking* nature –

His throat ached with the desire to cry aloud, the cry of a hawk or eagle on high, to cry piercingly of his deliverance to the winds. This was the call of life to his soul not the full gross voice of the world of duties and despair, not the inhuman voice that had called him to the pale service of the altar. An instant of wild flight had delivered him and the cry of triumph which his lips withheld cleft his brain.

. . . What were they now but the cerements shaken from the body of death – the fear he had walked in night and day, the incertitude that had ringed him round, the shame that had abased him within and without – cerements, the linens of the grave?

And Joyce had another gigantic faculty – laughter. His laughter, after some rumbles and false starts in *Dubliners*, after a check throughout the taut and burning *Portrait*, breaks out in the course of *Ulysses* into a sustained roar, and it sobs and wheezes and almost dies of itself behind the obscurities of *Finnegans Wake*. His laughter is disconcerting; people have edged away from it, as from a man laughing all by himself. When one was a child one used to be told: "It is bad manners to laugh for no reason, without telling people what you are laughing at." Joyce's attempts to tell us what he was laughing at produced the more contused passages of *Ulysses* and the almost lunatic reaches of *Finnegans Wake*. He pounded language to jelly in his attempts to make it tell us what he was laughing at. One may say that he ended by laughing so much that he could not speak. At the end of his solitary burning first phase, at the end of the racking ordeal of his long adolescence, the joke of the universe suddenly dawned on him, and, adult, he broke out into laughter so adult that it has been too much for most of us. He was, most of all, solitary in his mirth. And yet, it is in Joyce's own country that this cosmic devouring laughter is most heard. A door swings, and it hurtles out in a gust. Remember, in *John Bull's Other Island*,[1] how shocked the Englishman was when they all laughed when the poor pig died in the motor-crash.

In short, the contradictions of Joyce's nature ought not to perplex his own countrypeople: we have them all in ourselves. In the state of uneasy politeness caused by his death British critics, these last weeks, have been circling around him. *Was* the man kidding? What was he getting at? Had he, for the last twenty years and more, been leading young intellectuals up the garden path? The earnest cautiousness of the approach is marked – and from behind this emanates a relief that Joyce, the reviewers' nightmare, is now honourably hushed and will not make trouble again. Joyce has, by implication, been accused of having imposed himself craftily on the inter-war neurosis and disorientation of the young, of being a writer purely about the limbo for the too willing and desperate dwellers in it. To *Dubliners*, with its feeling objectivity, clearness, and strain of unhappy beauty, and to *A Portrait of the Artist as a Young Man*, with its universality and burning seriousness, all honest critics give praise. But waves of hostility can be felt breaking against the two later, obscure and in themselves "hostile" books, *Ulysses* and *Finnegans Wake.* Wartime England is in a state of reaction against what seems to her febrile or over-cerebral: she has only room, now, for the primary feelings, for plain speech and properly drilled thought. France is, at the moment, tragically silent, and slow mails hold up, for us, what America has to say.

An article in the *Times Literary Supplement* most fairly puts into words the general charge against Joyce. It speaks of him as "shirking his job of communication." Did he? Or was it that, as his years went on, he increasingly overstrained language, himself and us in the very efforts he made to communicate? I have (with *Finnegans Wake* in mind) spoken of him as (impatiently) pounding language into a jelly – strictly, the effect on our minds is that that was what he was doing. In fact, we know that Joyce had no impatience, and that his attitude to language was mathematical. He used authority to vary the formula. We know that every line of *Finnegans Wake* was the product of minute and exhausting care, and that, more than half-blind, he for sixteen years hung and hung again over every word.

Was this (as Arnold Bennett said, after *Ulysses*) a writer "playing the lout to the innocent and defenceless reader?" Or was it, this half-blind fumbling over a foreign writing-table, the end of the vision at which young Stephen Dedalus had wanted to cry aloud like a hawk or eagle, the "hawklike man climbing sunward above the sea . . . the end he had been born to serve and had been following through the mists of childhood and boyhood . . . the artist forging anew in his workshop out of the sluggish matter of the earth a new soaring impalpable imperishable being"?

Almost all of *Finnegans Wake* is, in the ordinary sense, unintelligible. It is unintelligible to the part of the mind that expects statement or narration. We are used to receive, from a page of print, *information*, of one or another kind, information that we could, if necessary, pass on to a friend in our own words: even a love-lyric is informative – as to the lover's emotion, as to his mistress's charms. We do not, on the other, expect *information* from a symphony or the sound of a waterfall. *Finnegans Wake*, like music or a long natural sound, acts on us. We are affected, profoundly, instead of being informed. Sense has been sacrificed to sensation. Is this wrong? – to the greater number of people it offends every morality of the mind. There seems no doubt that Joyce, in writing *Finnegans Wake*, used the whole of his, by then, complete mastery not only of language but of its associations against the defences of mere intelligence. The associations that reinforce his language are super-intellectual and sub-infantile. The esoteric levity of the scholar fuses with the trance of the young child chanting non-words to itself in the half-dark. The punning is packed with intellect; the schoolman swoops off into Jabberwocky[2] tongue. The maddening, watery book has a river theme; the images cast on it, as on a current, bend. There are names in it, and speakers, but no forms.

In fact, what happens in *Finnegans Wake* is that Joyce *does* communicate, but does not inform. To identify communication with information is to take a narrow view of communication. If art is not to stop, we shall have to widen communication. If art is not to stop, we shall have to widen our view. Joyce saw this widening as possible.

The charges against the Joyce of *Ulysses* have been more diverse. They have been serious enough to have, in this country, removed the book from our ken. Compared with *Finnegans Wake* the greater part of *Ulysses* is easy reading, though it has been found fatiguing because of its extreme length. Passages of it – notably the Dublin Bay sequence at the beginning – are so beautiful, and so in every sense inoffensive, that I wish they could be extracted from the rest of the book and made available to the public in Ireland. The theme of the book is well-known – the convergence, throughout the course of a Dublin day, of Stephen Dedalus upon Mr. Bloom, the puzzled and cheery little Dublin Jew. There are scenes in the tower overlooking the Bay, in the National Library, in a hospital, at a funeral, in an eating-house, in a low haunt, in Mrs. Bloom's solitary bedroom, scene of her monologue. Living Dublin figures appear. The middle of the book (after the hospital) is turgid with the first of those communication-experiments that were to culminate in *Finnegans Wake*. To be brief, the language goes funny, and undergoes a number of style-changes – we get a page or two of Olde-

Oake-ish archaisms, and a page or two of Ethel-M-Dell-ese.[3] Most of all, the stomach-turning physical ugliness of parts of *Ulysses*, and the failure of the internal narrative to be deflected by indecencies, have been denounced.

But – here is Stephen Dedalus on the seashore:

> Turning, he scanned the shore south, his feet sinking again slowly in new sockets. The cold domed room of the tower waits. Through the barbicans the shafts of light are moving ever, slowly ever as my feet are sinking, creeping duskward over the dial floor. Blue dusk, nightfall, deep blue night. In the darkness of the dome they wait, their pushedback chairs, my obelisk valise, around a board of abandoned platters. Who to clear it? He has the key. I will not sleep there when this night comes. A shut door of a silent tower entombing their blind bodies, the panthersahib and his pointer. Call: no answer. He lifted his feet up from the suck and turned back by the mole of the boulders. Take all, keep all. My soul walks with me, form of forms. So in the moon's mid-watches I pace the path above the rocks, in sable silvered, hearing Elsinore's tempting flood.

With Stephen Dedalus we go back in time to *A Portrait of the Artist as a Young Man*. This has been in the exact (not in the vulgar reviewer's) sense, Joyce's most powerful book. By those who do not like it and do not like adolescents, it has been called the bible of adolescents. But one might say the same of *Hamlet*. When Joyce perceived in himself and immortalised Stephen Dedalus, he defined not only the burning of one spirit, the desperate revolutions of one brain; he defined and seemed to create a type. He gave to male intellectual adolescence its lasting prototype in art. The sons of Stephen are many; he may be said to have bred a whole generation – but in Ireland they are most truly his sons. Across the quadrangles of old English universities, through the streets of London, New York, Paris have walked many self-seen Stephens, since *A Portrait* appeared. But to be truly Stephen one must be a born Catholic and Irish city-bred man.

"Crying aloud in the rain on the top of the Howth tram" – Stephen is undetachable from his place.

The writing of *A Portrait of the Artist* is straightforward, un-elliptical. The "stream of consciousness" writing that Joyce perfected – and with which he did much to infect Europe – has not begun yet. This is the one pure – or, one might say, classic – novel he wrote, and as such alone it would be admirable. The narration is direct, the dialogue telling, the characters three-dimensional. Here is Joyce in full daylight, and in the first phase of his strength. Why, we may ask, could Joyce not be content to use again this novel-form he had found that he could perfect? (For, here, he communicates fully, but *through* information.) I cannot believe him to be so fractious an artist that he despised whatever he could command. Nor was he so much of a virtuoso that he must seek new form for new form's sake. It was, simply, that he could not be static. As he found more and more to communicate he found, for this, the means that seemed to him best.

Europe and America have acclaimed Joyce. But it is in our power, as his people, to know him as other countries do not. His death, since he went away so long ago, need not estrange him from us, but rather bring him back. We have given to Europe, and lost with Europe, her greatest writer of prose. The shy thin man with the thick spectacles belonged to us, and was of us, wherever he went. He has not asked us for a grave – we have too many graves already. It is not with his death that we need concern ourselves, but with the life (our life) that, still living, he saved for us, and immortalised, line by line. In Ireland we breed the finest of natures, then, by our ignorance, our prejudice and our cruelty drive those finest of natures from our shores. Let us strip from Joyce the exaggerations of foolish intel-lectual worship he got abroad, and the notoriety he got at home, and take him back to ourselves as a writer out of the Irish people, who received much from our tradition and was to hand on more.

New Writers

O n the next page comes a story, "Three Talented Children," for which I feel a good deal of respect. I respect it because, though the author shows up his characters, he does so without a cheap wink. The decencies and the justice of art are, in the long run, the same as human justice and decencies – one must not expose a character to humiliation or one must not exhibit a character *in* humiliation, unless he has courted this by a course of action designed to humiliate someone else. In the case of the "Three Talented Children," the family's aspiration was innocent: modest, but given to self-expression through dancing and singing, the family are led by a friend to believe their accomplishments worth money. They hope to relieve their own extreme poverty – and if, beyond this, they figure out for themselves a brilliant worldly career, who is to blame them? Dreams are innocent things. The explosion of the dream by a hard fact – as when a child's balloon hits the spike of a gas-bracket – is sad, but it leaves the family honour intact. Also, this story has a wideness about it – it is a very well generalised picture of our people abroad: talented children all of us, unsure of our market value, at once defenceless and haughty, living in our own dream.

The technique of this story seems to me sure and sound. Domhnall O'Conaill seems certain, from the beginning, of an angle from which he wished to photograph. The story is told with no error of moral taste, and without undue exposure of painful feeling, *because* it is told by the youngest child. The little boy, passive throughout, emits, and remembers, no emotion, though he sees the signs of emotion in other people – his second sister's dropped eyelids of quick shame. I found the story's opening over-slow, and thought this a bit of a risk. But the writer's *intention* – the vital guide to all stories – appeared on the scene just in time, and got back my confidence.

Guy de Maupassant

Guy de Maupassant (1850–1893) is one of the few great masters of the short story. His work along this line has less atmospheric beauty than Chekhov's, but gains by sharp actuality, wide range of subjects and use of plot. Maupassant was not an intellectual; ideas did not interest him, and he preferred to deal with direct emotions. Born in a Normandy château, of landowning stock, he worked as a young man in a Paris government office: in his spare time he rowed, shot, travelled, and pursued women. His desire not only to write but to write well made him triumph over original vanity and laziness: he put himself to school, in the ways of authorship, with his older friend, the austere Flaubert, who pruned, criticised and sometimes suppressed his work.

As a writer, Maupassant exhibits the great French qualities, plus some particularly his own. Given craftsmanship, his temperament and his love of life were assets. Under the sophistication of the man-about-town, he kept the realism – sometimes savage, sometimes tender – of the countryman. His genius presents an extraordinary range of characters – city clerks, country priests, women of the world, provincial officials, peasants, playboys, squire-farmers, timid young girls and – as in this story – "little soldiers."

Some of his greatest stories deal with occupied France of the Franco-Prussian war. He can be over-harsh, even brutal; and some of his love-stories are overcast by what now seems to us tarnished cynicism. Towards the end of his not long life, he developed a vein of the hallucinatory and macabre: it is a fact that Maupassant died insane . . .

In "The Little Soldier," we have Maupassant at his most simple and human, and, consequently, at his most immortal. How well, in this tale of two homesick Breton peasant-conscripts, he makes us feel the *regionalism* of France!

Foreword to Tomato Cain and Other Stories, by Nigel Kneale

Within the last few years, readers have become less shy of the short story. That this form of fiction is also a form of art had fairly long ago been recognized; what is more important, from the point of view of popular favour, is that the high potential of entertainment in a good collection of stories may now be seen. There exists, too, a growing body of people who no longer turn to a book in search of "escape" but are genuinely interested in writing – who value craftsmanship and react to originality. To such readers, the short story – in its present rather fascinating position halfway between tradition and experiment – must particularly appeal.

The experimental story writer, lately, has in fact been given a good deal of rope: that the best use has invariably been made of this I cannot say. There has been a danger that, because of its literary privilege, the short story might fall under a certain literary blight, and become an example of too much prose draped around an insufficiently vital feeling or a trumped-up, insufficiently strong idea. The declared reaction against plot – as constraining, rigid or artificial – was once good up to a point, but possibly went too far: the fact that a story must be a story was overlooked. There are now signs of an equally strong (and, I think, healthy) reaction against plotlessness. Of this Nigel Kneale's stories are symptomatic.

Indeed, in one sense, these tales in *Tomato Cain* show a return to the great mainstream of the English story tradition – with which one associates Kipling, Wells, Saki, Somerset Maugham. When I say that Nigel Kneale's stories have plot, I mean that they make their effect by the traditional elements of invention, tension, a certain amazement and, ultimately, surprise. Like his great predecessors, he is impersonal, not using his art for either self-expression or exhibition. His art is the art of narration – the world's oldest. He knows how to rouse interest; and, which is still rarer, knows how to hold it. He is adept at giving a situation a final twist. These *Tomato Cain* stories vary in quality, as stories in any collection must; but, personally, I find the author guilty of not one single story which bogs down.

The writer of stories of this type must be bold; he disdains the shelter of ambiguity; it is essential that each of his pieces should come off. He is gambling – in an honourable sense, for are not Kipling, Wells, Saki, Somerset Maugham gamblers also? – on the originality of his imagination, on his power to grip, on the persuasiveness of his manner of story-telling. It might be too much to say that all the world's classic stories have had an element of the preposterous about them; one might safely say that any memorable story carried something which had to be put across. A part of the fascination of Nigel Kneale's story-telling is that he takes long chances; a part of the satisfaction of it is that in almost all cases he justifies the risks.

This writer is a young Manxman. He has grown up in, and infuses into his stories, an atmosphere which one can cut with a knife. He is not dependent on regionalism – not all of his work has an Isle of Man setting – but it would appear that he draws strength from it: his work at its best has the flavour, raciness, "body" that one associates with the best of the output from Ireland, Wales, Brittany, and the more remote, untouched and primitive of the States of America. He turns for his inspiration to creeks in which life runs deep, to pockets in which life accumulates, deeply queer. Is the Talking Mongoose a sore subject with the Isle of Man? That interesting animal – of which the investigations of the late Harry Price never entirely disposed – might well be the denizen of a Nigel Kneale story. Has he not made frogs avengers; has he not made a deformed duck a tragedian?

In far-off days [he says, at the opening of "The Tarroo-Ushtey"] before the preachers and the school-masters came, the island held a good many creatures besides people and beasts. The place swarmed with monsters.

A man would think twice before answering his cottage door on a windy night, in dread of a visit from his own ghost. The high mountain roads rang in the darkness with the thunderous tiffs of the bugganes, which had unspeakable shapes and heads bigger than houses; while a walk along the seashore after the sun had set was to invite the misty appearance of a tarroo-ushtey, in the likeness of a monstrous bull . . . At harvest-time the hairy trollman, the phynodderee, might come springing out of his elderberry tree to assist the reaping, to the farmer's dismay; for the best-intentioned of the beings were no more helpful than interfering neighbours . . .

This is the background atmosphere of one group of Nigel Kneale's stories; call them the local pieces. "Tomato Cain" itself, "The Excursion," and "The Putting-away of Uncle Quaggin" have (for instance) a naturalism not unworthy of Maupassant: the supernatural never raises its head, but eminent human queerness is at its height.

It is the function of every emerging writer to create, and stamp, his own universe. This Nigel Kneale has done. In his universe, love, in the sentimental or social sense, plays almost no part; but the passions stalk like those island monsters. Like the unfortunate bungalow in "Minuke," his characters are wrenched and battered and heaved up. What is remarkable, given the themes of many of the stories, is that the writer so seldom – if, indeed, ever? – crosses the bounds into extravagance; his *forte* is a sort of control, restraint. His "Quiet Mr. Evans," tale of an injured husband's revenge in a fish-and-chip shop, threatens at one point to approach in horror H. G. Wells' "The Cone," but the last twist gives a pathetic-ironic end. It would be fair to say that his children and animal stories, with their focus on suffering (e.g. "The Photograph," "Oh, Mirror, Mirror," "The Stocking," "Flo," and the semi-fantastic "Curphey's Follower") most dangerously approach the unbearable. It may, however, be found that Nigel Kneale knows how to relax any too great realism at the saving moment.

To the sheer *build*, to the something better than ingenuity of the best of the stories, attention should be drawn. "Peg" and "Bini and Bettine" would seem to me to be masterpieces in a genre particularly this writer's own. This is a first book: Nigel Kneale is at the opening of his career; he is still making a trial of his powers. To an older writer, the just not overcrowded effect of inventive richness, the suggestion of potentialities still to be explored, and of alternatives pending, cannot but be attractive. That the general reader will react to Nigel Kneale's stories, and that the perceptive reader will relish what is new in his contribution to fiction, I feel sure.

Foreword to Haven: Short Stories, Poems and Aphorisms, *by Elizabeth Bibesco*

The stories and poems of Elizabeth Bibesco bear, above all, the stamp of a personality – stories and verse are the overflow from a brimming-over capacity for life. One recalls, in the reading, that in good days "artless" was a term of praise, denoting what was spontaneous, uncalculated, natural and unfeigned. In this sense, the Princess Bibesco's was artless work – tutored, however, by keen intelligence and an intense reverence for art. One may observe, therefore, a continuous movement towards discipline: the spring, with its wayward ebullience, gradually gives place to the fountain – inside whose iridescence of blowing spray a determined pattern is to be seen.

This writer, vivacious and generous, in the first place inspired by sensibility, desired for her expression a language at which the intelligent should not mock. She was the child of a brilliant world – a world less rarefied and more sturdy than, superficially, it might now appear: it admitted dissonances and knew how to bite upon the grotesque. Such a world has a long European history: it began in Courts and found its later-day incarnation in groups of those drawn together by delight in one another's spirit, humour and company. By today's harsh reckoning, it might be found that such a world rested on guarantees which it took for granted, being the fine – yes, finest – flower of the old order which was in our century due to pass. That may be a fact, but it is not the point – the point, surely, is that there *was* a flowering. Civilisation is not merely a thing of structure; it must continue to owe much to the immaterial products of wit and heart, of grace, imagination and irony. Princess Bibesco's work is a written part of what was, in the main, an unwritten literature: conversations, with their felicities and their turns of phrase, have gone down to silence; intimacies, with what they bred of illumination, have – with the death of those who took part in them – been forgotten. These stories and poems, now reprinted, are examples of a manner of seeing life. Like the emerging points of an archipelago, they are linked by something we cannot see – a reef, or maybe a continent, engulfed by the waters of stress and time and change.

One may – and indeed one should – remind oneself that this writer's generation was not immune: the stories were written in the 1920s, while the psychic and social after-effects of the shock of the First World War were still present, and the poems mostly in the 1930s, while the Second World War (during which Elizabeth Bibesco died, abroad) was to be felt brewing. Those who lived, laughed and talked, who loved and analysed love, were consciously the survivors: they had looked over cliffs and were now using lightness and nonchalance as a sort of guard. This was a generation of which death had taken more than the full toll: faces were missing, remembered voices were mute. Can one wonder that such dwellers in those decades should be ultra-conscious of life, that they should have put such stress upon personality, that minutiae should have amused them or troubled them so (it seems now) inordinately, that their nerves and senses should have been so keyed up, that their vision should have been hyper-intensified? They spoke for the silenced; the life *they* survived to live – with its beauties, its incongruities, its fulfilments – had been snatched from their contemporaries, the dead.

Elizabeth Bibesco's earlier stories are perhaps written too much in a private language: they have the nature of work to be shown to friends. There is something impetuous, intimate, egocentric – in fact, engagingly personal about them. She wrote, at the start and throughout, for love of the thing – but never without real impetus, never in pure frivolity. The fact is, that to write at all is so difficult that (as this woman of brain, taste and temperament, friend of so many writers, knew) it is impossible to *be* frivolous about it. The earlier of the stories are aerial; yes, airy, even; but they are not airy nothings – the luxurious prettiness of the *mise-en-scène* may be deceptive. Not one of the stories is not about *something* – and, which I think is interesting, the interior drama (for each does contain a drama) could be, without loss of reality, translated into a different social setting. The gritting embarrassments of "I Have only Myself to Blame," the ironies of "The Dream" and "The Old Story," and the lit-up tensity of "The Ball" will strike any reader as "true to life." One does not have to be sophisticated to understand them.

A charge of over-sophistication, with regard to the work in general, may none the less be brought. These Bibesco characters may seem to be the inhabitants of a special *milieu*, in which the more ordinary taboos on feeling and brakes on speech do not operate. All these persons converse with a dazzling frankness. Their crises may seem to be self-spun, their sensibility to be over-luxuriant, their self-mockeries and their railleries at one another just too adept. One may admit that Princess Bibesco delighted in a semi-ideal world – a world which, though having a kind of counter-part in her experience, was to a great extent brought into being by her own temperament and, one might say, flair. One may hazard that she idealised her friends, and that a light which never was on land or sea played, for her, over conversations and moments. But is there not something compelling, something creative, even, in such idealisation? Who is the worse for being endowed, by their friend's vision, with an extra degree of beauty, honesty, subtlety, courage, grace or wit? For an hour, at least, one becomes as one's friend has seen one – a little more valuable, a shade more civilised, than before. This tendency to heighten, to rarefy, carries over into the style of some of her stories.

Others of them, however, are bleak enough. Not all the Bibesco characters are articulate; many become the prey of their own illusions. Herself articulate, the writer regards those who are in imperfect command of their thoughts and speech, and who cannot disentangle their own sensations, with a sort of helpful, chivalrous distress. Such persons become her butts only when their psychological handicaps make them actively cruel, oppressive or dishonest. For the innocent blunderer, bound to incur wounds, she feels an outright sympathy – to the middle-aged heroines of "Haven" and "The Whole Story," for instance, victorious endings are meted out. The young wife in "Red Hair" is another matter: not quite so innocent, full of petty malignancies, she is somebody else's tragedy, and a hopeless case . . . "Red Hair" is substantial: it ranks with "The La Perronnière Letters" (which has a grimness worthy of Maupassant), with "Villegiatura" (dedicated to Marcel Proust), with "While There is Life," "Auld Lang Syne" and "The Whole Story," as Elizabeth Bibesco's most acute, finished work.

One last point, with regard to the prose: this is cosmopolitan writing, which, though showing some of the English virtues, is not to be judged entirely by the English rules. Princess Bibesco not only lived many years abroad, knowing different cities, societies, ways of feeling: she was saturated in European literature. A great part of her sympathies and affinities are, obviously, with France. Her roots were always at home: as Elizabeth Asquith, the Prime Minister's daughter, she had felt not only the onus of high political life but, beyond it, the urges of her own people. That she kept alive so many contacts, that she succeeded in bridging the gaps and blanks left by her many and lengthy absences, must have been due to an almost preternatural quickness of insight and eager warmth of heart. Not easily, always, does one re-establish communication. "That was the worst" (reflects the returning lady in "Auld Lang Syne") "of being abroad so much. You were always either trying to tell things it bored people to hear, or else they were determined to hear things it bored you to tell. Her mind wandered to the tide-like quality of interest, the way it advanced and retreated in a conversation." Sometimes, perhaps, in these stories the author is trying to tell us things that (because of her gifts) never really bore us, but which we, with our island-bound vocabulary, are either slow or unwilling to seize or to comprehend.

The poems, still more than the stories, are personal; they have the merit of spontaneity and the ring of emotional truth. They are sad; here, one feels, is the natural lover of laughter confronted by the anguish of misunderstanding, loss, loneliness or the immutable fact of death. These verses were written some way on in Princess Bibesco's life; yet somehow they have the distinction of youth-fulness – nothing has been blunted, nothing lost; there have been no false reconciliations. The words, in their search for expression, are naïvely chosen: they often falter and sometimes fail. The poems are less accomplished than the stories; yet in them, surely, is exposed the philosophy which underlay, and gave spring to, the other work?

> Life is the sacrament of birth,
> A miracle and a vocation,
> The fire that warmed dust into earth,
> A currency for every nation.
>
> It burns as well as heats our way
> If we've accepted the divine flame:
> Sun-breathing joys on every day
> And pain must be welcomed into the same.

Introduction to The Stories of William Sansom

R are is the writer with command of his powers who absolutely cannot write a short story – if he so desire, or if (as may happen) it be desired of him. Few there must be who have not, at one time or another, wanted to try the hand at this form, or found themselves seized by an idea which could be embodied in no way other than this. The writer not sooner or later tempted to try everything, if only to prove to himself that he cannot do it, must be exceptional; might one not say, defective? Incidental short stories of writers by nature given to greater space, or by need bound to the synthesis of the novel, generally warrant attention and give pleasure. Some have the *éclat* of successful command performances. Few quite misfire. Few fail to merit the author's signature or to bear the particular stamp he gives any work. Yet such stories, recognizably, are by-products. One does not feel that they were inevitable. In this, they differ essentially from stories by the short-storyist *par excellence*: the short-storyist by birth, addiction and destiny. Such is William Sansom.

William Sansom, I do not need to point out, has extended himself into other fields. One could say he has experimented *with* extension, and that there has, moreover, been no experiment he has cause to regret. His by now six novels are in a position, a foreground, of their own. And of his equal command of the "short novel" (novelette or *novella*) has he not given us examples? His two travel books exercise a sharp, sensuous fascination: of their kind and in their own manner they are unrivalled. He has mastered the essay; he has manifested a gift for writing for children. It could be that these his other achievements eclipse, for some of his readers, his short stories – as achievements, these others have been substantial and dazzling. Yet the short story remains (it appears to me) the not only ideal but lasting magnet for all that is most unique in the Sansom art.

Here is a writer whose faculties not only suit the short story but are suited by it – suited and, one may feel, enhanced. This form needs the kind of imagination which is able to concentrate at high power and is most itself when doing so. The tension and pace required by the short story can be as stimulating to the right writer of it as they are intimidating to the wrong one: evidently they are stimulating to William Sansom. That need to gain an immediate hold on the reader (a hold which must also be a compulsive one) rules out the writer who is a slow starter: the quick starter, reacting, asks nothing better. There is also the necessity to project, to make seen, and make seen with significance – the short story is for the eye (if the mind's eye). Also the short story, though it highlights what appears to be reality, is not – cannot wish or afford to be – realistic: it relies on devices, foreshortenings, "effects." In the narration there must be an element of conjury, and of that William Sansom is an evident master.

Though all the short stories written by William Sansom are not, I find, present in this collection, the thirty-three which are present have been well chosen. (That a reader should be so conscious of those missing testifies to the power those pieces had to stamp themselves on the memory and, indeed, haunt it.) Those here are, one must concede, outstanding examples of their different kinds. Kinds? One had better say, types of subject – pedantic though that sounds. The wider a storyist's range, the more unavoidable it becomes that one should classify when attempting to take stock of his whole output. From his wartime London, N.F.S.[1] and fly-bomb period, we have, for instance, those two masterpieces, "The Wall" and "Building Alive." Portrayal of the terrible, or of the nature of terror, reaches three of its highest levels in "The Vertical Ladder," "How Claeys Died" and "Among the Dahlias." Comedy, canine in one case, human in the other, overflows with a cheering rumbustiousness from "Three Dogs of Siena" and "A Contest of Ladies." That extra dimension of oddness added to humans by their being in a pub or bar, or even in a hotel with the bar closed, appears in "Displaced Persons" (another masterpiece), "Eventide" and "A Game of Billiards." Of the pursuit of man (or woman) by a fatality, not to be given the slip or shaken off, there are several examples in stories here, the most memorable, and grimmest, being "Various Temptations." The resignation-reconciliation theme (very pro-nouncedly a Sansom one when he writes of courtship, engagements to marry, or marriage) carries to their conclusions two other stories, "A Waning Moon" and "Question and Answer."

Two of the greatest, at times awesome and certainly most curious powers of this writer appear in two kinds of story not mentioned yet. Where it comes to conveying hallucination, I know few if any who can approach him. (Kipling, possibly, though in another manner?) The fewness of "pure" hallucination stories in this collection to me is a matter of regret – above all, I hope that this does not mean that this author is reneging on this power? We have, however, the wondrous "A Saving Grace" . . . The other group, to be identified with the other power, are what one might nominate the great scenic stories: those in which what in the hands of another writer could be called "background" or "setting" steps forward, takes over, dominates like a tremendous insatiable star actor, reducing the nominal (human) protagonists to "extras," to walkers-on. In such Sansom stories, who, what, why and how people are is endlessly less important than where they are. How this can be made to come off, and come off triumphantly, is evident in "My Little Robins," "Time and Place," "Gliding Gulls," "Episode at Gastein," "A Country Walk," and, to a great extent, two stories already spoken of in another context (or, under another heading) "A Waning Moon" and "Question and Answer" . . . "Pastorale" is debatable: in a sense, the couple in it defeat the landscape.

To a point, all Sansom stories are scenic stories. Corsica, maritime Provence, Scandinavia, the Highlands of Scotland, the Isles of the West and the past-haunted, mountainous Austrian spa are far from being the only robbers. In this formidable and dismaying world of the Sansom art, no "inanimate" object is inanimate – mutely, each is either antagonist or accomplice. Influences and effluences are not only at work; they seem the determinants – to a point where mock could be made of human free will. The human is not only the creature of his environment, he becomes its plaything. For the moment, that moment, perhaps, only? But a Sansom moment, given extraordinary extension, so that during it hands may move round[2] the clock face, the sun set then rise, or leaves be torn from a calendar, is a Sansom story.

This writer's timing, with its expansions and contractions (as though he were playing on an accordion, or squeeze-box) is one of the instances of the trickiness he so well uses – trickiness which (I suggested earlier) a short story not only licenses and justifies but demands.

The need for the writer's obtaining compulsive hold on the reader (that is, the reader's imagination) has been referred to. Few, if any, are the occasions when the writer of the stories in this collection allows you or me to slip through his fingers. I suggest that what rivets one to a Sansom story is a form of compulsion, rather than "interest" in the more usual, leisurely or reflective sense. The characters, the men and women protagonists, are not in themselves "interesting" – or at least to me. In the main they are pallid; the few more coloured ones (like Miss Great-Belt, the Danish beauty-contestant in "A Contest of Ladies") are, often, handsome wound-up automata, jerking through their small ranges of looks and gestures. The fatalism shown by most of these people is, one feels, neither desperate nor romantic; rather, it is the outcome of an incompetence which may shade off at any moment into sheer impotence. These people do not appeal to us, or attract our sympathies. But to say that they "fail" to do so would be misleading. Why? Because it has not for a single instant been their creator's intention that they *should* (interest, attract or appeal to us, I mean). The enormous suspense element in a Sansom story is generated in no ordinary way. Since we care little for, or about, these people, do we greatly care what happens to them? Why, no! Then how are we held? We are held not by what happens but by how it happens. The substance of a Sansom story is sensation. The subject is sensation. The emotions are sensations of emotion. The crisis (to be depended upon to be "sensational" in the accepted sense) is a matter of bringing sensation to a peak where it must either splinter or dissolve because it can no more. Or it may, sometimes, simply, ironically and altogether subside . . . We accompany, thus, the nominal Sansom "character" throughout the ups-and-downs of fear, or infatuation, or suspicion, or daydream-success, or amazement, or apprehension, or whatever it be. We ease off during the inter-missions, let-ups and pauses allowed by the malady or the ordeal (or, it may be, the delight) only to quiver under the shock of renewed assault.

Held we are: either rooted, like the firemen looking up at the falling wall in "The Wall," or gummed, like the youth scaling the gasometer in "The Vertical Ladder."

A Sansom story is a *tour de force*. Readers who dislike, mistrust or resent that should turn to something other than this volume. In me these stories induce, also, suspense of another kind, call it sympathetic suspense – will they come off? It is staggering how they do. Their doing so is anything but a matter of fortuity. Nothing here is slapdash or "got away with." The writer has taken, and shown himself right in taking, a succession of calculated risks. He is not writing *for* effect, he is dealing *in* it, and masterfully. For his purposes, vocabulary is clearly very important – vocabulary in the literal sense, in the matter of words, yes; but also there has to be a complete command of the vocabulary of the senses. To have knowledge of, to be able to call up into what in the story is actuality, to be able not merely to convey to the reader but impose on him (almost, inflict on him) smells, tastes, sounds rendered complex or curious by acoustics or echoes, differences (as though under the touch) of surfaces, gradations of light and its watery running off into shadow – this was essential for the writer of the Sansom stories. Equally, the writing of these stories, these particular stories, as they come to us, must have been an essential for William Sansom – burdened, he would have otherwise been, with a useless faculty.

Weather is part of the vocabulary. "The day slate-dark, the air still, the cindertrack by the cottages without life in a watered middle-day light" – is the overture to "Something Terrible, Something Lovely." The visage of the house in "A Saving Grace" (the house from out of whose open door one by one the dead are to proceed, the dog and all, to group themselves smilingly on the lawn, as though for a photograph), is framed in "the hour before dusk . . . when the hot afternoon is grown old and cool." There are, again and again, in "A Country Walk," those weather-passages betraying the terrible animosity of Nature. Such as:

> The shadow of a cloud was passing over the map, it came towards him like a fast-moving tide, heaving the hills as it came.
> A simple matter? Not so simple. He watched it, he began to judge whether it would envelop him or not. It came at a fast windblown pace, eating up the fields, blotting out life like the edge of a dangerous sea moving in.
> The whole countryside grew more inimical. Every deep acre of this ancient sleeping earth breathed a quiet, purposeful life – and it was against him. Not now the simple material conflict with

animals – the grave earth itself and the green things growing in collusion with it took on presence and, never moving, breathed a quiet hatred on to the mineral air.

Animals, birds also are part of the vocabulary – they seem, at the moments of their emergences, long to have existed *within* it, behind all words. Corsican robins, the lion at liberty in the middle of the dahlia-edged path, and those dogs of Siena – Enrico, Osvaldo, Fa. And, in the Hampstead garden, "isolated at the very top of a tall sapling, crouched on the tapering end of this thin shoot so that it bent over under the weight like a burdened spring . . . a huge dazed cat."

The Stories of William Sansom speak for themselves. A peril of introduction is that it can go on for too long. So this breaks off, though there could be more to say.

A Matter of Inspiration

The British reader's concept of the American literary scene can but be limited, at the start, by the number and kind of your books which appear in England – appear, that is to say, under the imprimatur of London publishers. These do, on the whole, show an increasing flair, enterprise, confidence in their selection of American work: reciprocally, it is for the public to keep abreast of them, and, most of all, for reviewers to spotlight what is the best. Our book market and book circulation suffer both from the rise in costs of production and the shrinkage of reviewing space in our papers, due to the newsprint shortage: thus it is at once more risky to publish books and harder for books, having been published, to be intelligently discussed. The habitual book-buyer, these days, must think twice; the more mobile reader, looking for what is new, feels the lack of fuller critical guidance. This militates, sadly, against the writer, "foreign" or indigenous, who still has his name to make;

and our publishers may be a degree more cautious in the former, as opposed to the latter, case.

As against that, we have at present an author shortage, or what appears to be one; which leaves receptive space for an intake of work from outside this country. Literary isolationism – if such were ever desired – is of necessity broken down. Continental writers – French, Italian, and German – in translations which often come to us via you, are moving forward on our publishers' lists. On those lists, however, the major part of what is not British continues to be American – novels and collections of short stories, books on the world situation, works of humour, biographies (though these, I consider, are too severely limited), and "mysteries" ("detective stories" to us). On the scholarly side, we owe an increasing debt to American literary research. Your prominent critics, such as Edmund Wilson, Lionel Trilling, are on the ascendent with us – we should, though, also, have access to more of the bulk of your critical writing. We do not receive enough American history; nor does anything like enough American contemporary poetry come our way – though, as to that, one must take into account that our own younger poets have to combat neglect.

Are such American books as do come to us representative of today's American writing; or, are they more representative of our publishers' notion of British taste? The latter, to an extent, can but be true – as it must be true also in reverse: only such British books as bid fair to survive the journey are likely to make their debut in America. Ultimately, on both sides of the Atlantic, it rests with the public to exert positive taste – to be quickly receptive, hospitable, exploratory. Till then, the restrictive filter remains – or remains, at least, in its action on the average reader – dependent on book club, bookshop, or local library. He, here in Britain, receives his quota of London-published American books – reacts to them, ponders over them, likes them, is sometimes puzzled, and, above all, builds up out of them his personal, inner conception of America. The novel, the work of humour, the tale of crime, is to him also something of a document – he informs himself as to ways of living, manners, beliefs, traditions, food, sport, cities, and countrysides which are sometimes like, sometimes unlike, those he already knows. The sheer giant geographical size, and, within that, the infinite contrasts and variations of the United States are not easy for him to grasp: his final and – can one wonder! – confused and amazing image is put together out of a sort of compost of the late Sinclair Lewis, William Faulkner, Mrs. Frances Parkinson Keyes,[1] Raymond Chandler,[2] John Marquand,[3] James Thurber, Dos Passos, Ellery Queen.[4]

We have, however, readers, a smaller group, who discriminatingly pursue American writing – subscribe to your periodicals, learn from visiting friends, or, if they are lucky, receive as gifts American books not so far published here and not due to reach us for some time, if indeed at all. Such readers, with whom literature *qua* literature is a passion, are in a great number of cases writers also. As writers, they may have been among the fortunate who have been allowed (allowed, that is, in view of the present rigid British travel restrictions) to visit America. If so they will have headed, without delay, for the fascinating, dementing bookshops, to scan the output of the year and begin to realise what they have missed at home. They will have impinged on New York's or other cities' literary circles, heard the talk, marked the tendencies, traced the currents. It has been their right and duty, at the end of their stay, to return with some books in hand, and rumours of others – both are to be of value to untravelled friends of their own sort. Perpetual expectation is one of the joys of the literature-lover – what is emerging? – what is about to break? – who is to be the next of the radiant newcomers? All writers, all eager readers, however, may not be travellers. Those who remain in Britain must fall on, and make the most of, what comes to them, however slowly, through the accepted channels. It is on such a group, in the main, that our more adventurous publishers keep their eye – friendly critics, infectious talkers may do much to advance and support the fortunes of such of your *avant-garde* books as reach our shores. The influence of this alert minority is important.

Through them indeed, at the start, may have come about Britain's present, marked, if still just a trifle wary, predisposition towards American books; and, still more, this country's susceptibility to what may be called the whole force of American style – its mobility, its range, and its vividness. We have, first, the sense that here is something contemporary – a pace, a tempo, a psychic as well as verbal vocabulary which reflects, expresses the day in which we all live. With us, a whole tract of consciousness, of nervous sensation and mental flight (which is in fact our reaction to the twentieth century) still tends to reach beyond our means of expression – or, put it that our means of expression lags behind what we apprehend, know, and feel. A new language has to be found: we believe that America may be finding it. That such a style has its dangers, pitfalls, and possible limitations, that at its worst it may travesty and deride itself, we are no less, though also no more, aware than are the sterner of your own critics. Are we still seeking, has America found, a sort of shorthand of the sensations? But also, behind that, is there not about to be something more – an interpretation, the evidence of a spiritual search through the weight, glare, roar, and strain of a material world?

In writing, how shall one distinguish between matter and manner? Were one to attempt the distinction, it might be said that while the matter of American writing (the scenes depicted, situations unfolded, characters portrayed) interests, informs, and entertains us, it is the manner to which we react most strongly – the short, firm, sometimes elliptic sentences, the command of the visual (so that, in effect, a page is like a cinema screen), and the speed, shape, and vitality of the dialogue. Any of those three attributes can, we perceive, go too far, at peril of over-slickness and over-streamlining. At the best, there is tautness – a quality we are inclined to lack – at the worst (or at least good) an effect of feverish strain. Inevitably it is the extremes or exaggerations of American writing which tend to be imitated – and, unknowingly, parodied – by admirers here: the subtler precisions and rhythms, significant imagery, lovely evocations of your artist-writers defy imitation no less than they do analysis. One must allow for the time lag between country and country: the general British conception of American style dates back, it would not be unfair to say, to that of about twenty-five years ago. Slow (at least, until recently) in discovery, we are slower still in perception of the growth and change, the emerging potentialities, the newer disciplines. American fiction (and it is generally fiction we have in mind) in the first place broke on us by shock tactics.

The shock was agreeable: it was connected chiefly with the earlier novels of Ernest Hemingway. His, as technique, seemed to us revolutionary; and we may still fairly suppose it was. Hemingway impacted on England during that period, after the First World War, when we were at our most aesthetically susceptible – weary of old forms, harkening for new voices. He broke ground, here, not only for himself but for his American generation – the more difficult William Faulkner was to be next for us. For some time, it was hard to unclutter these writers' work from a haze of adjectives, such as "tough" and "sophisticated," or, in Faulkner's case, "torrid." The sheer fact of these two being so unalike suggested that they must be opposite poles, between whom stretched a terrain of so far uncharted creative power. Together, they changed our idea of fiction – already shaken out of its prewar mould by the upheavals of 1914–18. At the same time the French, with their Balzac-Stendhal-Flaubert tradition behind them, were, too, in throes of experimentation, and thereby communicated excitement to us: fuel was added to our creative wish as translation from Russian – Tolstoy, Turgenev, Chekhov – came pouring in. The world, to us who were young in the 1920s, seemed only to wait to be re-expressed – but, before that, we must re-animate our English language. Two young American writers gave us evidence that re-animation had already occurred.

The stimulus we got from you was immense; and not only that but it recurs. As to technique we, though fascinated by yours, must continue to struggle to forge our own – there is nothing, really, racial about technique, nor any general solution to its problems: at this, as on your side of the Atlantic, each individual writer works alone. What is encouraging is any sign of mastery – such as your writers give us from time to time. But American literature speaks to us, most of all, by that high, strange intensity of imagination which it holds at its best – sometimes in its mood of regional beauty, sometimes in unaccommodating fierceness, sometimes in prophetic craziness – e.g., Thurber. Thurber indeed now reigns amongst us, unrivalled.

We are commanded by the genius of your writers of the South; still by Faulkner, and by Eudora Welty; Carson McCullers, always known to a few, is beginning to enter, here, on a larger kingdom. In the field of the novel more classic and more direct, rediscovered Scott Fitzgerald excites us. And within the last year, in particular, two first novels, *The Trouble in One House*, by Brendan Gill,[5] and *A Long Day's Dying*, by Frederick Buechner,[6] have aroused us, and left a profound effect.

How far is your influence to be traced in our writing? It would be hard to answer. Creative writers of worth go through tuitional phases of imitation; they pass beyond that, find themselves – but they are always learning, quick to absorb what is in the air of the time, acquisitive of what they respect or admire. I cannot doubt that some of us have learned method from you. It has not been though, I think, between our two countries a matter so much of influence as of inspiration. Your impetus has refreshed and acted on ours; your vision adds to our power to see.

Introduction to An Angela Thirkell Omnibus

These three novels are vintage Thirkells – they mark, indeed, the opening of their author's career. *Ankle Deep* and *High Rising* both came out in 1933; *Wild Strawberries* followed a year later – and from then on, Angela Thirkell continued in full spate. Books came from her in an unbroken succession, one, sometimes two, a year: at the time of her death, 1959,[1] she was halfway through yet another. Yet – and surely this is remarkable? – there is nothing "torrential" about her writing. Nobody could have called it a headlong overflow: on the contrary, each of her books could seem to the reader to have been conceived with a greater deliberation and worked upon within a far greater leisure than her timetable can, in fact, have allowed her. Thus, in spite of her mighty production-rate, she escaped the fate of "torrential" writers – she never seems to have flooded her own market.

In another way this novelist was unusual, and fortunate. She lost no time in getting into her stride. That, one sees from these three, her earliest, novels: *Ankle Deep, High Rising* and *Wild Strawberries* are already technically, as shapely, sure, adroit and accomplished as any "Angela Thirkell's" that came later. Writers who having floundered through the "beginner stage" would fain have their early works consigned to oblivion may well envy her. Mrs. Thirkell, it would appear, simply began. True, she was not a young woman when she embarked on *Ankle Deep* – which could not have been written by a young woman. Two marriages, their accompanying vicissitudes, the in her case doubtful blessings of motherhood, and years of exile in an unsympathetic continent lay behind her. Life had more than provided her with material – that, however, can in no way account for the temperate dexterity of her pen. More to the point is, she had *written* already – during the time in Australia her output of satirical essays, critical pieces, short stories for Melbourne periodicals had been a fairly steady one. But to address oneself to full-length fiction, with its formidable, infernal, inherent problems was another and momentously different thing. Mrs. Thirkell's instantaneous success does not alter the fact that she showed courage. She set out with two assets: style (an inherited sense of it) and her own way of seeing things. Both helped.

Ankle Deep, High Rising and *Wild Strawberries* all have for some time been out of print. They now are re-published for the good reason that they make very good reading. They should revive the name of Angela Thirkell. They have considerable "period" interest, for they embody the atmosphere, manners, morals, conversational idiom and general outlook on life of the early 1930s in England (London and country). Their still greater interest – to me, at least – is, that in them we meet various Thirkell characters going for a preliminary canter. And there are as-it-were sketches of situations which will recur, perhaps more fully developed or quite differently handled, in the many more Thirkell novels time is to bring. In a sense, these three, with their totally different themes, can be ranked as prototype Thirkell novels – or, if you wish, try-outs (though expert ones) or samples. Back to one or another of these originals may be traced – I suggest? – the descent of all later works. *Ankle Deep* to me is the least pleasing. Thanks to the wonderful virtuosity of her story-telling, Mrs. Thirkell just gets away with her plaintive heroine – only just, though. Aurea is a temperature-lowerer, if ever there was one. That the full-blooded Valentine, her lover in name and would-be lover in fact, puts up with her whimsical dilly-dallying is amazing – and, somehow, faintly unholy. For all its Kensington cosiness (leafy squares) and clear-cut comedy portraiture (bouncy Fanny) *Ankle Deep* seems over-hung, therefore sinister. Has it that characteristic of most first novels, a too close involvement with its writer's past? . . . *High Rising* is a different kettle of fish. This is the first of the pastorals, although the main cast are non-indigenous literati: Laura Morland and George Knox, their children, respective publishers, and secretaries. *High Rising* is sterling comedy, with a touch of the knockabout (overturned car, lost hairpins) and – perhaps? – a streak of not quite agreeable cruelty: the hunting-down of the County Cork nymphomaniac. Lyricism has yet to appear; and does, intermingled with irony, in *Wild Strawberries*. In this third novel, too, we are to step over the line between the landless and landed gentry.

Wild Strawberries was the first of the great Thirkell endearing novels. It was with *Wild Strawberries*, I feel certain, that our author for the first time ensnared her public – as apart from challenging or amusing them. A sort of Circe strain appears in her writing. She unleashes upon us a host of enchanting persons; we are enclosed in a world of bewitching absurdity, graceful delinquency, serenity, undulant Christianity, effrontery. Above all, however, we are in the domain of order: living tradition. Chaos and doubt, alike, lie far from Rushwater House, in its golden landscape. There are no under-dogs. There is one toady. There is our first consignment of funny foreigners.

Lady Emily, of Rushwater, and her tribe of Leslies were to spark off a train of dynastic novels: setting, Barsetshire county. (Trollope would have been charmed by this graceful borrowing.) Angela

Thirkell's neo-Barsetshire topography becomes established, as by the hand of a master, compellingly, lovingly and entrancingly. So do its family trees. As time goes on (in the outer *and* Thirkell worlds) we are, more and more, riveted by these entrenched households. Deaths, inter-marriages, births – no waiting Nannie is ever left empty-handed . . . I believe, and hold the belief most truly, that it was the durability of these people, their staying-power, that fascinated Angela Thirkell. She has been called a snob. But mere snobbishness is barren; it's not creative. I would suggest, rather, that a passionate idealisation was at work.

Durability was to be the theme of her war-time novels: World War II. (In the novels in this compendium the "war" still haunting the air is World War I.) She chronicled; and I hold she has left behind her chronicles which are to be of value. With an eye sharpened by anger, she witnessed also social transitions, abandonments, disappearances. Alas, after the 1945 Labour landslide, cantankerousness was to infect her work and begin to chill her admirers – they so wished she wouldn't . . . ! And her attitude was to draw down upon her a scathingness from those who least knew her virtues.

I see Angela Thirkell as the last, and most memorable, of the Edwardians – and how good *they* were! She belongs to the time when novels were read for pleasure, and imparted pleasure through having wit. Her verve, her stylishness, her engagingness, her reckless funniness and her crystal melancholy remain unparalleled. She invites one to see, to savour, to discriminate, to enjoy – or hate! One charge against her has been, that she was "unfeeling." Was it that, in her novels, as also (apparently) in her life, she rode her emotions upon a tight rein? Or was it, as her eldest son believes, that "she was not able to give"? He goes on to say: "Hers was the tragedy of the inarticulate heart."

Here heart had no time, perhaps? A frenetic energy drove her along, as remorselessly[2] as she in turn drove others. Her production-rate as a novelist seems less startling when one glimpses her in her fierce pre-novelist days – thanks to that same son Graham McInnes's *The Road to Gundagai*,[3] a boy's-eye view of family life. Housewife in a ramshackle Australian-suburban bungalow, she kept her flag flying. High standards were (literally) beaten into her children . . . Leisure, gentleness, beauty were far from Angela Thirkell. That in her art she should dwell on them, bestowing them on the creatures of her fancy, was, I think, natural – and is moving. All honour to her.

A Passage to E. M. Forster

There was something to be said for first reading E. M. Forster when I did: 1915. I was then a schoolgirl. In those days, The Novel was not yet a classroom subject. One took notes on Fielding and Richardson, but there it stopped. The copious Victorians had been read aloud to many of us at home, or at school were part of the informality of the drawing-room evenings. In our free time we were, I am glad to say, left to ourselves: our recreational reading of living authors was hit-or-miss – with regard to anything in our own century our likings and judgements were not directed; which was to say, not tampered with. At the boarding-school I was at, a nominal censorship of books brought back after the holidays existed; I recall few collisions with that, and certainly *The Celestial Omnibus* (the 1911 Sidgwick and Jackson edition)[1] met no trouble. Absolutely nothing was known about the author, for or against. The importer, a friend of mine, lent the book round her personal circle. The format itself, fawn-grey binding indented prettily with a gilt pattern, nice-looking thick paper and large print, was promising and beguiling. The contents set up not only an instant enthusiasm but an *engouement*:[2] we were ready to go to any lengths, any expenditure of pocket money, to get hold of more from the same pen. A second-hand copy of *A Room with a View* was procured.

Not long after, I independently had a stroke of luck; investigating a half-empty valise in an attic at the top of an aunt's house, I came upon *Howards End*. Its bedfellows in the valise were, I remember, two books of poetry, Walt Whitman and W. E. Henley.[3] The entombment of these three was, I learned, accounted for by their being relics: they had been the favourite reading of another of my aunts, who was now dead. "Constance," explained her sister, looking at them with feeling as they returned to daylight in my hands, "was very intellectual." However, I was allowed to keep them.

That substantial, scarlet copy of *Howards End* bore the publication date 1910: can it have been, I now wonder, a first edition? After some years, with a then characteristic fecklessness, I lost it. I wonder in whose hands it is now.

The loss, under the circumstances, was catastrophic; it doomed me to remain without *Howards End* for I don't know how long. My passion for Forster novels had, in fact, formed itself during a time when they were increasingly difficult to obtain – the fourteen-year interim between *Howards End* and *A Passage to India*. Owing, one can only suppose, to the novelist's suspension of his activities, and so to a slackening of interest in him, the books for which I thirsted went out of print. The frustration was bitter. The sensation created in 1924 by *A Passage to India* having revived demand for its predecessors, they were reissued, bound to match in aubergine: the Collected Edition.

The lucidity of Forster's writing was, I suppose, what attracted me first of all. Adult fiction had hitherto riled and bothered me by being not only elaborate but, it seemed, fussily enigmatic. It appeared to go out of its way to avoid being straightforward. An Edwardian child, I had given a fair try to such Edwardian novels as came my way, or could be sneaked off tables. All of them had a sort of clique-ish alikeness. I see now, it could have been absence of this which made Forster novels disconcerting to my seniors – who, after all, constituted that vague yet powerful mass, "the reading public." In what other possible way did Forster transgress? The light was too clear, perhaps, the air just too bracing? Or was it that the novels were revolutionary in a manner impossible to pin down? There were few outright aggressions, none of the boldnesses associated with Mr. Wells and Mr. Shaw. Not a single overt hostility met the eye. As story-telling, the story-telling was of an adroitness which confronted no reader with hitch or obstacle. All was – one might have thought – in order.

And why not? For, it is interesting to reflect, the E. M. Forster of all the novels but *A Passage to India* was an Edwardian, and not only chronologically. His work, immaculately turned out, shows the engaging professionalism required in that day. The perfection, or perfectedness, of the novels, qua novels, is wonderfully and civilly inconspicuous: throughout, they are brisk, enticing and shapely. They could appear "light," from their execution being so light-handed. The desideratum for the Edwardian novel was, that it could be read easily and enjoyably. Tension, yes; but let the tension be alleviated by charm and humour. With this, surely, *Where Angels Fear to Tread* (1905), *A Room with a View* (1908), and *Howards End* (1910) comply. *The Longest Journey* (1907) does not; it not so much fails as refuses to; here and there there are affabilities, but the whole is daunting.

I, at any rate, came to *The Celestial Omnibus* with an open mind, the book having no connection with any other, or, for that matter, with anything else. In 1915 one was fortunate in being too young to have formed attachments, for the Great War, opening like a chasm, had swallowed up the immediate past – its tenets, its sayings, its personalities, its *idées reçues*. One was freed from those, at however dreadful a price. Landmarks were swept away, and one did not miss them: they had not been one's own. One began to require those that should be one's own. Where I was concerned, this book became one. The stories within it were revelations – come though they might to be looked back upon, afterwards, as foretastes. Each was a formidable entity on its own. I had had no notion that such things could be done. Few of them, actually, can have attracted me by their subjects: I loathed Pan,[4] for instance, and was inclined to look on the supernatural, other than in the course of a straight ghost story, as fishy. (I liked Miss Beaumont, in "Other Kingdom," however, because she bamboozled a pack of bores, and I ardently took sides with old Mr. Lucas, in "The Road from Colonus," against the dull daughter who cheated him of his fate, while the title story

confirmed my feeling for ancient alleys between suburban walls.)
No, the magic was not in the matter but in the manner, the telling,
the creation of a peculiar, electric climate in which *anything* might
happen. In itself, the writing acted on me as an aesthetic shock.
There was a blaze of unforeseen possibilities. For instance, the
welding of the inexplicable and the banal . . . At the same time,
banality was so treated as to make it appear not only fascinating in
itself but absolutely (one might have thought) impervious. With
each page, one was in the presence of a growing, not yet definable
danger, the blindness of those endangered being part of the spell.

There was a depiction of people in terms not of mockery but of
an irony partly holding mockery in curb, partly rendering it super-
fluous. There were types, I noted, to whom the author extended
no loving-kindness: they were his targets. The woolly-minded,
however fatuous, he let pass; but woe to the complacent, and above
all to the culturally pretentious! *Vide* Mr. Bons in "The Celestial
Omnibus":

> Yet even Mr. Bons could only say that the sign-post was a joke –
> the joke of a person named Shelley.
> "Of course!" cried the mother; "I told you so, dear. That was
> the name."
> "Had you never heard of Shelley?" asked Mr. Bons.
> "No," said the boy, and hung his head.
> "But is there no Shelley in the house?"
> "Why, yes!" exclaimed the lady, in much agitation. "Dear Mr.
> Bons, we aren't such Philistines as that. Two at the least. One a
> wedding present, and the other, smaller print, in one of the spare
> rooms."
> "I believe we have seven Shelleys," said Mr. Bons, with a slow
> smile. Then he brushed the cake crumbs off his stomach, and,
> together with his daughter, rose to go.

The gruesome death-crash of Mr. Bons is merited: justice is more
rather than less inexorable when it is poetic. The wicked are their
own executioners, impaling themselves, unaided, on their dooms

. . . Ultimately, though, for me, the central, most powerful magnetism of *The Celestial Omnibus* stories was in their "place-feeling." In each of them action was not only inseparable from its setting but seemed constantly coloured by it and, in one or two cases, even, directly and fatefully set at work by it; and of this there was to be, when I came to the novels, more, much more. E. M. Forster, in his introduction (1947) to the *Collected Short Stories*, admits that two of them – "The Story of a Panic" and "The Road from Colonus" – were inspired by their scenes. "One of my novels," he continues, "*The Longest Journey*, does indeed depend from an encounter with the *genius loci*, but indirectly, complicatedly, not here to be considered. Directly, the *genius loci* has only inspired me thrice." (The third case was a short story, "The Rock," excluded as an "ill-fated effort.") Intense sense of locality, and deference if not subjection to its power could in itself make distinguishable, did nothing else, the Forster atmosphere. My own tendency to attribute significance to places, or be mesmerised by them even for no knowable reason, then haunted by them, became warranted by its larger reflection in E. M. Forster. Formerly I had feared it might be a malady.

The conversations – in fact, the dialogue of which the stories consisted so very largely – whetted my appetite for more. I had met the like, for lifelikeness, only in *Alice's Adventures in Wonderland*. Here, if there was less diabolical repartee than in the Carroll universe, there was no less effectiveness. One was startled by the extent to which people are characterised by their own words, most of all by those thoughtlessly spoken. How they deliver themselves over to one another by so much as opening their mouths! And the more they do not intend to, the more they do so. That the greater number of speakers of Forster dialogue are either conventional or inarticulate (or both, sometimes) made, for me, their involuntary eloquence more memorable. I learned, also, from these premonitory stories, how great can be the striking-power of the thing said. Forster talkers are always precipitants of *something*. When (for the time being) they have done, a situation has changed for better or worse. Even a random, witless, wandering exclamation or observation has its potentially dangerous edge. Here or there, the voice of a lover, a rebel, a visionary, a juvenile or a simple person rises out of the trammels of its vocabulary into the empyrean of poetry. Yet all stays within the bounds of "ordinary" diction. That seemed to me to be semi-miraculous: I was right, it is. Untaught, I perceived in Forster the master dialogue-writer of our century. Variants and experiments continue to run their lively and harmless course. Basic – because, I imagine, instinctive – knowledge of the "how," not only the "why," of talking remains his . . . I look back on *The Celestial Omnibus* as an experience. Outside poetry, it was my first experience of originality – as such, unrepeatable. I mean, it could never again be mine with its original virtue. I do not know when last I reread the stories. They were an excitement; they were an incitement also.

Of the five Forster novels, the first four burst on the world in a sort of glorious rush, at a time (1905 to 1910) when I was too young to know what was going on. As I read them in no particular order, other than that in which I succeeded in getting hold of them, chronology plays little or no part in my indelible notion of Forster novels. As far as I am concerned, they remain phenomena. By which I do not mean isolated phenomena; their spiritual attachment to one another could not but be evident from the start, as one by one they entered into my cognisance. That their virtue is, in the highest sense, communal was not lost on me once I knew them all. I perceive now what I may not have perceived at first, that from each one sprang not only the impetus but the necessity for the one to follow. What was yet to be written would have been nascent, latent, in what was being written at the time; equally, what already had been written (or created) was present in what *was* being written, adding to the comprehensibility in depth. . . . I am debarred, as is to be seen, from tracing the "development," as a novelist, of E. M. Forster, even did I not feel, as I do, that it would be impertinent to attempt to do so. As a matter of fact, I do not believe that novelists do develop: they enlarge. Their area widens; their authority (in some cases) strengthens itself. I say "in some cases" because in that of E. M. Forster this not only was unnecessary but would have been impossible: the author of *Where Angels Fear to Tread* had, already, as much authority as the author of *A Passage to India*.

To revert to the striking-power I first noted in the dialogue in *The Celestial Omnibus*: I saw increasingly, as I came to the novels, how essential it was that the characters be armed – quick on the draw, at the ready. The E. M. Forster majority are more than effectively armed with words. The few who are physically aggressive (Gino, for example, in *Where Angels Fear to Tread*, Charles Wilcox in *Howards End*) are caused to explode into their aggressions by a rising and maddening pressure: their inarticulateness. The world of these novels is a world of conflict; its not being a world actually *in* conflict, fraught by battles and revolutions, makes the schisms within and oppositions between its people stand out more significantly and strongly. As does also, by contrast, the exterior gentleness: dramatically seldom is the surface – ironic, amiable, civilised, mannerly – cracked right across. True, few novels omit conflict, without which they would risk having no plot; simply, in many the conflict seems artificial, or manufactured to serve its purpose, rather than inescapable and inherent. Conflicts in Forster novels are inherent, radically inevitable. They are part of the continuous struggle for integrity. They are part of the way towards understanding: they desire solution. In this aspect the world of the Forster novel cannot but be instantly familiar, commanding and convincing, to a young reader. For me, it had more than verisimilitude; I arrived into it with a sense of homecoming. In this sense, Forster is a novelist for the young. He is no liar. He does not misrepresent.

He was, in fact, young when he wrote these books: twenty-six in 1905, when *Where Angels Fear to Tread* appeared; only five years older when *Howards End* did so, not far into his forties when, after the interim, came *A Passage to India*. One can now see, from the vantage point of one's own maturity (as no doubt he does) how capable he then was of injustices – sweeping, drastic, high-handed, high-minded youthful injustices. (Is it because he is now just that we have no more novels?) He is, was, an intemperate novelist; the intemperance of Dickens, whom I love also, stands out more conspicuously, but is hardly greater. E. M. Forster is not universally kind to people in the sense that people are taught to be kind to animals. Some of his leading characters he is drawn to (the Honeychurch family, all three); some he has a sterling regard for (Margaret Schlegel); some he cannot prevent himself from idealising (Stephen Wonham). He would *like* to like; in which he resembles the undergraduate Rickie Elliot. Here, from an early page of *The Longest Journey*, is an excerpt (cut) from one of those Cambridge conversations:

"Elliot is in a dangerous state," said Ansell . . .

"How's that?" asked Rickie, who had not known he was in any state at all . . .

"He's trying to like people."

"Then he's done for," said Widdrington. "He's dead."

"He's trying to like Hornblower."

The others gave shrill agonised cries.

"He wants to bind the college together. He wants to link us to the beefy set."

"I do like Hornblower," he protested. "I don't try."

"And Hornblower tries to like you."

"That part doesn't matter."

"But he does try to like you. He tries not to despise you. It is altogether a most public-spirited affair."

"Tilliard started them," said Widdrington. "Tilliard thinks it such a pity the college should be split into sets" . . .

"The college isn't split," cried Rickie, who got excited on this subject with unfailing regularity. "The college is, and has been, and always will be, one. What you call the beefy set aren't a set at all. They're just the rowing people, and naturally they chiefly see each other; but they're always nice to me or to anyone. Of course, they think us rather asses, but it's quite in a pleasant way."

"That's my whole objection," said Ansell. "What right have they to think us asses in a pleasant way? Why don't they hate us? What right has Hornblower to smack me on the back when I've been rude to him?"

"Well, what right have you to be rude to him?"

"Because I hate him. You think it so splendid to hate no one. I tell you it is a crime. You want to love every one equally, and that's worse than impossible – it's wrong. When you denounce sets, you're really trying to destroy friendship."

"I maintain," said Rickie – it was a verb he clung to, in the hope that it would lend stability to what followed – "I maintain that one can like many more people than one supposes."

"And I maintain that you hate many more people than you pretend."

Rickie's Cambridge was Forster's: it was, one is reminded, the Cambridge of the Apostles.[5]

But, when it comes to what I spoke of as comprehensibility in depth, the novels go beyond the capacities of youth. They contain more than the still-youthful reader requires, or knows how to look for, or would know how to handle were it come upon. The more often one reads them, and, still more, the later on into life one reads them, the deeper in one goes and the more they mean. These books at once expand and intensify, as does (or should) an individual human life. Did their author, even, originally realise their full content, or how much they involved? It would not shock me to think that he did not – at the time. He himself speaks, in *Aspects of the Novel* (1927), of the prophetic element to be sometimes found in it: the book may anticipate a consciousness yet to be. The Forster novels would seem to belong by nature to a time considerably later than their own (than, that is, the decade in which four of the five were written). They have characteristics which can have only slowly become apparent: they are, for instance, both more primitive and more religious than at first they may have been seen to be. What was once, I gather, known as their "paganism" easily brushes off; not so their physical mysticism.

Love. When is a kiss right, when is it wrong? Look from *A Room with a View* to *Howards End*. Why does George Emerson's kissing of Lucy Honeychurch, on the violet-blue hillside above Florence, bring about a solution and a redemption, and Paul Wilcox's kissing of Helen Schlegel, in the summery night of his father's garden, leave behind it a vacuum, to be filled only by "telegrams and anger"? Lucy reacts with injury, Helen with rapture; yet it is Helen who is to be the casualty. Both kisses were impulses – inspirations. Were not both, then, equally innocent? No; the Wilcox kiss had a tainted source. Falsification of what is between the sexes, and the possibility of fighting a way out of it, only just escapes being a Forster obsession. Actively present in all five novels, it is a constituent of their conflicts. Subsidiary in *A Passage to India*, it none the less brings about the main crisis: what *did* cause Adela Quested's delusion in the Marabar cave, and spark off the charge she brought against Dr. Aziz? . . . And yet the thing has its fearsomely funny side. Without it, where would be Forster comedy? Could one forego the train journey of the guests into Shropshire, for Evie Wilcox's wedding?

> The low rich purr of a Great Western express is not the worst background for conversation, and the journey passed pleasantly enough. Nothing could have exceeded the kindness of the two men. They raised windows for some ladies, and lowered them for others, they rang the bell for the servant, they identified the colleges as the train slipped past Oxford, they caught books or bag-purses in the act of tumbling on to the floor. Yet there was nothing finicking about their politeness: it had the Public School touch, and, though sedulous, was virile. More battles than Waterloo have been won on our playing-fields, and Margaret bowed to a charm of which she did not wholly approve, and said nothing when the Oxford colleges were identified wrongly. "Male and female created He them"; the journey to Shrewsbury confirmed this questionable statement, and the long glass saloon, that moved so easily and felt so comfortable, became a forcing-house for the idea of sex.

"The beefy set?" – cut down to size, polished up a little. It cannot be said that they transgress; they know nothing of the battle and the morality. They are without passion. The Forster *élite*, his central figures, are people of passion – without exception, I would say, were it not for *A Passage to India*: Adela, Ronnie, Fielding are cold fish. But then, there is Aziz. Very often the passions are submerged or muffled; they need to be – they are outlaw passions. They are called upon, also, to bridge gulfs. *Howards End*, the most violent of the novels, surges with them: hostility, pity, sense of injustice, hunger for knowledge are among those rocking the book. The Forster passions are not invariably sexual, or directly sexual. *The Longest Journey* is governed by passions which are not: Stephen Wonham's passion is for the earth on whose breast he sleeps at the very end of the novel. Stephen, the bastard half-brother, the doltish child of "poetry and revolution," at once complements Rickie and assuages him.

Above the battle, guardians of morality, are the elderly women. They have a Fate-like quality: Mrs. Honeychurch, Mrs. Wilcox, Mrs. Moore . . . Satanic Mrs. Failing and operative Mrs. Herriton rank just less highly. The great three are not only creatures of temperament but inject a further degree of temperament into the books they severally inhabit; two continue to do so after their deaths (Mrs. Honeychurch, fortunately, survives). They are capricious; they unaccountably veil themselves in huffiness. They are Nature. One passes directly on from them into weather and landscape. "Landscape"? – I mean, the formidable, ever-amazing shapes of pieces of country. The concern is with what these shapes give off, what they do to man. What do they not? They impart the sense of existence, of how ancient it can be, how volcanic it can be, and of how it continues. These are, therefore, the dominants in the novels – all the novels, not only *The Longest Journey* in its Wiltshire part. England, Italy, India, unalike, fascinating the pen as they do the eye by their singularities, have in common an underlying, impenetrable strangeness. In his unceasing awareness and awe of this resides, for me, no small part of the genius of E. M. Forster.

This piece of mine, called "A Passage to E. M. Forster," strikes me, now, that I near the end of it, as having had no particular bourne. I accepted the title, tentatively suggested by the book's editor, with no intention, or hope, of ever really converging upon the author. Who am I that I should? Neither do these pages qualify either as an appreciation or as a tribute. I have written, rather, a sort of auto- biography: the autobiography of an E. M. Forster reader. And when I say E. M. Forster, I mean the novelist, who was also the donor of the short stories. Some sort of recalcitrance makes me blind to him in any other capacity. Even within the bounds I have set myself, I should have done better than I have; I am aware of having been scrappy, arbitrary, over-impressionistic. I could be the first to point out glaring omissions. What, for instance, about the great part music plays in the novels? (The fact is that I am not musical.) Why have I referred less constantly, and more sketchily, to *A Passage to India* than to its fellows? I suppose because I resent its having stolen the thunder from them. But after all, autobiography is accorded the right to be disproportionate, prejudiced, and subjective. The main thing is that I am so saturated in the writing (the novel- and story- telling) of E. M. Forster that I find it hard to look on either the works or the author behind them objectively. I can think, also, of no English novelist who has influenced me more.

How lucky I am that it was he who did. It seems to me impossible for a writer, at his or her outset, not to be influenced. (Though, for the matter of that, who influenced *him*? One finds no traces.) I was reading him, and addictively, for some years before I thought of writing myself. (In those years I thought I was going to be a painter.) When I did begin, I do not mean that I copied him. More, he con- siderably affected my view of life, and, as I was to discover, my way of writing. For this influence I feel unqualified gratitude; without it, I should not even be what I am. I should like to close, however, by recording the joy he has given me, and by saying, I now see how this came about. In his 1925 Hogarth Press essay *Anonymity*, he says that when reading "The Ancient Mariner": "We have entered a universe that only answers to its own laws, supports itself, internally coheres, and has a new standard of truth." This is so, and has always been so, for me each time I enter a Forster novel.

Introduction to Staying with Relations, by Rose Macaulay

Staying With Relations is one of the most enjoyable, because in its own way most dementing, of the Rose Macaulay novels. A character comedy, it springs surprises at every turn. Nobody, or almost nobody, in the cast is, it transpires, what he or she had appeared to be. Nothing, it proves, can be so deceptive – or at least, so misleading – as human beings. But if we are bamboozled, so is our heroine. Catherine Grey, though by ten years senior to *Northanger Abbey*'s Catherine Morland, goes no less wildly astray in her suppositions. Catherine Grey is a novelist (now on holiday) with an occupational passion for "typing" people; through her eyes we see the nest of little-known relatives with whom she arrives to stay; with her misapprehensions we are to become entangled – to an extent which could be ideal in a detective story. (Rose Macaulay, one is reminded, delighted in detective stories.) This novel contains no actual crime, other than an attempted kidnapping, and – if that be ranked as a crime? – an illicit love affair, but a sense of tension, of impending crisis, of devious goings-on under the placid surface is ever there. Much, by the end, has dissolved in laughter, though there is a residuum that cannot.

Even had there been less combustible elements in Aunt Belle's household, the exotic-mysterious could not fail to surround it. For, the "little home" to which she invites her niece is in the darkest heart of Central America: an old Spanish plantation in a Guatemala forest. Isolation is absolute. Out of a long-derelict monastery, built on top of an ominous ancient temple, a blameless family villa had been constructed by Aunt Belle's first husband, a Texan oil king: the villa is in course of being transformed into a sophisticated baroque fantasy by her architect son-in-law and her stepchildren (all English: vintage, late 1920s). Three layers of culture, each at its most extreme: could anything more have fascinated the imagination of Rose Macaulay? The contrast between the cool, hyper-civilised junior group and their implacably primitive environment also is rich in possibilities; no one of which, the reader finds, has been missed. But it is Guatemala itself, its secretiveness, its suspended excitingness, its blend of the enormous with the claustrophobic, its pervasive psychic-physical climate, which has above all captivated the author. Guatemala is the dominant of the story. Where she writes of it, a dramatic sensuousness is released, full force. The characters *are* dwarfed; but how could they not be?

To commend, in a novelist, the "descriptive powers" is to evoke a somehow deadening idea. Out-and-out, categoric "description" is, in fact, a doomed and deadening activity – instinctively, genius has little truck with it. To cause a scene to spring so near to the eye that it almost burns, to affect the senses, to penetrate (as a scene can do) into the spirit, and, on some occasions, also delight the wits, is another thing. In *Staying With Relations*, a search-party's midnight flounderings through a forest still trembling after a shock of earthquake, foetid with overgrowth and darkness, alive, palpably, with inimical inhabitants, are unforgettable. No less, though, does the Macaulay magic work with an interior – in the following case, the (intellectually) bright young people's rehabilitation of the monks' chapel:

Claudia indicated with distaste a huge rood-screen which treated a painful theme with distressing realism.

"Latins like that sort of thing," Benet explained. "They're so strongminded. The English are too squeamish for it. That probably accounted for the Reformation in England. Anyhow, we thought we'd brighten the scene."

They had brightened it by adding two galleries like opera boxes on either side of the church, and filling them with male and female plaster saints of the most gentlemanly and lady-like appearance imaginable, apparently engaged in animated conversation, elegant adoration, or amiable interest in their surroundings. None of them either wore the smug appearance of many saints in churches, or clung morbidly to the instruments of their future decease like others. They behaved, in fact, like ladies and gentlemen, and their presence in the galleries, beneath gold-tasselled stucco curtains, gave to the little church the incongruous yet delightful quality of a Bibbiena opera house.

Staying With Relations was first published in 1930. It could be seen – though there is danger in seeing anything *too* simply – not only as a literary stepping-stone between one decade and another but as a transitional novel of Rose Macaulay's. In the Twenties, she had blazed upon the world as a brilliant satirist, wit, mocker, iconoclast – a writer more from the head than from the heart. *Potterism, Dangerous Ages, Mystery at Geneva, Told by an Idiot, Keeping Up Appearances* . . . She wrote for (or at least, was the delight of) a post-war generation on the rebound against emotion: one liked one's wine dry. Few among the enthusiasts knew, or may even have heard of, her more youthful novels, swept away in the deluge of 1914. And in their own day, even, *Abbots Verney* and *The Lee Shore* had been too ethereal, too individual, too internally "melancholy," or whatnot, to commend themselves widely to public favour. Could one say that, during the years when she was seen as diamond-bright, diamond-hard, another Rose Macaulay ran underground?

If so, re-emergence began with the 1930s. Significantly, the successor to *Staying With Relations* was to be the heroic *They Were Defeated*: tragic, austerely tender and wholly beautiful, set back in the century she best loved, fitly could have inhabited, and in many ways, in spirit, seemed to belong to.

From then on, the novels were to deepen in feeling. That they did so without loss to the edge of wit or lowering of the high spirit of comedy, and with an increase, if anything, of intellectual mastery is their triumph . . . How much of this is to be foreseen, or may be found to be already foreshadowed, in *Staying With Relations*? To begin with, I would suggest, there is less mockery: the most nearly ridiculous character, our heroine, incurs at worst a friendly-affectionate derision (poor creature, she was an incurable novelist, Heaven help her!). The agonies of the indeed injured but also hysterical girl-wife, Isie, and the dreadful scenes between her and her taut-nerved husband could not have been shown to be had they not been felt. The flashes of agony breaking through the almost super-human control of the futureless lovers are authentic. I have called this novel "a comedy": it ends up as one. In the whole cast, there is not one *âme damnée*: what is wild, what is inordinate, what is irreconcilable with any civilised theory as to existence is confined to, by being identified with, Nature, in Nature's limitless stamping-ground Guatemala. Bats whirl round; for moments, there are benighted silences. There are tremors. Something feverish even is in the sunshine. The utter descent of darkness is not more remorseless, or more unnerving, than the cold glints of dawn. We are not told, but may gather, that much the same goes on in the human soul.

FAIRY TALES

Comeback of Goldilocks et al.

A story must have a moral. Whether this axiom is based on the purest ethics, I have wondered. There being a moral – a point to be made, something to be demonstrated, or at least argued – ensures a firm grip on the story's audience. Should it fail to, our moral has been mishandled. Once felt, the moral makes for that sharp division known, at any game's outset, as "taking sides." (In this case, though, there is no doubt *which* side one is on!)

For excitement, one must have distinction, contrast – and what more clean-cut than those between Good and Bad, the Right and the Wrong? That, at least, was grasped in narrative's thriving days. Blurring of the distinction, or loss of certainty as to whether it does, or should, exist is detrimental to story-interest – bespeak as it may more fearless honesty or more complex sympathies. Stories (called novels) for so-called adults today more and more illustrate this. The fairy tale, primal juvenile fiction, remains immune from that sort of soft rot.

That fairy tales' morals may be peculiar, to the point at times of seeming defective, has been remarked. The fairy tale's move back into popularity – booksellers say they are selling more than ever today and publishers keep bringing out new and sumptuous editions – makes this important. What, then, is the effect on children who in increasing numbers turn (or return) to fairy tales? Do the raids made by Jack of the Beanstalk on the giant-ogre induce the notion that a boy's having shinned up an outsize beanstalk entitles him to *carte blanche* as to anything he finds at the top? And what was Goldilocks up to, making free with all that she found in the Three Bears' cottage, while its proprietors (socially unknown to her) were out?

Concealment of true fact, making of misleading statements (if not, indeed, outright fibbing), espionage, sly reprisals, unfair use of accomplices from the animal world, calculated trap-setting, tenacity with regard to grudges and grievances – with these, could not many a golden lad, and quite a representation of golden lasses of fairy tales' character-world, be charged? They could – but are they? By fairy-tale ruling, they not only get by but get by with laurels. Much is condoned.

Much is not. Disobedience, frivolity or forgetfulness, failure to follow instructions (and very closely), flouting of taboos, disregard of warnings, breaking of promises, defaulting from obligations, ingratitude – these incur severe penalties. The trend of the fairy tale is authoritarian. The prototype hero is, as often as not, acting under orders; the apparent free-lance, sooner or later, finds himself acting under advice. To ignore advice, as our lad soon finds, is as fatal as to contravene orders.

Who issues the orders, or deals out the advice? In all but a few cases, a supernatural being: a Good Fairy (usually of the female sex) or a male fairy-potentate – apt to make himself known from behind some grotesque or even repulsive disguise. Nonsupernatural order-givers – or advisers of the do-as-I-say-or-else kind, such as Good Kings – tend to have supernatural assistants, or what amounts to a supernatural warrant. The implication is – as I see it – that authority intrinsically is supernatural: accordingly, is not to be defied. It is, in intention, benevolent. It is all-knowing and all-seeing. By this reckoning, parents (other than Wicked Stepmothers) are, on the whole, built up. Not only anything *but* lawless but, on the whole, intimidatingly law-ridden, appears to be the world of the fairy tale.

Once get yourself into a hole by mistaken enterprise or by falling foul of your boss well-wisher and it's up to you to get yourself out of it. Here the wits must enter, bringing along with them, in their dubious train, the makeshift fibs, unpraiseworthy ingenuities and the seedy help-out allies above complained of. Those, as a child is able to see, are at once desperate measures and last resorts. Act right, then you won't be obliged to think, seems to be one of the morals of the fairy tale. (At the same time, if everyone *did* act right, there would be no tale: that we must face.)

For the grown-up, a fairy tale is a bracing vacation from sex interest; for the child, the immunity is normal. Little girls (or their seniors, beautiful maidens) take their chances along with the rest of the gang. How do feminine protagonists stand out – Red Riding

Hood, Goldilocks, Rapunzel, Snow White, Cinderella, the Sleeping Beauty?

The pick of them are resourceful and extra wilful. The marks go to Rapunzel for her use of her hair. The nerve showed by Red Riding Hood face-to-face with the Wolf in grandmother's bed, and the nippiness with which Goldilocks dodged the justly annoyed Three Bears, are also commendable.

Snow White, something of a cipher, might not have got as far as she did had she not been the adoptee of the Seven Dwarfs. Still more of a neutral seems to be Cinderella who, first mopey and later flustered, not only had luck her limpness little deserved but long-lasting fame (attendant upon her engendering of all "Cinderella stories"). An outstanding passive, the Sleeping Beauty demonstrates that you can't dodge predestined fate: asleep she was bound to fall, so, vain were precautions.

With the exception of my three favourites, most fairy-tale girls play the same role: they are first Victims, later Awards. (With Cinderella, the latter part is reversed – decidedly, she is an Award-recipient: award, the Prince.) Some, where the tale has chiefly masculine interest, keep right out of trouble and feature as Awards only (in which case, they are Beautiful Princesses). Few girl readers seem to object to this.

Fairy-tale morality, I contend, is child morality – child morality as it *could* be – untampered with (taking our child to be so far "average" as not to be, on the one hand, a moral defective or, on the other, an embryonic saint). Thus might a child see and judge, were a child left to see and judge alone and in peace. I not only doubt that a fairy tale is an "influence," I should call it a fortress *against* influence. Here's a universe peopled by extroverts, in which no Hamlet wrinkles his worried face, a world of Davids versus Goliaths, of young enterprise up against *force majeure* – the peculiar ethics of Jack (of the Beanstalk) and Goldilocks having this justification: that one robs a giant or skips about in the home of bears at considerable personal risk. That your child will be the better for reading a fairy tale, I see little reason to hope. But I see no reason to fear it will be the worse. It will be, largely, confirmed in its own ideas.

Are fairy tales rivals to or competitors with comics? Are they variants of comics (having basically the same formula), and would they be likely ever to drive the comic out of the field? A child who'd been a comic addict from young childhood would, one must imagine, be unlikely to switch to the fairy tale – which has yet to shake off the reputation of being sissy and has been further handicapped until lately by the sugary, drear insipidity of its illustrations.

Fairy tales and comics (some of the comics) have in common the David-Goliath theme and, not less, two major attractions: preposterousness and violence. To rail against violence, and children's liking for it, seems to me not only useless but disingenuous. "Sheltered" children (such as those of my own childhood) mimicked violence, revelled in the idea of it. But children in bombed cities, or exposed to still more scarifying horrors of war, continued to take pleasure (and it *was* pleasure) in violent games.

The horror, to me, of comics (out-and-out "horror comics" or otherwise) is their *drabness*, their visual ugliness, the lack – or, at any rate, the extreme rarity – of anything like or approaching wit in them and (for all their preposterous element) their prosaicness.

Is it possible that there sets in, in children today, a half-unconscious revulsion against them? Have children – do they increasingly have – a need that the comic fails to meet? Is that need, even in part, aesthetic? Do they, too, require an "other world" – a non-everyday, not only unfamiliar but totally *non*-familiar other dimension in which the fancy may have play?

If so, it is essential that they discover such a world for themselves. The hold, so far, of the comic has been, surely, that here is something children *have* found for themselves and therefore continue to enjoy – in spite of and, I imagine, still more because of, considerable counter-propaganda. Let a child come to the fairy tale in the same way, then we shall see. Already we *are* seeing to some extent. I cannot believe the present resurgence of the fairy tale to be due to grown-up pressure on childish taste. Even a docile child can be obstinate! By all signs, it is the children themselves who are leading the way back to the fairy tale.

Clearly, the aesthetic element is strongest in fairy tales of the kind

I have not discussed – and now, alas, have neither space nor time to. The supreme example is Hans Andersen. Many of such tales do, however, in a sense overlap on the adult world in that they introduce emotion – and thereby break one of the fairy tale's primitive, rigid laws. It is impossible to read a Hans Andersen story without risking heartbreak. Surely the fairy tale pure and simple, the fairy tale "proper," does by its very nature exclude such risk.

Nonetheless, the fairy tale pure and simple has an aesthetic of its own. It conjures up images and pictures which have, out of their very strangeness, a strange purity. Such tales as "Cinderella" and "The Sleeping Beauty" – singularly devoid of character interest – delight by their lovely paraphernalia: the pumpkin coach with its fantastic attendants, the tanglewood of overgrown roses through which the Prince goes hacking his way. Also, there is the aesthetic of the grotesque – the absolute of the "terrifying": ogres and witches, together with their fateful, weird habitations.

One final word: the fairy tale, in its extreme simplicity, is a supreme test of the narrator's art. This is a tale of a kind to be told, not read. If it is to be read, it should still seem to the reader a tale told (not, that is to say, a tale merely "written"). Fairy tales demand to be read aloud: they always have been, they still are – let us hope they will be more so rather than less. "The Three Bears" is an example of one which demands, and more than rewards, all-out vocal histrionics. Both demand and reward, however, go with any fairy tales that there are. The ideal is that these tales be (literally) *told* – that you and I should know them well enough, be acquainted enough with their possibilities, conversant enough with every turn of their dramas, to be able to tell them.

"What?" you may ask. "In only our own, dull words?" Never fear: the fairy tale is a formula for magic. Magic will take possession of your tongue.

Introduction to The King of the Golden River, by John Ruskin

Lucky are those who love fairy stories. You who will read *The King of the Golden River* are, I hope, eager for yet another. Already, maybe, you have your favourites, which you like so well that you all but know them by heart. If so, you may notice that while no good fairy stories are ever at all the same, many of them have something in common. How often, for instance, there are three brothers, of whom the youngest – modest, brave and deserving – is the one who wins his way to good fortune. Should there be a lovely princess (as there often is) it will be this youngest brother who wins her hand. But he has to go through much on his way to victory: terrifying dangers and dreadful monsters and snares of the trickiest kind beset his path. As we know, even in the everyday world an adventurous youth has much to contend with! But the fairy-tale hero has extra-powerful friends and enemies. The good fairies work for him, the bad against him.

In *The King of the Golden River* we have three brothers, but no princess. And the fairy personages are neither gauzy nor pretty: on the contrary, they are decidedly comic – an odd-looking, fussy, bossy pair of old men. Should we, indeed, call South-West Wind, Esquire (so bedraggled when he enters the story) and the little gold King, whose home is the furnace, "fairies" at all? Whether or not, they both wield strong magical powers, which can make them valuable friends but destructive enemies. The only out-and-out monsters in this story are, I am sorry to tell you, two human beings: Schwartz and Hans, the mean, cruel, black-hearted elder brothers of our young hero, generous fair-haired Gluck. A horrible end (which I won't divulge for fear of spoiling the story) awaits these bullies. Moreover, what brings them to it is not so much magic as their own hateful faults.

The King of the Golden River (unlike many fairy stories) is not set in a quite imaginary land. This marvellous region of beauties, perils and mysteries is a real one, to be found on the map – Styria, a province of Austria with tremendous mountains. Who knows? You may some day travel there and see for yourself the misted crags, the sinister glaciers and high-up cataracts flashing gold in the sunset. And still, today, in the lonely valleys dwell farmer families, making their living just as Schwartz, Hans and Gluck are doing when our story begins (though I trust there are no more types such as Schwartz and Hans!). That magical things should occur in a real-life place makes them, to me, *more* magical – how do you feel?

How came John Ruskin to write us this fairy story? He is famed for work of a totally different kind: learned, grave, sometimes fiery books on art and, too (since he was an idealist and reformer), on some of the problems of Victorian England. Yet *The King of the Golden River*, I'm sure, delighted him. What a vacation for him! And this Englishman gloried in natural scenery no less than he delighted in painting and architecture. He loved to breathe pure air (far from his dim-lit study) and sought it through travel and mountaineering. Ugliness he hated; to him it gave off evil, just as, no less, evil gave off ugliness. All things bad he embodied in Schwartz and Hans, under whose touch all loveliness shrivelled – whereas for Gluck, the innocent, birds sang and a devastated valley flowered again . . . Don't, however, form the idea that John Ruskin "preached" when he gave us *The King of the Golden River*. On the contrary: you are about to discover an exciting, semi-magic adventure story, with some eeriness but also some sturdy comedy.

No, there is no princess. But we bid farewell to young Gluck – back at last in his long-lost home, Treasure Valley, and now its master – certain that all good things are to flow his way. So when he *does* take a bride, she will be more fair than any who ever wore a crown. For that wise little golden King, having tested Gluck, saw fit to grant him, forever, his heart's desire – far better, far, than a river of molten gold!

Enchanted Centenary of the Brothers Grimm

Jacob and Wilhelm, the brothers Grimm, were only one year apart in age. Jacob, the first of a family of five children, was born in 1785, his birthplace (also that of the others) being Hanau, in Hesse-Cassel. The father, a lawyer, died while Jacob was still a boy, leaving his widow badly off – Frau Grimm would have been hard put to it to raise her brood had it not been for help from her sister.

The boys' benevolent aunt held a post at one of the small courts which then dotted Germany: she was lady of the chamber to the Landgravine of Hesse. Therefore, the fatherless five enjoyed if not the interest and patronage of the Landgravine, at least some of the pickings from her rich household. Even so, life would have been harsh, had it not been sweetened by affection and, for Jacob and Wilhelm, brightened by intelligence. Poverty bred something better than isolation. It made (as it did for the Brontës elsewhere and later) for the forging of almost uncannily close ties, and for the creation of a peculiar world.

Propinquity, in a small home crowded with children, is to be taken as a matter of course. For Jacob and Wilhelm, it had a psychic side. That these two throughout their boyhood shared the same bed and worked at the same small table was recalled, and given significance, by Jacob in his celebrated address to the Berlin Academy on the occasion of his brother's death. (Wilhelm predeceased Jacob by four years: it is Jacob's centenary we now honour – he died in 1863.)

With what could be called interlocking minds went what were certainly complementary temperaments. Jacob was the more positive and assertive, the more intellectually powerful, the more formidable. He tended to shun society; he remained a bachelor. Wilhelm had more evidently the makings of a Romantic; intuition mingled with his intelligence. His likings were quick, his impressions vivid; he enjoyed being in company, he engaged affections. His felicitous marriage in no way disturbed his relationship with his brother; on the contrary, Jacob shared the domestic joys. They continued to live in the same house, "in such harmony and community," said an admiring visitor, "that one might almost imagine the children were common property."

In youth, the two Grimms looked much alike – straight, thoughtful eyes and delicate features. In portraits, Jacob, as one might expect, seems the more authoritative and composed. The manner in which Wilhelm wears his hair is the more unruly – it runs to curls. These both were young men with careers to make. Non-frivolous though those careers were, are good looks ever a disadvantage?

Together, the boys attended the public school at Cassel. They then very properly – as their father's sons – were sent to Marburg to study law. In this, they were not to progress past the student stage, but their student days lasted for some time. And Marburg did not by any means go for nothing. Here it was that Jacob came under the exciting, inciting influence of the renowned Savigny. Listening to Savigny's lectures on Roman law, Jacob cunningly bypassed the legal aspect and settled for lasting interest in the antique. And then, still better, as a favoured student he was given the run of Savigny's private library, which was a rich mine of Old German writings. Here, first, Jacob encountered the *minnesingers*.[1]

Later, when Savigny transferred to Paris, he invited Jacob to join him there. That delirious Paris year, 1805, spent in assisting Savigny in his wide research, was to confirm, strengthen and aliment Jacob's taste for the literature of the Middle Ages. However, a living had to be made. Jacob returned (who knows how resignedly?) to Cassel, where Wilhelm and their mother had set up house and where he found a small clerkship in the War Office. Yet Cassel, too, was not for nothing. In spare hours, he and Wilhelm fomented their folk-tale project.

In 1806, the Napoleonic armies overran Cassel. "Those days," wrote Wilhelm, "of the collapse of all existing establishments will remain forever before my eyes . . . The ardour with which the studies of Old German were pursued helped overcome the spiritual depression . . . Undoubtedly, the world situation and the necessity to draw into the peacefulness of scholarship contributed to the reawakening of the long-forgotten literature; but not only did we seek something of consolation in the past, our hope, naturally, was that this course of ours would contribute something to the return of a better day."

So, again, two heads bent over the same table. The chagrins and hardships of occupation – "foreign persons, foreign manners, and a foreign, loudly spoken language" – burned a passionate patriotism into the Grimms' souls. If for the first time, certainly not for the last, this took as fuel the old mythology.

That being so, Jacob's acceptance of the post of superintendent of the private library of Jerome Buonaparte, "puppet" king of Westphalia, may for an instant surprise or puzzle one. It does not appear to have injured his good name; for after the expulsion of Buonaparte in 1813, he was appointed secretary of legation – in which role he accompanied the Hessian minister to the headquarters of the anti-Napoleonic allied army, and later attended the Congress of Vienna. Wilhelm made no such excursion into diplomacy; instead, he had niched himself into the Cassel library. Onward from 1817, when they removed to Göttingen, the brothers were to be never again apart.

Göttingen suited them. Jacob, as professor-librarian, lectured on legal antiquities, historical grammar, diplomatics, and literary history (in the course of which he explained and expounded Old German poetry), while Wilhelm, more modest under-librarian, unobtrusively married Dortchen Wild, a kindred soul in the matter of folk research. This halcyon period lasted for twenty years.

But 1837 saw Jacob in trouble for noble reasons. As one of seven professors who had signed the protest against the King of Hanover's abrogation of the constitution, he was dismissed from his post and banished from Hanover. Back went the Grimms to Cassel – though not for long.

Berlin, which already rang with the brothers' fame, came into the picture in 1840. The Prussian capital and its university could not have been more liberal in awards and honours. Jacob and Wilhelm received professorships and went on to be elected members of the Academy of Sciences. The more retiring Jacob did not lecture, but worked with his brother on a titanic dictionary which had, alas, to be finished by other hands.

No award could measure with Jacob's stature. Not only was he a great philologist, he was *the* great one, in being (as today comprehends) the first. He it was who had transformed philology from an errant study into an exact science by formulating Grimm's Law. What he set up could not be called a landmark – little had been the land in this particular field *to* mark. He was something between a bedrock and starting post.

From Grimm's Law to Grimms' Fairy Tales seems a far cry. There might seem, even, a contrariety between them, but on closer analysis there is not. The 210 fairy and folk tales collected by Jacob and Wilhelm Grimm bore the title "Kinder-und-Hausmärchen" (in English, "Nursery and Household Tales"). The collection was published in Berlin in two volumes – the first appearing (during Napoleon's retreat from Moscow) just in time for Christmas, 1812, the second giving a good start to 1815 by coming out in January of that year.

Success was immediate – for good reason – and the success was encircled by wide sensation. For the *literati*, the brothers were revolutionaries. How so? Why, in the manner of the telling. Here came tales still warm from the lips that told them. Here was the insubordinate, uncalculated beauty of the vernacular. Old, old, their origins lost in time, these tales had renewed their youth and recharged their batteries onward from generation to generation – their eager hearers having become vivid tellers, passing them on. Word-of-mouth tales, transmitted as word-of-mouth; tales unchastened (this is very important) by refining "literary" taste, tales which bore no stamp given them by the Grimms themselves.

The brothers wrote down these stories – that is to say, transcribed them. They did not write them – in so far as one means, when one speaks of "writing", that an act of imaginative invention has taken place. They found these tales, thereby rescuing many from the oblivion into which they might have fallen. Having found them, they presented them to the world. And what a gift! For the brothers, the giving was joy enough – personal "self-expression" they never sought.

The Grimms' criterion in the choosing of the stories was authenticity. They used no tales of which the (regional) origin could not be traced. Working together, they brought to a fine point an instinct which protected them from the specious. And Jacob brought also, to the selection, the developed faculties of the philologist. The vocabulary in which a tale was clothed, when it came to him, could in itself be a guarantee. Fairy tales for children contained more of the original soul of old Germany than anything else the Grimm brothers could find.

In insisting on this direct presentation, or transcription, the Grimms, with their interlocked, offbeat genius, fell foul of many of their contemporaries in the early nineteenth-century phase of the German Romantic movement. They seemed anti-aesthetic. Stylishness and refinement they seemed to scorn.

What bred this defiance in the Grimm brothers? Their contempt for "beauty" at the cost of excisions? Their support for spoken as against written prose? Ardent Wilhelm's reaction to the poetry of the spontaneous is understandable; but what part played the hardminded Jacob? Actually, it was Jacob's passion, the philologist's passion for the sound and nature of words, his regard for their virtue, his sense of their rootedness, his awe of their history, which determined the manner, and to an extent the matter, of the 210 "Nursery and Household Tales."

Some of the tales, it was true, had been disinterred from volumes or manuscripts in those time-darkened libraries which added a further dimension to Jacob's youth. But the main stream of them, the majority, had been transcribed direct from the lips of tellers native to the regions the tales haunted. One great source had been Frau Katerina Viehmann, tailor's wife in a village not far from Cassel. With delight, the student brothers frequented her home. "She recounts her stories," reported Wilhelm, "thoughtfully accurately, with uncommon vividness . . . Much was recorded in this way, and its fidelity is unmistakable. Anyone believing that traditional materials are falsified and carelessly preserved, and hence cannot survive for a long period, should hear how close she always keeps to her story and how zealous she is for its accuracy; never does she alter any part in repetition, and she corrects a mistake herself, immediately she notices it. Among people who follow the old ways of life without change, attachment to inherited patterns is stronger than we, impatient for variety, can realise."

What a Circe, this upright countrywoman! "She has a strong and pleasant face and a clear, sharp look in her eyes; in her youth she must have been beautiful." A priestess-grandmother. How long sat the brothers at her feet?

The Grimm brothers, I learn, were among those who have pointed out that folk tales are "monstrous, irrational and unnatural." And that goes for fairy tales, we may take it? The 210 released by the brothers Grimm, I refuse to discuss in scholarly terms. They hold me too close – I like them too well. Here is a boisterous, lusty, quick-witted world, with thickets of mysticism shot through by beauty.

Its inhabitants are children, robbers, huntsmen, discharged soldiers, tailors, peasants, fishermen, cowherds, goatherds and goose girls, kings and queens, and princes and princesses, malevolent witches and kind enchantresses, wicked stepmothers, tricky serving maids, horrid boys, ingenious little girls and inspired simpletons, giants, Tom Thumbs, good dwarfs and disagreeable gnomes. Its fauna consists of lions, bears, wolves, foxes, cats and, of course, dogs, also hares and mice – there appear to be no badgers and no tigers. There is almost every variety of bird, with the exception of blackbirds and peacocks. Frogs play a considerable part. Sole and herring are the more prominent fish. In a group to themselves are dragons and griffins.

The flora is headed by roses, which act dramatically. There are sinister lilies, and many innocent wildflowers. Fruit, particularly apples, is abundant, delicious and charged with magic. You cannot be too careful as to what you eat, what you promise to a stranger, or what you wish.

Much of the landscape consists of forests, and these are trackless, moody and very deep. Glittering and dangerous glass mountains may soar up into existence at any moment. Rivers are slippery customers; any ocean, you should think twice before embarking upon. Wherever a heath occurs, it is strewn with rock; glades are seldom not jewel-brilliant with flowers. Architecture is represented by castles, hung inside with crystal chandeliers, which appear or disappear at will; horrible incarcerating towers; intensely snug little houses in forest clearings; occasional churches and humble fishermen's huts.

Few dooms in this perilous world are permanent, it is consoling to remember. The prey of devouring carnivores, bolted whole, can be rescued alive from the brute's interior. Dismembered persons, pieced together again, walk away smiling. Birds, bears, lions and hideous monsters may at any time reassume human form. A maiden deserted, owing to a spell, by her dear lover almost invariably reclaims him. Only really evil schemers come to bad ends, and very excruciating *those* are . . .

Yes, this world of the tales is a blend of coziness and bloodthirstiness, of slapstick comedy, coarse-grained good sense and inadvertent, ethereal beauty. "The Girl Without Hands," "The Singing, Soaring Lark," "Frederick and Catherine," "Clever Elsie," "The Shoes That Were Danced to Pieces," "The Six Servants," "Donkey Cabbages," "The Devil's Sooty Brother," "The Young Giant" . . . Where must one now stop – and where next turn?

These are tales for all ages. They are tales for all. For children, they have the particular virtue of making sense. Everything that a child feels should happen *does* happen. In one if not another of these stories, rough justice rules – but may not justice be rough? Transformations, disguises fall into line with an infant's sense of the trickiness of the world. And, above all, here the extraordinary is the beautiful. Why not? Should beauty ever grow ordinary, what a sad affair!

ON WRITING

What We Need in Writing

Art is one kind of amusement, a game on a fairly high plane which the artist invites his public to play. The novelist and playwright offer art, or amusement, in its most immediate, likely and easy form; of all artists they exact least from their public; they must be topical – that is to say, in a felt relation to their own time and the general point of view – they cannot deal in high terms, and acceptability to an extent rules them. They must trap the imagination before they can command it; thus they dare not ignore, while they must not make evident that big element of craft in their art. To give themselves a wider scope they may work to enlarge comprehension, but must always defer to its limitations; the haughtiness of the pure artist – painter, musician or poet – is forbidden them; unintelligibility is fatal to the novel or play.

It is futile for the novelist or playwright to fight taste, to try to force it or to contemn it as an outcrop of unrelated whims: all whims are the emergence of a psychology, often pathological. Popularly, what are most wanted today are escape and affinity. The reader or theatre-goer desires to be exhilarated and lightened by non-existence, but at the same time to exist intensively inside a world, temporarily valid, in which his private susceptibilities and fantasies may uncurl like fronds inside heated glass. He likes to be at once absent and pervasive, on holiday and vicariously militant. So the comedy of pure manners, the satirical mirror, whether written or acted, has lost its vogue; the dream-world, censored and with an optimistic bias, becomes the commercial proposition now. The dope being handed out has a sickly quality: frankness, bogus in showing sentiment, end-of-the-party bravado and a tough-luck pathos that feeds and flatters universal self-pity characterise most novels and plays today. Mawkishness flies up from the dry speed of the American novel, and blots whole tracts of English "exquisite" prose. *Pure* escape literature – detective fiction, the vast Scandinavian romance, the picaresque novel – and drama – crook melodrama, the costume play – are so plainly functional that they keep a minor honesty of their own. It is the pretension to seriousness, to pertinence, of more high-class writing that makes so much to deplore.

This pretentious weakness and invalidity is not wholly the writer's fault. He is the child of his age, feels his way in its general fog and shares its democratic timidity. Like the solitary Paris pedestrian, he waits by the kerb for a little group to gather, not daring to cross the street alone. Too muddled or honest to generalise, he occupies himself nervously with the particular. If his thought attempts any unfamiliar track it loses itself and comes back in a panic. His self-knowledge and knowledge of other men is derivative, literary. He must cultivate his garden inside a small, cleared space: this has been widened a little, but also too many others have been gardening there. His profession provincialises him; he thinks, he feels, he remembers *like* a writer: Trigorin's troubles[1] were not only the penalty of success. So many words have to go to make up a book, so many sensations raised like crops of cress on flannel, that he must school himself to dread simplification. The plainness of fact, the unliterary quickness of men in action cannot but be his enemies. He dare not strip life; he is expected to add to it; he has been put into power and invited to practise by the emotional *il faut vivre*[2] of a dissatisfied and uneasy class – his public – who wish to see life other than as it is, to be flattered, to be condoled with, to be explained. He cannot say: "*Je n'en vois pas la nécessité*":[3] he is sworn to keep a doubtful, a more than half factitious emotion in play. Dare he see himself harshly, he must see himself there to promote and market bunk.

His range of subjects is limited. The exceptional writer only dare send up a new dish, if his skill be superlative and the dish intriguingly dressed. There are startling few things that the public cares to hear about. Sex, or love, is a popular subject because self-love and the private imagination luxuriate round it. Adventure, being fantasy, is safe ground. Children, animals and the upper classes appeal to tenderness and to curiosity: it is impossible for the reader to document himself fully about them, so that the writer has free scope. Class – with the class that largely pays the piper – is as a subject fatally unpopular. There is little temptation to write up the class struggle palatably: possibly it would be impossible to do so. Only exceptional novels show it by implication. Middle-class repugnance to an essential subject must exercise the strongest possible censorship over the artist while he remains the pensioner of middle-class taste. He feels something iron behind the received suggestion: *Parlons d'autres choses*.[4]

So at present the theatre and the novel keep up their nervous patter about the immaterial. The public is dissatisfied, and naturally: there is a streak of natural irony in the most self-deceiving person, and the first reflex is to reject bunk. In the traffic between writers and their public one must admit the remains of some good faith, though a wasted, misused good faith. A good deal of second-rate writing – with an aesthetic, with a morality even, that is at first sight impressive – is turned out sincerely, and with high aspirations, and received sincerely, and with aspirations to match. The critics do much to further this hanky-panky; they bleat, they exalt or they deride, but few critics attempt to stabilise their currency. They preach, implicitly, resignation to inflated dullness or trumped-up internal drama; and that we are not to expect, would be unfair to our age in expecting another *War and Peace*, another *Madame Bovary*, another *Emma* – or, in the theatre, even another *Cherry Orchard*, another *Way of the World* or *Lady Windermere's Fan*. I quote these two last plays because things would not be so bitter if accomplishment had not been sacrificed to an untrue morality. Most novels, most plays now kick up what appears to be significant dust: they leave the plain man or woman agreeably flustered but not at all vitally discomposed. There are packed houses for plays about the difficulties of parents with adolescent, highly passionate children, the hesitations of sub-Hamlets, the tenacious mother, the right of a woman of any age to love. But the root of their matter, which is in most cases largely and plainly economic, is seldom attacked. If we must dissimulate, better be elegant. Trouble now lies in the purse, not in the heart.

What we want, in novels and in the theatre, is the work of writers more normal and disengaged – normal in not being warped by their profession, disengaged in their point of view, from their background, as to their prospects, who have not so much to lose, or who do not care what they do lose. Objectiveness is impossible for the imperfectly free. Also, freedom – from self-interest, from obsession, from nostalgia, from arbitrary loyalties – is necessary if life is to be examined and the result shown. Our writers fail now in flexibility, in the coldness Flaubert desired, and in perception. There are too many imperfect artists; the imperfect artist cannot grip a subject that has to be followed, that does not offer itself or whose acceptability is not guaranteed – hence the present hedging timidness, the re-translation of *clichés*. It is not that subjects do not exist, but that writers are not empowered to tackle them. At present the greater number of novels and plays are claustrophobic – one feels as in a dream, a ghastly, unreal constriction. Modern French and Russian novels are giving the lead towards a greater plainness and vitality: is there any reason why that should not be followed here? The Americans, though still not without sentiment, embrace the everyday widely and make everything their province. Our novels and plays need both deeper seriousness and higher frivolity: it is impossible either to be tragic or to be funny without a profound sense of the relation between things. Love engages the fancy because it is irrational: it would not be half it is if reason were not present, but fiction and drama tend to isolate it. Character is important as it affects plot, action; exalted above plot it is artificially complex, dead. Domestic crisis only becomes important where there is a lively sense of what lies beyond its stage.

We want, if novels and plays are more than merely to detain us, a more natural approach to life on the part of their authors, and at the same time a more unflagging devotion to art. We want more emotion implied (not merely written up), more relevant fact stated, more vital relations shown. We want pain disabused of sentiment, fun of facetiousness. We cannot have this, or can only have it rarely, until the public go halfway to meet the writer, and go to meet him with a more active mind, with sensibilities open, with prejudice pocketed. Expecting more from him, we are likely to get more – or, at least, to be clear about what we have not got, and so end this unfocussed discontent.

The Short Story in England

The development of the short story in England has been interesting to watch. As an art form, it is still fairly new – roughly, the child of the twentieth century. Before 1900, short stories – and often, great ones – had indeed been written; but there was, I believe, a tendency to regard these as by-products, chance overflows from the brimming imaginations of novelists. Fine short stories, while they might delight the public, were not yet of technical interest to the critic. Kipling – the main body of whose prose work was in this form – *was* Kipling: unique, unquestioned, with a place of his own.

The freshness and force of his style, the variety of his subjects, his wide knowledge of men and countries, his equal command of the comic and tragic muse – it was those that struck contemporary readers. They did not pause to examine *how* the stories were told. And Kipling the artist tended to be obscured by Kipling the national institution. Only lately – only, that is to say, since the awakening of artistic interest in the short story form – has there been what one might call a delayed-action appreciation of Kipling's technique. Now we see him as not only our first but also as one of our greatest artists in that particular line.

Yes, we took Kipling for granted. Ironically, perhaps, English interest in the short story was to wait to receive its impetus from abroad. Late nineteenth-century Europe had given birth to two outstanding short-story writers – French Guy de Maupassant, Russian Anton Chekhov. The Maupassant stories, with their strong Gallic flavour, appealed only to a special public in England: none the less, their reputation spread. As with Kipling, the Maupassant stories' subjects were, at the time, more striking than was their concealed art. The impact of Chekhov on us was very different: no sooner were his stories translated into English than he began to be felt as an influence. Why? Because the Chekhov stories deal more with mood than with action. To us in England that was something quite new; and it opened infinite possibilities. Mood (though it may be mood of a different kind) is, I think, as strong a factor with the English as with the Russians; the idea of expressing it was fascinating, and the suitability of the short story for this purpose soon came to be seen. The short story promised to do in prose what had, so far, only been done in poetry. Isolating some perhaps quite small happening, it emphasised its significance by giving it emotional colour.

The first, and brilliant, exponent of Chekhov's technique in England was Katherine Mansfield – be it clear that she added to her discipleship a genius altogether her own. The work of that young New Zealand woman, settled in England, appeared at a time that could not have been more propitious – the years following the First World War. A swing-back to reflectiveness, a revulsion against action, violence, and any form of systematised energy is, I imagine, characteristic of any postwar period. Individual feelings reassert themselves. Like small spring flowers, personal loves, pleasures, and fancies appear again, after the harsh, repressive winter of war.

Katherine Mansfield's tragically early death left her not lost to us as an inspiration. Throughout the 1920s, and into the 1930s, her imitators, inevitably, were many. What was better, quite independent talents found themselves encouraged, by *her* achievement, in their own belief in the short story. A. E. Coppard[1] and H. E. Bates,[2] with their lyrical but at the same time virile tales of the English countryside, showed that the English "atmospheric" short story need not stay only in the feminine sphere. Another woman short-storyist, Ethel Colburn Mayne[3] – who had, I believe, been writing prior to Katherine Mansfield – began to come into greater prominence; though never quite the prominence she deserved.

William Plomer, before he was twenty, published his first collection, *I Speak of Africa*. Plomer (who has now much other work to his name) is, I think, still the English short-storyist whose development has been most continuous and most steady: he is now in his prime as a writer. More and more, as in the decades between the two World Wars the short story has become a literary cult, one has had to distinguish between the mere good technician (the writer, one might say, for writing's sake) and the man or woman of first-class imagination, who has something wholly original to say. High in this class comes D. H. Lawrence, whose short stories are unweighted by any of the redundancies that may slow down his novels. All the vision, the fire, the gentleness, and the sheer observation of which Lawrence was capable come out, pure, in his stories. He was writing during the 1914–18 war; and the stories in the *England My England* and *The Ladybird* collections seem to me to have captured, as truly as anything in our literature, the psychological atmosphere of that time. And his postwar stories were to show no decline. Arguably (and I could support the argument) Lawrence is our finest short-story writer. He is certainly in the rank of the first six. With him I should place Kipling, Somerset Maugham, Aldous Huxley, William Plomer and Katherine Mansfield. But here, I fear, I risk being controversial. Walter de la Mare's position is indefinable: he belongs more than half, always, in the poetic province. And James Joyce, Frank O'Connor, Liam O'Flaherty,[4] and Seán O'Faoláin, as Irishmen, are outside my present scope.

As the short story has gained in literary prestige, "over-literariness" has become a danger with it. Of this danger, Somerset Maugham – perhaps because of what one might call his, in the good sense, man-of-the-world qualities – has steered clear. And Aldous Huxley, in whom the aesthetic exuberance of the 1920s found high expression, steered clear too – perhaps by sheer mental vigour. But, alas, several writers who showed promise later "bogged down" in over-ambiguities. Their contempt for plot went too far. The Chekhov influence, as I have tried to show, had at the beginning been excellent. But soon a reaction against it must set in.

This reaction showed itself as the 1930s advanced. The tenseness and seriousness of that decade, in which England could not ignore the troubles of Europe or the storm clouds darkening her own horizon, began to reflect itself in our short stories – as they did in our drama and poetry. Social consciousness succeeded to aesthetic susceptibility. The general feeling that we must begin to act brought action back into prominence in our stories. Charming descriptive passages yielded place to quick-moving dialogue; and characters, instead of being poetically generalised, had to be clear-cut, perhaps prosaic, identifiable by the reader as types in everyday life. I say, "had to be." The art of the short story showed itself truly to *be* art in that it felt compulsions from the outside world. And also, in that, like a magic mirror, it was already reflecting what was to come. Spareness, energy, a respect for the fighting spirit (rather than for the luxurious sensibilities) of man, and a tendency to question the social order – all these appeared in the more representative stories written for some years prior to 1939.

Who were the writers who showed this immediately pre-war trend? Arthur Calder-Marshall, Leslie Halward, James Hanley, G. F. Green[5] are names that come most immediately to my mind. Hanley's sea stories have, it is true, a horrific, phantasmagoric quality that entitles them to a place apart. Arthur Calder-Marshall is, in the main, a novelist: his short stories are not many, but are first rate. Several isolated fine pieces – often, for instance, about the war in Spain – came from writers whose output remained small. The short-storyists of the 1930s were fired by their subjects, and less concerned with technique for its own sake. Or perhaps one should say, they strove to avoid showing that technique *had* been used. They were influenced, if at all, by the Americans – principally Hemingway. It may well have been Hemingway who, already admired here in the 1920s, first threw the slow motion, Chekhov-style story into discredit.

An alternative type of story was, it is true, still produced through-out the 1930s. Stylish, memorable in theme and highly imaginative in treatment, such stories were most often written by poets. The ever distinguished work of Osbert and of Sacheverell Sitwell shows, for instance, little deflection by world events – though, be it said, Osbert Sitwell's *Defeat* has embodied the whole of the tragedy of 1940 France. Peter Quennell,[6] Dylan Thomas, and Stephen Spender (whose collection *The Burning Cactus* is to be recommended) also made experiments in this form.

Curiously enough – or is it so curious? – the actual outbreak of the long-dreaded war sent the English short story soaring, with a new kind of hardy exuberance, into realms of humour, satire, fantasy, and caprice. Artistic release could not but follow the long tension. I do not but say that tragedy and duress have not, also, imprinted themselves in our wartime stories. Nor do I mean that the short story has contributed, in any *unworthy* sense, to "escape" literature. No – but is it not fair to say that true art never underlines the obvious? In peace time, our short-story artist had for subject those uneasy currents beneath the apparently placid surface. In wartime, the surface being itself uneasy, he plumbs through to, and renders, unchanging and stable things – home feeling, human affection, old places, childhood memories, and even what one might call those interior fairy tales (sometimes, perhaps, ridiculous; often touching) on which men and women sustain themselves and keep their identities throughout the cataclysm of world war.

The Horizon Book of Short Stories offers a fair cross-section of short stories written since 1940 – and, I think, bears out my generalisations. These stories, selected by Cyril Connolly, have all appeared in *Horizon*, from month to month. Very important, since war began, have been the number of periodicals or book-form publications ready to welcome, and make known, new short-story writers. Besides *Horizon*, I instance *The Cornhill*, *Life and Letters*, *English Story*, *Penguin New Writing*, *New Writing and Daylight*, *Orion* and *The Windmill*. Seldom, in England, can the literary scene have been more propitious for fresh talent. But alas, ironically, few of the young are free to write – or to write much. The Forces, or exacting strenuous war work outside the Forces, have claimed them. Under the circumstances, it is amazing how many manuscripts (these travelling, often, from the ends of the earth) *have* reached the London editors. It has been striking, also, how much imagination *has* been able to add to experiences that might, one would have thought, exceed it. I instance the N. F. S. firemen stories of William Sansom; also *The Last Inspection* – which, left us by Alun Lewis,[7] shows what a tragic loss this young Welshman's death in India has been to the art of the short story.

I have said how those two collections of D. H. Lawrence's captured the time-spirit of the 1914–18 war. It would still appear to me that the short story is the ideal *prose* medium for wartime creative writing. For one thing, the discontinuities of life in wartime make such life a difficult subject for the novelist. For the novelist, perspective, and also a term of time in which to relate one experience to another, are essential – I suggest that we should not expect any *comprehensive* war novel until five, even ten years after hostilities cease. The short-storyist is in a better position. First, he shares – or should share – to an extent the faculties of the poet: he can render the great significance of a small event. He can register the emotional colour of a moment. He gains rather than loses by being close up to what is immediately happening. He can take, for the theme of his story, a face glimpsed in the street, an unexplained incident, a snatch of talk overheard in a bus or train.

Wartime London – blitzed, cosmopolitan, electric with expectation – teemed, I feel, with untold but tellable stories; glittered with scenes that cry aloud for the pen. So did our other cities, our ports and seacoasts, our factory settlements, our mobilised countryside. Already, the first of the harvest is coming in: I foresee a record crop of short stories now that the European war is over. Of all the arts being practised in England now, none, I think, responds more quickly to impetus than does the art of the short story

Introduction to Chance

To introduce this opening number of *Chance* is a privilege – warranted, I may hope, by my continuous interest in the short story for over thirty years. This magazine is well named: it takes the field at a time when the fortunes of younger writers seem overcast, and fresh talent finds it hard to make itself known. This is a young enterprise – built up, as its friends have reason to know, on enthusiasm, devotion and good faith. The editors, and most of the contributors, are still in their twenties – the second half of our troubled but interesting century lies before them, and upon it, one may believe and hope, at least some are likely to leave their mark. The magazine, and its appearance now, sound a ringing, engaging note of confidence – a confidence both in art and in life. As we know, to the person truly alive the one has never been separable from the other. Indeed, without the creative wish, existence would be a dejected and poor affair.

There is a splendid riskiness about the launching of any magazine. *Chance* is taking a chance, and it also offers one. Here is an opportunity for the reader, and for those interested in promoting writing, to watch new writing in its initial stage. In America they have writing schools, which enable the potentially creative person to make his experiments, show his paces and, above all, profit by formative criticism. Here, for better or worse, we have none of those: the only education is publication – the ordeal by cold print, the transformation of the personal manuscript into something im-personally offered to the world. I – like, I imagine, other writers some way into maturity – have always felt, and have tried to stress, the important literary function of the *reader*. The writer cannot work in a vacuum, quite alone – he is all the time addressing himself *to* someone. If the intelligent writer cannot communicate with an intelligent reader of his own kind, it is as though he were trying to telephone with the line dead. Therefore it is up to the readers, to that conglomerate of them we call "the public," to give ear and under-standing to new voices. Every writer is forging – sometimes through words themselves, sometimes through ideas or the notation of impressions – a language of his own: his aim, it must be remem-bered, is so to use that language as to say something in it which has not been said before, and which could have been said in no other way. Intelligibility is the aim of every sincere writer: if on his way to intelligibility he has to pass through curious phases, he ought none the less to be suffered with, honoured, and met halfway. As to this, perceptive critics should give the lead; but, in the long run, it must be the general readers, the public, who have the decisive power. The development of a writer can but depend on the degree to which he is understood. If we are to continue to have creative writing, we must develop the art of creative reading.

The stories in this first number of *Chance* are, on the whole, straightforward: we find, so far, no revolutionary or chaotic experiments with prose. Each, however, of these "straight" narratives intends to convey a unique idea, pin down an unobvious impression, or drive home a freshly felt emotional truth. The return to conservatism in style – coming, as it does, halfway through a century which has seen so many violent experiments – may in itself be found interesting, or significant. The editors of *Chance*, we may conclude, have no peculiar directive, no special policy – simply, they are drawn by, and have given preference to, what is clear in expression and spontaneous in feeling. They would seem to support intuitional rather than cerebral writing.

The short story, to whose furtherance *Chance* devotes itself, lends itself to intuitional writing. It demands visual sense, and at least an equivalent of the poetic faculty. At the same time, because it *is* a story, it must be shapely, mobile and interesting: it cannot afford to overload itself with language, nor should it try to carry too much analysis. It can be a fine vehicle for fantasy, but should keep whimsicality at arm's length. It can offer, also, an ideal commentary on human behaviour, i.e. on human behaviour seen as a whole, but exhibited in some small, special incident. There are, as we by now know, no hard-and-fast set rules of technique for the short story – each writer must evolve, for himself, the technique which best suits his powers and serves his purpose. We can tell when a story is marred by poor technique; few of us, probably, could offer other advice than: "Recast this, overhaul it – see where emphasis *should* lie, and replan and reweight your story accordingly." My view of the writers in this number of *Chance* is that, one and all, they are on their way to technique: some are well in sight of their goal, others, perhaps, a little further behind. Not one has shown himself or herself unconscious either of the exciting possibilities or the testing difficulties of the short story as a form of art.

Chance deserves to be watched along its way. Its character as a magazine cannot fail to declare itself further as it grows older. We who are associated with it ask the reader's attention – here is a source of writing, and who knows from this beginning what may come? Who knows whether, in the future, we may not count ourselves lucky – we who possess this opening number of *Chance*?

Introduction to The Observer Prize Stories

On October 14th, 1951, *The Observer* announced a Short Story Competition. The stories, not to be longer than three thousand words, were invited to "deal in any mood with any subject connected with Christmas." No writer was to submit more than one; the entry must be work not previously published, and the manuscript must carry only a pseudonym, the writer's name and address being attached in a sealed envelope – this not to be opened until the judges had made their choice. By the closing date, November 26th, six thousand seven hundred entries had been received. The winning story, "The Seraph and the Zambesi," was published in *The Observer* of December 23rd, and twenty runners-up also received prizes. The chosen twenty-one now, as promised, make their appearance in book form.

This book will command attention – would do so, one is inclined to think, even apart from the interest of its history. Here are twenty-one pieces linked by the same theme, but surprisingly various in their play upon it. All are of the given length; and all were, one may take it, conceived and written within the same six weeks. Here is the final selection from a great, an all but overpowering, spate of entries; encouraged by *The Observer*, one must reflect, nearly seven thousand writers took up the pen. The competition stimulated a vast creativeness, which the rules served to keep within helpful bounds. In so far as these stories were written for, and specially for, the competition, they might be considered command performances: recollect, however, that no command can elicit what is not potentially there. The competition provided impetus, context, direction, aim – such, indeed, was its purpose. It caused writers to write. But these twenty-one out of the stories it called forth are, in essence, something more than performances: they express something which already *had* been there, awaiting expression. Not one of them gives the feeling of being forced; some are ingenious, none show sheer ingenuity. Each bears a touch of temperament; each has been the occasion of the

318

writer's releasing stored-up material. These are, in fact, stories which had become due to be written. Unequal in merit, all merit their winning place by showing inner inevitability. Some may have been brought to their final form not so much for as because of the competition.

The short story requires fancy, then technique – the first must be unique and forceful, the second apt. No other prose form can, without distortion, let itself be so rich in fantasy, or concentrate so much sensation into few pages, or be stamped to such an extent by vision. The narrative can be shaped to the ruling idea, suited to, soaked in the prevailing mood; indeed, this form has an inherent freedom. With the freedom go dangers: there is a risk of formlessness and, sometimes, of over-subjectivity. Nothing else saves a story which is incomprehensible – the matter-of-factness of the reader must, as a foe to be won over, be kept in mind. A story must *be* a story, a tale told, on whatever plane – remote perhaps, unsubstantial – the action is to occur. Suspense must be set up, emotion stirred, interest engaged. And the factual frame of the story should be unmistakable – there should be mystery, but not unnecessary puzzles. The writer, entitled though he may be to poetic licence, ought not to feel himself quit of all rationality: he must impose a reasonableness of his own. His aim should be to make the incredible credible.

Here technique comes in. Is it too much to ask that the opening paragraph, or at any rate first two paragraphs, of a story should impart what it is necessary for the reader to know in the way of facts – the time, the place, the identity and circumstance of the characters? Almost all, not quite all, perhaps, of the stories in *The Observer* collection meet this suggested requirement – the opening of "The Seraph and the Zambesi" is a particularly admirable example. Most of the stories deal (as short stories of our day do tend to do) with cases of oddness or deviation, of solitude, crisis, forlorn hope or, at least, eccentricity. It is therefore imperative that the reader, with his ignorant and presumably normal starting-point, should be introduced to the story in such a manner that he may understand what is going on – know, in fact, what the story is likely to be *about*. According to the success with which that is done, the stories here may be ranked in artistic order.

Economy, not least vital part of technique, was enjoined by the competition's word-limit. These twenty-one writers are where they are – in this book – through their having known, or learned, how best to employ economy to drive home points or suggest volume. One must admire those who have not allowed one word out of their three thousand either to go to waste or to fail to tell. In some cases, word-distribution may be queried: have there been sacrifices of force or clearness to "atmosphere" or decorative effect? The laconic naturalism of William Goldman, Deborah Newton's airy tautness, W. J. Pyne's all but harsh restraint, and R. A. Lippy's mocking touch on the literal are reassuring; and Miss Spark's Seraph gives out the more light because of her glass-clear prose. Among the other stories, one or two are on the tenuous side. How, why? This invites analysis, which may be rewarding.

Christmas – what a subject! It was well found. "No one who has not still the heart of a child can look forward to Christmas without fear: it is a terrible time," remarks Mrs. Debono, leading in to her Malta 1942 tale. It *is* a searching-out time – should one say that, as a subject, it drops a depth-charge? Fragments of foregone feeling, tendernesses, associations, remorses swim up; memories and neurotic rebounds from memory thicken the psychological air. Convention, fled from, lays unexpected traps. At the same time, always, the touch of blessedness! The honest man hardly knows where he stands, or how, in regard to Christmas; and, if so, what of the honest artist? He must sound around him, listening for what rings true, open to what may be disconcerting. Our twenty-one contributors, taking the invitation to write "in any mood" at its full latitude, may be found to present, between them, a Christmas compost. Writing unaware of each other, and far apart, they do here complement and explain one another, oddly. Further value accumulates around their relationship, in this book. The collection is to be read as a human whole.

It is, also, likely to be a landmark in the modern history of the short story. Here are examples of what is being done – a cross-section of the imaginative mind of the 1950s. The form of literary art to be studied here is, by its very nature, experimental; there is a suggestion of progress in sheer fluidity. The short story reflects contemporary consciousness more immediately, sensitively, than does the novel; it has the means to capture what could be transitory, but is not so, quite. The short story *is*, now, necessary for expression. Ironically, however, it also is, now, in economic peril – work in this field is lost for lack of market; fresh talent finds it not easy to come to light. In giving these stories prominence, and their writers support, *The Observer* has done an important thing, not only for writers but for writing.

English Fiction at Mid-Century

In general, something is expected of, or at, the turn of a century. A term of time by being demarcated acquires character, which, as such, makes itself evident as it matures. So a century halfway along its course may be considered due to declare maturity, to have reached culmination-point, to make seen the fruition of its inherent ideas. The twentieth century's development, however, has been in some directions so violently forced, in others so notably arrested as to seem hardly to be a development at all, or at least to be difficult to recognize if it is one. In European countries, certainly, life and art are still seeking their footing in their actual time – both have the stigmata of an over-long drawn-out adolescence.

The mid-century call for an exhibition may therefore be said to have taken us by surprise, and found us unready, in disarray. As to art, it is *not* that there is nothing to show; the difficulty is rather in presentation – arrangement, classification and rating order. Individually, no potential exhibit is not expressive: now, however, is each so to be placed as to bring out its relationship with the others? For the warrant for and point of an exhibition must be its overall significance and expressiveness. In this case, one is tempted to ask, of what?

In England – if one may press the display analogy further – there would be particular difficulty in arranging the fiction stall. The novel, onward from 1914, has in different ways reflected the sense of flux. The cracking and splintering of the social mould during and after the First World War accounted for a shift, as to the subject, from outer to inner – from man as a public being, in public play, to man as a seat of isolated and in the main suffering private sensibility. For the greater part of the inter-war years, subjectivity hazed over the English novel; there was disposition to follow the stream of consciousness "from caverns measureless to man down to a sunless sea."[1] With this went, it may now be felt, a misuse or perversion of some influences – the overheated for-or-against reaction to D. H. Lawrence, the attempted segregation of Henry James and Proust from their *beau monde*, of Tolstoy, Chekhov and Turgenev from their thriving social-sensuous universe, of Thomas Hardy from his Wessex exuberance.

The intellectually respectable English novel for some time concentrated upon, insisted upon, the victim-hero – whether at school, in love or at large in the jungle which by overgrowing the ruins of fixed society succeeded to what that used to be. There was almost a convention of disillusionment. The forte of the novelist was analysis. The alternative to the analytical was the caustic – the iconoclastic novel of ideas: for this, the still young Aldous Huxley gave the prototype.

The English inter-war novel, it seems now, was somewhat "out" in its concept of what makes tragedy. It did not finally diagnose the modern uneasiness – dislocation. Dorothy Richardson (still owed full recognition) and Virginia Woolf did best, in their stress on the interplay between consciousness and the exterior world; but these two delicate novelists of the senses cannot be called, in their last implication, tragic. The salutary value of the exterior, the comfortable sanity of the concrete came to be realised only when the approach of the Second World War forced one to envisage wholesale destruction. The obliteration of man's surroundings, streets and houses, tables and chairs sent up, for him, their psychological worth. Up to now, consciousness had been a sheltered product: its interest *as* consciousness diminished now that, at any moment, the physical shelter could be gone.

The Second World War halted already-working novelists, and for obvious reasons produced few new ones. Few reputations, however, actually foundered (as had happened between 1914 and 1918). Graham Greene, for instance, and Evelyn Waugh, having begun to be prominent during the thirties, emerged from the war years to become still more so. It is they who have headed the novel's trend towards what might be called moral drama. Independent participants in this move have been Joyce Cary[2] and, in his very different way, L. P. Hartley:[3] both of these were writing before the war, but it would seem that the ensuing decade has given them special focus. Drama involves plot, action; on whatever plane, in whatever sphere – into the present picture, therefore, comes the intellectually-written adventure story, of which Hammond Innes[4] is one exponent. P. H. Newby[5] – like, again, Joyce Cary – is a dramatiser of character; both write about extroverts, domestic or social buccaneers. And one-man character-drama was epitomised in V. S. Pritchett's *Mr. Beluncle* – upon which followed the almost simultaneously written *Mr. Nicholas* of Thomas Hinde.[6]

Those two novels, in each the father viewed by the son, link up with yet another development: family drama – as, indeed, does the L. P. Hartley *Eustace and Hilda* trilogy. This field, the English seldom desert for long. In the I. Compton-Burnett masterpieces, the dialogue keeps shifting veil after veil from obsessions or passions bred by the blood-tie. But the main run of family novels now shows a blend of pleasure in idiosyncrasy with a far more adverse regard for the institution – the Rosamond Lehmann and Elizabeth Taylor novels exemplify this. Indeed, the attitude to institutions *as* institutions is more clement than it was, say, twenty-five years ago. A sort of aesthetic neo-conservatism may be found to have set in.

That, maybe, is helping to reinstate the social drama novel, which, having suffered eclipse in the twenties, began to make its way back, thanks to Evelyn Waugh, under the guise of burlesque or satire. A pre-1939 sequence of Anthony Powell novels made merry at the expense of coteries: this admirable writer's return, after twelve years' silence, has lately given us the more mellow, retrospective *A Question of Upbringing* and *A Buyer's Market*. Society, as it now provides material, might be described as the pattern formed by any frequentation of persons by one another through affinity or in pursuit of pleasure – dance, cocktail or weekend party, but equally the gathering in the pub or attendance at dog racing come under this. Henry Green, outstanding social novelist and, like I. Compton-Burnett, dialogue-expert, illustrates this necessary versatility: his *mise-en-scène* varies from the Mayfair drawing-room to the castle servants' hall, from the girls' school to the fire station. William Sansom has moved from firemen stories and Kafka allegory to the study of the upper or lower suburban rock pool. Nigel Balchin,[7] master of hard-built plot, personalities the office and the laboratory.

Jocelyn Brooke is to be watched as a roving talent with, as yet, no special territory – he has, if anything, a semi-hostile addiction to type, as shown by his *Passing of a Hero*. Rex Warner[8] continues to combine tautness with poetic distinction. Philip Toynbee[9] is, of the younger group, probably the most interesting to his fellow-novelists: his *A Garden by the Sea* has been a controversial high point. Thomas Hinde and Emma Smith,[10] who impacted with *The Far Cry*, seem so far to have no serious rivals among their young contemporaries.

At the moment, it is the political novel which is in eclipse. The ideological novel also is infrequent. As a general verdict, it might be fair to say that English fiction at present is at its most English: as an export, its value should rightly reside in that. A good deal may be felt to be germinating during this phase of apparent self-regard. What will have come of this, say, in ten years' time? Ideally, the exhibition should not open before then.

Rx for a Story Worth the Telling

I can imagine no age, however scientific, in which mankind will be contented by plain fact, however impressive, or by direct statement, made with whatever authority. Of fact we say, "That is that, that is so." We accept it. But there is some errant part of us which cries, "What next?" and "What then?" We are insatiable children: "Tell us a story!"

What is the need behind the demand? It may have different facets; it may be complex. For one thing, we require to be transported, to transcend boundaries – not, I think, merely with a view to "escape" but out of a necessity for enlargement. Positive rather than negative, this wish carries us to the portals of a world that is at once "other" and our own, a terrain with potentials we barely sense in the everyday. A story deals in the not-yet-thought-of but always possible.

We have within us a capacity, a desire, to respond. One of the insufficiencies of routine existence is the triviality of the demands it makes on us. Largely unused remain our funds of pity, spontaneous love, unenvious admiration or selfless anger. Into these, a story may drop a depth-charge.

We need to marvel. Overhung as we are by the nominal, concrete "marvels" of our century – the triumphs of science, the masterworks of technology – we are creatures of numbed fancy and stunned senses. Or could be, did we not resist and hope. Nothing *is* truly marvellous that is not Man. It is his diversity, his passion, his soaring and his endurance, which stir our amazement. Yet we await, it seems, the storyteller's cry of "Behold!"

Finally, we are born with a thirst for myth, its heroic simplicity, its bright air. A story provides life with an ancient prototype, in which action is fearless, decision swift. Vanished, banished as may be the gods and heroes, they bequeath their mantles. Who is to wear them? We need today illusion's reviving touch.

What are the essentials of a story? To begin with, it need not necessarily be untrue, that is to say, invented. I am not thinking of fiction only. Biography, history, folklore, Biblical narrative and, no less, the happening recounted by friend to friend, the memory given voice, or the flash of gossip: all these are stories. I would say, however, that if a story *be* true, it still cannot take its stand on its truth only. To act on us, it needs to be truth plus art; no small part of a story is in the telling. Conversely, when we have invention (fiction), the telling must impart an air of truth; art is summoned to substitute for veracity. Willing though we are to be moved and held, none of us can be held by the unbelievable. Great novels have an inspired lifelikeness. They *could* have been true; they outrage no real-life law.

In the main, a story does two things. It confers importance: characters in it are given stature, and are moreover spotlit, so that their gestures are not only clearly seen but cast meaningful shadows. Enhanced, the characters seem singled out from ordinary men, yet not wholly, for we perceive ourselves in them. Similarly, the settings of the story (the scenes within it), whether rooms and their furniture, city streets and parks or stretches of landscape, become endowed with a sort of super-reality, which causes them, often, to surround us more nearly than do our own surroundings, and burns them deeply into our memories. Something extra also attaches to words and actions, which have about them a touch of fatefulness; for nothing once in a story can be undone. We have this in mind when we say that some real incident has affected us "like something in a book."

A story moves, advances, and it not only can and does do this, but it must. If it stood still, it would cease to be a story and become a picture. As the story moves along, it gains in significance. What we are being shown is cause and effect. If the chain were broken, if the story's movement were altogether inconsequent or at random we should not read with the eagerness that we do. We encounter crises, situations, out of which something is bound to arise – but what? The degree to which we react to the advance depends upon the powers of the narrator.

Is a story, then, wholly within the narrator's power, circumscribed (as that would imply) by one individual's outlook, mind, pen or voice? Surely not. It enlists a series of faculties which are, no less, ours. In acting upon us, the story is drawing upon us; our responses contribute; our contributions create. The reliance of the narrator upon his audience may or may not be conscious, but it is immense. The reality (for us) of the story is a matter of how much it has elicited from us. We enter in, and through this entering in know ourselves to be active. We cooperate.

Sometimes the cooperation may be unwilling. Then we have an uneasy sense of compulsion. One may feel "against" a story on account of its errors, fatuities, lapses of taste, floutings of judgement, distortion of emotions, yet be slow to disengage one's self from its hold. To a point, we incline to lend ourselves; we are loth not to. Once under way, a story sets something going, and that is not only true of a "good" story. We allow our doubts to be stilled, our fancies exploited, as I say, to a point. Past that point, cooperation does break down, but this happens wonderfully rarely.

Why so rarely? Let us admit: the story's primary power is through suspense, the lure of "What next?" and "What then?" By literary convention, the suspense story is assumed to be the thriller or mystery. I contend that no story fails to invoke suspense, and compel us by it; the question is, simply, what kind, and on what plane? Straightforward adventure or science-fiction restricts itself to physical risk together with the physically spectacular; the more subtle mystery blends in the psychological. The play on emotional suspense throughout a love story does not need comment. Novelists know how to arouse what is more complex by revolving their plots around questions of conscience or of equity (such as race or class issues) or by bringing their characters to peaks (of success, exaltation) from which they seem liable to fall or plunging them into morasses (disaster, obloquy) from which the means of their rescue is uncertain. The psychological novel, outwardly more austere, focuses suspense on the inner conflict: the protagonists are, as it were, battlegrounds – what is to be the outcome of the day?

Suspense may account for the primitive hold on us of a story. But when the end is known, when the suspense evaporates, what then? Were there nothing left, one might speak of the story's magic, its power, even, but not, surely, of its strength. The idea of strength is indivisible from that of endurance: in that sense, strength constitutes an inherent virtue.

So far, we have been discussing the story only within the terms of its first telling. After this telling, what is left? The answer to this query, in every case, is the test.

A story may act on us while it runs its course, and for that time only. It is ephemeral. Another story, when its nominal end is reached, is only at the beginning of its term of life; from now on it will continue to make growth, extend, deepen. Rooted in our imaginations, it induces reflectiveness. In itself an experience, it stays at work within us, affecting experiences we may later have. Take the extreme case, the formative power of stories assimilated in childhood. Of a story we have either read or heard, I think we may legitimately ask: to what degree did it transform the world for us?

Great stories have basic themes; the lesser rely on devices and ingenuities. Basic themes, when one numbers them, are few; their recurrence is proof of their immortality. They are traditional, having a touch of lore and at the same time a father-to-son authority. The wonder is, that having been born knowing these themes, we continue to want them and wonder at them. Recollect, however, that they renovate themselves in their outer guise. In effect they reincarnate, donning the different languages, taking in the ideas, embracing the usages of different generations, different countries. Each time, they take colour afresh from time or place. Also they renew their expressive quality; they voice, as, it seems to us, nothing else can, the spirit of a century, or of a society, or of a region. The great story is one that remains true.

Conflicts or rivalries and their resolution, pride and its fate, estrangement and reconciliation, revenge or forgiveness, quests and searches rewarded or unrewarded; abidingness versus change, love and its proof – these are among the constants, the themes of the story. The story is a form of history; nothing we are involved in goes unrecorded. Having by nature shape, it imparts that, thereby lessening our chaos. By perceiving nothing to be unmeaning, it enlightens us. It arrives, by its end, at a harmony that is not impossible. For the story is vision turned upon reason, with nothing to fear from reason: therein lies its strength.

Preface to Critics Who Have Influenced Taste

How far does the critic influence taste? This succession of essays has been inspired by the assumption that he does; each of the twenty-four has as its subject a critic who, whether immediately or by delayed action, disturbed thought, undermined conventional values and, in his own way, in his own time, on his own level and from his own angle, made for a breakthrough into areas hitherto unexplored. Such critics recognized taste as a potential; they were for it as a form of discrimination, against it as anything rigid or dictatorial; they were aware of it as a capacity for sheer liking or a means for the perfection of enjoyment. In some cases, whatever was in its day revolutionary in the expression of such a critic was inadvertent; he was stating, very often sedately, what for him were the commonplaces of honest minds. In others, there was a consciousness of attack. All of these critics were discursive, remarkably few of them analytical. By all of them, an engaging familiarity, sometimes, it could be said, a furious intimacy with the mind of the reader was established. It may be found (and indeed the author of one essay has pointed out) that the actual taste of a critic could be questionable, have root in obsessions or show blind spots. What matter? – none of these twenty-four set up to be God. Faulty or not in choices, inconsistent in judgements, they stimulated. That they did so gave them their point, and gives point to this book.

One may distinguish, and it is interesting, here, to attempt to do so, between criticism as a give off or by-product of creative energy (that of the poet, playwright or novelist) and criticism as a *métier* in itself. One might say of the first kind that it is less considered, less disengaged, that it is so many sparks sent flying by creative experience, that there is a repartee element in it sometimes. Ben

Jonson, Dryden, Coleridge, Shelley, Virginia Woolf . . . The other pole, the pure or *métier* critic, would seem to be represented in this volume by Hazlitt, Sainte-Beuve, Macaulay, Croce, A. C. Bradley, Desmond MacCarthy, James Agate. How, though, can the distinction be hard-and-fast? In these pages, borderline critics confront, confound us. Samuel Johnson, as critic, gave criticism itself a severe wigging, and in general refuses to be involved – it affected character. "There is often to be found," he noticed, "in men devoted to literature a kind of intellectual cowardice." Pope, Pater – and Matthew Arnold, at present more highly rated (wrongly, *I* think) as critic than poet – had a foot in both worlds. How classify the ruminative and reflective, such as De Quincey? One has to think again. For, who loving literary art with the passion necessary for a critic has not, at some time, essayed to practise it also? To the making of major critical reputation went how many abandoned hopes, what forgotten outpourings? Or a critic may set up other substantial monuments: see Macaulay. Rare in fact is the critic who has not literary sidelines, or (better) parallel activities. The gross error is to think of the critic as a failed artist, or to regard "taking to criticism" as a step down. The pre-eminent critic is one who, after, it may be, a phase of trial-and-error, has found his *métier*. Into that, from then on, proceeds his creative force.

Our concept of creativeness has been narrow; wrong teaching (the unnatural awe of the teacher for any "artist") may further narrow it. At the same time, the idea of creative criticism has been accepted, or has succeeded in inching its way in. However intellectual, and intellect is necessary, the creative critic is not intellectual purely. He acts intuitively, as befits one who has dealings with intuitive matter. He is affectable, whereby he affects others. One may take it that criticism is more and more read (may it not be *more* read, one begins to wonder, than the literature which authorises it?) because of identification of critic with reader. For the latter, this is elating. It can be dangerous, when or if the critic imposes his own reactions – no more than a possibility, but a possibility viewed in some quarters with grave, not silent, concern. Exception is taken. Critics, and their lesser train of reviewers (the complaint or attack runs) are becoming worse than arbiters, dictators: an Establishment in themselves. This complaint rebounds from the critic, but hits the public, in whom it argues an utter and prone passivity. That *I* cannot accept: throughout the patience, the concentration, necessary to take in a book of criticism must run a live-wire intelligence; and intelligence is capable of dissent. I cannot believe that readers, in these competitive days, can be prone and passive; nor can I, which is endlessly more important, believe that anything but a venal critic believes that either. Would any critic *par excellence* (money or not) consent to remain in action if that were so? Such a critic, the proper critic, salutes taste as a constituent of our human nature. He invites it forward. In so far as he "directs" it, he does so only as a native may direct a wandering motorist. He respects taste; he does not attempt to "form" it.

(It is interesting that no or but scant objection was taken to the two "king-makers," ace reviewers, James Agate and the otherwise-novelist Arnold Bennett – both of whom, I am happy to see, are discussed in this book. Those two dealt with what could be taken to be ephemeral. The more serious, long-term critic, with his probing of values, remains the target.)

Each in his own time (or in one case, her time) these twenty-four were critics of the free kind. If perhaps from a distance, for some were shy, they were humanity-lovers. I find how many of the writers of essays on them emphasise their subjects' instinctive wish to break down the barrier, or, put it, bridge the gulf between life and literature. That they did do so, some for their own generations, all for succeeding ones, is the reason why they made and have left their mark. To an extent also they were prophetic. Samuel Johnson's: "We are formed for society, not for combination; we are equally unqualified to live in a close connection with our fellow beings, and in total separations from them" pin-points today's predicament novel and the *cri du cœur* of the anguished and puzzled lyric. Shelley stated: "A man, to be greatly good, must imagine intensely and comprehensively; he must put himself in the place of another; the pains and pleasure of his species must become his own. The great instrument of moral good is the imagination." And, further on in *A Defense of Poetry*: "We want the creative faculty to imagine that which we know; we want the generous impulse to act that which we imagine; we want the poetry of life." Croce discovered that poetry was an activity common to all men: "The poetic state was experienced to some degree by everyone, and wholly by no one." Matthew Arnold saw the future of poetry to be "immense"; Pater saw, further, that the poetry of the future would take the form of prose. "Art," Oscar Wilde held, "expands one's sense of possibility." Virginia Woolf, meditating on what could yet be done in the novel, remarked: "The process of discovery goes on perpetually. Always more of life is being reclaimed and recognised." One is reminded how Flaubert (not here, and why should he be?) foresaw the novel of the future, the novel pending, as being a "psychological overflow."

How far can such critics, these critics, be held accountable for the psychological overflow of the 1960s, a decade distant from some of them by some centuries, and which even the latest-born of them did not live to see? Do *we* face another false dawn, or a culmination? On the surface, there has been a vast break with continuity, a to some minds shattering reversal in matters of language, imagery and theme. *Is* this a revolution (it has been called so) or one further try, the most desperate so far, to encompass "the poetry of life"? Is this the future we heard was coming? How dynamic is all this, where is it leading? Is disruption total, or does there continue stretching beneath the surface, submerged reef, the unbreakable-with past?

In its own way, often enough gracelessly, the 1960s novel embodies poetry. Its stuff is sensation, generic, mankindish, common to one and all. The fraternalism, or classlessness, of the present novel is, as an innovation, far more important than are its sexual escapades – of the latter it might be said, they are somewhat sinister: such writing was not required by our lusty forefathers. So, what is the matter with us: are we under-sexed? True, a ban has been lifted; but think how brief that ban was, compared to the length of history. However, there may be method in this off-madness. More of life *is* being "reclaimed and recognised": should a hush surround modern man's most nagging predicament, though it be, from most of the evidence, his most futile one?

Freedom is hard to envisage, though right in principle. Literary freedom can be chaotic if it shakes off the restraints of order and style; should it fail to do so it is not quite freedom; should it successfully do so, is it still literature? Would the critics we are about to study hold themselves accountable for the 1960s? That seems the question to ask. Would they do so gladly, and how gladly? We remain in their debt, whatever the answer – they opened our eyes, taught us the virtue of pleasure, put their faith in intensity. These critics desired a merging of art with life; and in our day the two are running closer together, for better or worse. For better, in that we are aware of the miracle of existence, our own and others'. For worse, in a sense that those good ones could not foresee: our world spawns visionaries and criminals. We expect from life, and may seek to extract by savage experience, the satisfaction, meaning, glow and intensity which belong to art.

AGE

Modern Girlhood

The French First Communicants cross the page,[1] and cross my imagination. At the first glance, this seems to be a procession of little brides. But inside the white falls of gauze pierced with sunlight, their faces are shadowed by concentration; their eyes are downcast, and these girl-children seem austere, mysterious and remote. All are young, some are very young; but all are the daughters of a very old race. And their sex is innocently and plainly written across their features: not for a moment, since they emerged from babyhood, have they been unconscious that they are to be women.

The procession, for all I know, may be taking place in some obscure provincial town; the young girls are not the daughters of famous[2] families. None the less, all are heiresses to two great things – the Latin culture and the Catholic mystique. Both have moulded their faces into a humble sureness. They are born to the expectation to live in a certain way. Yet – I remind myself – France is the least Latin of the Latin countries. Intellectually, she is in advance of the world; reason and revolution have, for centuries, been at work in her; with her Revolution dawned the era in which we are all still living. Under the Third Republic, the forces of secularism have been strong.[3]

Will these young First Communicants, as they grow older, falter in their Catholicism and be disturbed? Looking again at their faces, I am struck not by any particular spirituality but by a sheer capacity for *devoutness*. This devoutness, if it should be turned away from religion, will not fail, I feel, to be turned towards something else – family life, love of country, or even the running of some small business in which the wife, with the husband, has equal share. It may even – and this will be something quite new – be turned into the channel of politics. For has not General de Gaulle announced that the Frenchwoman is to be enfranchised?[4]

Will the promised vote mean much to these young girls? To look at them is to wonder – and to be left wondering. Since France was

France, her women have had a tacit power equalled, perhaps, in no other land. These girls I am looking at stand on the brink of an all-absorbing career: womanhood. In expecting to step into the places of their mothers and grandmothers, they expect much, not little. The full demand will be made on their energies, their characters and their heads. The meeting of this demand has, for centuries, seemed to be satisfying. The vote may be one thing more – but France, up to now, has shown wonderfully few discontented women. The sufficient *dot*;[5] the early, usually "arranged" marriage; the domestic, social and often business prestige of the wife[6] – are these, then, to be all?

Surely not. No answer is so simple, even in France. Authority and security are not everything. Outwardly, these young girls may – to a degree which seems to us Oriental – have few decisions to make. Strict chaperonage, up to the time they marry, will render impossible for them even the most innocent, tentative experiments in love. For the girl of any "position" (and few French families lack the sense of position) cinema-going, dancing or country walks with the most blameless young man will be out of the question. Intimacies even with other girls are discouraged. Reading is carefully supervised. Are they, then, not trusted? It is not so much that: more, there is a feeling, on the part of their elders, that human nature[7] is too fundamentally serious to be trifled with.

The French do not underrate sex: we have always tried to. The girl is not only watched; she is brought up to watch herself. She moves, she speaks, she goes through her daily duties with a controlled precision, without adolescent gangling. "*Soyez sage!*"[8] – the words seem to hypnotise her. So much for her outwardly. But, inwardly?

Acquiescence has the effect of sealing her up inside a sphere of dreams. Inwardly, she is a deep, if still, pool of emotion. Her reserve is immense: it comes partly from discipline, partly from an unbreakable sense of solitude. She may go through her whole life – as wife, as mother, as mistress of a household, as a respected matriarch – without ever, in the full sense, *speaking*. She may or may not encounter that great invitation to break one's silence – realised romantic love. *Inside* marriage – the marriage she is likely to make –

the chances are against it. Mute, she lives in a country that is still full of nightingales and that once gave birth to the troubadours. ". . . *What do young girls dream of?*"[9] A Frenchman asked it: and the artist, Marie Laurencin,[10] who as a Frenchwoman probably knew,[11] painted the dream in the eyes of her young girls without ever giving away the mystery.

This incommunicable, sealed-up, intensive existence of the young feminine creature, as perceived by the artist, has made itself felt in all French Romantic literature. To the man-mind, its appeal is at once voluptuous and aesthetic. Flaubert's Emma Bovary brings to illicit passion the fervour and, in a strange way, the innocence of a whole youth of solitary dreams – and Flaubert said in a letter: "My Bovary weeps in a thousand villages of France." The extremities of the dream, in religious terms, dominated St. Thérèse, the Little Flower of Lisieux.[12] For Jeanne d'Arc, the sturdy peasant, the dream took the form of heroic instigation. Sometimes, the dream fixes itself, and perhaps breaks, on a public figure: in the novel, *Les Jeunes Filles*, by Henri de Montherlant, lonely girls in different parts of the provinces write a succession of letters, each one more self-revealing, to an inhuman novelist in Paris. He reads few and answers none. "I am telling you," writes each girl, "what I have never told anyone in my life before."

In America, I should fancy, there is not much time to dream – not much time, at any rate, for "the teenage girl." She makes, enjoys and rules a world that is all her own. She has her own status, her own fashions, her own ideas. She is the child of young parents in a young, vast country. Sunny lawns, cool porches, rumpus rooms and capacious lounging chairs (with radio knob within easy reach) are her domestic province. Outside home she has high school, the ice cream bar, the music shop (enshrining, with portraits and records, her favourite crooners) and the movies.

The "teenager,"[13] once named, has become a type. More – ousting her elder sisters, the deb and the college girl, she has come into prominence; so much so that a leading American picture paper has "featured" her. I have thus been able to study four or five pages of captioned photographs of teenage life.

Each teenager wishes, fanatically, to behave, to dress, to look and in fact to be exactly like all the others in her set. She wears – they all wear – bobby sox, loose sweaters, casually pleated skirts, swinging topcoats, flat-heeled moccasin shoes, and a mane of shoulder-length hair. For homework and lounging (which look synonymous) she does a quick change into her brother's shirt and slacks. Ease and unrestriction show in every line of her attitudes. She is the reverse of solitary; she moves in a shoal of contemporaries, girls and boys. She is articulate: probably nothing she has ever felt or thought remains unsaid – where language, even the American language, gives out, she invents and puts into circulation her own words.

She lives in the present; not as a policy but because *her* present could not be better. She puts on a hat and stockings only to go to church – which is all, by the way, that I know about her religion. "She likes boys," says a caption, "but not too much." She likes girls a good deal better: she and her fellow teenagers form a closed circle, to whose edge the boys are admitted on sufferance.

She is, I am told, unaware of the teenage boom – which is to an extent promoted by her astute papa. But she profits by it: today she has her choice of several teenage radio programmes; and the department stores bid for her favour by running special teenage lines.

The apparent ideality of the American teenage world is almost frightening. Must there not, one asks, be a catch *somewhere*? Can the young female spirit really expand so painlessly, without a complexity or a hitch? Is everything extroversion[14] and sun and fun? Are no tears shed – those terrible tears of youth, that tear out the vitals – alone in the muslin-and-chintz-hung bedroom, when the last of the girl friends has gone home? Could so much freedom not possibly give you a vacuum inside?

I don't say the teenager has thought this out, but she must have instinctively sensed the dangers. For she and her contemporaries, in their apparent play, have reverted, in fact, to the close formation and stern dark laws of the primitive tribe. Taboos – to whose breaking dire penalties, even ostracism, attach – surround them. Rites that might have interested Sir James Frazer[15] attend initiation into high-school sororities. Behind the teenage crazes lies something atavistic. One jingles with charm bracelets, improvises strange dances at midnight, walks with a coin in the shoe . . . The French young girl turns from the outward law to the secret dream. Does her American sister turn from the outward dream to the secret law?

And in Britain?[16] About a year ago I walked down the gangway of a cinema straight (it seemed) into a pair of enlarged, direct young eyes. They were Princess Elizabeth's. She was, I believe, in the course of reviewing the Grenadier Guards, of which she is the Colonel; but the troops had, for the moment, marched out of view, leaving her alone in a large grass space under a sky of scudding grey clouds. The wind which made the clouds scud blew strands of Princess Elizabeth's front hair up against the upturned brim of her hat. I wondered whether the hat would blow off, and the same thought may have passed through her mind. But she did not touch the hat: she continued to eye the camera with candour and with a touch of humour in which preoccupation hardly appeared at all. Amazing, I thought. – It was not, of course, so amazing: it showed the force of a royal upbringing. Still, amazing *I* thought. A young English girl who, in spite of all provocation, forbears from fidgeting with her hat!

The young English girl fidgets and gangles her way through society, in which she is conscious of having no place. She comes in round doors sideways, bashfully, like a crab. She can be very annoying or very touching: I think she is chiefly annoying because she *is* touching. She is as humble as a puppy and as self-conscious as a peacock. She hasn't got a formula – either the classic, sculpted, disciplined formula of the Old World French girl, or the relaxed, gay, loose-limbed formula of the New World American. Since "flapper" died, she hasn't even got a generic name: usually, she is referred to as a "schoolgirl" – with the suggestion that, if at the moment she is not actually at school, it would be better for everyone if she were. She does not feel funny – in fact, she often feels tragic – but she is conscious that most people think her funny. Indeed, many of the heartiest and jolliest English jokes centre round the miseries of adolescence. "Laugh 'em out of it," is the attitude.

The English young girl tends to be boy-type: this, I think, is largely protective, from not yet feeling confident as to femininity. She affects brusqueness and gruffness. Many would rather die than show how much they care about what they do care about. Appearance and clothes are such a profound worry that the gym-tunic, the cropped hair or the tense pigtail are a welcome let-out.

When she is all alone, the girl goes to the looking-glass, looks at herself with a sick smile and says, "Gosh . . . !" She is convinced that nobody is ever going to fall in love with her. At the same time, if someone *did* fall in love with her, might she not perhaps feel rather an ass?

She is very good, however, herself, at falling in love. Actually she prefers a one-sided passion. For this (I should say) the rarest possible object is any man who is at all young. Mark Anthony is more attractive than Romeo. She can also fall in love with a character out of a book or history, with a celebrity or with a school friend. In the presence of the beloved she has glorious feelings of abjection, turns scarlet all over and cannot speak . . .

This may sound as though I shared the general opinion that English young girls are funny: I do not. Their internal lyricism seems to me very grand. I have seldom met a young girl that I did not love; though I often do not know what to say to her. And I am happiest with the friends who were my school friends.[17] For suddenly, from behind the composed surface, looks out at me the familiar face of sixteen.

Teenagers

Under no other name would teenagers be quite so engaging. The American teenager problem came into being once that name was found – as in all other countries containing young, which is to say all other countries, there had of course always been a problem, but not yet specifically that. Once docketed, the teenager sailed into prominence, to provide a major national topic. So popular are teenagers in the Press (which may claim to have discovered, if not invented, them) that it must be seldom that one of them picks up a magazine or newspaper without finding something about himself, or herself.

On that scale, publicity is unknown to the equivalent age-group in our land, where it is still more or less anonymous – the flapper, who once did not do so badly, disappeared with the big back bow and the switch of hair: upon her bobbing or shingling the curtain dropped. Anyhow, flapperdom was confined to one sex. Law takes august notice of "young persons"; "young people" sounds some-how woolly-benign. "Adolescents," though favoured in novels, are not what our friends between twelve and twenty would gladly, actually, claim to be. So, our unfortunates labour through seven years of, virtually, an age without a name. So far, they fail to be put across. Different is the lot of the teenager.

Teenagers are not merely a group, they are a race – never extinct, perpetually re-supplied. Intake from below, from the over-twelves, makes good any loss at the top, as the seniors are forced out by becoming twenty. Seniority does not confer prestige; indeed it may mean a slight falling-off, for the absolute, the meridian of teenager-ship is at about sixteen. Growing up is not numbered among the tribal aims. It *is* possible – though not, I think, well seen – to dress and act like a teenager for a good while longer, if one finds one still likes oneself best as that: lingerers-on are to be spotted in mixed State colleges, beach resorts, ice cream bars. The pure or out-and-out teenager, however, is usually still attending high school, which entails living at home: or rather home is the base for sleeping, feeding and telephoning. Sleep is brief, feeding hasty; telephoning, very much more protracted, is followed by once more rushing out of the house. Teenagers are regarded by adults with fatalism and awe. Adults are, as they are aware, by teenagers not regarded at all.

Anthropological study of these nomads reveals much that is constant in their customs – troopings, assemblies and choice of locale. Movement, usually in numbers, is achieved by piling in and out of cars; the feet, however, do not atrophy, being used for scuffing at things, pointing at things or marking rhythm, whether dancing or not. Hands are put to less use. Sitting singing is one nocturnal activity. Dress, much the same for both sexes, is so worn as to seem on the point of falling or blowing off – preference going to what flaps, such as shirts with their tails not tucked in, or what is susceptible to being hitched or rolled up. Limbs are notably bare. As to ornament, the bizarre is sought. But the constant in fashion is only one rule: it must never stabilise. Teenagers are fashion-pioneers – and this goes for crazes, taboos, vocabulary. They are America's unpredictables.

This, in fact, constitutes the teenager problem. Who knows what they are going to do or say next; or still more, why they are going to do or say it? Who knows whether they know themselves? – it is generally, however, supposed they do. Their inscrutable motives are much delved for. Now and then a teenager arms himself and commits crime, or heads a religious revival, or burns up his or a friend's home, or takes himself off, then telegraphs home for money. Or a pair detach themselves and elope, to be come upon drinking coke inoffensively in an hotel or motel. The bang with which these hit the headlines results, almost every time, in a questionnaire: what are teenagers' views on crime, God, family life, sex? Wisely, teenagers make few statements – at most, they consent to let it be known that everything is still under consideration. They continue to lie or crouch around, supposedly either thinking for themselves or not thinking because they see no necessity to do so, while rumour lengthens in their wake a trail of wrecked cars, empty bottles and stumps of marijuana cigarettes.

The sexes are addicted to one another, but not to a degree which should cause alarm. None the less, it is felt by the community that a teenager is always upon the verge of an extreme act, which no one can hope to stop in time. At the same time, one would hesitate to check their development, even had one a notion how to do so. Parents also console themselves by the American fallacy that one can only be young once.

Teenagers officially feel fine. As what they are they are successes, and they are not expected to be more. All that is asked of them is to exhibit unconcern and nonchalance, and as to this they put up a good show: they represent the non-suffering version of adolescence. At the same time, adolescents are what they are, call it what you like, like it or not – and they suspect something is wrong somewhere. They have misgivings. They guess the world needs improving; they guess they would like to feel secure. They suspect that life is not all it is shown to be in the glossy magazines. Worse still, a day will come when the gang will break up: how is one going to make out, all the rest of one's time, as an individual? This is what they say when compelled to talk, or in some way communicate, with a stranger – teenagers tolerate visitors; they were good to me. Possibly one's oddness gets past their guard. Unaccustomed but totally civil smiles (they seldom smile at each other) extend their faces. They put me at ease by assuring me *they* were not so much at ease as they might appear.

"The way we act," they said, "is considered funny."

"Why?" I asked.

"Have you not been told about us?"

I said I wondered if they were misreported; after some thought they said, oh no. They had a collective dignity, and rightly – are they not a composite celebrity? I was hobnobbing with a unique feature of contemporary American life.

Mental Annuity

Youth, they say, lives for the future, old age in the past. And the middle years? I do myself doubt whether youth takes more account of the future than can be coloured by the mood of a day. Not till the middle years does one look ahead, with lessening illusion, and objectively. Only then, when one already knows what it means to live, does the future take shape as a probability. Subject to world events, it is none the less personal, ours, and for our making. A path to be trodden, a term of time to be lived by us, individuals, you and me. More than half of life, not impossibly, still awaits us. How is it to be met?

There *should* be a halfway pause, a taking of thought. Yet, ironically, it is now, in our middle years, that we are most driven by hurry, beset by claims. We have a feeling of crowdedness – it is this which renders evaluation so difficult. Affections, duties are valid; but outside those what *are* the essentials? May we be missing them? What are we to lay by out of experience? – Time is not to be endless, and we know it. Hours, days, weeks: ought we not, perhaps, to be in some way checking on our expenditure? We have, it may be, a haunting sense of improvidence, of time paid out for short-lived returns. Ultimately, what *will* remain of worth? The query continues, the misgiving disturbs us. Unstated, the problems of our maturity are more complex than any which confront youth.

What, in the castings around of our middle years, are we in search of? Many might say, security; some, fulfilment. Is it too much to ask the advancing years that they should show us not loss but gain? To age, should that not be an adventure? Today, thanks to art, fashion, and science, the physical age-terrors are laid low; we need not lose our looks, we should keep our health. Materially, we are most of us taken care of, shored up against any reasonable future by somebody else's foresight if not our own – the economic principle of investment. Capital, the dividend or annuity, so far, so good: in fact, very good indeed. To continue to look well, feel well, and be maintained – can one ask more? Yes.

What of the inner fund? Mind, heart, spirit, what shall *they* have to draw on? Our returns or lack of returns show early: among our contemporaries, already, begin to appear emptying faces, unexpectant eyes. Automatic talk, unconvincing laughter but thinly bridge over the psychic void. Few of us, probably, are not haunted by a picture of somebody left with nothing – the man or woman with no incentive, no joys, no interests, it may seem no memories. That last pitiful, most common of tragedies, negativity. Old age, while it accentuates this state, cannot wholly account for it: seeds were there. Old age excuses it – "So-and-so," one hears charitably explained, "has outlived his (or her) day." That I always doubt, and for this reason: if one has *lived* one's day, it lives on within one. Witness the glow, the authority of great-aged people. Only the superficialities desert one.

Good investments don't always bring quick returns. To build up an inner life needs patience, discrimination, and, above all, faith. To pursue essentials may lead one some way off the beaten track. Valuable people are not always easy people to know – they may seem forbidding or inaccessible. Great books, which germinate in the mind, may involve a tussle with one's intelligence. Places which speak to one, little ancient cities almost unheard of, a plateau with a battered solitary church, a landscape with unexpected poetry, lie hidden in the crease of the world, out of reach of the more orthodox tour. One cannot say that the test of the worth of things is *always* their aftereffects – when what is to be a lasting impression comes, the moment often is in itself intense. Yet one feels, also: "This I must revisit. It is more than I can take in now." And revisit one does, unfailingly, in memory.

The filling and furnishing of memory is, undoubtedly, one great means of inner resource. Yet one would not look upon memory as a museum – in fact, it refuses to be one, utterly. The charm, one might say the genius of memory, is that it is choosey, chancy, and temperamental: it rejects the edifying cathedral and indelibly photographs the small boy outside, chawing a hunk of melon in the dust. What one can do for memory is to offer it fair fields out of which to make its gleanings, not compel it forever to choke itself with dusty ephemeralities and trash. One can make a friend of one's memory, one can school it; to memorise – a face, a poem, an idea springing from talk, a lovely room, the play of light on a landscape – is a rewarding, voluntary act.

One fallacy injures the name of memory – the idea that living on constant terms with it condemns one to "living in the past." That could not be less so. The fact is, memory is vitally interconnected with all experience; just as it takes in, it gives out. Lively associations are its language. It *is* continuity – linking moments, imparting meanings, suggesting comparisons, throwing light. It is an integral part of the fabric of friendship, love – are not our affections like living books, in which each fresh page gains from the one before?

How many of one's choices are instinctive? What is it that leads one, in the first instance, to what will come to seem the predestined friend? Many relationships in life are a matter either of chance or of obligation – family, business, social. There are people one has to know, and does well to like. Quite a number of us, by the middle years, find ourselves occupying a social framework from which it is not easy to step clear: success and[1] established position have their price. Acquaintances tend to run to type – one meets new people, but seldom different ones. There begins to appear to be a set pattern, or formula, for knowing people: one settles down to it – though not, I think, without disappointment and a sense of growing inert and passive. Yet, humanly, miracles still happen, and happen before it is too late. A face arrests one's attention, or something said pierces the surface, becomes significant. One bestirs oneself. The unmistakable signal of a friend is that, from the start, they ask something of one – some greater degree of intelligence, candour, feeling. In return, they may proffer a rich new world.

So much has been said and written about falling in love, so little about the gentler approach to friendship. In this case the dynamism is quieter. Lovers may flash into being, friends are *made*. It is less easy to make friends in middle life: other ties, responsibilities, affections make felt their claims on one. A friend, in fact, has to be worth the making; when one judges a man or woman to be that, one is, I think, usually proved right. It takes some exceptional quality to attract one – in addition, there almost certainly is some mutual interest waiting to be explored, or common sympathy ready to be deepened. A friendship is generally *about* something. And, unlike youth's, the friendships of one's maturity have a tempo and temperance of their own. Times to meet may be brief, few, far apart; but the good overflows, fills up intervening spaces.

Nor, let us remind ourselves, are all friends new friends. To maintain an existing relationship means no less, asks no less, but also rewards no less than to embark upon a fresh one. Something dies in one if, out of inattention, one lets an old friend go. Both to make and to keep friends does take time – but the time is invested in immortality. Inwardly, one need never remain alone.

Books offer illimitable wealth. Their multitude, when one looks back and back, may also occasionally be baffling. "To enter a noble library," a friend confessed to me, "makes me burst into tears. It's not that I couldn't finish reading all this, but I don't know where I should ever begin." She was honest. A difficulty of reading is not only selection but continuity – disjected fragments of literature, like torn pages flapping around in a draughty attic, may settle to nothing within one, so go to waste. One may hope to have carried from school or college a general notion of what is classic, of what carries the universal stamp. Most of us have within us potential taste. But taste is not all: there's requirement, there's affinity. Certain books come to meet one, as do people. They speak out to one, they enlarge one, they remain with one. I say, one should read what one enjoys; saying this, I base upon the belief that one can educate, tune higher, experiment with, extend one's inherent faculty for enjoyment. Poetry is less out of normal reach than one's day-to-day trivialities make it seem. Conflict, in the expenditure of our reading time, may arise between "good" reading and what is current. The wish to keep up with what's written today is spontaneous, sociable, and human; to exclude what is "popular" may be snobbish. Should one, all the same, be debarred from the company of majestic imaginations and timeless minds?

There is much to be said for *two* books on hand – one to be savoured slowly, a page a day; the other for recreational reading. Literature, one may recollect, is a whole – a compost being added to continually. Ancient august books fructify what is newer. Experience, yours and mine, is at once individual and general – a clue to your being or mine, an assuaging touch on the soul, or a thought to live by may come from a pen laid down thousands of years ago. And nothing one reads deeply has ever gone – strange are those reassurances, from the depths of memory!

"They flash upon that inward eye which is the bliss of solitude," Wordsworth said of the crowd of daffodils.[2] With what same benevolence scenes and places return to one. If, as a traveller, one from time to time leaves a little of oneself behind, feels unaccountably heart-rent by the departure from some valley one has only viewed for an hour, or small town where one has only stayed for a night, how one is requited! The film of memory, as we have noted, is intermittent, but oh how dear is that series of pictures it can immortalise. Such pictures, nothing but hurry blurs – let us be lingerers, where we can. Out of a dozen, one place holds out its arms to one; I can't feel its invitation should go for nothing. Great cities have, too, their speaking moments – why should the fountain-filled silence of a square, or the bye-street beneath the cathedral's flank suddenly seem one's own – and one's own only?

Scenes to be dwelled upon, years after, do not lie by necessity off the map. In essence they're seldom exotic; they seem familiar as though already known in a dream. They may connect with child-hood – they may indeed be some lost paradise revisited. The aim of travel – whether over the hill or to the extremes of some other continent – is not the *deliberate* collection of mind pictures. Yet that these form themselves, find us, stamp themselves on our hearts is, I am certain, travel's truest reward . . . To observe and to love, to learn and to[3] reflect, and perhaps even a little to understand – is not this how to travel into the future? The fund built up, drawn on, again renewed. We need much to live by – and live we must.

The Case for Summer Romance

Summer is a fiesta. Burnished with colour, pungent with scents, soft with heat-muted sounds, summer is youth's rightful, rewarding heritage. Hazy early mornings, lit through by a gleam from ocean or lake, are fresh, every one of them, with promise. Noons, whether on the shadeless beach or the shadowy patio, are spellbound: dark-blue nights are tense with unfathomed mystery. All things seem afloat in this dazzling weather – and there can be a charm even in freakish days: scuds of rain, salt gusts whipping the grass on the rippled sand dunes, clouds sailing the sky in a slow procession, the uncanny hush before the electric storm. The setting of the vacation is the more vivid for being not too familiar – it gazes back at the eye like a living picture. Maybe, too, there is something dramatic about the background – a touch, one might say, of the painted stage-set: the shore colony with its rainbow awnings, jetties, and bobbing craft . . . the valley with its icy, swift little river, overhung by the majesty of the mountain range . . . the camp in the forest . . . the ancient village, sunk in the sleep of years, unstirred by the youthful rush of summer invaders . . . the foreign hill town, vine-trellised, clustered around its castle, girt by battlements with an immense view. Yes, a stage *is* set.

And set for what? Romance.

At the start of a vacation, sheer contented bliss is enough – the ease, the sense of having all time to play with, the exhilaration of being "out of school." To breathe, to *be* – to swim, to wander, to lie in a daze of sun. Those first days, could one desire more? For a while, well-being itself, with a thousand lovely sensations, is enough to drink in: a brimming cup. But after that comes, "What more?" Happiness stirs up the anticipation of being happier still. Surely this, all *this*, was meant to be shared? Like a child on the beach looking round for a playmate, the girl instinctively looks around for some particular playmate for her heart. This sweet and sensuous world of summer, at once so idle and so intensified, seems her temperament's dancing-floor; who is to be her partner? Not so much conscious search as the welling up of an unconscious and wonderful expectation causes her to glance at the faces round her. Never was she more ready to be entranced, never more in the mood to be found entrancing. And she *is* entrancing. Even herself delights her – the bronze of her bare limbs, the coursing of the blood in her veins, quickened by the air of the hills or the tingle of the sea. In her looking-glass, she smiles at her own reflection: how ready she is for the mirror of Someone's eyes!

She has not, let us suppose, very long to wait.

Possibly, even, there was no waiting. It happened the first day, at the first glance. He and she singled each other out; there *could* be no mistake surely, for this was magic. Right from the start, it appeared, they were in tune. Together they take the floor – the actual dancing floor of sapphire evenings, outdoor, lamp-hung, also the day-long floor of twin, shared activity – cutting the water in a speed boat, goggling at one another in deep-sea depths among goggling fishes, horseback riding along the edges of woods or on mountain tracks. Their sports car, headed into the sunset, tears along the curve of the bay road. Or there is laziness: elbows buried deep in the forest mosses or fingertips seeking each other, touching, as the two lie side-by-side on the beach like bright spars of sentient driftwood, washed up together.

And, in a sense, they *are* two creatures washed up together, caught on the same current. Both are bound by the same idyllic and golden spell. The present is enough; they are saturated in happiness. They are one in mood, and this mood enclosing them is an iridescent bubble become a universe; for the time being, nothing exists outside it. Forgotten is the banal, the everyday. Still more than half childish, these two are playmates. Romance, in passing, brushes them with the tip of its bright wing. Lightly in touch, they are dancing partners; youth and the joy of holiday are their music. Summer is their *now*.

Often the young are wise – they are wise instinctively. They know what they are doing, though they don't tell you. An onlooker, watching the boy and girl, might wonder, "Is there no risk of heartbreak?" Yet these two, for all their radiant abandon, are apt to be more wary than they appear. They are playing fair, in their own way, by one another. Born players of life's most rapturous game, flirtation, they abide by its one rule – hurt not, and be not hurt! By their code, it's more than a blunder, it is a crime to "spoil things." To go too deep, to ask too much, to be *serious* . . . Yes, there is danger (a hint of it) in the offing. At any age, the heart is incalculable. Also, happiness is not only a heady wine; it has a way of drawing up more emotion than the young foresee. No, neither has hurt the other. Yet *something* hurts. What has happened?

Young summer lovers go suddenly shy of each other, when it comes to parting. They feel, perhaps, a shock of bewilderment. Till now, they did not know the meaning of the word Goodbye.

Till summer catches her unawares, a woman may not realise how young she is. Marriage, she thought, put a term to girlhood, its rhapsodical gaieties, dreams, and attendant pitfalls. The coming of children, and her delight in them, has given her – surely? – all that woman can ask. Her home grants a thousand rewards for the tasks it brings. She has steadied into companionship with her husband; their loving mutual loyalty is her fortress. As they promised each other when they were first lovers, they make an ethical effort to "keep young." From time to time they go dancing, they brisk their minds up by an intellectual argument or so fix things that they can take the car for a tour. One would be a fool (she tells herself) to expect now the freshness, the stimulus, the initial thrill that, long ago, gave an extra lift to those pleasures.

Now, she is adult, satisfied, and fulfilled. She reasons to herself that this must be so – for lack of any cause to find it is not. So far as she can be conscious, she has no yearnings. Now and then aware of left-over daydreams, she laughs them out of existence (or so she fancies). Summer now means chiefly a move to the beach cottage, a transference of the family pattern to a stripped-down, salty, and sunshiny other setting. Taking her children swimming, she's remotely amused by watching the boys and girls sporting like couples of young dolphin. Lying in the sun, she may roll head sideways, with an indulgent smile, to note the trances of nearby juvenile lovers. She herself, she cannot but reflect, is still hardly less slender, and just as brown, as her nineteen-year-old neighbour. But, now – what matter?

It's sad enough, when the day comes, taking her husband to the train to go back to town, to business. His vacation over, she stays on here with the children; he'll make it, whenever possible, for a weekend. Now sets in a period of – what? A state of mind she's unable quite to define: something between liberty and loneliness. Her children have joined a group; they make few demands on her. She's likely to take a book with her to the beach, but may not read it. Restlessness gets a hold on her. Has she forgotten how to be alone? She supposes, yes . . . And now it is, ironically, that summer (lagging a little, so far) comes to perfection. Never, it seems to her, has the ocean reached so burning a blue, never have the extending sands been more dazzling, the pine woods behind them more aromatic. Later, all things reflect the flamingo sunset – finally there come down the gauzes of evening, through which flit the boys and girls, hand-in-hand. Wafts of distant dance music come to her through the trees.

On one such evening she makes her way, unaccompanied, to a party some friends are giving at the club. Most of the faces are familiar, but there's one stranger – or if there *were* other strangers she did not notice, for this one claimed her. He and she were, she supposed, introduced; what she did remember was that, from then on, he never left her side. A man of around her age, maybe a year or two younger, here for a while on his own – that's to say, unattached. An overflow guest of one of the neighbour cottages, making do at the inn.

Dancing with him, she remembered what dancing could be – what once it was. Outdoors, they found themselves in the other-worldly light of the full moon: when the music stopped, there was nothing but the murmur of the ocean. Standing there in the milky-white of her chiffon dress, she allowed herself to be conscious of his gaze, though she no more than said to herself, "Yes, he's very charming." Before they returned to the others, the crowd, the ballroom, she stole a glance into the curious mystery of his face. At the end, he walked her back through the woods, as far as her door, outside which they stood smoking last cigarettes. That was the beginning.

The weather became more beautiful, if possible. He made friends with the children. She never knew, when she opened the screen door, whether she might or might not find him there on the porch, waiting for her to be ready to come out. Always was there this slight, delightful element of suspense (a sensation till now all but forgotten). He never took her for granted, or she him. Always, there seemed to be some new plan for the day or evening, or something further to laugh about: a surprise! Not for – how long? – had anyone been so observant of her movements, so perceptive of her ideas, her thought, and her wishes. Yet he teased her as often as he flattered her. Free, without ties, he had the fascination, for her, of a creature from another and wider world. Picturing his experiences, listening to his stories, she felt her wits quickening, her imagination again stirring alive. Principally, gaiety was the thing: they shared some delicious, secret source of amusement. Even small "family" doings, in his added company – taking the children for a picnic, going marketing – took on a touch at once of comedy and of magic. And now, with him as escort, she either went to more parties or found the parties she went to still more fun. Music was no longer distant; it was in her ears.

She did not run wild.

All the same, when he said, "You're looking lovely, you know, this evening," it meant something. She realised, just with a little start of the sense of danger, how much it *might* mean – in so far as it differed from what she had never-failingly heard for the last years: her husband's placid, "You always look good to me." Making comparisons . . . Now was the time to pull herself up, she thought. So she began wondering where to, when to, how to. However, as it turned out, she need not have worried. There arrived a long distance call, or maybe a cable, terminating his holiday three days sooner. That was that.

On the day after his going, the weather breaks: the sky chills, rain begins to fall. The beach empties. Yet, lighting a fire in the cottage, with the children, she cannot feel that anything is over. On the contrary, she feels miraculously in tune with herself, her life, and the round of routine which has begun again. That week of happiness has been to the good, and the good stays. She is left more confident, more generous, more honest with herself, and with more to give out to the world round her, by that unspoiled idyll. She gives thanks. Whether the illusion would have lasted, she does not ask; for so long as it did last, it remained untarnished. Nothing to regret.

Summer, showering down on us its bounty, deserves well of us – let us misuse nothing it gives or brings. Let earth's generous season close with a sigh, not tears. Tears mean summer romance has over-flowed bounds.

The Beauty of Being Your Age

Beauty's a thing of youth, fleeting; Age lies in wait, its relentless enemy . . . That's been a concept drilled into us women, to the point, maybe, of setting up an obsession. Dread of advancing years goes deep, is not merely a matter of surface vanity; more, it speaks resistance to change – must not change mean loss?

But *must* change mean that? – moreover, in fact does it? Look at Nature, the drama of changing seasons; each of the four (and winter, I think, not least) having a peak of perfection of its own – and, with its subtle transition through to the next, a power to stir the imagination, elate the heart and quicken the pulse. Phases, contrasts, differentiations, pages turning over, new chapters opening: is it not those which bind us to life, as to an absorbing tale, which enliven the long, long day of existence for us? Why, then, fear new chapters in our personal being? Each decade is, surely, a fresh beginning – a challenge, yes; but also an invitation to adventure further, to experience more.

As women, we need recourse to the art of living. Our "seven

ages"[1] are more inner, less arbitrary, than those which Shakespeare outlined as the fate of man. Each has its intrinsic style, its special kind of allure, its own possibilities . . . "Yes, fine," I hear women object, "but how about looks? How am I to view the years as a big adventure, if for many, yes, most of them, I'm to look like nothing on earth?"

The mistake is, probably, that of thinking in terms of Age, as an abstract bugbear, rather than of ages – of which each is to be welcomed, when it falls due, as a further addition to the identity. For beauty, once its early dazzle is past, *is* very very much a matter of identity; ease, poise, the gentle brilliance of individuality in expression, gesture and tone of voice. Youth, real youth, is an ability to be charmed by the world around, to respond to things as they come. That, we need not lose.

Only a fool would decry, or expect to rival (or, worst of all, would attempt to imitate) the lyric and glowing beauty of a young girl – the artless physical glow, the dynamic movement, the aura of more-than-conscious expectancy. Yet, watching the flower-like swirlers on a ballroom floor, one sees the "I" already define the faces: already, the modelling touch of the thumb of Life, that artist never the same, and never unsure. In the later years, there'll be only one kind of face which both spells negative tragedy and lacks beauty. What kind? The unmarked, "unknowing," totally null one.

The "later years" – later than what? The "after years" – after what? Life is never over; never is it a book to be closed and set back, with a sigh, upon the shelf. And, too, *are* we right in thinking life grows more difficult? Youth as a state of being is far from easy: that we either remember or can learn, again, from the young who are dear and near to us. With middle age comes a slackening of early tensions, a lay off of emotion's more wild demands. Problems don't vanish, but take more manageable proportions. Leisure, were there ever enough of that, can be valued at its actual, golden worth. Now is, therefore, the time for relish, for exploration: unread books to catch up with, countless new friends to make, fresh horizons to view and, it's hoped, traverse. Elasticity, eagerness in the spirit renews an elasticity in the body. And add one good word for our century: never was there one more propitiously kind to the "young-old." Atmosphere, way of living, dress, make-up combine to provide an expressive style for her. Dead, today, as the dodo is that piteous guy of the Victorian novel, the wheezing and flaccid lady "past her first youth."

The move through, from the thirties into the forties, *is* a test. Maturity, now asking to be assumed, is a garb at first not always easy to wear. Before that, that transition from girlhood into young womanhood was helped, maybe, by accepted pattern – whether that of early marriage and motherhood, or the stimulus of a "to make" career. It's when major decisions have (it appears) been taken, that a woman may sense anticlimax, or at least aftermath. Or, outward adjustments hide an inner bewilderment. Yet what an epoch this ought to be: life's high noon! To expand and glow in it should be natural. Recall, the idealised goddesses of antiquity all had the attribute of *matured* beauty.

From the fifties on through the sixties, to – who knows when? For women who learn how to live them, or know instinctively, these ages hold unforeseen treasure. Detachment, one secret of happiness, strengthens daily; egotism, that nagger, becomes less – the "I" now no longer a tyrant, proves a trusty companion. Life, there's no doubt, becomes more interesting the more you know of it. Best of all, the years are no longer enemies; they are conquests – there's triumph in having lived them. These, I suppose, are reasons why I see such a steady light in the faces of many of my con-temporaries. Their good looks, their manner, their way of being, suggest they are having *their* kind of wonderful time. They are. By some paradox, on the eve of old age they have repossessed themselves of essential youthfulness. Nor, found, is that liable to be lost again.

The woman I know best in the world declares that, so far, she likes her sixties so well that she hopes her seventies may do even more for her. What is good is always apt to be better. Must she live, she wonders, to eighty, ninety, a hundred, *quite* to realise the beauty of being the age she is?

Was *It an Art?*

Seen from without, *their* ways and manners of love could look to be, largely, a matter of tribal custom. The tribe? – their own: themselves. I mean, the young of today – or, one could put it, youth's more conspicuous section. As a tribe, they have been in business for several years: how almost over-familiar becomes their image! In shoals they move, along streets, across college campuses. Their garb, for all its vagaries, has basically the similarities of a uniform, and thereby serves a requisite purpose. It stamps them, proclaiming their dedication to their idea of themselves: a generation which holds itself to be like no other, and glories in that belief. *How* they look is more than a matter of whim or fancy, it is a manifesto – in itself a declaration of independence.

Something, though, has been sacrificed to this "general" look. While good for the differentiation of the tribe (as a tribe) it causes a lessening of identity in the tribe's individual members. Not always, even, are the sexes easily to be told apart, so alike is the flow of the hair, the cut of the jib. Only the male beard and feminine mini-skirt, when worn, at the first glance establish out-and-out certainty. In the main, characteristics have been pooled, and this makes for a sort of egalitarianism in regard to looks (as apart from "look"). Goodlookers, of either sex, stand out less strikingly – surely? – than they normally would; tending rather to merge into, and be lost in, the homelier rank-and-file. Maybe this is due to the cult of amorphousness, together with the current adoption of "granny" spectacles. Could it, though, also be part of the ethics of the tribe: "One must be the *same*"? By that reckoning, star-quality could be a form of disloyalty. I am left to wonder – that is, I have not yet asked.

I may do so, in time. For I have found these young, in spite of the occasional savagery of their appearance, to be kindly, inclined to react willingly to any question not put with hostile intent. In so far as they have time over for you or me, they are glad to give it – they feel for us *others* (so far as I can make out) a kind of pity which makes for tolerance. Not only do they enjoy talking about themselves, as do and have all and any young people at any time, but they feel they ought to. They have a creed to expound, and this they proceed to do with the greatest earnestness. Unlike the young of my day, the flippant Twenties, they are not inhibited by self-mockingness, or objection to being pompous. They *are* pompous – how can they not be? For not only have they a creed, they have a doctrine. Though that doctrine passingly touches on other matters, it begins with, reverts to, and largely revolves around sex.

Sex is a problem they have solved – I am glad to tell you. They indeed find it hard to see why it *was* a problem (only the infinite perversity and unutterable misguidedness of their forebears can have made it so). In reality, nothing could be simpler. Cut out all artificialities: be *natural. Act* natural. Everybody is looking for somebody to have sex with, nor need that somebody be far to seek, for that's true of everybody in your crowd. So you meet up. So then, the rest follows. If nothing happens one time, it will happen the next: all you need to do is keep on the move, with the crowd, and await developments. Sex is right. It is a salvation. It does good. It's fulfilment. Without sex you'd be sick, or schizoid, or something.

No, *not* always fulfilment with the same person. You might get with a person who wasn't right for you. Or they might start right, then after a while not be – so then you tell them. You don't have to feel obligations to any person: after all, you gave as good as you got. You don't want to tie yourself up – that's not fair to you.

Love . . .? Well, I guess we all feel lovingly, one way or another, to all the kids in our crowd. Kind of universal. We all see things the same way, and act the same way, so of course we're all of us close. That's what keeps us going. Love's not *special*, with us. *We* don't want things special. Thinking of love *that* way could be how you people ran into trouble . . .

Possibly . . .[1]

All we people – the young of a vanished day. The more the young of Today knew about us, the more we would shock them. Conversely, the more I hear of the contemporary stark sex program, as outlined, the more uneasy I feel – not on my own behalf but on that of its glib and convinced participants. Something tells me, there's a catch in it somewhere. Tears ahead? – I should hate to think so: who could desire these virtual children to be unhappy? Yet I feel tears pending, hanging about in the atmosphere like coming rain. And not only that – I envisage torrents shed, at midnight, into solitary pillows. The awful, despairing sadness of the deserted ones, made worse by having to be unadmitted, kept dark – it's against tribal rules. I somehow cannot believe that the sex program, in its carrying-out, does not leave behind it, often, heartbroken casualties. *Is* it possible for human beings, and above all young ones, in whom emotions are at their height, to be as invulnerable as these experimenters set out to be? A meeting, a mating: all but synonymous. To follow, a week (two, three?) of company-keeping, entailing drastic mutual exploration on every plane. Then, what? A walk-out, ruthless, often abrupt – the he or she in the matter having decided truer "fulfilment" is to be found elsewhere. Are all break-offs made by common consent? I should be happy to think so – but I doubt it.

The exponents of this creed, which idealises fulfilment (intense, temporary) and denounces involvement (a threat of permanence) do, by their own profession, live for Today. Which is to say, in the moment, and for the moment. So do most children. But *these*, I need to remind myself, are not children – they are young adults, encased (for all the enduring childishness of their outlook) in high-powered, quickly maturing bodies. They have no idea of the forces within themselves that their sex-experimentations could stir up – forces of which their elders have learned (often learned by experience, the hard way) to stand in awe. Awe is a[2] faculty lacking in this group – as, too, is foresight. No, *we* cannot warn them.

Did we, they would not listen. They have all the answers, pat. "It's all so simple. We see that – you muddled the thing; we don't. It is all *natural*." Heaven help you, you wise ones! – have you, then, no conception what Nature *is*? A very demon, a tyrant latent within you. Involvement – you repudiate involvement. You recoil from any kind of responsibility. Easy enough to shake off another person, or so you claim (though, watching some of your[3] cases of stifled conscience, I've come to doubt if *that's* as easy as that). Worse, and absolutely more unavoidable, is involvement with the being YOU are: yourself – your own unexpected complexity. Your passions, your senses, are a full-sized, elemental inheritance you can't shake off: they, with the frenzying memories they engender, the dismaying confusions they set up, will not easily let you out of their grip . . . To which one might add: What a waste of your youth! Can't you be . . . gay?

We were gay. One era of my now distant past remains an ingenuous melange of dancing-shoes, indecipherable telephone messages, shreds of flowers which put in their appearance the day after. Curling-up faded snapshots immortalise picnics (all those faces in the groups, whatever were their names? – where can *they* have gone?). In the world I moved in, none of our families were rich; none of us girls were "debs" – our social occasions, largely, were improvised: none the worse for that. Now and then came a grandiose event: we would find ourselves whirling round some vast, dazzling ballroom – chiefly, though, our young men took us out dancing: one dined first, sipping at white wine. It was very charming indeed to be taken out, and such evenings had a delicious bloom. In the taxi, on the return home, a light kiss, in which affection and gratitude mingled, might or might not be exchanged: there never was more than that. Pleasure was the thing, and it seldom failed. Yes, we frivolled about together, we opposite sexes. We enjoyed one another: it was as simple as that.

Ought I to have my and my friends' frivolities on my conscience? They were endemic to our generation, like it or not – nor did those immediately following on our own either eschew or depart from them. I look back on our pleasures with a defiant fondness – and I say "defiant" because of the dark way in which, be certain, they would today be looked upon, by the stern banner-bearers in what comes to be called the sexual revolution. When I said, at the start, that part of my slight uneasiness with the present young resides in the fact that I could unwittingly shock them, that is what I meant. I could outrage their principles. Inadvertently, I could drop some remark, or embark on some giddy generalisation, which could be regarded as blasphemous – quite the end! "Artificiality" would appear, at its most offensive. The idea that the opposite sexes should, chiefly, amuse, beguile and, to a degree, enchant one another, and be content with that, could constitute vilest and blackest heresy. What *should* we have been doing? Seeking fulfilment.

At the very least, they would feel, we wasted our time.

How indefensible, to those who do not practise it, is flirtatiousness! Yet after all, *was* it – perhaps – an Art?

I can't feel that, by it, we dodged reality. Love always was in our minds, as a beatitude that sooner or later might come our way. We awaited it. Till it should come, with its enormous fatefulness, we were content to enjoy our playtime: from which in itself, maybe, we were learning something? One could be all *but* captivated – yet, not completely! Yes, some of us fell in and out of love, and how could we not? An iridescent veil of enchantment hung over the dancing and the chattering, the moonlight picnics, the rides through woods; but what I do know is, that through that veil we perceived something – something of the actual being of man, and of woman, and the basic nature of the relation of man and woman. As to that, one could not be irresponsible: we dared not. There *was* something too serious to be trifled with. We did not trifle.

Every "new" generation is, I realise, something of an enigma, something occasionally of a nightmare, to its predecessors. My own, in its own way, was no exception – our tastes and ways were open to criticism, and stood up to it. Our manner of dancing, for instance, was considered "extreme." Exception was taken to our slouchy attitudes, and our wispy dressing. We also lost no opportunity to voice our views (unfortunately, I cannot exactly remember what those were – except that we were against convention, and for our frankness, and wished to sweep away anything "artificial"). We differed from the current "new" generation, I should say, largely in one thing: it would have embarrassed us to go streaming around in shoals or crowds, or congregating in masses. And, too, we were anxious to be as *unlike* one another as possible.

Distinctly, it is a burden to be young – enviable though that state may appear. My lot bore its burden more lightly, and also took its vocation less earnestly, than now do others. We lived in a world which, though never quite satisfactory, gave as yet no cause for total dissatisfaction. For Today's young, it must be anything but easy to make out – which ought to excuse their somewhat overconspicuous manner of doing so. No wonder they close their ranks, tribalise themselves, fetishise juvenile sex, with its tribal harshness. "When will they ever learn?" – they have no desire to. All I hope is, the whole thing won't end in tears. Whether or not we were wiser, we fared better.

WOMEN

An Enormous Channel of Expectation

Today there was no daybreak: who was to say when today began? It was in the senses of sleepers before they woke – waking or woken before there had yet been a note from a single bird. Awareness was in the pre-dawn darkness of summer London; one by one, down streets far from the route, windows sprang alight; the humid shadowy trees just stirred as a breath met us hurrying out of the houses. Today was born to be a reality. Footsteps for some time were the only sound. No apparent sun rose; only, as the Palace came into reach, the sky lightened over the people who had been out all night, as though it were they who had willed the day to come – to these encamped ones along the curbs of the route something of the morning was old already. Dozing shoulder to shoulder, making tents of their coats, lying waiting with their heads on each others' knees, they have long been familiar with flags and triumphal arches. We, climbing up into our places on the stands, were the newcomers – latecomers, though the air was still dawn-steamy and smelled of grass.

The grandiose Mall is like nothing else in London, as London is like nothing else in the world. The Mall seldom seems wholly everyday, seldom quite ordinary: but today, already at this hour, it is transformed into something new again – an enormous channel of expectation. That it runs, deadstraight, from the Palace to the Admiralty Arch makes the Mall, this morning, seem to be drawn taut. And this tautness is of extreme length – a length extended by being flagged and peopled, flowery, spanned by delicate golden hoops, and overhung by the newly dazzling façades. Carlton House terrace indeed has the air of being erected for today – what a pattern of balconies and windows! Tier by tier below them the stands also fill with faces. June-fresh, ranks of plane trees stretch out their branches; under the sheltering leafiness, at ground level, packs in a crowd immobilised by itself. Indeed nothing appears more solid, more irremovable, either side of the Mall, than these living walls. (It was between these, by this way, that the Queen not only went to but came from her Coronation.)

Everything – though it is still so early, though nothing is yet in prospect but long waiting – photographs itself dramatically on the pale air. Glare comes from any striking colour; if it was a moment when the Guards cheered, marched in, taking up their position lining this section of the route (the Navy are further down), it was still more of a moment when the Guards let drop their wet weather cloaks from their scarlet tunics. The Guards further stamp the scene with attentive stillness. Broadcast music, now and then interrupted, makes one aware by its way of sounding that acoustics too are peculiar to the trafficless day. Something *will* have begun once the bands strike up. The only palpable restlessness is the weather – the varying luminosity and occasional curdling of the sky, which now and then spills splashes of sunshine, while little runnels of wind, never quite chilly, draft their way aimlessly through the plane trees. This is very English. Mounted police jogtrot up and down; a Royal Parks van patrols, clearing the route of débris. Everybody is waiting with equanimity, under the spell of a sense of timelessness – time is not, till there may be hope of processions.

The Mall has the first view. Here takes place the confluence, the ordering, once or twice, the halting – when it is not a matter of car-smooth speed – of processions due to precede the Queen's to the Abbey. It is not, indeed, long after nine o'clock that the first applause breaks out, at the Palace end, and from then on it continues, if somewhat fitfully. Now do we feel our magnitude as a crowd of thousands, our distinct personality as one crowd of London's – throwing ourselves upon the beginning of the spectacle in a captious or a hilarious unpent morning mood – for it *is* only a spectacle till we are disposed to consider more; that is, when it is a matter of the Whole Family. Something enters with the later carriage processions; each of us reaches out to those Royal *known* faces. Aunts, uncles, cousins – what is today to them? The Queen Mother smiles at us out of the glass coach: her paleness leaves in its wake a hush, a muting of some of us by emotion.

After a pause, Her Majesty's procession . . . There is an

incredibility, now that it is in view, about the advancing state coach, the eight grey horses, the four golden tritons. Hearts, as though not ready yet for the moment – not perhaps able yet for the moment – stand still. This is pure fairy tale. That impression of radiance left by the young beauty seated beside her husband, who seems to accompany her on a joyous journey, makes us want back the moment to live again.

One can hardly wait for the Queen to return, this way.

The coach takes its golden, surrounded way down the perspective, vanishes with a final gleam under the Admiralty Arch. For a little while longer its course onward is traced by sound: but she, for the time being, is gone from more than view. Have we, till now, envisaged her destination, or, still more, the isolation, in any human sense, of the journey she is about to make? Today we are not dealing in charming fairy tales: there is a spiritual sternness about her calling. What has to be the extent of her dedication, only she knows. How dare we compute the weight of the Crown? Though by love surrounded, she is not to be accompanied on her whole way. We thousands left behind in the Mall are now let know that the Queen has entered the Abbey – here, now, in the open air, under the changing sky, we must consider the sacrament of the Coronation. Broadcast, the words of the service sound here as if everything were taking place where we last saw her, between the double lines of the Mall plane trees – and yet, no, listen; the beautifully spoken words carry ancient reverberations of the Abbey – which we have only to turn to see behind us, not so far away, high up over the hazy foliage of the park. With awe we follow. As the Queen is being anointed, the sun comes out and for a minute floods over everything: thousands of us together do not speak – before we know, rain has begun to fall, sighing soft at first, glistening on the umbrellas crowdedly unfurled on the speechless stands; then thickening, muffling the forty-one gun salutes at the Queen's crowning. This rain, earlier so much dreaded, seems to enhance a sort of reconciled calm; we have it in common with one another. Rain *now* does not matter; one cannot say why – has the afternoon gone with us into some new dimension? We have perhaps touched upon some fringe of the experience of the Queen. For whatever has happened is unforgettable.

Waiting these hours for her to come back, while cheers and music proclaim her elsewhere in London, we wonder if she will be aged by the crown, or stripped of herself by the mystical ceremonial. Will her hands, having held and supported Orb and Sceptre, wave to us with the same unconcerned, easy and speaking grace as they did this morning? Look, the rain has stopped; the late afternoon Mall – wet flags and crowds, glistening trees and arches – stands out in dauntingly splendid and candid light. Her Majesty's two-and-a-half-mile long procession begins to enter, at the Admiralty end of the cleared length. There is the pulse of the endless marching, rank on rank, race on race, uncased colours, medals, men mounted, unswerving horses, bearskins, turbans, bayonets, bands. This is her blameless mightiness and her fearless force.

Eight home-going grey horses; four gold tritons. Seen through alternate windows of the coach is the head bowing the steadily balancing crown. All the long taut straight way to the Palace gates is a continuous moment of Recognition: we behold ELIZABETH, our undoubted Queen.

Enemies of Charm in Women, in Men

My old friend X remains young in her vivid, unfailing interest in new people. She favours the thought of them, is disposed to seek them. Those she does not herself meet, she delights to hear about – any fresh acquaintance I made, I must quickly sketch for her. This time, she's back from six weeks abroad.

"*Well,*" she inquires eagerly, "what's been happening?" I let drop I have a new neighbour – likely, from now, to play some part in my life. As a neighbour, she's bound to. Yet, all the same . . . X detects the pause. Swiftly she says: "You like her? – what's she like? I expect she's charming?"

I hesitate. "N-No. No, I don't think I'd quite say that." I hastily add: "She's energetic, she's well-read, she has great integrity." . . . I go on to list other sterling virtues. X hears me out with a twinkle, then delivers her verdict, "You'll grow to like her!"

Charm: how unmistakable it is – how indefinable. One ought not to say, how necessary: one *can* live without it. It enlivens and gilds the atmosphere like sunshine: like sunshine, it is to be rejoiced in unthinkingly, gladly, without analysis. Instantly, we react to its presence in another person; to whom (unless we are quite un-generous) we cannot begrudge a gift that mellows the world. Myself, I cannot conceive of "charm" in the abstract – it is unique each time, in each manifestation, endlessly various in the forms it can take, for this reason: being in essence personal, individual, it gives forth something peculiar to the woman or man from whom it emanates. Yet do we incline, perhaps, to be over-orthodox, narrow, in our notions of what does constitute charm?

If so, we tend to see its possessors as a rare *élite*, an enviable minority, set apart from the rest of us by the part they play. I maintain charm is less rare than some of us think – often, because its action may be original, it affects us before we know it for what it is. In some natures it may not be on the surface, but, rather, is waiting to disclose itself. Love, we observe, or sympathy may bring shy, latent charm out into bloom; or it may be among the discoveries in the course of friendship. To a degree, in our social dealings with people we take charm for granted more than we realise. On the whole, it is its absence that strikes us.

Marked lack of charm is a handicap that we recognize – in our instinctive pity for the person in whom such a lack stands out. To be honest, does not also slight irritation have a place in our attitude to that person? So-and-So is withholding some contribution owed to society in general – life, with its rubs and strains, is far from easy to live: let us heighten all possible pleasantness for each other.

Charm helps – to put the matter perfectly simply. But then, maybe, we reproach ourselves: is not So-and-So hampered by, as it were, some psychic deformity, some equivalent of tragic physical gracelessness, cause unknown? It's not his (or her) fault, we attempt to tell ourselves. The generous impulse is right: we ought not to "judge" – none the less, our verdict may be too lenient. In nine out of ten cases, charmlessness, if not a fault outright, is a sort of failure for which So-and-So deserves to be brought to book. As a human being, he or she may be taken to have inherited at least a modicum of the human outfit, in the way of wishes, willingness, and powers. High among those we reckon the wish or at least willingness to please; which *should* be linked with the capacity to do so. It seems, however, that sometimes the capacity goes astray.

Charm is more than pleasingness. Or should we say, it is that, with an extra glow from some mysterious source?

What "prevents" charm? What militates against it? One enemy I detect is, over-anxiety to *be* charming. Into most women, as social creatures, the desire to be charming has been inculcated, and rightly. But charm, we must realise, has no mechanics; it cannot be put consciously into action. Interknit though it is with physical personality, it can be no more than enacted outwardly (at the worst, mimicked or even parodied) by smiles, intonations of the voice, gestures or attitudes, *unless* those be harmonised from within.

For the wish to be charming there are often innocent, altruistic reasons; in itself the wish is neither wrong nor absurd – but it must not show. Once endeavour comes to be noticed, it sets up tension: too evidently, the person is concentrated upon herself, the im-pression she hopes to make, the effect she wills to produce. And that is ruin, at once, to charm's essential element, spontaneity. The truly charming woman is self-forgetful, lost to all but her pleasure in what is round her: any company she is in becomes good company. Eager and ready to *be* charmed, she creates in others, strangers or friends alike, as though by some magic touch, the power to charm. She neither asserts nor seems to exert herself. Be easy, have faith in the hour in which you find yourself. Do not the Scriptures warn against "taking thought"?

So much for over-activity. Yet its opposite, extreme passivity, may be no less an enemy. Who does not know the obstinate non-participant, the wary and guarded egotist who will take no chances? One might ask, does or can such a person lay claim to charm? It's to be feared that she does, in her perverse way. She has got it into her head that silence is "interesting"; she attempts to centre attention by being cryptic. She relies on a static pose, striking immobility, a rare and therefore dramatic turn of the head, and a reflective, often critical smile. She regards, and shows she regards, almost any remark as a poor security risk – let some other, more foolish than she, expose herself. To a point, this lady attains her end: she does, by her power to discountenance others' efforts, succeed in adding prestige to her own cool, and it may be decorative, remoteness – which is why, I suppose, she continues to be found at so many tables.

Absolute is her self-possession; at less than a glance she can be distinguished from the truly tongue-tied, or the shy, cramped outsider. Many envy her; no one can overlook her; what she has may, accordingly, *pass* for charm – "of a subtle, mysterious, odd and disturbing kind," her supporters tell. Let's demolish that fallacy – she's a bad model, on no account to be copied. Fascinate she may, slightly; but charm, never. Charm is outgoingness: generous, responsive, human. It takes chances; it risks a leap in the dark. Evident cautiousness is fatal. And more than caution, fear (though concealed by art) does in fact inhabit this cryptic lady – a fear that we need not pity: its root is vanity. Loth is she to venture forth from her own ground.

Grant her this – she can at least *act* repose.

Real repose is essential – at once, one senses its presence beneath the surface. Inner lack of it shows in an arid restlessness, foremost among charm's enemies. Exaggerated, jumpy physical mannerisms, talk which is over-rapid and discontinuous, abrupt and wayward changes of mood – these are the stigmata of the restless person. Moving from group to group, from party to party, she unsettles the air wherever she goes. Pity her as one may, she is hard to bear with. At her extreme, she is what Victorian nurseries knew as "a fidget" – tapping with her fingernails, recrossing her legs, swinging a foot, darting glances around and behind her. Visibly, she is impatient for something better, uneasy lest she miss it by being here. Gone awry in her are several attractive qualities: eagerness, quick if fleeting responses, willingness to give (though she knows not what). Touchingly, up to any age she seems childish; though a fretful, adult dissatisfaction begins, as time goes on, to shadow her eyes.

Why, when she *was* a child, was her hair-trigger temperament no more guided? Did no one so much as say to her, "Sit Still!"? We know bodily quiet helps to induce psychic equilibrium. She needs to centre herself. Often, this type is the victim of too much leisure, or a woman upon whom there are too few claims. One dominant interest, or objective, or outlet, ought to be the solution. Meanwhile, the exasperation she causes us is, perhaps, a sort of charm in reverse? Within her derelict restlessness there is lost, somewhere, what should have been vivacity.

Gaiety . . . One hears of "sombre charm," but to me that's a contradiction in terms. Wistful, I've known it be; or, in some appealing people, a touch plaintive; it can shine from under the shadow of grief or sadness – it remains incompatible with gloom. Humour or tenderness, grace or sunny intelligence: of these, one or another may predominate, or, they may all blend.

In general, we look to charm for a smile, are most conscious of it as social radiance. Is there, perhaps, the danger – because so very many charming people *are* gay, adding sparkle and animation to any company – we take it that by arriving at being "gay" we ourselves can by no means fail to be charming? Hence, the recourse to haphazard, unmeaning, unnecessary laughter? Who does not know her, the woman laughing because she feels she ought to? Everything *should* be pleasanter if she does (she imagines – honour her good intention). The carefully modulated peal, or agitated series of little gasps, how fatiguing to utter, alas, to hear. "Social" laughter somehow deals death to mirth. And what an irritant, to the kindliest ear, is the titter due to constant nervous compulsion.

The test of the "real" in laughter could not be simpler – is it or is it not infectious? Spontaneous, the thing spreads like a happy wildfire whether the first outbreak ring out, clear and impetuous, or be a throaty chuckle. How endearing, how *human* . . .

As a sound in itself, I seldom think laughter pretty; rare (outside fiction) is the woman actually gifted with a musical laugh – though the outright "unfortunate" kind, ruin to charm, is almost always the forced, or the habitual. Gaiety can be quiet. As a contribution, does it not more often, come from a smile, lighting up the face?

Charm, where it is present, tends to create good humour and good accord. In reverse, a most grievous enemy is aggressiveness. The aggressive instinct is said to be more developed in men than in women, but that women have their share of it, who can doubt? Arguably, in women it's on the increase: competitiveness fosters it, widening fields of activity multiply the conflicts which give it cause. The measuring of our powers against men's may make, on our side, for an angular self-assertion. The outright "unpleasant" woman, bully and quarrel-picker, need not delay us – *she* has nothing to lose – one is worried, more by the forms aggressiveness takes in those who should otherwise be agreeable.

Outwardly, there is stridency – the strident voice, the over-emphatic manner, the "crashing" colour scheme, dress or make-up. The offender in this way wields her personality at one like a battle-axe – there's nothing to fear, one soon finds, but, oh dear, she jars on one . . . Yet a deeper, more complex, troubling kind of aggressiveness is, frequently, sheathed in a quiet woman. At first glance, she's the opposite of the battle-axe type: dress incon-spicuous, manner guarded – conversationally, sometimes a slow starter. All at once, out she blazes. You or I have said something she can't let pass. Colouring, all but trembling, she whips up the easy talk of but a minute ago into a crisis-ridden, fiery argument. She is a case, literally, of painful honesty – make her views known she must, at whatever cost. And there *is* a cost, to her. Tense internally, apt to be rendered more so by the loneliness that surrounds a "difficult" person, she yields again and again to a nervous impulse which, later, she knows to be unfortunate. She's a person of worth, she deserves friends, unavowedly, and how she would like to have them. She continues to alienate, by her fierce sincerity. Need for affection makes her spikiness worse.

Charm is common to both sexes; rightly, each looks for it in the other. These days, are there fewer charming men? More than one

ENEMIES OF CHARM IN WOMEN, IN MEN

critical woman has been heard to say so. There rings in my ears, also, one young woman's furious exclamation – "I charm men, do I? Then why don't they do more about charming me?"

Not *quite* fair, I think. There is, as there ever was, a specific race of male would-be charmers in circulation. "Would-be," however, is often the fatal word – for we women grow, with each generation, more sharp-eyed, more quick to be seers-through. We've touched on the woman given to "charm mechanics"; no better fares her masculine counterpart. "When he has ladies to please, every feature works," remarks Jane Austen's observant Mr. John Knightley of his pet aversion, the parlour-frequenting clergyman Mr. Elton. *That* type is now, possibly, somewhat dated; in its place are the shoals of youngish young men, in movement through *mondain* cocktail parties. Each of these is afloat (or so he believes) on a charmingness proved to be irresistible; by now, the exercise of it is automatic. Ought not you and I to be gratified, all the same, that he does favour us with this exhibition? (Worse if he sized us up, then turned his back.) The trouble is, we sense that the good impression he makes, or imagines he makes, on us is chiefly food for his own vanity. Nothing's more honouring, indeed in itself charming, than a man's taking genuine trouble to please *us*.

What acts against charm in men we should like to like, and could have liked better? Where I'm concerned (I've decided) a touch, or more, of any of these three qualities: pomposity, pettiness, un-straightforwardness.

Pomposity may root in one form of shyness, or be frontage for a diffident temperament – it afflicts quite often the intellectual young, in whom it can be comical, not uncharming (none the less, girl or mother should gently tease the sufferer out of it). Should it increase with years, one cannot but connect it with self-importance, resent it as egotistical overbearingness. There is the man no power can stop laying down the law. Conversationally, he kills the most likely subject by treating you to the benefit of his whole opinion. Though he fixes his gaze on you, this is not flattering: you are not *you* to him, simply a captive audience. The pompous man inclines also to be fussy; in all things, he has a mania for the just-so. Paralysing as he is to prove to be, one may not have warning of this at the first moment: often his looks are impressive, his carriage upright, his eye arresting. Prosperity tends to irradiate his person (insecure men can seldom afford pomposity). Kindly if tedious host, he may show himself possessed of an excellent heart.

Pettiness (or small-mindedness) is consistent with surface agreeability. Often, it is not at once apparent, entertaining cleverness may conceal it – symptoms show themselves as acquaintanceship ripens. The cause is a jealous, perpetual self-concern. Biased judgements, ungenerous or slighting comments on others, suspiciousness, harping on minor grievances, quickness to take affront – why, in man, are these to us so irking? They conflict with our inborn notion of masculinity: we expect a man to have "a mind above things." The man giving way to pettiness (if he did but know it) can only shrink in a woman's eyes. How can he charm *as* a man, when he's not one – wholly?

What I call unstraightforwardness by no means denotes the official crook. The business and social record may be impeccable. Simply, when one is in the company of this particular kind of character, one misses what in a man *is* charming: unequivocal frankness and simplicity. Though he makes a point of looking one straight in the face, one cannot shake off an impression of *jake*[1] sincerity. His manner is confidential, or, if at all encouraged, conspiratorial; he relies, for effect in talk, on "For *your* ear only." *Why* is he telling me this, one begins to wonder? Calculation, some possibly devious motive, can be felt behind what he does or says. (Is one, oneself, suspicious? This never seemed so – one hates to think so.) Directness, single-mindedness are unknown to him; amuse though he may (to a point, he does), round him there's an atmosphere of uneasiness . . .

His case points to one universal truth: real charm has always some moral quality. Lovely as we find it, in man or woman, it has *stuff* to it: it is no mere lovely illusion. You'll protest, "But 'bad' people can be so charming!" Truly they can, for moments together. For those moments, I boldly say, these people seem to me good.

Woman's Place in the Affairs of Man

Today vitally alters our sense of history – no longer is it "the past," a book on a shelf; we live in its midst, it is in[1] the making, a making in which we share. Vast threats drive home, more and more, the value of life, its marvels, enigmas and possibilities. We envisage,[2] we have an increasing picture of what life *should* be, and what – maybe? – it could be made to become. A picture partly in outline, in part filled in. And to it women contribute – indeed, so largely that its character shows their touch, their outlook, their work. Nor has this contribution of women's been, only, that of the idealist or the visionary. They have not merely dreamed, but effected; and thanks to this the picture is merging into reality. For the better, women bring change about. Overshadowed the civilised world may be; but at least in desire, intention, advancing practice, it is nearer to *being* civilised than it was. Once, to accomplish anything, woman's sole hope was to "inspire" men; now it is she who acts on her inspiration. Result, our society breathes a less deadening air.

Amazing to realise, looking back, with what a blend of concern, mistrust, apprehension, the emergence of woman was first viewed! Emergence from what? – sheltered living, private concerns, the home. What more could she want (it was asked): had she not her time-honoured sphere, in which she, esteemed and unchallenged, reigned? To do men (the better men) justice, I don't think they so much feared that woman would now attempt to usurp their powers, as that she would abdicate from her own – at what a loss to humanity, and society! One must recollect, men accorded woman that "sphere" – a traditional, semi-sacred, intensely human one. The home, as generations had come to see it, *was* to be honoured; and that was woman's creation, area of activity, fulfilment of being, outlet for gifts and skills. The ancient, noble Roman idea of the *domus*,[3] surviving, ranked high the domestic virtues: serenity, balance, tenderness, intuitive wisdom, justice, patience. That these were woman's attributes, warrant for her high status, was, be certain, doubted by few good men. What *was* doubted was, whether woman could usefully (or, it might be, even without disaster) bring her specialised faculties into the common market, man's domain of affairs. Moreover, what a disturbance she might cause! Loyally, lovingly willing to work for women, men showed no great disposition to work with them. The male preferred to pursue his unaided way.

I am not, and never shall be, a feminist. I should be sorry to think that women's achievement, their soaring prestige, their present central position, was due to men's inadequacy or failure, or, even, to lessening masculine self-confidence. "Men messed things up, were powerless to avert wars, were paralysed by the growth of evils they should have grappled with, *then* cried aloud to women, 'Come, put things right for us!'"? . . . It's been neither so simple, I think, nor so bad as that. Rather, two questions have by now answered themselves: – Woman, amid the affairs of man, genuinely *was* needed; her place awaited her. And, the particular faculties she brings with her more than prove their mettle in public life – making for quickened energy and a fresh viewpoint.

Not disrespectful or hostile to institutions, women do none the less feel free to examine them. Nor is any and every law, to them, a law of the Medes and Persians. To be told, "That has always been done," evokes from them, often, a ringing, "Why?" They tend to short-circuit discussions; they like to meet abstract problems in concrete form. There's something of the free-lance in most women – reason, perhaps, why they made good in the arts while still debarred from entering the professions. Intellect is outside the mould of sex; yet there's no doubt that a woman brings to scholarship or creative thought a rare precision, patience and concentration, plus unique flashes of insight: her intuition! And often, women outstand through boldness of mind. Their gaze is unblinkered; nor do they fear to be stirred by feeling, compassion or indignation.

Generations of home-makers are in a woman's ancestry, and not for nothing. Through her, though she may be scholar or artist, runs a deep inherited streak of the practical. And, strangely, when she is at her most practical, she is, too, creative. Domestic are her ideals: she loves order, light, and the warmth of kindness – the more, now that walls no longer confine her. The home *was* her sphere, and now the world is her home. Her arrival into the forefront comes late in time; but not, we have reason to hope, too late!

Outrageous Ladies

Truth stranger than fiction? I never think so. Amazing as facts may be – and, in our day, are – magic still pervades an invented story. When real-life oddness passes a certain point, we exclaim: "It's like something out of a book!" Surely it is by imaginative daring that fiction holds us? Look at any acceptedly great novel – work, say, of one of the Brontës, Dickens or Balzac. *Can* this be found to be no more than a literal, sober transcript of everyday reality? Jane Austen builds up her flawless comedies by touches of subtle exaggeration; Thackeray, together with Thomas Hardy, works on a larger-than-life scale. Even Trollope, apparently so straightforward, often idealises, often caricatures. And, if this be so with the masters, how much more is it with the ranks below them. In a sense, it is fiction's business to *be* strange.

Art, after all, is a form of make-believe. And how willing are we to fall in with the game! How insidious is the art of the story-teller, one can see by observing his hold on children – and are adults less susceptible, if it comes to that? To the novelist, grown-up story-teller, we grant considerable licence – but not endless licence: there is an understanding that, in return, he play fair with us. He must not overstrain our credulity, or transgress our notions of commonsense. His plot must not be too wildly farfetched, his characters must bear some basic resemblance to people as we know them to be in life. In fact, while the make-believe element in a novel attracts us, and whets our imaginations, the make-believe must not go too far – what we want is a story which *could* be true.

If a novelist does not play fair, can he get away with it? At the outset, one would suppose not. The penalty for unconvincingness is failure: either the story does not get published, or, even if published, it finds no favour and sadly dies out, all but unread. Yet, on second thoughts, do not successful novels – whether today's best-sellers or the recognized classics – contain, sometimes, flagrant improbabilities? And if this be so, how is it that we accept them, enjoy them and (in the case of the classics) honour them? The answer is, I suppose, that we are won over – the novelist having exercised something akin to the skill plus effrontery of the conjuror. The great Victorians, in particular, might be described as master illusionists: in the light of their achievement, it would appear that a story depends for its hold on us, first and last, chiefly on the convincingness of its telling. We seek Victorian novels partly for their vitality, partly for their unaccountable spell. Contemporary writers have far less virtuosity.

Today, our criticism of novels directs itself, most of all, to character-drawing. A great part of our modern interest is psychological. We analyse ourselves and dissect our friends more thoroughly and calmly than did our ancestors: accordingly, we apply more searching tests to the men and women whom we confront in stories. And inevitably, knowing our own sex best, we are most observant of our own sex in fiction. Outrageous improbability in a heroine (or, indeed, any feminine character) is likely to be dropped upon by a woman; men, provided the creature be charming, may let her pass.

Now which, I ask myself, are the ladies who fill me with most misgiving? And why do they?

First, there are the "impossibles" – that is, those who never could have existed, on land or sea. In any century, was it humanly possible for a girl to have been so silly as child-wife Dora in *David Copperfield*, or so at once vapid and obstinate as Amelia in *Vanity Fair*? I remind myself that these two nonentities were products of male Victorian sentimentality – and that it's likely, too, that Dickens and Thackeray could never really be bothered to think them out. (Poor little Dora's early death would be sadder if one *could* believe, for an instant, that she had ever lived.) Again, there are the beauteous and blameless heroines who bevied forth from the pen of Sir Walter Scott, to remain for us as static as paper figures – *they* served their creator's romantic purpose: one would not look to Sir Walter for realism. A character fails to live (where I am concerned) when the author has endowed her with only one trait – dazzling loveliness, innocence on the one hand, guile or active malevolence on the other.

Granted, even under this handicap, villainesses are better value than heroines: vengeful, obsessed Rosa Dartle in *David Copperfield* and evil Madame de la Rougierre in *Uncle Silas*, excite and impress one by their sheer monstrousness. They belong, however, less to authentic fiction than with the dark tribes of the fairy tale, witches, ogres . . . None of the ladies so far named (too flimsy, too pure or too wholly vile to be credible) had, we may notice, women creators. It took Jane Austen, Charlotte Brontë, George Eliot and Mrs. Gaskell to point out how complex woman can be, or follow the to-and-fro of her inner conflicts.

Outright "impossible" characters are one thing – for the moment they rile us, soon we forget them. As readers, we probably suffer more from those who at first seem totally real to us, then go on to do some unbelievable thing. The better we like our heroine, and the more we know her, the greater the shock if she behaves wrongly – out of accord, I mean, with our idea of her. (In itself, the action may be blameless.) For my own prime instance of this, I must turn to drama, and query Shakespeare – *would* Ophelia, image of youthful honesty, have consented to act as decoy duck in order that her father might spy on Hamlet? Unlikely betrayals, improbable blind-nesses, uncharacteristic choices or decisions may be, in all sorts of fiction, attributed to those of whom we know better. Then, either we quarrel with the author, or the novel loses its former hold – we become uneasy. "*She* would not have done that . . ." True, in real life we meet baffling inconsistencies; but in a novel, for some reason, we mind them more.

Sometimes, one suspects, an author alters his characters, or forces an inappropriate action on them, in order to build up a better plot – in the long run, I doubt that this ever pays!

Worse still is it – or at least, more disturbing – when a character does what not only *she* would not do, but what could not be done by anyone living. Only when this occurs, or seems to occur, do we realise how strong is our sense of the human norm. Outside that norm, there is nothing but aberration. Yet, look again – is it not genius novelists who take the longest chances? Fearless, they confront us with aberrations. Would Thomas Hardy's Tess, of *Tess of the D'Urbervilles*, have turned back to kill her betrayer Alec when reunion with Angel Clare was at last in sight? Whether or not, Hardy asserts she did: his conviction carries the day with us. Would Tolstoy's Natasha in *War and Peace*, have planned to elope with a young officer on the eve of her adored Prince Andrew's home-coming? Tolstoy's all-knowing sureness is our authority. And Jane Austen no less persuades us that Emma, of *Emma* (a girl no fool) could be so far the dupe of her own illusions as to overlook a string of intrigues and dramas which were plain for almost anyone else to see . . . Great novels challenge our fixed ideas – they cause endless argument; thus, they forever live.

Lesser novels leave our ideas alone and, instead, pander to passing daydreams. Hence the absurdity, very often, of the day-before-yesterday's best-seller – and, still more, of its once glamour-ous heroine. Fashions in ladies change; when the tide goes out, grotesqueries are laid bare. Long, long dust is the charmer of the tiny lily-white hand and rosebud mouth – yet in her time, for her public's taste she could not blush, flutter or sigh too much. And since her, generations of favourites have gone their way. During the pre-1914 heyday of Mrs. Florence Barclay,[1] heroines' age-level steadily rose: the Little White Lady, of *The Broken Halo*, attained the record – she was winsome at seventy. Ethel M. Dell's[2] pale, masochistic brunettes would today seem ripe for psycho-analysis: time was when their misadventures enthralled the world. I recall, too, a long run of expensive sinners, headed by the lady of *The Green Hat*,[3] a host of *gamines* (imported, I think, from France) and a hell-cat dynasty, founder Scarlet O'Hara[4] . . . It was the triumph of those dream-queens that they *were* outrageous, in one way if not another. Readers were naïve, were they – in the past?

And the future – are we, both readers and writers, due for reform? We are told that the novel should sober down, be concerned with fact, make a break with make-believe. Should it, I wonder? There would be fewer dangers, less wild flights, less risk of the preposterous. Better, you may say, safe ground than thin ice. Yet is it not, in a way, the triumph of fiction that it *does* so narrowly sheer clear of the impossible? Reformed, subdued, the novel would cease to be – this bold art is in herself, all but, an outrageous lady. Yet far afield from truth, for long at a time, she has wonderfully seldom wandered. There is more sense in this just not nonsense than many know.

VARIOUS ARTS AND
DISAPPOINTMENTS

A Way of Life

Arguably, the person one knows least is oneself. One can live for years without forming more than a fragmentary concept of the person one is. Sometimes, as when in some large public place one finds oneself walking towards one's own reflection in an unexpected mirror, one gets a fleeting impression – often disconcerting, powerful always, but not lasting. Any casual comment from a friend – "Of course, *you* always do this or that" – sets up, as a rule, surprise. Anyone who, having made a recorded broadcast, hears his own voice played back to him for the first time listens to it less with embarrassment than with complete amazement: he hears the voice of a stranger. To be confronted, on a cinema screen, by oneself, photographed by a concealed camera, walking down a street or about a room would, I imagine, produce the same result. But it is not only one's exterior self – gestures, gait, intonations, and cast of countenance – that one is unaware of: the ignorance goes deeper. Perhaps it is not so much ignorance but unconsciousness. The habits, desires, and ruling trends of the inner person are the real mysteries; most mysterious in that – though they work within one, make one, in fact, *are* one – one is seldom reminded that they exist.

When one is reminded, the reminder is sharp. Usually brought about by an outside crisis, it becomes an interior crisis in itself: one realises that one has acted, spoken, or made a choice as though under direction from some authority – rightly or wrongly, for better or worse, one could not, apparently, have acted, spoken or chosen otherwise. "That," one thinks, with a sort of curious awe, "was *I*." And the moment, like a flash of lightning over a dark landscape, has the effect of illuminating one's whole past, throwing everything that can be remembered and much that had been forgotten into relief, casting event and feeling into a new but conclusive relation with one another, making the whole a pattern, giving the pattern meaning.

As to individuals, all this is a commonplace – this prevailing unconsciousness of the self, this tendency to live almost automatically, between those, in most lives, infrequent shimmers of revelation. It would not be worth comment were it not an analogy of what can also happen to a country or a nation. I have in mind the British, in whom collective unselfconsciousness is most marked – it is, I think, a factor in what from time to time seems, infuriatingly, to be our complacency. It is not merely that we are not self-analytical; we are almost stupendously unaware not only of, as it were, our outward appearance, the impression we make on the world, but of our own inner character as a people. We feel, only half know what we do feel, and never know why; we act, are prepared to support the action almost fanatically, but are slow to justify the action even to ourselves, and slower to explore its roots. We live, we have always lived, in our own way. We have not even been particularly conscious that it *is* our own way: it is the one way *to* live as far as we are concerned – that has been enough for us. Why should we ask ourselves what that way of life is?

Why, indeed, till now? Now we are being told that our way of life is in danger. What was originally a phrase, sharp and grim enough but liable, like so many other phrases, to begin to sound hollow by repetition, has gained meaning: it has seeped down into the intuitional part (which is the only really operative part) of the mass of the people. Danger – it is a presence; it is to be felt. Not the queerly stimulating, exciting, stringing-up, dramatic physical danger almost every city civilian knew in the air raids: something more sinister and oppressive for being less immediately palpable and more quiet. Something is in danger. But what is in danger? Our way of life. But what is our way of life?

The reaction in Britain to a defined threat of a not yet defined, but deep-down and generic *something* has been curious. The stress, with most of us – at least, so *I* feel – is less upon the danger than upon the endangered. The Britain of this year is way-of-life conscious. Or perhaps, better, conscious of the desire to know what this "way of life" *is*. What is its nature? In what does it consist? What are its realities and what its fictions? How far is it traditional? And how much of the tradition still holds good? How much, and what, in it is to be held onto at any price; how much should be, however reluctantly, sacrificed; how much should have been discarded before now? How much of our part in it is acceptance, superstitious acceptance, and how much is active will? In short: what is it, why is it, and what does it mean to us?

These questions, or rather these different aspects of one question, are being ruminated rather than put and answered. The pre-occupation is on the whole a silent one: we are not articulate. It crops up rather in random talk than in analytical conversation. It is an abstraction which has boiled down to concrete things, and seems to overshadow, and make momentous, what could have been the most trivial decisions. As a woman, I naturally am most conscious of how this rumination, as I call it, affects and acts in women – in fact, I am not sure whether we, as a sex, are not the principal ruminators: we have less time for conscious, but more for unconscious, thought.

We are not, in the main, economic thinkers: up to now, the family bankbook has constituted for us the single, sufficient, and ruling economic reality. We are aware that everything costs money, and that there must therefore be money; but actually our so-called *sphere* is made up of psychic by-products of objects or processes which have been bought and paid for; e.g., the china on our tables, which stands for style and gaiety; the electric gadget in the kitchen, which stands for time saved, therefore time gained, therefore leisure; the schooling, for yet another term, of the children, which stands for growth in them, therefore growth in their relation to us.

Whatever even the most practical woman does has always some emotional connotation. By life, we mean practice: the things we – daily, yearly, and lifelong – do or cause to be done. Such things – many of them in themselves repetitive and fatiguing – add up, how-ever, to something more – something which has a quality. Life itself.

Life, in the sense that it has for women, is a thing men may pay for but women make. (The independent career woman must play the man's part also: that is all.) I myself believe that, certainly in Britain, it is women who are the custodians of the way of living. This being so, I have never been able to understand why some of them grumble that this is a man's world. In women's triple world – the personal, the domestic, the social – what they will should stay, stays; what they will should go, goes. As the daughters of their mothers who have become the mothers of their daughters they have been at once receiving and handing on something – inside, it is true, up to now, an economic structure which they did not examine but could assume was firm. Not only the home but society has taken colour from women's notions of what it ought to be.

In America this, I imagine, is axiomatic: in Britain it has been a submerged truth that is only now beginning to reach the surface – women, here, find themselves touched to the quick by the way-of-life question. Why? Because in a very great part, they understand, suddenly, that it *is* their affair.

Politics quite apart, as a sex women have heard themselves charged, in this country, with an undue conservatism of two kinds – emotional, social. There are many things, men say – rules, obser-vances, formalities, small extra taxes on the routine of the day – which they would be glad to let go, but that women stand by them. (At the same time, one hears the Britisher say with a certain pride: "It's my wife, you know: she keeps me up to the mark!") *Is* it, in this country, the women who continue to insist upon class-distinctions? I do not think so – real and malignant snobbishness usually is the hallmark only of the warped or frustrated woman: in our dealings with one another, irrespective of class, it takes remarkably little to bring the sisters-under-the-skin feeling into play. As against this, women of gentle birth do love what might be called the aesthetics of their tradition: they find it hard to forego courtesy or to relinquish any kind of grace. Thus a woman is anxious as to the friends her children make: she finds it hard not to wince at some threatening new little proletarian vowel-sound in their speech. (But then, equally, the working-class mother does not want her children to grow up "rough.")

There are aesthetics – though *that* we should never call them – not only of manners but of the home routine which women will almost kill themselves (and the war years already have almost killed them) to maintain. Queer little ceremonials in connection with the service of meals; open fires (even when a back-breaking half day must be spent in the woods gathering fuel); the polishing of silver; the putting on of something different for evening dinner (vestigial trace of the "dressing" habit); evening dinner itself – irrespective of what there may be to eat. One sees this shadow-battle, still so poignant, reflected in the novels of Angela Thirkell – she, it is true, writes of a restricted class: none the less, I can but believe that in every home in Britain there is a woman battling not to let *something* go. If it goes, it is gone forever.

But is it better gone? The children coming back from the wars may say so. There is a goodbye-to-all-that[1] attitude in the young. Or so they protest – but, is there? Is it possible that beneath the noisiness of our young people there is a conflict: they are half revolutionaries, half nostalgics. Denouncing this and that as absurd and anachronistic, they are gruffly susceptible to the graces: they are shy of showing how much they would like security. A proportion of them spent the war in the New World: they come back, here, to shabby and shadowed homes – maintained, it can but seem to them, at the cost of more stress and effort than any home is worth.

Stress and strain – in the question of sheer survival they are at the moment, we know, involved. In the question of not merely keeping alive but living they can but be involved for a great deal longer. This transition time for us, under the pressure of our crisis, is dark with confused issues which we must face and clarify. It seems symbolic that in our houses, even, we are hampered, and being drained of our needed energies, by an outmoded plan: the average middle- and upper-class British home was built for, and remains the expression of, an order, a *material* way of living, now gone for good. Segregation of children; work by servants; importation of ton upon ton of coal. Now the dusky, distant servants' quarters are empty: as for the children, they are amongst and on top of us in a tribal closeness. Dust-gathering staircases, draught-conducting corridors, unheatable halls stretch, echo, between our living and sleeping quarters. No, we did not re-architect our houses while we could, although their coming impossibility foreshadowed itself as early as World War I. (Did we take some oblique pride in their very unmodernity?) Now, we cannot.

Now, right now, what we must do is something more fundamental: re-architect, as a people, our conception of living –
perceive and stand by the essentials, for Britain, of our "way of life."
If the sacrifices must be fearless, the refusals to sacrifice must not be
less doughty. For we do not, we know, live by bread alone.

The Forgotten Art of Living

Life, it seems, is not what it used to be: much less pleasure
accompanies the sensation of living. How is one to rid oneself of the
idea that the fabric of existence is wearing thin? People confess, all
round, to an increasing dismay in their private life: the matter has
not often been aired in print for, I suppose, two reasons – fear of
saying anything disaffecting, fear of incurring the obvious rebuke:
"How expect to be happy? – Look at the world!" The dismay, of
course, must have one exterior source, public, rational. But it has
another, private one – always apart from war threats, vistas of ruin,
political uneasiness, shortages, the grotesque fatigues attendant on
every day. It set in decades ago; it has remained apparent in the
outlook of more than one generation; it is at its peak now. No, our
sense of impoverishment cannot altogether be charged to war, ruin
or economic change. The world is bad now, but it was bad before.
We may think we dread mass extinction; what we dread more is
vacuum. It is the possibility of breakdown in our inner, rather than
in our outer, world that troubles us.

The world has been bad before – but did that, till lately, prevent
the individual from conducting his life with a sort of secret assurance, a devout energy? That curious immunity of our ancestors –
was it inhumanity, or genius? Against everything, they maintained
the assertion of their humanity, that obstinate expectation of good
from life, that capacity for liking life for its own sake. They did
expect to enjoy themselves. So, still, to be frank, do we.

At the moment, however, we do not. Conceivably we have

forgotten how to – what has become of the nerve of pleasure, the capacity for play: have these atrophied? We dread being thrown back on our own resources. Indeed, how many sneers at "planning" arise from mistrust of what should be, intrinsically, its good effects? Should catastrophe not again submerge us, we are due, in a reckoned number of years, each to be dealt out his or her accredited slab of leisure, leisure vested in safety. The emergency-stimulus will be lacking; the hypnotic rush for survival will have died down. We shall have no alibi. For hours of a day, not impossibly for days of a week, a benevolent State will require of us only that we should be ourselves. Liberty, and the pursuit of happiness . . . what were desiderata become perils. Mechanically, home life will proceed with increasing smoothness: no more drudges, no more sacrificed persons. We shall be confronted, at every turn, by means to express and complete ourselves – but how if, writers who can no longer write, we falter more every day at the sight of the blank white page?

This is our apprehension – the white, too quiet morning on which we wake to find we have lost the power to live. Absolutely unmeaning, furniture round the bedroom would, that morning, meet the waking eye; knowledge of the routine of the day to come would remain stamped on the brain, but without evoking a stir of liking or disliking, hope or fear, attraction or repugnance from the sensibilities – which would have, having gradually run down, stopped.

Neurotic exaggeration . . . How is it, however, that such a morning should be in even remote sight? Is it that we have been thwarting, ignoring, warping or starving our sensibilities till it *could* be that they take their revenge by striking? They have been asking us for a better time. Is it not due to them that we live more rewardingly, more stylishly, more fully? Agreed. But then, if so, how? Why not? What is holding us up? How, once again, is not only pleasure but sense of worth to attend our conduct of a day? Have we mislaid some formula, or have we lost illusion?

If so, it must be for that illusion that we envy the past, that we hope to rifle the past. The sickly dominance of nostalgia in our talk, writing and reading becomes accounted for. We cannot hear enough, apparently, about childhoods – provided those are set anything more than forty years back – nor is it childhoods only: the reading market is flooded with diaries, memoirs, family letters, reaching the printer from backs of bureau drawers. Letters from home to the son abroad; patient love-letters; the diary-chatter of the young lady on the move; the retrospections, penned flowingly evening after evening, of the lady in the sunset of life . . . The trivialities of yesterday have become our literature. Uneventfully intimate, these documents were in their time put away: sentiment expected for them no other future. *We* fall on them with an eagerness which should make us pause. Up from those pages flows illusory light; magic exhales from their banality.

Mary and the children over from Cheriton in the wagonette. Cousin J. still with us. Strawberry picking. B. read aloud letter from Edward, no more of his headaches. Delightful day.[1]

Dear dead dull people – what was that element in which they were afloat? What was the source of it: for us, has a spring dried up? We want the prosaic in happiness: lives we search for the secret are the lives of the mildly amused obscure, the tranquil, not the lives of the great – the lives of the great were too full of stresses and imperatives, too tense and demanding, too like our own. We envisage places where history never set foot; where it was an adventure to go nutting and enterprise to be setting out on a visit. A new face, a letter, a little misunderstanding, a bishop to lunch: any of those set off a delicate pendulum of excitement, not to swing either too wildly or too far.

There could be no end to idealising the past: in vain we call up its darker side – the inhibitions, the banishments, the snobberies, the consuming grievances – in vain we recall that, as Proust said, art with its sublime trickery is at work in memory. Idealisation apart, it remains a fact that, for people, life – the living of days – did once maintain a balance and hold in itself a charm. There was not only gusto, there was discrimination. There was behaviour; there were the accomplishments. Not unadmirably, those people idealised themselves; their lives were innocent factories of illusion: we receive the impression that the good life was most of all an aggregate of spontaneous moments, unsought sensations. Wonderfully seldom the scene changed; familiarity was a merit; objects seem to have taken on a peculiar virtue from having been often or even always seen.

One point it would be dishonest not to admit: this gift for living went with gentle birth, or at least gentle education. Outside one class, it was to be come upon only in the exceptional person. The aristocracy used themselves more roughly; the new rich seem, from evidence they have left, to have felt void, uncertain and gloomy – the gift, therefore, was not by any means the prerogative of wealth; it was enhanced by but not always dependent upon security. In Gorky's *The Artamonov Business*,[2] I stopped at the passage where Peter Artamonov, freed serf and rich self-made man, caught in a thunderstorm, turns for shelter into the small manor house. I quote the passage, inevitably cut for the sake of space:

> So there was Artamonov, in somebody else's clothes, wrapped so that he was afraid to stir, sitting shamefaced, as if in a dream, at table in a warm room, in a dry, pleasant soft light. A nickel-plated samovar was purring, and a tall, thin woman, with a turban of auburn hair, and dressed in a dark, loose-fitting frock, was pouring out tea . . .
>
> Artamonov cleared his throat and, peering cautiously around him, was envious . . . Here was a kindly atmosphere, everything was just right. A large lamp with a pearl globe poured its milky light over the cups and silver on the table and on the tightly drawn-back hair of a little girl with a green shade over her eyes; there was an exercise book open in front of her, and she was drawing in it with a thin pencil and purring to herself, so softly though that it did not prevent him from hearing all the mother said.
>
> It is not a big room, and it was tightly packed with furniture, but everything looked as though it had grown naturally; yet each separate thing spoke for itself, about itself, just like the three very

bright pictures on the walls. The picture opposite Peter depicted a fabulous white steed with haughtily curved neck, and mane unbelievably long, almost to the ground.

Everything in this house was amazingly comfortable and soothing, and the lovely voice of the mistress rang like a pensive song coming from afar. Now with such surroundings you could live all your life without a real care, and never do anything evil . . .

He left at daybreak, tenderly bearing with him the impression of a peace which caressed, an impression of comfort, and the almost disembodied image of the grey-eyed woman, who had created it all. Swaying through the water-logged potholes, which equally reflected the gold of the sunlight and the dirty blotches of the wind-torn clouds, he said to himself with sorrow and envy; "That's how people really live."

But yet, the pleasure of envy – of the pang, the disturbance set up by the received illusion! *That* is not at an end: almost every lighted room, seen at night through an open window, still has a momentary ideality of its own. Suddenly, from a face, from the shadows of a newly entered room, from a tone of voice or a phrase in somebody else's talk, the enviable, the troubling, the illuminating shines out – we are Artamonovs in our susceptibility.

How many of us take pleasure in our own rooms, or regard them as anything more than boxes encasing and reflecting our anxieties? We think out our interiors (spacing, lighting and colour), but then dread to feel them: the amiability of almost all objects and pieces of furniture fails to reach us because we are over-concerned with their shape. Possibly if in the arrangement of things round us there had been less calculation and more sentiment, we might feel better – in anyone else's room, one would admit, there is something immediately sympathetic about any giddy little outbreak of bad taste that is personal taste. Do we allow enough for the claustrophobia set up by the completely correct? Or for the strain on the nerves from the morgue-like stillness of the room in which there is nothing moving but the hands of the clock – no fire flutters, no canary hops in its cage, no flower drops a petal? I suppose there is this for pet-keeping: the presence of an independent will.

Our studied rooms may be symptomatic: there is more and more to be said for being foolish, artless. And again, we show our rigidity in the matter of time: we are clock dominated. It is terrible to hear oneself say: "I will now relax for an hour." How can one relax if one is thinking about the hour? And, also, how dull, how null merely *to* relax! How is it that we never open an exercise book, pull up to the table and draw cats, even if we cannot draw? Why not the Meccano set or the lump of plasticine? It is not we who should be childish; it is the child making something who is adult. Why should we never do anything for which there is no reason? If we cannot enjoy time, waste time and enjoy wasting it, our interior tension will tighten until it snaps. Nothing exceeds the happiness of the person uselessly employed. No, it is a nightmare to think of time, all the time, economically. If one must be a little useful, one can make a scrap screen.

Decidedly we are riding ourselves too hard: could we not loosen up and be more irrational? In the matter of surroundings, habits and company we shave the grass close, then wonder why there is no longer that mysterious rustle.

In our choice of company we are restrictive, owing to inertia, or choosey, owing to snobbishness (intellectual). How if one broke the circle and went further afield? Round and round we go, in our little set, like goldfish in a bowl of exhausted water – where are the handsome, the dashing, the vital, the honest of other worlds? Provinciality has settled upon us without our knowing: we are possibly more worn down by our friends, with their terrible similarity to ourselves (and they more worn down by us) than we care to state. To be amusing, society should be composite: there is nothing like the variety of the neighbour or the new acquaintance, nothing like the monotony of the intimate. To break new ground involves a fascinating discovery: how many matters one did not know of occupy how many people one did not know! A weight lifts – one matters less than one thought.

On the one hand, a greater romantic irregularity, more carelessness; on the other, a greater impersonality – are these possible to combine? The more formal façade, the more gothic interior? We miss Society (as opposed to company) and it would be something to reconstruct it. As to that, the difficulties – beginning and ending with the economic difficulty, but comprehending those of time and space – are immense, admittedly; but it is worth trying. If we let slip forever that concept of people in a relation to each other which, purely social, is an affair of gaiety, dignity and style, our children will never find it again, and the loss of grace will be irreparable. Real society (as opposed to the little playgrounds of *embusqués*[3]) still does survive in pockets – in the provinces, in parts of the country, in corners of cities: it is worth frequenting, studying. Social intercourse does need staging, however modestly: it is the aesthetic that is the charm, the discipline that is (for us) the repose. Once, the futilities of Society were the target – nowadays, one finds one must think again. The Englishman in his dinner jacket in the jungle – was he so ridiculous, after all? There is much to be argued for dressing up.

Is living a lost art, or a lost gift? Say, it was once a gift but must now be art. The gift was restricted; the art is open to all.

The Art of Respecting Boundaries

In this present-day clouded, uncertain world, the value of people for people has gone up. The affections become our one abiding reality. Friendship, love, yes, and genuine social pleasure are to be prized as perhaps never before – these reassure and warm us: we have need of each other. We invest more and more of ourselves, and of what we inwardly have, in personal relationships – contacts, communications, understandings. We seek the fixed star, the perpetual comforter, the kindred spirit who shall never vary or cool or fail. Yes, people matter, perhaps they matter too much. We risk disillusionment, tragedy, when we pursue them wrongly.

Do we always realise, for instance, that relationships most worth having are built up on a basis of things unsaid?

Not so long ago, that was a commonplace: one expected the deeper sympathies to be tacit. Our parents or grandparents, possibly, were either less eager than we are or less impulsive. They gave more time, all time, to getting to know their friends; they were reticent or more adroitly guarded; and intimacies, such as there used to be, were rarer, more temperate – were they perhaps more lasting? One hesitated before one opened the heart; formality, the tradition of manners, a whole flock of considerations and codes and loyalties interposed between lover and lover, or friend and friend. To us, looking back, that may all seem frigid and false – did not many lives, we may ask, remain unfulfilled? Did not human relations lose by being conducted with the stilted intricacy of a gavotte? We, in our reaction, swing to the other extreme, making all but an idol of spontaneity. "*I* have no time," how often one hears it said, "for shillyshally, conventions, or false reserve! When I meet some new person I like, I put all my cards on the table, and of course I expect the other to do the same. By now, if one cannot be natural and frank, where are we?"

As a sentiment, splendid: but can this involve some error? Must reserve always be "false"? And, exactly what does our speaker mean by "natural and frank"? May not he or she (more generally she, I fear) project yet another campaign of ruthless intrusion upon the privacies of someone else's life, combined with a total advertisement of her own? Declare all, ask all – simple; but does it work out? "Intimacy," said one of the wisest of my friends, "has to be wooed, not ravished." And this holds good, one can see, with regard to friendship no less than passionate love. Impatience, emotional restlessness and, it may be, vacuous curiosity lie behind those verbal assaults we make; while the urge to seem "interesting," at any cost, prompts disclosures which could be better timed. We rush, we storm our approaches to other people. What is at fault – the age we live in, fever, and insecurity? Or are we, inside our gloss of sophistication, less adult, more adolescent than we have the right to be?

THE ART OF RESPECTING BOUNDARIES

One can but respect those who are straightforward truly – the child with its naïve, disconcerting questions, the simple-spoken, primitive country person. Nothing asked in innocence can offend, and nothing stated in innocence is unseemly. Indeed, from young children's dealings with one another much, it occurs to me, might be learned – one observes them in a sort of tribal propriety: the serious gaze, the ceremonial approach. It is as though they employed an inherent technique – are we born, perhaps, more discreet than we grow to be? Yet, the *child* is "natural." We, adults of today, are the ones who try to sweep aside age-old laws. Society gained its structures and drew its grace from the underlying idea of the private right – one entered where one was invited, and there only. One did not attempt to pluck out the heart of mysteries.

There is something destructive and, still worse, dull, about extravagant frankness as we now know it. For the crowning irony is, we defeat our ends: ultimately, the most interesting people are those about whom we continue to know the least – not because they surround themselves with elaborate mystery, pose as inscrutable, or put up "keep out" notices, but because some unconscious dignity in them forbids intrusion, and modesty keeps their lips from the easy confidence. To them, with their shadowy backgrounds and untold secrets, the imagination, fascinated, returns. Such are the characters, glimpsed perhaps long ago, who most often haunt and inhabit the books of novelists; they inspire yearning romantic memories. They never vanish. By contrast, see how the tracks of so many lives are strewn with the husks and shells of abandoned friendships, of intimacies which once flared up so fast, to gutter out when the early excitement died. "Once I used to find her so interesting: I'm afraid now she bores me." Yes, so it finished: no more was left to say. What next? The search for another face, another series of secrets, another story?

Friendships, and all the affections, were meant to be long-term things. "Fine!" it may be protested, "but *we* have no time, no leisure, no certain hold on the future. One must live in the moment; one must seize what one can!" What one can – how much that is precious eludes the too-hurried grasp! In handling objects of art, jade, crystal, or porcelain, we are careful; we have an instinctive feeling for preservation. Ought we to use personalities more roughly? Human beings, and the relations between them, are a blend of delicacy and strength: like instruments, they reward the sensitive touch. Should not art – which means skill and reverence – have its place in our immediate dealings with one another?

Art, in so many senses: most, the art of reserve – the sense of when not to ask and what not to say. The art, perhaps, of oblivion. Is it not better, sometimes, to forget the rash declaration, the heated outburst, the frantic confidence? That which my friend may regret having said to me, may I do my best to believe I have never heard! Let us not be over-infected by the idea of urgency; happiness, which is always somehow miraculous, creates its own calendar, sets its own clock. The infinite possibilities of happiness within a single human relationship unfold slowly, with a deliberation of their own – magical silences, delicious chance meetings, the evening by the fire, the sudden talk by the window looking out at the snow. We grow to know one another: gleam by gleam, intimation by intimation the truth blossoms; the story comes to be told.

Let us know, or learn, how to pause, to discriminate, to respect the boundaries. This revival of honour for private life, for the unique mysteries hidden in each existence, must begin to be manifested by you and me. Publicity, at its monster extreme, wheels at all angles its dazzling searchlight. Yet those who are in the complicity, who are far too willing to figure, far too unashamedly hungry to be informed, dare not denounce such publicity. Too many people are crude interviewers of those they seek as friends, brash broadcasters of feelings and personalities. There is more than charm in reticence, there is virtue. The enlargement of knowing another person, the reassurance of feeling oneself known, requires all that we have of restraint and balance, patience and intuition. What *do* we truly value? That, we have to discern. The art of reserve, what is it but the will to wait for perfection until the perfect time?

The Virtue of Optimism

Optimism is one of the slighted virtues – perhaps it seems too ready-to-hand? Indeed, that it *is* a virtue has been contested; it has been seen, rather, as the happy endowment of some temperaments. On the whole, it is felt, the optimist gets off light, so should agree to rank as a light-weight character, well enough liked, but disregarded. "Oh, one cannot possibly go by what X says! X simply says what is easiest, or what will make one like him. For his own sake, he wants to have everyone in the best of moods!" Such, often, is the satiric verdict. Optimism is charged to the wish to please or, when not that, to escapist policy.

Yet the real thing is neither facile nor superficial. Genuine optimism is hard won, needs courage, is based on staying-power. And, unlike the synthetic product, it does not advertise. Ostentatious "cheeriness," the automatic, slightly-too-bright smile have little connection with what is, in reality, a deep-down and sober belief in life. Does it seem too much of a contradiction to say that the genuine optimist is serious, or, at least, reserved? Hopeful, yes; but a certain amount of suspense attaches to even the strongest hope. When one cares, everything matters. The optimist does not merely believe that the good will win, he is intensely concerned that it should do so. One cannot stay passive and simply expect the best; the best needs active cooperation.

There may be something dangerous, or false, about this stated idea of the good "winning." Life, unlike a game or a campaign, seldom shows scores or arrives at declared results. Day by day, our objectives alter; values shift and change with the changing scene; so much so that what once we most desired may have come to mean less, or almost nothing, by the time fate places it in our hands. The optimist learns not to be disconcerted by the extreme slowness, or still more by the inscrutability, with which destiny works out its underlying pattern for the nation, the group or the individual. Expectations or hopes, if they are to be valid, must be long-term. One may say, indeed, that optimism involves the long-term view;

one believes (albeit, with sobriety) that ultimately matters will work out well; but, what will *ultimately* prove good may be far from what seems good today!

So far, I have referred to the optimist as "he," as one tends to do when speaking in the abstract. In fact, though optimism, like other virtues, is not the special prerogative of either sex, it is needed and should be sought by women. We need it not merely for our own support but for the sake of those with whom we are in contact. Rare, and perhaps unfortunate, is the woman whose fundamental attitude to life does not affect at least one other person; and generally it is a matter of several more. In the home, it is the woman who sets the mood; husband or children can but react to variations in the emotional weather-chart. Domestic relations, it must be said, are a most searching test of the true or false; in dealings with one's own flesh-and-blood, in weathering the crises of the home, superficial optimism is fatal. The methodically cheery and smiling lady, the automatic looker upon the bright side is likely, by sheer power of irritation, to provoke gloomy resistance in those around her. Worries and griefs will be hid from her, troubles not brought her way, for it seems evident that she cannot (or still worse, that she simply *will* not) plumb them. To ignore, deny or underrate suffering is to insult the sufferer; thus one drives away confidence. The man, the child or the adolescent are all likely to bring their troubles to one by whom they will be understood. Help, advice, consolation are only possible where there has been realistic sympathy – that is, where the extent of the trouble and, still more, its particular grievousness for a particular person, has been fearlessly faced out and computed. It is in the matter of "facing-out" that genuine optimism comes into play and for this, too, is required the long-term view. The professional problems of the man, with those obsessing anxieties that attend them, are almost certainly capable of solution; what he must have are time, courage, a certain amount of vision and, above all, confidence in himself. Time only time can give him; the other three can be reinforced by the friend who most truly loves him, knows his position and shares his fortunes: in his wife he is right to seek such a friend. The emotional agonies of adolescence are, as one can well see by middle age, disproportionate; the best one can probably do for the young victim is to recall one's own memories of those growing pains, but to add, "All the same, it's extraordinary how one lives through things and how, gradually, things do fall into place." One may also, in bad cases of love, suggest that the power of other persons to hurt one is far, far less than one's power to hurt oneself. "*You* can take this; *you're* not going to let this break you up!" The savage dramas of childhood, whether connected with play-time competitiveness or school work, need, above all, sympathy, plus a sense of proportion: one seldom in vain addresses oneself to a child's good head; in fact, in some issues it may appear that children are more reasonable than adults.

In all, the optimism that helps most is the expression of confidence in a person. Life is a compound of events, many of which cannot but be outside one's own control. When one speaks of confidence in life, one means, really, confidence in the power to live it. It is easier – or, should one say, more natural? – to be aware of that power in other people (and to remind *them* of it, when they need aid) than to rely on it constantly in oneself. We women, if we are honest, are self-critical, rather too quick to feel that we have failed. Perhaps we are too much given to self-searchings. A degree of optimism, *not* of the blind kind, does no harm in one's view of one's own character. One may not be much, but at least one has made out so far. At home, in her social relationships and her friendships, and in, if any, her professional or her public work, a woman is the better for self-reliance. Of herself, she can at least hope the best! On that hope, however modest, she bases good morale; and good morale, like its opposite, is infectious.

At almost every moment, more than we are aware, we affect and work upon other people – not so much by "influence" (which is always suspect) but by generating around us, wherever we go, the psychological air in which we live. Of men and women this is equally true – indeed, it is masculine ethics and staying-power which have, so far, moulded the exterior world. The more personal, intimate world remains woman's province; not only the home but society are our domain. Need it sound reactionary to suggest that what a woman is – that is, is in herself – almost always is more important than what she does. Our being, our existence from day to day, and not less its effect upon other people, is a matter of what we believe and feel. We act out an unworded philosophy. And just that, just such a philosophy, is optimism – *where* it genuinely exists. There are natures, often fine in themselves, for which belief of any kind is impossible. One must salute, when one meets such cases, the grim, dire courage with which they survive at all. But most of us are endowed with belief and hope; we not only should not deny these, we should apply them. Instinctively we are turners towards the sun; the sun may be hidden, but not forever.

Disappointment 1

Disappointment is a harsh emotional blow. For the eager child nothing softens it; for the young,[1] disappointment spells outright tragedy. The adult reaction is more guarded – yet has not the wreck of a hope or plan even now the power to cast us back into the disproportionate world of childhood? Utter dismay may last for a moment only – after that we strive to regain control. Sometimes a disappointment is of a magnitude which cannot be immediately taken in – painful are the phases of realisation. Till we can master ourselves, we require solitude: few of us are willing to meet the world till we can put on some sort of face. When we do feel ready for consolation, we turn to friends or allow them to seek us out; but few, we may find, either know us or know the facts of the case well enough to grasp what this blow means, or to compute our sense of disaster. Kindly intended sympathy may fall short, leaving us with a feeling of isolation.

True, as we grow older we expose ourselves less often to disappointment. We come to aim less high, expect less or take fewer chances. We become more cautious as to how or where we invest our hopes. Should we not therefore be safe? We fancy we are

– till, from some unpredictable quarter, the blow falls! The carefully thought out project collapses, the reward for effort is snatched away. Something has slipped up, someone has let us down. In business or love we experience a point-blank reverse – a reverse which may even appear incredible. *Had* we miscalculated? We cannot think so. The bitterest disappointments are those which seem, by all human reckoning, unmerited. We have been taken unawares.

Not all disappointments are sudden. Many are of the kind which operate slowly, over a term of years or (it may seem to the sufferer) a lifetime. Failure to realise objectives or make grades in business or the professions,[2] continuous social frustration, or non-achievement of happiness with another person in the course of a love affair, friendship or marriage are instances of gradual disappointment. What is undergone, in such cases, is not a single blow but a series of checkmatings, defeats, rebuffs – which, small or large, tend to mount up into a dire whole. On a man or woman, repeated little frustrations may have cumulative effect, undermining morale or corroding character. Disappointment may be a sort of process – going all the deeper because it *has* acted slowly. Hard is it, if such be one's own case, not to come to see oneself as a victim: one is threatened by defeatism and self-pity. There is danger of becoming that sad type, the recognizably "disappointed" person – condoned with, but liable to be shunned.

None of us can evade disappointment – no degree of age or experience, no policy can render you or me quite immune. Indeed, a life planned for immunity would have to be so negative in its outlook as to be hardly a life at all – empty of projects, bare of feeling. "Nothing disappoints me now" is either a vain boast or a tragic saying – for it could but mean, if it were true, that the speaker has not only withdrawn right into his shell but begun to die in it. *Is* it possible really to care for no one, to wish for nothing? At the lowest, a self-centred person sets his heart on his own small range of gratifications – the special dish at the restaurant, the armchair or newspaper at the appointed hour. Yet the dish may be "off," the chair gone, the delivery late – what then? For almost all of us, being alive means to love and hope, to plan and aspire. And is it not through our loves, hopes and aspirations that disappointment is ever able to strike? To be human is to remain exposed to the tricks of fate, which may affect our schemes, and to the behaviour of those we love or count on, which affects our feeling. We never can be insured against disappointment. This being so, what we must aim to learn by living is not how to evade disappointment but how to take it. Nothing is wholly bad till we let it be so. It is in the surmounting of disappointment that the crux comes.

Disappointment – how is it best surmounted? In each case, a certain part of the answer only can be provided by you or me – each of us has to reckon with his own nature. We may, however, be guided by a few general rules. One of these is, surely, that we should seek clear-sightedness – try, that is, for a realistic view of what has happened, its possible causes, its exact meaning to us. We do well to ask, "How far may this be my fault?" Is it a fact, for instance, that you or I *have* been living in something of a dream world? If so, there was almost bound to be a collision with reality: what else is disappointment? Self-delusion, vanity or egotism may have caused us to take unconscious risks: now, at a high price, we learn a lesson! Or it may be we have overrated our powers, or sought too much to dominate other people. A test case may be parental disappointment – a son or daughter makes a career choice or marriage which runs dead against cherished hopes. It is open to the father and mother to see this as a disaster, and feel accordingly, *or* to admit: "This was not what we had wished, but maybe we tried too hard to force a young life into our own mould."

Still more is clear sight needed (though it may be hardest then to attain) when disappointment occurs in a love relationship. We experience all the pain of a lost illusion. But how far was the illusion of our own making? Self-deception may play a part in romantic love. Have we, through over-idealisation, created as the object of our affections someone who in reality never was? Have we insisted on being blind to the true nature of the man or woman on whom we set our hearts? If so, a false situation has arisen: the loved one sooner or later[3] *must* give us pain by no more than being himself, or herself. By trying to force another person to conform with our notion of him or her, we virtually force them to disappoint us – in fairness, we should take that into account. Let us be slow to bring that terrible charge, "You have disappointed me!" Who knows but a life may be shadowed by that reproach? To admit one's own share in what has come about not only makes for justice, it serves to heal what might otherwise fester: the sense of injury.

In a case of career or social disappointment, clear sight also does calming work. At all costs let us measure the situation. The block in promotion, the withheld success – are those always due to ill will or indifference on the part of others? We are tempted to feel the world has combined against us: reasonableness comes with our second thoughts. Continuous failure to be accepted, repetitive failures to make a grade – may or may these not be traceable, if we search, to some deficiency in our own character, blind spot in our outlook or error in our approach? In future, cannot we make good the lack? Disappointment may be found to come as a challenge – a call for realism, a spur to effort. Profited by, it loses much of its sting.

But there are disappointments for which we are *not* to blame – the type which may strike from a blue sky. These show the action of forces outside our own control: we are made to feel our helplessness in the hands of fate. An enterprise, personal or commercial, may founder under unforeseen competition or be sunk by some unpredictable world event. Hard work, attention to detail, meritorious patience are all in a[4] moment cancelled out. What can we be but bewildered? Or, we have been building upon the promise of someone we had the right to trust: he or she backs down. And are there not emotional disappointments in which the sufferer *is* a victim truly? – cases of outrage to tender love or infidelity in return for good faith? Disappointment is present when we confront ingratitude. Disappointment is an element in the grief which submerges us at an untimely death – with the child killed in an accident or a son in battle has there not been snatched from us also a precious future? There are the disappointments which hit us doubly because of the pain they involve for another person;

someone near, dear and as innocent as ourselves – the husband who somehow has missed promotion shrinks from telling his wife the disheartening news; the boy who has flunked the examination dreads his return home. Yes, there are dealt out to the most blameless of us what cannot but seem to be crushing defeats to hope.

The fact that a disappointment is undeserved by no means renders it easier to take. For one thing, we are assailed in our sense of justice – the best in us seems to have gone for nothing. How are we to be reconciled to this grievous wrong? Not only have we to rally to the moment; somehow we have to come to terms with what now seems altered forever and for the worse. Immediate courage is not enough; to sustain us we need a long-term philosophy. We must try to see *around* what has happened, not let it block our entire view. A friend may chance to help, by some saying drawn from his own experience; and up to a point we react to sympathy. But ultimately only you or I can really come to our own aid. Alone we must set out to rebuild ourselves. Recuperation may be painful and slow – be that as it may, the essential is to *wish* to recuperate from a disappointment.

The hurt grows less once we can regain our sense of proportion. We re-find proportion as soon as we can cease to be self-obsessed – as soon, that is, as we take note of the vast scheme of human destinies around us. Bad as our own reverse or disaster may be, let us measure it against those large-scale ordeals undergone by the world. Once our trouble assumes a less inordinate size, we begin to be able to see it in perspective. Now we can see beyond it. We look ahead – is it not still in our power to shape *some* future? We look behind us – have we not in the past overcome other disappointments? Called upon to view our lives as a whole, we may well take heart from the picture shown us. And what of the overall pattern of human history? How has mankind survived but through readjustment? – and what is readjustment but the power to adapt to a changed position, the ability to cut losses and start anew? In you and me the unfailing life force is waiting to do its work – restoring, as it does the cells of the body, fundamental energies and hopes.

No disappointment is final; something goes on beyond it.

Nor does a frustration or failure, once taken stock of, appear so complete as it did at first. On a particular aim or person we had maybe concentrated our thoughts and feelings – to the exclusion of most things else. But did and does not life contain alternatives? Let us look again. For it is a curious fact that often in the aftermath of disappointment we find ourselves receptive to new ideas; our minds having become as it were clean slates. Unforeseen possibilities disclose themselves, opportunities offer, or inspiration directs us to our next move. An author whose manuscript[5] has been rejected conceives in a flash the theme for a better story; the let-down lover finds promise in some new face – or in a face well known but not *seen* before. And there are careers in which a disappointment turns out to have been a major turning-point.

At such a time, none the less, we do well to watch ourselves. We have been thrown off balance: balance we must recover. There may be danger in a too quick rebound, a too hasty grasping at compensations. Let us not embark on a fresh course simply for the sake of "showing the world," distracting our thoughts or healing our vanity. Disappointment has to be faced out, not run away from. No shame attaches to it – taken honestly it will raise, not lower us in the eyes of men. Like all other forms of primal experience, disappointment has about it a sort of dignity. As experience, it can both test and teach us – in so far as it does so, it has value. To have lived through and lived down a disappointment deepens our knowledge both of ourselves and others. As life continues, we find we have drawn strength from every inner crisis we have surmounted.

Disappointment 2

There are experiences which seem to belong to no one age, because they belong to all – one continues, that is to say, to feel them, and with intensity, right through life. Outstanding among these is disappointment. To undergo that takes one straight back to childhood – fresh as ever seem the particular stab and ache. In the eyes of a suddenly disappointed person, caught off guard, a sad and infinite youthfulness appears: never is the emotion not somehow childish. To the wrecked plan, the snatched-away pleasure, the vanished hope all of us who are sentient stay vulnerable.[1]

It is true that in the process of growing up one acquires safeguards, or learns to make out something of a philosophy: one becomes more foreseeing as to the whims of chance. To set the whole heart on anything is to court disaster, we tell ourselves, trying to act accordingly. Yet, secret happy expectancies go on; and indeed how should one live without them? To outgrow the capacity to be disappointed might make for peace, but peace of a barren kind. Stoicism can be at too high a cost. And one loss might be that of touch with children.

Being in touch with children, in tune with children, means sensing their emotional magnitudes. The child has no guard against disappointment; the whole heart sets itself on a project; a promise means the world. What we may find it hard to compute is childhood's absolute single-mindedness, or the way in which the whole eager being attaches itself to an envisaged joy. Few of us, we may be fairly sure, would disappoint a child knowingly or willingly; but what about what is inadvertent, those heartbreaks we hardly know we cause? By habit, we adjust our plans to necessity; how is the child to know or take account of the cause of changes which bring his dreams for a whole day toppling down? Life, it can but seem to him, should be within our power; why do we fail to make it as it should be? Again, there is the literalness of the child-mind: one thing is not much the same as, or just as good as, another. Substitutions of subterfuge fail to work. Who is to plumb the bottomless dismay behind the blurted-out, "But you *said* . . ."?

Disappointments are unavoidable – the car fails to start, rain falls on the picnic day, the awaited friend-visitor falls sick, or the child himself sickens on the eve of an outing. Who has not heard sobs which seem to shake the whole house because they shake one's heart? How is one to help this despair at blankness?[2]

First, by so understanding it as to enter in;[3] by sharing, and by making the sharing felt – for to the child, no less than the adult, woe brings a frightening isolation. Next, reason may start on its careful work; things seem a shade less grievous if they can be talked over. Last, may there not be an invitation, not to deny or minimise disappointment but to, somehow, surmount it and brave it out?

In fact, it is with this matter of the surmounting of disappointment that the crux comes: may not the child be aided to learn for himself what we have, in the course of experience, learned for ourselves?[4]

Disappointment is a harsh emotional blow, which must, like blows of all other kinds, be rallied to. Rallied to, "taken," it should not – and indeed must not be allowed to – breed a permanent state of mistrust, cynicism or insecurity. Disappointments are dangerous to psychic health only when they are, successively, taken wrongly. Does not that form a temperament with a lasting predisposition *to* disappointment? That sad adult figure, the officially "disappointed" man or woman is one into which one could wish no child to grow. "Disappointed" folk lay a blighting touch on society: at times we are tempted to ask ourselves, did Miss X really suffer worse from a faithless lover than other spinsters who learned how to smile again?[5] Was Mr. Y more baulked in his young ambitions, or frustrated in his later business career than those many cheerful men who pursue dull rounds? With relief, we applaud modest flags kept flying.[6]

We ought to be just: it appears that Nature, from time to time, sends fated cripples or victims into the world. Susceptibility to disappointment varies and, with that, varies recuperative power. To recuperate, to outface, to throw off may be the soundest aim one can give a child. That said, let us never underrate disappointment. It is seldom distant. It always hurts.

How to Be Yourself – But Not Eccentric

"I want," declares the young person, "to be myself!" And one smiles and answers: "There is nothing to stop you." Yet then there follows a qualm, a certain misgiving – this *should* be true, but is it? And in the clear gaze meeting one's own, is there a touch of wonder? – "If it's so easy, what happened to you, then?" The young are puzzled by our conformities; as they show, they fail to see reason for them. Confidently flying their own flags, they suspect us of having lowered ours. How is it, they ask, that people tend to become so all-of-a-pattern as they grow older – and, still more, seem content to let this happen? We could tell them that life as the years go on becomes less straightforward than it seemed at the start; constantly it is subject to pulls and pressures. True. Yet that question youth raises is not lost on us; it disturbs, haunts us more than our children know. For is it not one we have asked ourselves?

So many of our conformities are skin-deep only; they cost us nothing and matter little. A general wish for smooth-runningness accounts for them; seldom are ethics or loyalties at stake. When talk, for instance, takes a turn towards subjects as to which you or I lack any particular interest or conviction, it seems at once simpler and more civil to fall in with opinions expressed by others. Some of our agreements are due to laziness, but others to actual diffidence or humility – "Who am *I* to know?" And there are pacts we make with the rest of society: on the whole we dress, behave, run our homes, and conduct our outside existences in the accepted manner – to do otherwise could involve us in needless trouble, or cause us to rile or perplex our neighbours. Overmarked self-assertion could, we see, border on self-advertisement. We break with convention, depart from custom, only for some authoritative reason. Altruism, too, can make for conformity – have I the right to expand, to express myself at the expense (as it could be) of those around me?

So far, so good. But where should this stop?

We slip into many acceptances unwittingly: do we know *when* we begin to begin to give way too much? Danger signals, some infinitesimal, others sufficient to cause us shock, show when individuality is threatened. Such, for one, is the moment when we find ourselves no longer making decisions – no longer comparing values, weighing alternatives. Choice is not choice when it fails to be quite our own, calling upon taste, will, and indeed temperament. And yet another warning is boredom – we are bored when our existence grows automatic; when impulse, enterprise, the stimulating element of uncertainty no longer play even a little part in it. Or, our likes and dislikes lose their spontaneity; even our pleasures lessen in flavour – where are the incentives which moved us once? We feel brought to a standstill. Then it is that, within us, something makes heard a half-stifled cry: "Let me live, let me *be*, before it is too late!"

This cry of the self is not egotism. Let us be clear as to the immense distinction between egotism and identity; otherwise, in our efforts to curb the one we may end by extinguishing the other. The ego by nature tends, as we realise, to be grasping, aggressive, and antisocial; whereas identity, on the other hand, puts forth but one deep insistent quiet demand – for outlet. Outlet means expression, and *that* tends to enrich rather than harm society. In the best of the world we live in, civilisation, art, we see the splendid achievements of self-expression; countless creative identities, back through time, have greatened our concept of humanity. Not all of us are artists or thinkers, statesmen or pioneers; we are none the less each born with one priceless attribute – we are each unique. In each of us therefore resides the power to leave our own individual marks on life. Small as these may be, they are never trifling: they count.

What they count for, we should know – for how quick and happy are our reactions to the "expressive" in other people! The most fleeting evidences remain memorable – the face glowing with character on the crowded street; the room unalike to a thousand more through the atmosphere given it by its owner; unusual breath from a perfume, flash from a colour, inspiration in the pinning-on of a jewel; the fresh and lively turn of a phrase in talk: these affect us like miniature glints of genius. And what else are they? . . . In love and friendship, the predominant moments are those when those we care for are "most themselves"; equally we, when we can be natural, cause a release all round us of personality – feelings are unsealed, thoughts find words, affection and gaiety well up. To be treasured in memory are such days or hours – how sad, by contrast, seem our constraints, our half-wary shynesses, our small-talk made trite by conventionality! Why are we not ourselves, we wonder, all of the time – or at least, more of it?

Possibly, we don't give ourselves enough chances. There is the matter, for one thing, of opportunities: some occasions, like some persons, ask something special of us, offer us special scope – those are the ones not to let slip by. Life's unexpected small invitations, are we too routine-bound to take them up? The impromptu party, the sudden purchase, the unplanned journey: who knows what might not have flowered out of them! And again, many of us have hidden interests, likings, capacities to be amused or charmed, which we disavow because of their seeming "childishness" – exactly these could go to the making of our own individual inner world. Furthermore, there can be good in daydreaming. We are warned against what can be its insidious dangers – gone too far, it could weaken our hold on fact. But in happy rovings of fancy, I see no harm – I maintain that in our middle years many of us do not daydream enough. Endless, for one thing, are the delights of building castles in the air; if they never become reality, we have still enjoyed them! The "I" in us, eager and many-sided, is capable of living more lives than one – imagination, often, can supply them. I have a friend, a contented woman, who remarked to me as we passed a neighbouring home: "Mrs. So-and-So may not know it, but for years *I* have been living in her house!" Having fallen in love with the place, knowing full well she had never a hope of owning it, my friend had found the solution: she had moved in and was serenely dwelling there – in fancy.

Let us want what we *do* want, not what we feel we ought to! Our genuine wishes, choices, and tastes express us, even apart from their realisation – though, let us realise them if we can. Choice – or call it selection, discrimination – is the most eloquent of all (which is why I call it a bad day when that power in us threatens to atrophy).

In dress, in home decoration, shapes, textures, colours, the "I" finds a concrete vocabulary. Fashion, today, no longer is a dictator, rather a would-be ally of the identity; it deals no longer in "musts" but in possibilities. There are an infinity of ways of avoiding the mass-produced look. Even what may seem to be universals, the grey suit or the black dress, subtly are invitations to personality; everything depends on the way of wearing them, the unique touches, the language of the accessories. Anything more out-of-the-way, more striking, issues a more uncompromising challenge; there *are* times when one should take this up. How we appear is a great part of what we are, and the same holds good in the making of our surroundings – grouping of objects, lighting, and use of colour. It is up to us to arrive at our own harmonies; there is not an expert in the world who can more than suggest how this may be done.

Decisions we make when we go shopping have their psychological equivalents all the way. At every turn, the question is put to us: "Do *you* wish this? – is this what *you* really like, love, require, prefer to other things?" None of us desires to be the prey, entirely, of our instincts and impulses; nevertheless do we not do wrong if we endlessly disregard and thwart them? We ought, I'm sure, to analyse the reasons for our conformities. Convention is a good guide, but a deadening ruler. It may be that we restrict ourselves out of over-deference to unreal standards: for instance, I have known people in whom a genuine urge towards hospitality (and, almost certainly, a potential gift for it) was balked by the fear that they could not offer enough. That what counts in entertaining is warmth and grace, that thought taken achieves more than money spent, were truths they had not the courage to act on. Immense is the value of spontaneity – in a flower arrangement, in an impulsive visit, in a remark. Slight risks of oddness – *do* they matter so much? Even those who smile at them, they may well delight.

It is infinitely rewarding to be oneself. It is not easy. How much is involved in the undertaking, the confident young speaker has yet to know. Ego, crashing head-on against authority, is miles from identity seeking its gentler way out. Aggressive, offensive eccentricity is its own warning; only slowly, by experiment, do we learn the quiet art of the personal in behaviour. Born to our individualities, as to destinies, we have in us the power to fulfil them – small or great, the means lie everywhere to our hands. What we are is, most of all, what we have to give.

The Thread of Dreams

Our thoughts, like buildings standing up out of water, are at their base washed by tides of dreams. Who dares deny this? From out of the depths of a night's sleep, a dream pursues us through the following day. Then, there is daydreaming, with its many allurements. Is the break between these two dreamings really so sharp? These two, between them, compose a universe of desire and envisagement – a lordly background, in whose presence our thought-out "design for living" struggles to carry itself out. A losing struggle. For, we are to discover, no action has not a misty emotive source, no decision, however cerebrally taken, is not swayed by a mysterious undertow. To oppose dreams is to find ourselves swimming against the current of our being. We are dreams' creatures, like it or not. True, in the night dream with its absolute power there may be an element of dread – we wrench ourselves free by wakening, though not completely. That, we call nightmare. The daydream, enticing our will, flooding our leisure, is in essence rewarding, glowing and pleasurable. Yet had not the night dream, in its very enormity, also a tint of desire – however inverted? Both kinds of dreaming conjoin: they fulfil for us whatever surface existence leaves incomplete. They blend, for instance, in any passionate love. They are the dark-and-light harmonised by supreme art: poetry, painting, music. They are the twin extremities recognized in the contemplation of the mystic: to reconcile them would indeed be the triumph of a religion. Just as, unchecked, dreams may make for obsession, they enter also, strongly, into ambition. The sustained dream becomes a determining force – for worse or better. The world may feel its effect; it indents history, history being man-made. The monster-dictator, with his criminal record, and the sublime national hero, mainstayer and maybe saviour of his country, alike had nourished a dream: it came to be realised. Spectacular, the career of a famous person has about it something phantasmagoric – however much discipline, calculation, cold hard work and fanatic austerity did, actually, go to the making of it. Why is the "star," the celebrity, not more bitterly envied by the mass of mankind, by those hundreds of thousands of persons whose dreams aborted? Because their dreams triumph in him, vicariously . . . For the ancients, a dream had divine authority. See how, in the Bible, sleeping prophet or patriarch was visited by a messenger angel, or heard, direct, the commanding voice of his God. In a dream, the agitations of good St. Joseph, husband-to-be of Mary, were laid at rest: "Fear not," the angel said. And dreams acted as warnings to noble pagans: in the face of one, Julius Caesar went to his death. The idea of a dream as a dictum, not to be flouted, or omen, not to be disregarded, has hold on many of us: how can it not? Fateful or not, how dreams rejoice – in the main! Rare is a dream which is not dramatic, vividly visual. At night by chance and by day at will we command a great, secret, internal cinema – where should we be without this entrancing extension of our existences? Fantasies architect themselves, forms float, the lyrical mingles with the comic. Friends or lovers, figuring in our dream, accumulate further magic around them. Dreams have a lovely frivolity – a sheer opalescent and stylish prettiness overflows from them into our tastes and wishes, engendering, when we waken, caprices, *engouements*, crazy and innocent adventurings without which the world would be a degree more dull. "Dreamlike" is how we speak of our purest happiness. Little wonder, in our day, that the dream extends its domain into art and fashion – we need its triumphant irrationality. Here is one great "No" to the computer age.

Notes

Modern Lighting

"Modern Lighting" appeared in the *Saturday Review of Literature* (27 October 1928): 294. Somewhat overwritten, this essay is the first piece of non-fiction that Bowen published. Showing off her modernity by contrasting electrical lighting with candlelight and gaslight, she draws examples not from life, but from literature, both English and French. Erratic capitalisation and spelling have been amended. "Shops" and "Method," for example, are put in lower case.

1. The published text has awkward punctuation: "We can control shadow, place, check, and tone light." The first comma has been altered to a colon for coherence.

2. "Lead Kindly Light": the words to this Christian hymn were written by John Henry Newman in 1833; John B. Dykes composed the tune in 1865.

3. "The Dong with the Luminous Nose": a nonsense poem by Edward Lear published in *Laughable Lyrics* (1877). The nose of the Dong, a fabulous creature, glows luridly in the dark.

4. "Markheim": Stevenson's short story about murder and the supernatural was published in 1885, then collected in *The Merry Men and Other Tales and Fables* in 1887.

5. Balbec: the published text gives "Bulks bedroom," which is probably a typesetter's error. In *À la recherche du temps perdu*, Marcel stays at a seaside hotel at Balbec.

6. Albertine: mistakenly spelled "Albutine" in the published version. Albertine plays the pianola in the bedroom of the narrator in *Albertine disparue*.

The 1938 Academy: An Unprofessional View

This "unprofessional view" of the 1938 Academy exhibition appeared in the *Listener* (4 May 1938): 952–3. Reviewing the annual exhibition at the Royal Academy for the *New Statesman* two years earlier, Bowen excoriated the insipidity of the paintings on view: "The blandness of the whole is unnerving" (*Collected Impressions* 211). As Bowen specifies, the Royal Academy was founded to create and disseminate a national school of painting. Respecting the dictates of Sir Joshua Reynolds, first president of the Royal Academy and author of *Discourses on Art*, Bowen emphasises the national parameters of art. In "Discourse XIV," Reynolds considers artists who exemplify "the English School" (248). Having attended art school in London as a young woman, Bowen retained a life-long interest in painting.

She occasionally went to galleries to "look at some pictures" with William Plomer (HRC 11.8; note dated "Monday"). Her interests took in the avant-garde as well as academic painting. Plomer and Bowen intended to meet at the opening of the Surrealist show in London on 27 June 1936, but they missed each other in the chaos (*Mulberry Tree* 201). Keri Walsh, summarising Bowen's differences of aesthetic opinion with the surrealists, concludes that "Surrealism was both a source of creative inspiration and an ideological movement demanding critique from Bowen, and her work provides a rich archive of the complex and fruitful dialogue between French surrealism and Irish modernism" (144).

1. John Constable (1776–1837): English painter best known for his landscapes. He was elected to the Royal Academy in 1819.

2. Sir George Clausen (1852–1944): English painter elected to the Royal Academy in 1906 and knighted in 1927. Clausen studied with Bouguereau in Paris, but the impressionists also influenced his style. He painted landscapes and scenes of peasant life.

3. Alfred J. Munnings (1878–1959): a war artist during the First World War, he subsequently concentrated on equestrian subjects. He presided at the Royal Academy from 1944 to 1949.

4. Wilson Steer (1860–1942): English painter Philip Wilson Steer studied under Cabanel in France and later became an impressionist of the English school.

5. Chantrey Bequest: Sir Francis Leggatt Chantrey (1782–1841), a sculptor and member of the Royal Academy, bequeathed the residue of his personal estate, after legacies to his widow, in trust to the Royal Academy for the purchase of British fine art in painting and sculpture. These works were first displayed in the Victoria and Albert Museum, then moved in 1898 to the National Gallery of British Art (now the Tate Gallery).

Christmas at Bowen's Court

This evocation of "Christmas at Bowen's Court," Bowen's country house near Kildorrery in County Cork, was published in *Flair* 1.11 (December 1950): 20–1. Bowen had previously rehearsed the history of this Georgian country house in *Bowen's Court* (1942). The spiritual meaning of Christmas preoccupied her throughout the 1950s. The ringing bell – a favourite motif in Bowen's stories, novels, and essays – recalls the jubilant, clanging bells at the end of *The Heat of the Day*. Erratic capitalisation in this essay has been regularised for consistency.

The Light in the Dark

"The Light in the Dark" was first published in the American edition of *Vogue* 116 (December 1950): 89–90, 157, 158. It was reprinted in the British edition of *Vogue* (January 1951): 25, 84. Subsequently it was anthologised in *The World in Vogue*, edited by Bryan Holme (New York: Viking, 1963): 291–2. Childless herself, Bowen recalls her own childhood and the meaning of the Christ child in this essay. The mystery of Christ's nativity inspired more than one modernist writer, as T. S. Eliot's "The Journey of the Magi" and Bowen's own *Nativity Play* attest. Bowen heightens the Christian content of the essay by capitalising "Story," "Holy Night," and "Child." These capitalisations have been kept, but other, less consistent capitalisations have not.

1. Year's midnight: an allusion to John Donne's "A Nocturnal Upon Saint Lucy's Day, Being the Shortest Day," which begins, "'Tis the year's midnight, and it is the day's."

Ecstasy of the Eye

First published in American *Vogue* (December 1968): 189–90, "Ecstasy of the Eye" is a Christmas rhapsody. Illustrated in *Vogue* with a Piero della Francesca head and a Fernand Léger painting entitled "Woman with Book," the essay recalls Bowen's fondness for visual art and the eye as a mediator of emotional states. Capitalisation has been regularised; after colons, some words are capitalised and others are not, so they have all been put in lower case.

1. "The moon doth with delight": from William Wordsworth's "Ode: Intimations of Immortality."

2. "Walk with eyes cast down": the "puritan" would seem to be John Bunyan. This exact passage, however, does not appear in *Pilgrim's Progress*, where it would most likely be found. The "puritan" may be generic rather than specific. The statement recalls any number of biblical injunctions, especially, "Let their eyes be darkened, that they may not see, and bow down their back alway" (Romans 11:10).

New Waves of the Future

One of Bowen's very last essays, "New Waves of the Future" appeared in *American Home* 72 (October 1969): 70–1. It addresses the decorative and interior aspects of lighting in a manner that recalls "Modern Lighting." Bowen distinguishes the modernity of her generation from the timidity of the Victorians. Tanning is one proof of modernity, a show of fearlessness in sunlight. Such modern attitudes do not prevent Bowen from welcoming the return of candles and fires.

1. A comma appears in the published version, although the sentence is more intelligible without it.

Britain in Autumn

"Britain in Autumn" is an earlier version of "London, 1940," which Bowen included in *Collected Impressions* (217–20). She may not have wanted to extrapolate the blitz in London to a general experience of warfare in Britain; hence the change in title, with its narrowing from "Britain" to "London." The carbon typescript of "Britain in Autumn" has ten pages (HRC 2.2). The censor cut two small pieces from page five, and two large sections on page six. On page six, the typescript was sellotaped on to another page for support; the typed words "CUT BY THE CENSOR" appear inside one excised box. Before publishing this essay as "London, 1940," Bowen revised it heavily. She creates, for instance, a blasted scrap of prose in the first sentence: "Early September morning in Oxford Street. The smell of charred dust hangs on what should be crystal pure air" (*Collected Impressions* 217). "London, 1940" concludes with the terrifying sentence, "We have no feeling to spare," whereas "Britain in Autumn" continues for some pages further with political commentary and observations on the atmosphere of the city. The "theatricality" of events and of the city during warfare is raised several times. I have signalled differences between "Britain in Autumn" and "London, 1940" in notes. Obvious spelling errors have been corrected: "fundementals," "becasue," and "frig" instead of "fridge." For quoted speech, Bowen sometimes leaves off commas, an idiosyncrasy that I have not retained, even though the omission creates a sense of urgency that suits the subject matter.

1. Central Park: the reference to New York suggests that Bowen is addressing American readers.

2. A.R.P.: Air Raid Precautions was formed in 1924 as a result of German bombing in England during the First World War. During the Second World War, the A.R.P. was responsible for handing out gas-masks, ensuring the upkeep of bomb shelters, enforcing the blackout, and locating people after bomb attacks.

3. Tank-like: the typescript reads "tank-life," a typing error. In "London, 1940," this phrase changes to "aquarium-like" to avoid confusion about what sort of "tank" is meant.

4. The typescript reads, "have been bombed." This is rectified in "London, 1940."

5. In "London, 1940," this paragraph begins differently: "This is the

buoyant view of it – the theatrical sense of safety, the steady breath drawn" (*Collected Impressions* 218).

6. Bowen types "sideways," a spelling that has a dislocating unorthodoxy about it. The word "bubbles" is a noun. In "London, 1940," the sentence is clearer: "Chatter bubbles up; or there is a cosy slumping sideways, to doze" (*Collected Impressions* 219).

7. The last four sentences in this paragraph are cut from "London, 1940."

8. *Ewigkeit*: eternity. Bowen transforms this paragraph completely in her revisions.

9. The censor cut a few words from the beginning of this sentence. In "London, 1940," the sentence reads, "For one bad week, we were all turned out on account of time-bombs: exiled" (*Collected Impressions* 220).

10. Initially Bowen capitalises "Time Bombs," then writes "time-bombs." I adopt the latter orthography for consistency.

11. Whatever short sentence the censor cut, it was perhaps some version of the single sentence that appears in "London, 1940": "Regent's Park where I live is still, at the time of writing, closed: officially, that is to say, we are not here" (*Collected Impressions* 220).

12. An excision of about five lines occurs here and the defaced page has been taped on to another page. "CUT BY CENSOR" is typed into the gaping space. In "London, 1940," the shrapnel-collecting postman does not appear and Bowen discusses the beauty and brittleness of the terrace houses.

13. Where this excision occurs in "Britain in Autumn," the following sentence appears in "London, 1940": "Now and then everything rips across; a detonation rattles remaining windows. The R.E. 'suicide squad' detonate, somewhere in the hinterland of this park, bombs dug up elsewhere" (*Collected Impressions* 220). R.E. is the abbreviation for "Royal Engineers," responsible for ordnance disposal.

14. In "London, 1940," a one-sentence paragraph concludes the essay at this point: "We have no feeling to spare" (*Collected Impressions* 220), a version of the third sentence in the next paragraph of "Britain in Autumn."

15. The typescript reads "usual," but the nonchalance during warfare would seem "unusual," which Bowen probably intended.

16. Bowen writes "Democracy" and "democracy" to indicate the differences between the political ideal and its manifestation.

17. Narvik: in the early months of 1940, Winston Churchill realised that taking control of the Norwegian coastal town of Narvik, which had a rail link to Swedish iron-ore fields, could disrupt the supply of iron ore to Germany. Battles for control of the city occurred in the spring of 1940.

By the Unapproachable Sea

"By the Unapproachable Sea" was published in the *Christian Science Monitor Magazine* (5 February 1944): 10. I have collated the printed version with the longer typescript version, which appears on the recto and verso of one legal-size page (HRC 2.5). As far as possible, I have used the *Christian Science Monitor* version as the base text, but a long section of the original essay was edited out, probably for reasons of space. The ending was redrafted for publication. This essay, because it exists in two quite distinct versions, presents a complicated editorial challenge. I have created a hybrid essay using the typescript and the published versions, in part because the typescript is longer and has fewer awkwardnesses. To be sent to the US, the essay had to pass before the censor. At the top of the typescript, the censor's approval is typed in: "(Not available for Canada) *Length 1,050 words. Passed by the British Censor Quote No.Q.3656.*" As in "Britain in Autumn," Bowen comments on civilian solidarity under wartime duress. In the typescript, Bowen included two headlines: "How Life Goes on In One of Britain's Typical Front Line Towns," followed by, "'Look At Our Babies!' Said The Mayor." These do not appear in the printed version. Two other headlines have been removed from the body of the text as well; in the notes, I have indicated what these headlines stated and where they appeared. American spellings have been converted back to British orthography.

1. The published version omits the next four paragraphs, which concern the history of the coastal town. I have included them for the sake of completeness.

2. The headline, *"Winston Is The Warden,"* appears after this paragraph.

3. The headline, *"A Street That Suffered,"* was inserted here in the typescript.

4. Housewives: the published version reads "shopwives," a neologism. I have therefore opted to use "housewives," which appears in the typescript.

5. Has been: the published version gives the untruthful verb tense, "had been extra quick." I follow the typescript for verb tense because, as the subsequent passage makes clear, cleaning up after bomb raids is a present perfect activity, not a pluperfect one: "Hythe . . . has been extra quick."

6. The typescript and published texts deviate at this point. The typescript, which I have followed, is more elaborate. In the *Christian Science Monitor Magazine* version, everything after "bomb damage" was cut and two sentences were joined together: ". . . clear away bomb damage. The sneak raider is barely gone again, the Mayor told me, when all hands fly to work . . ."

7. Exploring, again: this sentence is omitted from the published version.

8. After Sunday service: this sentence is omitted from the published version.

9. The published version ends at this point. The typescript has two further paragraphs – restored here – that emphasise the future and babies, rather than return and continuance.

Foreword to *The Cinque Ports*, by Ronald and Frank Jessup

The Cinque Ports belongs to a series of books on "British Cities" published by B. T. Batsford (London, 1952). R. F. Jessup had written *The Archaeology of Kent*, *Little Guide to Kent*, and *South-Eastern England: A Revision*. F. W. Jessup had published *Problems of Local Government in England and Wales* and *Local Government in Outline*. Illustrated with maps and photographs, *The Cinque Ports* provides historical information for touristic purposes. The chapter on Hythe (90–103), where Bowen lived as a young girl and where she again settled at the end of her life, features commentary on military and religious architecture. Shores and coasts appeal to Bowen, as in the Waikiki episode in *The Death of the Heart* and her comments on seeing the coastline of France for the first time in "The Idea of France."

The Idea of France

The six-page carbon typescript of "The Idea of France" bears the date "23.11.44." (HRC 6.3). I have not been able to trace it to a published source. Bowen added a few emendations in black ink to the typescript. She maintained a lifelong interest in France. She especially monitored politics and culture in France in the years leading up to, and culminating in, the Second World War. Poignancy in the essay stems from Bowen's wondering what the country will look like in the postwar period. She yearns to be embraced by France, which she identifies with her mother.

1. The word "adventure" was deleted and "undertaking" added in the typescript.

2. The typescript reads, "she already travelled," but the pluperfect makes more sense.

3. While revising, Bowen accidentally deleted "of."

4. Bowen uses a semi-colon, but a comma before "which" makes more sense.

5. La Bibliothèque Rose: a collection of children's books published in French by Hachette from 1856 onwards.

6. The original gives "impassible," which means "incapable of suffering, pain, or emotion." Bowen probably means "impassable."

7. Fourteen years: by this account, Bowen first travelled to France in 1920, when she was twenty-one years old, which corroborates what she states earlier in the essay.

Paris Peace Conference: 1946. An Impression

Bowen's seven-page essay on the Paris Peace Conference is a draft for three articles that she wrote for the *Cork Examiner* (HRC 8.7). Certain ideas and phrases reappear verbatim in the published essays: Molotov's deadly way of speaking; the relation of the Luxembourg Gardens to the deliberations inside the Luxembourg Palace; Bowen's description of being in Paris, then in Ireland, as close and distant perspectives on the proceedings. The Paris Peace Conference negotiated postwar frontiers and reparations from 29 July until 15 October 1946. Charles Ritchie, a member of the Canadian delegation and Bowen's lover, saw her regularly during the conference. "Her being here," he wrote in his diary on 15 October 1946, "is the reality which shows up for me the unreality of this sad charade of a conference" (*Diplomatic Passport* 12–13). This version is typed with handwritten corrections in ink, although corrections are relatively few. Some type-overs and inter-lineal additions have been transcribed as Bowen's intentions (as against the cancelled material). Minor alterations in punctuation, mostly added commas, have been made for intelligibility.

1. The word "which" has been added.

2. Queen: the Luxembourg palace was laid out for Catherine de Medici, wife of Henri IV; construction began in 1615 and continued for some 15 years.

3. Renascent: Bowen spells this "renaissant."

4. Hemicycle: at the front of this grand room, currently the senate chamber for the French Republic, is a semi-circular alcove lined with statues.

5. The typescript ambiguously reads "afternoon after-noon."

6. The question mark, which may indicate a rhetorical enquiry, appears in the typescript.

7. Congress of Vienna: from September 1814 until June 1815, statesmen met to redraw the political map of Europe after the Napoleonic wars.

8. The word "the" has been added for sense.

9. *Le smoking*: dinner jacket.

10. Lubitsch: Ernst Lubitsch's films include *Ninotchka* (1939), *The Shop Around the Corner* (1940), and *Heaven Can Wait* (1943).

11. The word "the" has been added.

12. Lief Egeland: South African Minister to Belgium and Holland, Egeland was a member of the South African delegation.

13. The word "in" has been added.

14. Vishinsky: Andrey Yanuaryevich Vishinsky, member of the Soviet delegation, was Deputy Minister for Foreign Affairs in the Soviet Union.

15. Bebler: Ales Bebler, Deputy Minister of Foreign Affairs for Yugoslavia, was a member of the Yugoslav delegation.

16. Jordaan: Jan Ruiter Jordaan, an officer in the South African Department of External Affairs, advised the South African delegation. Bowen misspells his name as "Jordan."

17. Hodgson: William Roy Hodgson, member of the Australian delegation, was Australian Minister in France. Bowen misspells his name as "Hodgeson."

18. Connally: Tom Connally was a member of the American delegation. A senator from Texas, he was chairman of the Senate Foreign Relations Committee. Bowen misspells his name as "Conally."

19. Molotov: Vyacheslav Mikhailovich Molotov, Minister of Foreign Affairs for the Soviet Union, headed the Soviet delegation.

Paris Peace Conference – Some Impressions 1

Bowen's first article on the Paris Peace Conference appeared in the *Cork Examiner* (12 October 1946): 9. Although most articles in this newspaper were unsigned, Bowen published this, and its two companion pieces, under her own name. In a 1959 radio interview, Bowen commented on her journalism: "When I was reporting a peace conference there was a good deal of photography of the situation, photography of particular characters as I saw them, the atmosphere of a particular occasion, the circumstances, the surrounds, whatever you call it, of a particular conference room where small debates were taking place. But I had enough sense to know that I ought not to waste space in the columns of the paper by laying down any theory or appearing to act on any information which I would not have, and you would" (HRC 2.3). In addition to her preliminary draft for these three articles, two versions of each exist: the *Cork Examiner* version and the typescript (HRC 8.7). I have used the printed newspaper version as a base text, but have consulted the typescript and combined variants for all three articles. Inter-titles that the *Cork Examiner* inserted to break up the body of the text and to create proper spacing on the page during typesetting have been omitted, but I indicate in the notes where they were placed. The principal differences between the typescript and newspaper versions concern capitalisation. The newspaper, applying house style, capitalises "Press," but Bowen does not. Bowen capitalises "Bar," as in "Press Bar," but the newspaper does not. "Plenary Sessions," "Palace," and "Conference" retain upper case in both versions.

NOTES

1. General Smuts: Smuts was Prime Minister of the Union of South Africa from 1919 to 1924 and again from 1939 to 1948. A British Field Marshal in both wars, he represented South Africa at the drafting of the United Nations Charter in San Francisco in May 1945, before attending the Paris Peace Conference. In a summary of war events in *The Heat of the Day*, he is cited by name (348).

2. *Amende honorable*: in French, *faire amende honorable* is to make amends.

3. Bowen writes "Paris" rather than "French" in the typescript.

4. The inter-title "IN HEAT WAVE" appeared after this paragraph in the newspaper version, and "UNCANNY" after the paragraph ending "her way."

5. The word "the" has been added for sense.

Paris Peace Conference – Some Impressions 2

The second article in the series, "The Paris Peace Conference – Some Impressions," appeared in the *Cork Examiner* (15 October 1946): 7. In the same issue, other journalists reported on Soviet Foreign Minister Molotov's accusations that Western Powers, specifically the US, Britain, and France, were changing their stance on agreed-upon decisions concerning Trieste and the Greco-Bulgarian frontier. This shift in stance, according to Molotov, would allow the Soviets to view the Peace Treaties, already negotiated and drafted at the conference, as null and void. While the *Cork Examiner* conscientiously reported on official negotiations, Bowen personalises and humanises them in her "impressions." As in the first article, capitalisation between typescript and newspaper versions of this article varies; nor is capitalisation consistent from one article to the next in the newspaper versions. While making some typesetting errors, the compositor at the *Cork Examiner* retains, by and large, Bowen's copy. Using the newspaper version as a base text, I have incorporated elements from the typescript – occasional commas, semi-colons, colons, or capitalisation – that enable sense.

1. The newspaper version gives "you," not "we," which creates inconsistency with the "we" in the next sentence.

2. The newspaper inserts the inter-title "A BAD PATCH" after this paragraph, and "A BETTER PHASE" after the paragraph ending "electric drill."

3. The newspaper version gives "the end," but "its end" makes more sense.

4. Punctuation in the newspaper version could be a dash or a colon; it is illegible in the copy that I consulted in the British Library. Bowen uses a

semi-colon in the typescript version. The typesetter for the *Cork Examiner* often replaced colons with semi-colons.

5. Bowen writes "adherents in the Slav *bloc*," but the newspaper version, which I have adopted, reads, "with their adherents, the Slav *bloc*," which implies that all Slavic countries are adherents.

6. The newspaper version places a semi-colon after "source," causing incomprehensibility in the latter part of the sentence. Bowen more sensibly uses a colon in the typescript, which has been adopted here.

7. The newspaper version places no commas around "exactly" but the typescript does; the latter version has been adopted here.

8. Friend: possibly Charles Ritchie.

Paris Peace Conference – Some Impressions 3

"Paris Peace Conference – Some Impressions 3," the last of Bowen's brief essays on the reparations negotiations, ran in the *Cork Examiner* (22 October 1946): 4. As with the preceding two reports, the compositor changed some colons to semi-colons, altered capitalisation, and switched "press" to "Press" most of the time. The compositor erroneously spells "Grande Salle" as "Grand Salle." I use the published version as a base text, supplemented with variants from the typescript that make better sense.

1. The newspaper prints "also dealing," but "also" creates a redundancy with "another." Bowen does not use "also" in the typescript.

2. The inter-title "TRIBUTE TO CHAIRMAN" appears after this paragraph in the *Cork Examiner*; "SLAV CHARGES" appears after the paragraph ending "by the Russians."

3. A comma appears after "human" in the typescript, but "human" modifies "survival" rather than "necessities." Therefore, no comma seems logical. Bowen might also have intended "human-survival necessities."

4. Dominions: within the British Commonwealth, Canada, New Zealand, and Australia were "Dominions." These countries had the status of nationhood while retaining the British monarch as the titular head of state.

Prague and the Crisis

"Prague and the Crisis" was published simultaneously in British and American *Vogue*. The base text is the version in American *Vogue* (April 1948): 156, 195–6. Visiting Prague in February, Bowen sums up the atmosphere in the city immediately prior to the coup in which the Czech Communist Party seized power. Her reportage depends on talking with people and sensing the course that "destiny" will take. The essay concludes ambiguously on a note of solidarity with, and abandonment of, Czecho-slovakia. Certain words seem translated from other languages, especially "nervosity," reminiscent of the French *nevrosité*, and "outlander," a close approximation of the German *Ausländer*, or foreigner.

Hungary

The ten-page typescript of "Hungary" is dated 29 November 1948 on the last page (HRC 6.2). Sellary and Harris call this an essay, but it may have been written, like "Impressions of Czechoslovakia," for radio broadcast. Its importance lies in Bowen's exposure to Soviet influence in Hungary and Europe generally. The tone of the essay approximates the casual, informative tone of the political observer in "Notes on Eire," Bowen's reports about Ireland during the Second World War. Bowen habitually capitalises "Government" and adds an accent to "régime"; these words have been altered to "government" and "regime," except where the latter is used in the French phrase, "*ancien régime*."

1. Debrecen: the second largest city in Hungary after Budapest, 220 kilometres east of the capital.

2. The plural subject, "the hall's being packed and the audience's being . . . attentive," requires the plural conjugation, "were."

3. A comma after "survival" has been removed.

4. The typescript reads "Communist," in the singular.

5. Rebecca West also noticed that books in German bookshops after the war were out of date. As West writes in *A Train of Powder*, booksellers licensed by the Allies "had been forced to restock their shelves by exhuming remainders of books which had been published before the war, had fallen flat, and had therefore been warehoused" (35).

6. The comma is Bowen's, but the clause would be more fluent without it: "however desperately."

7. This typescript gives the misspelled word "Britian."

8. In the typescript, the word "power" is capitalised.

9. Hortobad: a national park with protected flora and fauna near Debrecen.

Without Coffee, Cigarettes, or Feeling

Illustrated with photographs of students haunting bookstalls, campuses, and pubs, "Without Coffee, Cigarettes, or Feeling" appeared in *Mademoiselle* (February 1955): 174–5, 221–3. While acknowledging the tensions produced by Nazism and attributing the deadening of feeling (alluded to in the title) to the repression of the political past, Bowen concentrates on youth culture, and more specifically student life. As with her other essays about Europe, especially "Hungary," she discusses the university as a promise of hope for the future. Despite being a republic, West Germany was not technically a democracy, as Bowen notes in passing. Allied occupation officially continued until May 1955, but full sovereignty was not conferred on Germany until 1991, after the reunification of East and West Germany in October 1990.

1. Children, kitchen, and church: a direct translation of the German expression, *Kinder, Küchen, Kirche*, widely used during the Third Reich to define women's roles.

2. Free University: the Frei Universität in Berlin was founded in 1948, in part because Humboldt Universität was located in the Soviet-controlled sector of the city. American money, including a donation from the Henry Ford Foundation, helped to pay for university buildings.

3. Time-spirit: a literal translation of the German *Zeitgeist*.

Regent's Park and St. John's Wood

"Regent's Park and St. John's Wood" was a commissioned essay for *Flower of Cities: A Book of London* (London: Max Parrish, 1949): 149–58. Surveying the neighbourhood in which she herself lived from 1935 until 1951, Bowen recalls scenes from her own novels, including *The Death of the Heart* and *The Heat of the Day*, which both open in Regent's Park. Emphasis on painters and visual art begins in the first paragraph with a reference to the park as an "abandoned sketch." Bowen loved the park. As Charles Ritchie reports in his diary, on 29 September 1941, he and Bowen "went to see the roses in Regent's Park. For days we had been talking of those roses, but I could never get away from the office before nightfall, and it seemed as if we should never go together to see them" (*Siren Years* 118). In a phase of reconstruction after the blitz, London is lovingly evoked – railway stations, palaces, neighbourhoods, museums, galleries, institutions – by twenty-two writers in *Flower of Cities*. Leonard Woolf submitted a chapter called "Bloomsbury" and Stevie Smith wrote "A London Suburb." Line drawings illustrate each text.

1. Sir John Nash (1752–1835): architect who designed private and public buildings. A favourite of the Prince Regent, Nash designed various buildings for him and refurbished the Royal Pavilion at Brighton.

2. John Summerson (1904–92): architectural historian and museum curator. His biography, *John Nash: Architect to King George IV* (1935), received universal acclaim. Bowen might be confusing *Georgian London* (1945) and *Architecture in England* (1946), for Summerson did not write a book called *The Building of Georgian London*.

3. Joanna Southcott (1750–1814): prophetess and pamphleteer with a considerable following in the early nineteenth century who kept her sealed prophecies in a box. The box passed to her followers upon her death, then disappeared.

4. John Sell Cotman (1782–1842): an artist known for his watercolours and etchings. He taught Dante Gabriel Rossetti.

5. Ackermann's pages: possibly George Ackermann (1803–91), publisher and artist. Ackermann & Co., located in the Strand, published prints, lithographs, travel books, and panoramas.

6. R.A.: member of the Royal Academy.

7. In *To the North*, Emmeline and Cecilia keep a house in St. John's Wood.

8. Clare Leighton (1899–1989): an artist and author who wrote about gardening and the working classes. She evokes her childhood in *The Tempestuous Petticoat: the Story of an Invincible Edwardian* (1948).

9. Sir Edwin Henry Landseer (1802–73): painter and sculptor whose lions grace Trafalgar Square.

10. Charles Badlaugh (1833–91): political activist and atheist.

New York Waiting in My Memory

This essay appeared in *Vogue* 116 (July 1950): 78–9. A corrected typescript, nine pages long, exists as well (HRC 9.1). The original title was "Thoughts in America," which Bowen amended to "Thoughts in New York." Editors at *Vogue*, selecting a line from the article, probably determined the final title. Editors modified Bowen's syntax by altering punctuation, and by changing some verbs to present perfect from the past emphatic or pluperfect. In certain instances, the microfilm version of the *Vogue* essay was illegible. To supply missing words, or where punctuation was doubtful, I resorted to the typed draft.

1. The typescript reads "awesome" rather than "ageing."

2. The typescript reads "hallucinated state."

3. The typescript reads "sounds" in the plural.

4. In *A Time in Rome*, Bowen mentions her sense of alienation in a Roman hotel room that is *too* quiet; she asks to be put in a noisier room on a lower floor (3–5).

5. The typescript reads differently: "I retreated from the overpowering morning into a dark-blue calico nighttime, through which I drowsed or slept." Bowen means that the darkness resembles a deep-blue calico.

6. The typescript reads "trifles" rather than "minutiae."

Miss Willis

The date "11/6/52" appears on the first page of "Miss Willis," a three-page carbon (HRC 8.4). Although it was apparently never published, this brief recollection of Miss Willis is a companion to two other essays by Bowen: her foreword to Anne Ridler's *Olive Willis and Downe House: An Adventure in Education* and her foreword to the *Downe House Scrapbook*, both reprinted in this volume. In tone this brief portrait resembles "The Mulberry Tree." It is possible, but not provable, that this brief portrait was a preliminary sketch for one of those three published pieces. "Miss Willis" shares no exact phrases with those other recollections about Downe House and its headmistress, even though it shares certain details, such as Miss Willis's serenity and her ubiquitous dogs. Only three small corrections in ink appear in the text.

1. In the typescript, Bowen placed an asterisk against the date and attached a note at the end of the essay: "Please check the actual year of the foundation of Downe: I *think* it was 1909."
2. *Faux bon*: false goodness.
3. The word "her" has been added.
4. In the typescript, Bowen altered "appreciation" to "discernment."

Paul Morand

This short character sketch of Paul Morand, somewhat indebted to the tradition of "characters" of the sort inaugurated by Theophrastus, then practised by Overbury in England and the Duc de Saint-Simon in France, was sent to Lady Ottoline Morrell in 1937 (HRC Ottoline Morrell Collection 35.3). Morand had a tumultuous literary and public career. He sided with Vichy during the Nazi Occupation; he was ambassador to Switzerland. Although his candidacy for the Académie Française was opposed by de Gaulle in 1958, Morand was elected ten years later to that prestigious institution. He published numerous books, including *Lewis et Irène*, *L'Homme pressé*, *Le Flagellant de Séville*, and his memoirs.

Mainie Jellett

This eulogy for the painter Mainie Jellett (1897–1944), appeared in *The Bell* 9.3 (December 1944): 250–6. A seven-page typescript with some handwritten corrections also exists (HRC 8.4). Jellett's sojourns in France and Spain legitimate her art in so far as Bowen preferred continental artists, whether painters or writers. As she indicates by citing several of Jellett's paintings by title, Bowen understood and approved of the painter's abstract, cubist style.

1. The published version reads "Mainie and I have first met." I have added "must" because the present perfect tense makes little sense in context.

2. Elizabeth Yeats (1868–1940): printer, print-maker, and designer, she was a sister of William Butler Yeats and Jack Butler Yeats. With her sister Lily, Elizabeth Yeats set up Cuala Industries in 1908, a workshop devoted to printing and embroidery.

3. The typescript reads "weariness" rather than "fatigue."

4. Dorothy Richardson (1873–1957): novelist and journalist, best known for her thirteen-volume novel, *Pilgrimage* (1915–38).

5. The typescript reads "present" rather than "palpable."

6. Walter Sickert (1860–1942): painter, who specialised in landscapes, theatre settings, interiors. He was helped by Whistler early in his career and knew Degas in France. As a teacher, he had a lasting influence on British art.

7. Theodor Leschetitzky (1830–1915): a Polish pianist and teacher. Bowen spells this "Leschititsky." I have opted for the more usual spelling.

8. André Lhote (1885–1962): French painter and sculptor, with a speciality in still life, portraiture, and landscape influenced by Fauvism and cubism.

9. Albert Gleizes (1881–1953): a painter who migrated through several styles, including cubism and abstraction. He collaborated on murals with Robert Delaunay in the 1930s.

10. Dynamicism: Bowen may mean "dynamism," or she may intend the neologism.

Foreword to *Olive Willis and Downe House*, by Anne Ridler

Perhaps out of fondness for her former headmistress, Bowen provided the foreword to Anne Ridler's *Olive Willis and Downe House: An Adventure in Education* (London: John Murray, 1967): 1–5. Ridler's biography covers the major events of Olive Willis's life from schooldays to retirement. In "The Mulberry Tree," Bowen discusses the architecture of the house, the sociability of the girls, school games, and other subjects, but not Miss Willis.

1. *Schwärmerei*: derived from the German *schwärmen* (to swarm), the word means a rapturous enthusiasm for a cause or person. Sometimes it refers to an erotic crush, especially of one adolescent girl for another.

2. My own age: Bowen was born on 7 June 1899, which means that her age was not exactly that of the century.

3. Adolescence: according to the Oxford English Dictionary, the word dates back at least to Caxton's usage in the fifteenth century; Bowen means "adolescence" as a clinical, psychological term. She mocks school mistresses who read up on adolescence and its problems in both *Friends and Relations* and *To the North*.

4. Angela Brazil (1868–1947): author known for her novels about schoolgirls, including *A Pair of Schoolgirls* (1912), *A Patriotic Schoolgirl* (1918), and *A Popular Schoolgirl* (1920).

5. To imagine that which we know: from P. B. Shelley's "The Defense of Poetry."

6. Lerici: Bowen may be thinking of Shelley, for he moved to Lerici in Italy in 1822, and drowned there off the coast the same year. Leopold disparages Shelley in *The House in Paris*.

The Christmas Toast is "Home!"

"The Christmas Toast is 'Home!'" appeared in *Homes and Gardens* 7.24 (December 1942): 20–1, 76. Sellery and Harris do not list this essay in their bibliography. *Homes and Gardens*, a monthly magazine marketed to middle-class women, ran an annual Christmas number. The editorial commentary in the December 1942 issue reminds British readers to invite Americans into their homes for an "austerity meal," because dining with a family "means far more to an American soldier than being entertained lavishly at an hotel or club" (9). The editor's note, in full consciousness of the restrictions imposed during the war, further states that "travelling may be impossible, none but the plainest food may be procurable and the Xmas holiday itself may make unexpected demands on our time and energy" (9). An illustrated article by Cecil Beaton on his wartime photography appears in the same issue. In tone and idea, "The Christmas Toast is 'Home'" anticipates both "Calico Windows" and "Opening up the House."

Opening up the House

"Opening up the House" exists in a draft and a published version. The carbon typescript, in five sheets with inked-in emendations (HRC 8.7), corresponds quite faithfully to the published version in the British edition of *Vogue* (August 1945): 38, 75, 82. A few variants do occur. The editor at *Vogue* broke long paragraphs into shorter ones. Numerous hyphens were added: "war-time" and "criss-crossed," for instance. Bowen gave considerable thought to the continuity of houses and the lineage of those who inhabit them. Destroyed houses feature in short stories such as "In the Square" and "Oh, Madam . . ." The poignancy of returning to houses that had been appropriated for billets or because they were too close to the coast echoes the rediscovery of the seaside house in the short story "Ivy Gripped the Steps." Bowen achieves a virtuosic rhetorical effect in this essay by making houses all over Europe seem like a single house.

1. And they returned again into their own place: this passage, with its biblical ring, is not an exact allusion to anything biblical. Bowen, a faithful Anglican, may be remembering scripture: "I will return into my house from whence I came out" (Matthew 12:44). Less probably, she quotes Latter Day Saints scripture: "the land of Jerusalem and the land of Zion shall be turned back into their own place, and the earth shall be like as it was in the days before it was divided" (Doctrine and Covenants 133:24). However improbable, the allusion is applicable.

2. The typescript reads "rusted," which avoids repetition with "rusty" several sentences further on.

3. The phrase, "you put them back there," appears in the typescript, but not the published version. Putting objects in harm's way is counter-intuitive, but the gesture suggests a reclaiming of the house.

Home for Christmas

"Home for Christmas" appeared in *Mademoiselle* 42 (December 1955): 57, 120–3. In a severely abridged version, it was anthologised in *The Family Christmas Book*, edited by Dorothy Wilson (New York: Prentice-Hall, 1957): 2–3. This essay should not be confused with the short story that bears the same title (*The Bazaar* 309–19). While ostensibly talking about returns and reunions that happen at Christmas, Bowen divagates on friendship. The peal of bells that concludes "Home for Christmas" is a call to a higher plane – spiritual, Christian, social – that remains undisclosed.

1. The published text erroneously gives "are," but the verb must read "am" to agree with "I."

2. "They shall return": Psalms 126:5–6.

Bowen's Court

"Bowen's Court" appeared in the Philadelphia-based magazine *Holiday* (December 1958): 86–7, 190–3. In title and content, this essay recalls the extensive family history recounted in *Bowen's Court*. As in *Bowen's Court*, Bowen numbers her ancestors (Henry III, Robert I) as if they sprang from a monarchical dynasty. The fond description of exterior disposition and the interior layout of the property is a presage of doom, for Bowen sold her ancestral pile in 1959. The farmer who bought the property pulled down the house. In the 1963 "Afterword" appended to *Bowen's Court* for publication in the US, Bowen writes: "It was a clean end. Bowen's Court never lived to be a ruin" (459).

1. The word "the" has been added.

2. Eudora Welty (1909–2001): the American short story writer stayed at Bowen's Court on several occasions throughout the 1950s. In a letter written on 4 April 1951, Bowen mentioned to Blanche Knopf that Welty was "working away at one of her great short stories in another room" (HRC Knopf Collection 685.14). Welty was writing "The Bride of Innisfallen."

3. Evelyn Waugh (1903–66): visited Bowen's Court in 1931 or 1932, as he acknowledges in an imprecisely dated letter (HRC 12.1).

4. David Cecil (1902–86): author and a professor of English at Oxford, became one of Bowen's closest friends after they met in 1926. He wrote books on Jane Austen, Sir Walter Scott, Thomas Hardy, and other subjects.

5. Isaiah Berlin (1909–97): philosopher and Oxford professor, first visited Bowen's Court in 1935 and returned to work on his book, *Karl Marx*, in the summer of 1938. He visited often. A lavish and gossipy correspondent, Berlin was not always sincere, or certainly did not prove to be in later life. Berlin described Bowen as "a wonderful talker, highly intelligent, very sympathetic, charming and interesting and agreeable [. . .] she was Christian, she was religious, she liked mainly men, she liked joking and she voted Conservative and wanted people to be masculine and no nonsense, hated pacifists and vegetarians and that kind of thing [. . .] she wanted a clashing of swords" (Berlin 705). Berlin told Michael Ignatieff that, despite his enthusiasm for Bowen's novels in the 1930s, he later found them "unreadable" (Berlin 705).

6. Virginia and Leonard Woolf stayed one night at Bowen's Court in late April 1934. Cyril Connolly might have forgotten the key to his diary, but Virginia Woolf had not forgotten hers. She records, with the gimlet eye of the ungrateful, everything that is wrong with the house, her host Alan Cameron, and the other visitors: "one can see, after Bowen's Court, how ramshackle & half squalid the Irish life is, how empty & poverty stricken. There we spent one night, unfortunately with baboon Conolly [sic] & his gollywog slug wife Jean to bring in the roar of the Chelsea omnibus, & it was all as it should be – pompous & pretentious & imitative & ruined – a great barrack of grey stone, 4 storeys & basements, like a town house, high empty rooms, & a scattering of Italian plasterwork, marble mantelpieces, inlaid with brass & so on. All the furniture clumsy solid cut out of single wood – the wake sofa, on wh. the dead lay – carpets shrunk in the great rooms, tattered farm girls waiting, the old man of 90 in his cabin who wdn't let us go – E[lizabe]th had to say Yes The Ladies are very well several times [. . .] Talk too much of the Chelsea bar kind, owing to C[onnolly]'s – about starting a society called Bostocks, about Ireland with Alan [Cameron], a

good humoured bolt eyed fat hospitable man" (Woolf 210–11).

7. The published text reads "themic," but "thematic" might be intended.

8. Seán O'Faoláin (1900–91): born Jean Francis Whelan, he adopted the Gaelic form of his name around 1918 while studying at University College, Cork. A prolific writer, he founded *The Bell* in 1940, and edited that magazine until 1946. He had an affair with Elizabeth Bowen from 1937 to 1939.

9. Frank O'Connor (1903–66): Irish writer known for his short stories, collected in *The Stories of Frank O'Connor* (1953). Among other books, he wrote a biography of Michael Collins and a memoir called *An Only Child* (1961).

10. Carson McCullers (1917–67): American author of *The Heart is a Lonely Hunter* (1940) and *The Ballad of the Sad Café* (1951), she stayed twice at Bowen's Court in the spring of 1950. Glendinning reports that she was intensely bored by the quiet of the country house and spent her time drinking excessively (237–8).

Letter from Ireland

"Letter from Ireland" appeared in *Night and Day* (28 October 1937), the short-lived magazine that Graham Greene edited. Sellery and Harris do not include this essay in their comprehensive bibliography. Although she was the regular theatre critic for *Night and Day*, Bowen also submitted two travel articles: one from Salzburg and this one from Ireland. Her letter about Salzburg was reprinted in *Collected Impressions* (214–17).

1. Jimmy O'Dea (1899–1965): Irish comedian and actor. A pantomime artist who became a household name in Ireland and England. He was known for his character role, "Biddy Mulligan, the Pride of the Coombe."

2. *Va et vient*: bustle, comings and goings.

Ireland Makes Irish

"Ireland Makes Irish" appeared in both British and American editions of *Vogue*. The British version bore the title "Irish Country Life." The American version, used as the base text, was called "Ireland Makes Irish" (15 August 1946): 180–1, 214–17. Bowen's essay was part of an eight-page spread about Irish castles and country houses. Perhaps because of the context in which it appeared, the article connects twentieth-century Eire with the feudal past and the history of successive invasions that Ireland withstood. As in her other essays about Ireland, Bowen's sense of the country is informed and mediated by books.

1. Strongbows: Anglo-Norman mercenaries who invaded Ireland in

1169, led by Richard de Clare, Earl of Pembroke, nicknamed Strongbow.

2. *Folie de grandeur*: megalomania.

3. Constantia Maxwell: Bowen reviewed Maxwell's *Dublin Under the Georges, 1714–1830* in the *New Statesman* 12 (25 July 1936): 128. Maxwell made a career of writing about Ireland in books such as *A History of Trinity College, Dublin* and *The Stranger in Ireland*, both reviewed by Bowen in the *Tatler*.

4. The published text erroneously reads "are." The verb, to agree with "I," must be "am."

5. Twenty-Six Counties: by excluding the six counties that comprise Northern Ireland, Bowen makes clear that she is speaking of Eire only.

How They Live in Ireland: Conquest by Cheque-Book

"How They Live in Ireland" was a two-article feature on Eire that ran in *Contact: Points of Contact* 3 (1946): 84–6. Bowen's article preceded Kate O'Brien's "The Daily Life of Mick Mac," a profile of a farm labourer named Michael MacNamara, a man with eight children and a subsistence living. The two articles were meant to be read in tandem. Bowen's reference to "Mick Mac's wages" explicitly points the reader to O'Brien's article. *Contact Books* actively promoted internationalism in more or less quarterly issues between 1946 and 1949. Each issue had a subtitle, hence "Points of Contact" for the third issue. In the same issue as Bowen's essay, Stephen Spender, freshly returned from a conference on "the Spirit of Europe" in Geneva in September 1946, enumerates elements that unite Europe: Christianity, eighteenth-century French rationalism, the catastrophe of the Second World War. Spender, a member of the editorial board at *Contact*, advocates international cooperation – political and economic contact – as the way forward from the debacle of the war. In a letter to the Curtis Brown agency on 25 June 1945, Bowen expresses enthusiasm for the *Contact* agenda: "my interview with Contact Publications (before leaving for my visit to Ireland) was most satisfactory. It followed the lines of their original conversation with you and I am to do a story and an article for their September number. Contact sounds to me a very interesting experiment" (HRC 10.5). On 26 November 1945, Bowen mentions in a letter that *Contact* sent her a cheque for an article (£25) and a story (£40), but I have not been able to find a story among the issues. She did, however, publish "Façade at Folkestone" in *Contact: First Spring of Peace* 1 (1946): 49–52, which was reprinted in *Collected Impressions* (225–30). Bowen's reference to Irish airports connecting to North American and European destinations sustains the note of worldliness favoured by *Contact*.

NOTES

1. Imitation Sheraton: copies of furniture designs by Thomas Sheraton (1751–1806), known particularly for his cabinets and chairs.

2. *Tatler*: the popular magazine (1901–40) absorbed the *Bystander* to become the *Tatler and Bystander* (1940–79). While flying to Paris, Markie and Emmeline scribble notes to each other on the back of a *Tatler* issue in *To the North*.

Ireland

"Ireland" appeared in *House and Garden* 105 (June 1954): 92, 158. Instead of emphasising political history and literature, this essay promotes the country as a tourist destination. In this regard, it resembles "Ireland Makes Irish." Bowen covers many of the same topics in these two essays – Irish weather, landscape, literature. In both essays she recommends Constantia Maxwell's *Country and Town in Ireland Under the Georges* as preparatory reading for a trip to Ireland. Among the other books that she recommends, Bowen reviewed Frank O'Connor's *Irish Miles* in the *Tatler* (2 July 1947): 22–3.

1. *Plage*: beach.

2. The published text hyphenates "august-provincial capitals," which implies that the capitals are only august in a provincial way. A comma instead of a hyphen would make the adjective less ironic.

3. Penguin edition: an imprint series begun in 1935 at Allen Lane, Penguin books became an independent company in 1936.

4. O'Connor . . . Maxwell: O'Connor's *Irish Miles* was published in 1949; O'Faoláin's *Irish Journey* in 1940; R. Lloyd Praeger's *The Way That I Went* in 1937; and Maxwell's *Country and Town in Ireland Under the Georges* in 1949. Either Bowen or the editor at *House and Garden* accidentally reversed the first two nouns in the title of Maxwell's book and called it *Town and Country in Ireland Under the Georges*.

Introduction to *The House by the Church-yard*, by Sheridan Le Fanu

Bowen wrote this introduction for the Doughty Library edition of Le Fanu's novel (London: Anthony Blond, 1968): vii–xi. Recalling her preface to *Uncle Silas*, she conjures up the specifically Irish aspects of *The House by the Church-yard*.

1. Burning: perhaps "burying" or "burrowing" is intended.

2. *Âme damnée*: damned soul.

Toys

"Toys" is a seven-page typescript with handwritten corrections (HRC 9.6). The date "7.12.44." is inscribed at the end of the carbon copy. I have not been able to locate "Toys" in any publication. Bowen, an acute observer of children and their toys, makes much of Henrietta's stuffed monkey named Charles in *The House in Paris*. Comments on shopping anticipate later essays on shops, shopping, and objects in essays such as "New York Waiting in My Memory" and "For the Feminine Shopper." "Toys," written apparently for Christmas ("this or any season"), may have been published with parents' shopping in mind. Curiously, Bowen, although childless, positions herself as a parent; because toy psychology differs from age to age, she writes, old-fashioned toys "do little to your or my girl or boy."

1. Bowen accidentally writes "husband's families," when it should be plural.

2. Valhalla: the dwelling place of the gods in Richard Wagner's *Ring* cycle.

3. Kewpie: illustrations of Kewpie dolls appeared in *Ladies' Home Journal* in 1909. As Bowen surmises, the dolls went into production in 1913. "Kewpie" is a deformation of "Cupid."

4. The typescript reads "a," but "one" is more exact.

Calico Windows

A small contribution to the war effort, "Calico Windows" appeared in *Soho Centenary: A Gift from Artists, Writers and Musicians to the Soho Hospital for Women* (London: Hutchinson, 1944): 19–20. In his introduction, editor James Laver sounds the note of heroic rebuilding of London after the Blitzkrieg bombings: "Soho was hard hit by the War. Many of the Italian shops were closed and the rest were cut off from the source of their supplies. The district was not spared by the bombers. Many old houses were demolished and of Soho's fine old church only the quaint spire was left standing. But Soho will revive and continue to be not only a monument of English history but one of the most foreign districts in London" (8). The essay rhetorically and ritually invokes "you" as someone who lives through the blitz.

1. Calico windows: translucent calico material was used to replace broken glass panes during the war.

Introduction to *The ABC of Millinery*, by Eva Ritcher

An admirer of fashion and style, Bowen introduces Eva Ritcher's *The ABC of Millinery* (London: Hurst & Blackett, 1950): 13–16, with a certain expertise. Victoria Glendinning mentions Bowen's love of jewellery: "she always had a penchant for large earrings, necklaces of false pearls or great glass bobbles, and flashy fake jewellery that on her looked neither flashy nor fake" (47). Her 1946 short story, "I Died of Love," is set in a dressmaker's shop (*The Bazaar* 143–51). In *The ABC of Millinery*, Eva Ritcher devotes chapters to the beret, the turban, the straw hat, trimmings, and other refinements of millinery.

The Teakettle

"The Teakettle" was published in *House and Garden* 123 (January 1963): 70–1. The article kicked off a series in the magazine devoted to "the simple, humble things of daily life," as a headnote to Bowen's essay states (70). The biographical blurb that accompanies this essay in *House and Garden* singles out Bowen's predilection for representing objects in terms of their colour, shape, function, and finish. The note mentions that her books "are rich in little things that have caught her own roving eye: lozenged doorknobs, fringed towels, sauce-bottle stoppers ('buttons of bright red') as well as the spiked gilt leaves on the mirrors and the brass plate on the front door of the house in Dublin where she was born" (71).

On Giving a Present

"On Giving a Present," apparently never published, comprises eight carbon pages (HRC 8.7). It may have been a draft towards "The Art of Giving." Yet differences make the essays complementary rather than clearly related. On the other hand, Bowen often reworked her prose extensively – cancelling sections, reformulating points – between first draft and final publication. The essay, like "The Art of Giving," recalls Seneca's *De Beneficiis*, one of the *Moral Epistles* that concerns the giving of gifts. As in the essay "Toys," Bowen relates vanished or ungiven presents to Valhalla.

    1. The word "is" has been added.

    2. The typescript reads "This," rather than "Thus." The letters "i" and "u" being adjacent on the typewriter, Bowen may have accidentally substituted one for the other. On the other hand, the whole sentence is ambiguous. She typed "the emotion use pure," but "is," which I have adopted, makes better sense.

    3. "More blessed": Acts 20:35.

The Art of Giving

Bowen sold "The Art of Giving" to UK and US magazines through the ministrations of her agents at Curtis Brown. Such sales maximised her exposure on both sides of the Atlantic and doubled her revenues. The essay appeared in *Mademoiselle* (November 1953): 74, 135–8; and in the *Spectator* (18 December 1953): 732–3. Late-in-the-year publication suggests that the essay was meant to remind shoppers of the intention behind Christmas gift-giving. The last paragraph confirms this intention.

1. The published text reads "in," but that may be a typesetting error for "an."

Mirrors Are Magic

"Mirrors Are Magic" appeared in *House and Garden* 132 (August 1967): 112–13. In this essay, as in others where Bowen contemplates specific material objects, she considers the mirror in narratives, poems, social contexts, history, architecture, and personal anecdote. This method, while loosening the structure of the essay, creates comprehensiveness of treatment.

1. Roman emperor: Domitian. In *A Time in Rome*, Bowen writes, "Domitian had another companion: fear. Certain, and rightly, of being sooner or later stolen up upon, he caused the walls of the *peristyle*, phengite marble, to be polished till they became mirrors – reflected, he watched what went on behind him" (90). The detail derives from Suetonius's gossipy history, *The Twelve Ceasars*: "The gallery where he took his daily exercise was now lined with plaques of highly-polished moonstone, which reflected everything that happened behind his back" (310).

2. *The mirror crack'd*: from Tennyson's "The Lady of Shalott."

Jane Austen

"Jane Austen" appeared in *The English Novelists: A Survey of the Novel by Twenty Contemporary Novelists*, edited by Derek Verschoyle (London: Chatto & Windus, 1936): 99–113. Under the title "Jane Austen: Artist on Ivory," the essay was reprinted in *Saturday Review* 14 (15 August 1936): 3–4, 13–14. Putting together essays, reviews, and broadcasts for *Collected Impressions*, Bowen considered including "Jane Austen" along with her essay on James Joyce (HRC Knopf Collection 685.14). For whatever reasons, both essays were excluded from that volume. Sensitive to nationality, Bowen locates Austen's novels within English and European traditions, as when she remarks that Henry Crawford comes across as an exile from a French novel and that Mr. Darcy is a Proustian character.

1. In a letter to her sister Cassandra, Jane Austen explained that she worked on two inches of ivory, by which she meant that the scale and scope of her novels were quite specific: the rural gentry of Regency England.

2. *Partis*: good matches, suitable for marriage.

3. Let other pens: the opening sentence of the last chapter of *Mansfield Park*.

4. *Beauté du diable*: devilish handsomeness.

Introduction to *Pride and Prejudice*, by Jane Austen

Bowen wrote this introduction to *Pride and Prejudice* for a postwar edition of the novel (London: William & Norgate, 1948): vii–xv. Bowen held Jane Austen's novels in high regard for their comedy, their situations of disappointment and marriage, and their witty heroines. She notes in more than one essay that Austen understood men as if from a distance, or from the outside. In 1942, Bowen dramatised sections of *Pride and Prejudice* and other novels for a radio broadcast on the BBC. The segment was re-broadcast in August 1948.

What Jane Austen Means to Me

"What Jane Austen Means to Me" appeared in *Everybody's Weekly* (10 May 1954): 19, 39. A sidebar offered a quotation from *Pride and Prejudice* under the headline "My Favourite Passage." Bowen's article appeared in a series devoted to "famous writers of today" talking "about their favourite author of yesterday," as the lead to the article announces. The choppy paragraphs are not characteristic of Bowen's capacious paragraphing style; no doubt an editor at *Everybody's Weekly* subdivided longer paragraphs into shorter ones.

1. *Quality Street*: J. M. Barrie's four-act play opened in New York in 1901, followed by London in 1902. Two sisters in the play start a school, while Captain Brown, the erstwhile suitor of one sister, fights in the Napoleonic wars.

2. *Cranford*: Elizabeth Gaskell's novel was published serially in 1851 in Dickens's magazine, *Household Words*, and as a book in 1853. The novel concerns two spinster sisters, which explains why Bowen links it with *Quality Street*.

3. The published text reads "are," which does not agree with the subject, "fear."

Persuasion

Bowen's appraisal of Jane Austen's *Persuasion* appeared in *London Magazine* (April 1957): 47–51. Two typescripts also exist: a heavily revised nine-page carbon, and a clean copy that does not deviate in any substantive way from the published version (HRC 8.12). Several of Bowen's friends, including William Plomer and John Hayward, sat on the editorial board of *London Magazine*, which was edited by another friend, John Lehmann. The magazine positioned itself as a defender, even an arbiter, of culture. In this regard, this essay locates *Persuasion* within the central lineage of English novels, and Jane Austen among the most astute of English novelists.

Introduction to *No One to Blame*, by H. M. Taylor

Although she was not usually drawn to autobiographies, Bowen introduced *No One to Blame* (London: Jonathan Cape, 1939): 7–12. Discreet and *bien élevée*, Bowen rarely wrote of herself at length; *Seven Winters* and the opening section of *Pictures and Conversations*, both memoirs, contradict this reticence, while avoiding racy disclosures. When she writes in the first person, Bowen speaks about others: Olive Willis, Sarah Barry, friends, acquaintances. Moreover, Bowen expresses impatience with psychoanalysis; she declares in "Portrait of a Woman Reading" that her set did *not* read Freud in the 1920s. Uncharacteristically, Bowen shows tolerance for Taylor's interest in psychoanalytic therapy.

1. Anthony Trollope (1815–82): the Victorian novelist published *An Autobiography* in 1883. Acclaimed at the time of publication, it later led critics to question Trollope's facility, for he compares novel-writing to shoemaking. Bowen wrote *Anthony Trollope: A New Judgement* for radio broadcast in May 1945; it was published as a booklet in 1946.

James Joyce

"James Joyce" was written for Seán O'Faoláin's Dublin-based magazine, *The Bell* 1.6 (March 1941): 40–9. Addressing an Irish readership, Bowen rhetorically positions herself as Irish in this summing up of James Joyce's career. In his biography of Joyce, Richard Ellmann does not mention that the two Irish writers met in Paris. Despite their divergent writing milieus and styles, Bowen never ceased to praise Joyce for his experimentalism. In "Portrait of a Woman Reading," she calls *Dubliners* "the best book of stories ever written" (10). She clearly perceives Joyce as a comic writer: his cosmic laughter may not always be intelligible, but it reverberates. Reviewing

Finnegans Wake for *Purpose*, she untangles strands interwoven in the book and warns readers that Joyce's "anti-literariness is formidable" ("Fiction" 178). She also remarks on Joyce's "hilarity, hilarity arising from some, however obscure, self-torture, *not* the virtuosity, that bears one down. The sheer force and drive of the fun is a gale to stand up against. The language has two violent intimacies: the child-talk (the talk of the self in the half-dark) and the lover-jargon, a terrifyingly urgent melting, slurring and dislocation of words" ("Fiction" 178). Developing a special line in Joyce criticism, she reviewed Herbert Gorman's *James Joyce* (1941) and Patricia Hutchins's *James Joyce's World* (1957).

1. *John Bull's Other Island*: George Bernard Shaw's play about Ireland and Home Rule was commissioned by W. B. Yeats for the Abbey Theatre. Yeats, however, rejected it. It opened in London in 1904.

2. Jabberwocky: Lewis Carroll's nonsense poem filled with portmanteau words published in *Alice Through the Looking-Glass* (1871).

3. Ethel-M-Dell-ese: best-selling British novelist Ethel M. Dell (1881–1939) wrote passionate romances in hyperbolic language. In unison, critics reviled Dell's novels, the first of which, but by no means the last, was *The Way of the Eagle* (1911). She wrote prolifically between the 1910s and the 1930s.

New Writers

In "New Writers," Bowen introduced and commented on Domhnall O'Conaill's "Three Talented Children" for *The Bell* 2.1 (April 1941): 54. The assertion that writers should not expose characters to humiliation suggests that fiction has its proprieties and those proprieties should be observed. The writer has an ethical duty towards character and representation.

Guy de Maupassant

Maupassant's story "The Little Soldier" immediately follows this brief, biographical introduction, published in *Literary Digest* 1.1 (April 1946): 26. Not unusually, Bowen positions Maupassant in relation to Flaubert. Proust and Flaubert form the twin poles of French literary accomplishment in Bowen's opinion. Despite the brevity of this introduction, Maupassant was Bowen's touchstone for clarity and virtuosity of effect in the short story.

Foreword to *Tomato Cain and Other Stories,* by Nigel Kneale

Tomato Cain and Other Stories may have been given a boost because of Bowen's foreword (London: Collins, 1949): 9–12. In her biography of Bowen, Victoria Glendinning claims that she "was a notoriously kind reviewer of novels; she preferred not to write about a book she could not praise, and was known in the business as a very soft touch" (146). By and large, this statement is true. But this foreword to *Tomato Cain* expresses, through double negatives and qualifications, a high degree of ambivalence about the quality of Kneale's prose. Although *Tomato Cain* won the Somerset Maugham award in 1950, Nigel Kneale (1922–2006) did not live up to the promise that Bowen detected in him as a fiction writer. He did become an influential scriptwriter for television, producing both original material and adaptations.

Foreword to *Haven: Short Stories, Poems and Aphorisms,* by Elizabeth Bibesco

Bowen's foreword to the collection of Bibesco's previously published pieces appeared in *Haven* (London: James Barrie, 1951): 7–12. As Bowen explains, the Princess Bibesco (1897–1945) was the daughter of Prime Minister Herbert Henry Asquith and a friend of Marcel Proust. Bibesco was also sister-in-law to Cynthia Asquith, for whose various anthologies Bowen wrote the short stories "The Cat Jumps," "Brigands," and "The Unromantic Princess." As if to recall that higher standards exist for the short story than perhaps Princess Bibesco exemplifies, Bowen evokes the name of Maupassant as a master of the genre, an evocation that she also makes in her introduction to Nigel Kneale's *Tomato Cain.*

Introduction to *The Stories of William Sansom*

Hogarth Press published *The Stories of William Sansom* in 1963 with Bowen's introduction (7–12). Sansom (1912–76) wrote short stories and novels, including *The Body* (1949) and *The Loving Eye* (1956). Influences on his writing include Henry Green, Franz Kafka, and Edgar Allan Poe. Sansom's and Bowen's careers intersected in various ways. Sansom selected Bowen's story "I Died of Love" for *Choice: Some New Stories and Prose,* a volume he edited in 1946. Bowen reviewed eight of Sansom's books in the *Tatler,* and a ninth in the *New York Times Book Review.* In "English Fiction at Mid-Century," Bowen writes, with less exuberance than this introduction displays, "William Sansom has moved from firemen stories and Kafka allegory to the study of the upper or lower suburban rock pool" (212). The titles mentioned throughout the introduction refer to stories in the volume.

1. N.F.S.: National Fire Service, a single fire-fighting service created for Great Britain in August 1941. Stephen Spender and Henry Green also fought fires during the war. Spender and Sansom collaborated on a book, *Jim Braidy: The Story of Britain's Firemen* (1943). Green's novel *Caught* (1943) also concerns firefighters.

2. There is ditto on "round" in the published text.

A Matter of Inspiration

"A Matter of Inspiration," an assessment of American literature as perceived in Britain, was published in *Saturday Review* (13 October 1951): 27–8, 64. When she returned to the United States in 1950 after a hiatus of seventeen years, Bowen cultivated friendships with Welty and McCullers, who both visited Bowen's Court (see notes to "Bowen's Court"). She often undertook to interpret American culture for British readers in essays and commentary.

1. Frances Parkinson Keyes (1885–1970): American novelist, whose various works concern Washington politics, New Orleans, and Catholicism. Bowen reviewed *The River Road*, a novel about sugar plantations in the Mississippi Delta, for the *Tatler* in 1946.

2. Raymond Chandler (1888–1959): crime writer, whose hardboiled novels feature the protagonist Philip Marlowe. Bowen reviewed Chandler's novel *The Little Sister* for the *Tatler* in 1949, alongside George Orwell's *Nineteen Eighty-Four*.

3. John Marquand (1893–1960): American novelist who wrote about upper-class East Coast society. He is better known as the author a series of spy novels with a protagonist named Mr. Moto. Over the years, Bowen reviewed four of Marquand's novels for the *Tatler*.

4. Ellery Queen: the name of a detective, as well as the pseudonym of a writing duo who created the fictional detective. The Ellery Queen mysteries had their heyday from the 1930s to the 1950s, and generated numerous spin-offs on radio and in magazines.

5. Brendan Gill (1914–97): writer, best known for his association with the *New Yorker*. Bowen reviewed his book *The Day the Money Stopped* in the *Tatler* in 1957.

6. Frederick Buechner (1926–): American author, whose books include *A Long Day's Dying* (1950) and *The Season's Difference* (1952).

Introduction to *An Angela Thirkell Omnibus*

This foreword appeared late in Bowen's career (London: Hamish Hamilton, 1966): vii–ix. Largely forgotten today, Angela Thirkell (1890–1961) was admired for her novels of manners and decried for her snobbishness. Bowen was well placed to write an introduction as she had reviewed a host of Thirkell's books for the *Tatler*, including *Miss Bunting*, *Peace Breaks Out*, *Private Enterprise*, *Love Among the Ruins*, and *Never Too Late*.

1. Thirkell died in 1961, not 1959.

2. Remorselessly: the published text reads "remorsely."

3. Graham MacInnes: MacInnes wrote four books of memoirs, including *The Road to Gundagai* (1965). Thirkell's other son, Colin MacInnes, established himself as a novelist with three novels, most notably *Absolute Beginners* (1959), about swinging London.

A Passage to E. M. Forster

To celebrate Forster's ninetieth birthday, Oliver Stallybrass edited the collection of essays called *Aspects of E. M. Forster* (London: Edward Arnold, 1969). "A Passage to E. M. Forster," Bowen's introduction (1–12), precedes essays by Benjamin Britten, William Plomer, Malcolm Bradbury, and others. As Bowen acknowledges, her engagement with Forster's fiction was life-long, especially in terms of the English short story.

1. Sidgwick and Jackson: Bowen's short story collection, *Encounters*, was published by Sidgwick and Jackson in the same series as *The Celestial Omnibus*. Years later, teaching a course on the short story at Vassar College, Bowen considered assigning stories from that volume.

2. *Engouement*: passing fancy, infatuation.

3. William Ernest Henley (1849–1903): editor, critic, and poet, he was known as a great encourager of young talent. He championed the sculptor Rodin in England; he befriended Robert Louis Stevenson; he edited the *Scots Observer*. His first volume of poems, *A Book of Verses* (1888), led to others, including his last book, *A Song of Speed* (1904), about the experience of being driven in a car for the first time.

4. Pan: "The Story of a Panic" in *The Celestial Omnibus* concerns the Greek god Pan.

5. Apostles: an exclusive Cambridge group founded in 1820, called "The Apostles" because they were twelve in number. A footnote at this point in Bowen's text directs readers to Patrick Wilkinson's essay, "Forster at King's," which follows hers in *Aspects of E. M. Forster*.

Introduction to *Staying With Relations*, by Rose Macaulay

This introduction appeared in a reprint of Macaulay's novel (London: Collins, 1969): 1–5. As Bowen acknowledged numberless times, Rose Macaulay introduced her to Naomi Royde-Smith, editor at the *Saturday Westminster Review*, where Bowen's first stories were published. Macaulay and Bowen remained friends and correspondents until the older writer's death in 1958. Repaying debts, Bowen reviewed many of her mentor's books for the *Tatler*, including *They Went to Portugal* (1946), *Fabled Shore* (1949), *Pleasure of Ruin* (1954), and *The Towers of Trebizond* (1956). She generously reviewed Macaulay's critical book, *The Writings of E. M. Forster* (1938), for *The New Statesman*. William Plomer, in a letter dated May 31 [1938], wrote to Bowen that he had been to a party thrown by the publisher Jonathan Cape: "Rose Macaulay, breathing purposefully in my eye, wished to know what I thought of her book about Forster. As I hadn't read it, the occasion called for as much tact as you displayed in reviewing the book, but I don't know whether it got it" (HRC 11.8). While diagnosing *Staying With Relations* as a transitional book between the 1920s and 1930s, Bowen could not have ignored that her novel with a similar title, *Friends and Relations*, was published in 1931.

Comeback of Goldilocks et al.

"Comeback of Goldilocks et al." was published in the *New York Times Book Review* (26 August 1962): 18–19, 74–5. This essay recalls Bowen's own fairy tales, such as "The Good Earl" and "The Unromantic Princess," and anticipates her illustrated children's book, *The Good Tiger* (1965). In "Notes on Writing a Novel," she tersely declares, "Much to be learnt from story-telling to children" (*Collected Impressions* 250).

Introduction to *The King of the Golden River*, by John Ruskin

This introduction accompanied Ruskin's *The King of the Golden River*, illustrated by Sandro Nardini (London: Macmillan, 1962): iii-v. The book belonged to a series in which contemporary writers wrote about classic fairy tales. John Updike introduced Oscar Wilde's *The Young King and Other Fairy Tales*; Isak Dinesen introduced *Thumbelina and Other Fairy Tales by Hans Christian Andersen*; Randall Jarrell translated and introduced *"The Golden Bird" and Other Fairy Tales of the Brothers Grimm*. Although

Bowen points out that Ruskin's tale has only male characters, she holds out the hope that Gluck will one day marry. Her view of *The King of the Golden River* as having a tourist element – "the sinister glaciers and high-up cataracts" in Austria – may partly derive from Bowen's travels to Austria before and after the Second World War.

Enchanted Centenary of the Brothers Grimm

"Enchanted Centenary of the Brothers Grimm" was published in the *New York Times Magazine* (8 September 1963): 28–9, 112–13. The article may have been written to order, for it dwells on factual coverage of the Grimms' lives and devolves into long lists near the end. Nevertheless, it demonstrates Bowen's obsession in the 1960s with oral tales and transformations in the period just prior to the publication of *The Little Girls* (1964) and *Eva Trout* (1968).

1. *Minnesingers*: the German counterparts of French troubadours, these medieval minstrels sang about love and valour.

What We Need in Writing

"What We Need in Writing" appeared in the *Spectator* (20 November 1936): 901–2. The call for something vigorous and natural in writing to counter the "weakness and invalidity" of 1930s writing is consistent with metaphors of illness – social and political – in that decade. Although she appeals to classics of drama and narrative fiction, Bowen does not fully specify what she wants from contemporary writing.

1. Trigorin's troubles: Trigorin is a writer in Anton Chekhov's *The Seagull* (1895) who leaves his lover, the actress Arkadina, for Nina, a young provincial girl. After two years, he leaves Nina and returns to Arkadina.

2. *Il faut vivre*: one must live.

3. *Je n'en vois pas la nécessité*: I don't see the reason for it.

4. *Parlons d'autres choses*: let us speak of other things.

The Short Story in England

"The Short Story in England" appeared, just as the war ended, in *Britain Today* 109 (May 1945): 11–16. It was reprinted in August 1945 in *British Digest* 1.12 (August 1945): 39–43. I have used the reprinted version as the base text. As a summary of the modernist short story, this essay traces a lineage from Kipling and Lawrence through Mansfield and Plomer to the generation writing during the Second World War. If anything, Bowen displays her immense reading in the short story repertory and her up-to-date knowledge of its development. Bowen implies that the connections required for a novel yield to the instantaneous and transitory effects of the short story – "the great significance of a small event."

1. Alfred Edgar Coppard (1878–1957): poet, short story writer, and Bowen's friend. He edited *Consequences*, to which Bowen contributed a chapter (*The Bazaar* 77–82). With customary aplomb, Bowen wrote to Coppard about his story collection entitled *Polly Oliver* on 31 August 1935, "As for *Polly Oliver*: it gave me the extreme pleasure and sense of amazement and at the same time of actuality your stories always do. I like best 'Gone Away' – 'Ring the Bells of Heaven' and 'Crippled Bloom.' But then, I like all of them, startlingly much. I say startlingly because I haven't been able to read much, lately: most print seems to slip over my mind, like water over an oiled surface. And your words don't" (HRC Coppard Collection).

2. Herbert Ernest Bates (1905–74): author known for his short stories; he often wrote about country life. He comments on the short story in *The Modern English Short Story: A Critical Survey* (1950).

3. Ethel Colburn Mayne (1865–1941): Irish-born author who published in *The Yellow Book* and became a sub-editor for that journal. Her first collection of stories, *The Clearer Vision* (1898), led to five others.

4. Liam O'Flaherty (1896–1984): Irish novelist and short story writer, best remembered for *The Informer* (1925).

5. Arthur Calder-Marshall (1908–92), Leslie Halward (1906–76), James Hanley (1901–85), George Frederick Green (1911–77): writers active in the 1930s. Halward, the most obscure of the four, published *The Money's All Right and Other Stories* (1938) and stories in *The Best British Short Stories* (1936, 1937). As Bowen points out, these writers are linked by their interest in social milieus, especially working-class characters and situations.

6. Peter Quennell (1905–93): known as a biographer, he wrote *Byron: The Years of Fame* (1935) and *Byron in Italy* (1941), which might be two of the books, of the many written by Quennell, that Bowen has in mind. He was a biographer and historian rather than a fiction writer.

7. Alun Lewis (1915–44): Welsh poet and short story writer. He died young, of malaria, while serving in India during the war.

Introduction to *Chance*

This introduction appeared in the first issue of *Chance* 1 (October 1952): 6–7. Although the editors sought new talent, they neither excluded William Sansom's work nor avoided Bowen's conferral of quality through her introductory salvo. The magazine contains drawings, book reviews, and poems. The unsigned editorial in the first issue claims that new talent exists: "We thought that it was not the dearth of talent that was responsible for the decline of magazines, but the prohibitive cost of paper and printing: with the encouragement of an outlet for it, we hoped the talent would reveal itself" (10). The journal promotes youthfulness, from which Bowen may have wished to dissociate herself. She introduced; but she never wrote for the journal again.

Introduction to *The Observer Prize Stories*

This introduction appeared in *The Observer Prize Stories: "The Seraph and the Zambesi" and Twenty Others* (London: Heinemann, 1952): vii–xi. In her comments, Bowen lays out the rules of the competition as it was run by the *Observer*. Stories had to be about Christmas. Indeed, Bowen herself entered the fray of Christmas writing with gusto in the 1950s. Muriel Spark won the competition, the beginning of an auspicious career. Bowen served several times as an *arbiter elegantiarum*, at least in matters literary. In addition to commenting on the winners of this competition, she judged the Sanditon Competition and the Tait Prize. In this introduction, her comments on the short story – its technique, its economy – reveal her notions of what makes an effective example of the genre.

English Fiction at Mid-Century

"English Fiction at Mid-Century" was published in the *New Republic* (21 September 1953): 15–16. It was reprinted in *Highlights of Modern Literature*, edited by Francis Brown (New York: New American Library, 1954): 30–2. In her evaluations of authors, Bowen shows a shrewd sense of their relative merits. Having read widely in contemporary fiction for reviews, she sifts away the worst and retains the best – albeit her friends and admirers frequently number among the best. Among names that she drops in this essay, she personally knew V. S. Pritchett, Rosamond Lehmann, Elizabeth Taylor, Ivy Compton-Burnett, Henry Green, Jocelyn Brooke, and Evelyn Waugh. Jocelyn Brooke interviewed Bowen on the radio in October 1950; he published a short, informative book called *Elizabeth Bowen* in 1952.

1. "From caverns": from Samuel Taylor Coleridge's poem "Kubla Khan."

2. Joyce Cary (1888–1957): Anglo-Irish author, known for *The Horse's Mouth* (1944).

3. L. P. Hartley (1895–1972): novelist and reviewer, Hartley published eight novels and six collections of short stories. He is best remembered for *The Go-Between* (1953) which opens with the quotable line, "The past is another country; they do things differently there." He reviewed *Ann Lee's*,

The Hotel, Joining Charles, and other books by Bowen. In turn, she reviewed The Sixth Heaven, Eustace and Hilda, A Perfect Woman, and other books by Hartley.

4. Hammond Innes (1913–98): thriller writer, whose Wreckers Must Breathe (1940) and Attack Alarm (1942) draw on wartime situations. The 'Mary Deare' (1956) was immensely successful and turned into an equally successful film (1959).

5. P. H. Newby (1918–97): author of Journey to the Interior (1945) and Agents and Witnesses (1947), he also served during the war in France and Egypt. He was fiction reviewer for the Listener and, in 1958, became controller of "Third Programme," the BBC arts network.

6. Thomas Hinde (1926–): pseudonym of the author Sir Thomas Willes Chitty. After Mr. Nicholas (1952), he published fiction and non-fiction, including Capability Brown: The Story of a Master Gardener (1986).

7. Nigel Balchin (1908–70): writer who worked as a psychologist during the Second World War, and wrote Darkness Falls from the Air (1942) and The Small Back Room (1943), based on wartime experiences. In addition to novels, he wrote screenplays later in his career.

8. Rex Warner (1905–86): classicist, author, translator, Reginald Ernest Warner began his career writing fiction, but increasingly turned to non-fiction. He discusses political regimes in The Cult of Power (1946).

9. Philip Toynbee (1916–81): during the war, Toynbee contributed to Horizon. After the war, he briefly edited at Contact. Bowen may have crossed his path at either magazine. A weekly reviewer at the Observer, he also wrote novels and verse.

10. Emma Smith (1923–): author of Maiden's Trip (1948) and The Far Cry (1949), which won the James Tait Black Memorial Prize that year. Smith subsequently wrote children's books but did not persist with writing novels.

Rx for a Story Worth the Telling

"Rx for a Story Worth the Telling" appeared in the New York Times Book Review (31 August 1958): 1, 13. The biographical blurb that accompanies the essay states, "Miss Bowen, British fiction writer, critic and essayist, lectured on the story this year at the Universities of Virginia, Chicago and Wisconsin." This essay may combine some of the aspects of the lectures given at those universities. Indeed, Bowen lays out a notion of compulsion and momentum in narrative that applies to her own stories as much as to others'.

Preface to *Critics Who Have Influenced Taste*

This preface appears in *Critics Who Have Influenced Taste*, edited and introduced by A. P. Ryan (London: Geoffrey Bles, 1965): vii–x. The twenty-four short essays in this volume cover critics, mostly English, from Ben Jonson to D. H. Lawrence. Unlike Matthew Arnold or T. S. Eliot, Bowen rarely spoke about criticism as an activity separate from literary creation.

Modern Girlhood

Two versions of "Modern Girlhood" exist: a typed draft and a published text. The undated carbon draft, eight pages long, bears a pencilled note at the top of the first page: "For: *The Leader*" (HRC 4.6). The essay appeared in the Easter number of the *Leader* 2.24 (31 March 1945): 8–9, 22. A photograph of a young, female communicant graces the cover. The *Leader*, which ran from 1944 to 1950, emphasised British relations with the US, Russia, France, and other countries. This focus partly explains Bowen's comparative analysis of French, American, and English girls. The unpublished typescript is called "Girlhood," as against "Modern Girlhood." The editor at the *Leader* corrected grammatical errors and amended punctuation that appear in the typescript, in addition to inserting numerous paragraph breaks. Hyphens have been excised from "teen-ager" and "teen-age." The March 1945 issue of the *Leader* included a profile of Elizabeth Bowen under the title "Leading Story-Writer" (14).

1. The typescript reads "this page." Two black and white photographs of devout communicants accompany this article in the *Leader*; Bowen may be commenting on them.

2. The typescript reads "great families," not "famous families."

3. Third Republic: the Third Republic ended in France on 10 July 1940. The Fourth Republic did not come into being until 1946. Bowen's present perfect tense, "have been," may be the result of confusion about what to call de Gaulle's provisional government that followed Vichy and preceded the Fourth Republic. On the other hand, Bowen may be asserting, as did Churchill, British solidarity with the French government during the war.

4. Enfranchised: women were finally granted the vote in France in 1944, largely because of their contribution to the war effort. After much parliamentary debate about whether women should be allowed to vote *before* deportees and prisoners of war returned to France – women, it was thought, might skew the general vote – de Gaulle signed an ordinance conferring full citizenship, including the vote, on women in April 1944.

5. *Dot*: dowry.

6. The typescript reads "mature woman" instead of "wife."

7. The typescript reads "sex" instead of "human nature."

8. *Soyez sage*: behave.

9. *What do young girls dream of?*: in the typescript, Bowen cites the French version, "*À quoi rêvent les jeunes filles?*" The Frenchman in question is Alfred de Musset, who wrote a play by this title. Bowen also generally alludes to Henri de Montherlant, whose novel *Les Jeunes Filles* is cited later in the essay; Bowen reviewed Montherlant's novel for the *New Statesman* on 30 October 1937 when *The Young Girls* appeared in English translation. The reference to *les jeunes filles* also recalls Proust, whose *À l'ombre des jeunes filles en fleurs* Bowen unquestionably knew.

10. Marie Laurencin (1883–1956): French painter who often depicted doe-eyed young women in pastel colours.

11. The typescript reads "probably knew the answer."

12. St. Thérèse de Lisieux (1873–1897): canonised in 1925. She advocated "the little way" of holiness, namely the expression of piety in small, private ways, not heroic, public ways.

13. The OED records the first usage of "teenager" in 1941 in the US.

14. Both the typescript and published text read "extraversion," which was a viable spelling of "extroversion" in the early decades of the twentieth century.

15. Sir James Frazer (1854–1941): assembled various myths in *The Golden Bough* with a view to their anthropological rather than their theological value. The first edition in two volumes was published in 1890. The comprehensive third edition of *The Golden Bough* appeared in twelve volumes between 1906 and 1915.

16. The typescript reads "England," not "Britain," which makes more sense in light of subsequent statements about English, not British, girls.

17. There is a paragraph break in the published text, but that break orphans the last sentence of the essay.

Teenagers

"Teenagers" was published in *Punch* 225 (19 August 1953): 226–7. Bowen's business correspondence indicates her sensitivity to the differences between American and British readers. On 15 April 1953, she wrote to Colin Young at Curtis Brown, "I wrote the 'teen-age' article, for *The American Weekly*, on my return from Italy, last week. Herewith a copy of it. Would it, do you think, as it stands, be slightly incomprehensible to English readers? I *could* – if there were a reasonable offer for it – insert a paragraph describing the appearance of the American teen-ager (this, the American takes for granted.) If the occasion arises, let me know" (HRC 10.5). On 25 April 1953, she wrote to Edith Haggard in the New York office of Curtis Brown: "I'm *delighted* to hear that *The American Weekly* likes my teen-ager article – I said to Colin Young, in my letter to him, that maybe before he can place it in England I should add a brief descriptive piece: the American teen-ager doesn't jump (pictorially) to the British eye" (HRC 10.5). Bowen's curiosity about teenagers has a sociological, even anthropological, keenness about it.

Mental Annuity

"Mental Annuity" was published in *Vogue* 126 (15 September 1955): 108–9. The reiterated phrase, "the middle years," alludes to Henry James's short story and memoirs of that name. The editor at *Vogue* who worked on this essay was not especially vigilant. Several grammatical solecisms occur in the essay. "Cannot" is divided into two words.

1. The published text reads "or," not "and," which creates both verb and pronoun agreement errors.

2. Crowd of daffodils: from Wordsworth's "I Wandered Lonely as a Cloud."

3. "To" has been added to preserve parallel construction.

The Case for Summer Romance

The vacation-mindedness of "The Case for Summer Romance" is due perhaps to its initial publication in *Glamour* 43 (June 1960): 94–5, 180. The structure of the essay, doubling youthful romance with a married woman's dalliance, creates an uncanny effect; the rhythms of boredom, dancing, and sudden departure are common to both affairs. The essay, with its present tense and detailed exposition, verges on being a short story.

The Beauty of Being Your Age

"The Beauty of Being Your Age" appeared in the English edition of *Harper's Bazaar* 64.4 (July 1961): 22. Bowen turned sixty-two just prior to publication of this essay. Ageing preoccupied her throughout the 1960s. Whereas she refers to the "middle years" in "Mental Annuity" in 1955, she speaks of the "later" and "after" years, not without irony, in "The Beauty of Being Your Age."

1. "Seven ages": Jaques's speech in *As You Like It* (Act 2, scene 7) outlines the seven ages of man from infancy to old age.

Was It an Art?

"*Was* It an Art?" has nine typed pages (HRC 9.10). It may or may not have been published. A directive to "begin" at the paragraph starting "All we people" might be Bowen's note to herself or a note to an editor. Other than that, the essay is free of handwritten corrections. From internal discussion, the essay was written in the late 1960s, certainly after Mary Quant created the mini-skirt in 1965. The further reference to granny glasses, which became fashionable circa 1968, means that this essay was probably composed that year. The rhetorical positioning of an older "I" against the young is uncharacteristic of Bowen's self-conception. In this essay, Bowen's favours her generation and its habits over the youth of the 1960s. Nevertheless, she ironically identifies with the young through the pronoun "we" when she discusses love: "We all see things the same way." Immediately thereafter she reverts to "we" to mean "the young of a vanished day." "It" in the title appears to be "flirtation," although it includes love and sex as well.

1. After the space break, Bowen writes in "Begin" at the head of the paragraph.
2. The word "a" has been added for sense.
3. Bowen writes "you," but she probably intended "your." Or she may have intended to put a comma after "you" to create an apposition in the clause that follows.

An Enormous Channel of Expectation

"An Enormous Channel of Expectation" appeared a month after Elizabeth II's coronation on 2 June 1953 in *Vogue* 122 (July 1953): 54–5. An admirer of ceremony, Bowen attended the funeral procession of George V in 1936, as she reminds William Plomer in a letter dated 6 May 1958: "I *can't* believe – though I'd believe it if you say so – that I went to tea at Virginia [Woolf]'s, and met you there, on the afternoon of George V's funeral. My cousin Noreen, who was staying with us, & Billy Buchan & I had got up at 4 a.m. to watch the procession in Edgeware Road; and I remember nothing else about the afternoon except being anaestheticised by tiredness, plus in vain looking for food for that night's dinner (to which I do remember you and Tom Eliot came) with all shops shut: a condition I'd forgotten to foresee" (Plomer Archive MSS 19/15). The coronation in 1953 was a cause for widespread jubilation. Bowen roughly sketches the procession route from Buckingham Palace, along the Mall, to Westminster Abbey. Her interest in royalty is not entirely separable from her willingness to undertake quick-study journalism. She wrote this article at top speed, as she predicts that she would have to do in a letter dated 16 April 1953, to Colin Young, the agent at Curtis Brown who handled commissioned articles for Bowen:

> Excellent – I'm so glad English *Vogue are* taking the Coronation article. Fee, as you say, not vast; but I congratulate you on having improved on the terms proposed: English *Vogue* have never been princely payers! And conceivably the 2nd serial rights might go somewhere else, later.
>
> The article's got to be rush work: I've promised to deliver it by 12 noon on the 3rd June, day after the Coronation, at the English *Vogue* office, who are to cable it through the night of the 2nd–3rd! Had I better hand the carbon of the article in to English *Vogue* at the same time, then notify you, formally, that it has reached them? (HRC 10.5)

Bowen could not have been unaware of paying obeisance to a queen who shared her own name; the capitalised "ELIZABETH" in the last sentence twinkles with a purposeful irony.

Enemies of Charm in Women, in Men

"Enemies of Charm in Women, in Men" appeared in *Vogue* 134 (15 September 1959): 158–9, 201. The difficulty of defining charm leads Bowen to a discussion of what traits *defeat* charm. Literature about charm is woefully deficient, although Bowen may have remembered Anthony Blanche's diatribe against charm in *Brideshead Revisited*: "Charm is the great English blight. It does not exist outside these damp islands. It spots and kills anything it touches" (260).

1. Jake: American slang, meaning, as an adjective, excellent, admirable, fine.

Woman's Place in the Affairs of Man

"Woman's Place in the Affairs of Man" is a four-page typescript (HRC 9.12). A letter from Bowen to "Mrs. Morris" accompanies the typescript. The note, on letterhead from The Hampton House in New York, is dated 21 October 1961: "Here is the article; I hope it is what you wanted. It has been interesting to write; and thank you for waiting so long!" The article was evidently commissioned, probably by a women's magazine. Bowen's declaration, "I am not, and never shall be, a feminist," should be read in the context of her war work, her journalism, her service on the Royal Commission on Capital Punishment, and numerous other activities that took her outside the *domus*. She explicitly states that women are no longer confined to the home; "the world is her home." Bowen wrote extensively about the history of Roman houses in *A Time in Rome*, and in a lecture given at Barnard College, "The Idea of the Home" (HRC 6.3). Some hand-written emendations to the typescript have been incorporated into the present version.

1. There is a ditto on "in" in the typescript.

2. Bowen frequently replaces "that" with a comma in this essay, as happens here.

3. *Domus*: in *A Time in Rome*, Bowen defines the ancient Roman *domus* as private houses patriarchally organised and given over to the idea of the family (104–15).

Outrageous Ladies

"Outrageous Ladies" exists in two versions: a pink carbon of six pages with extensive corrections in ink; an eight-page fair copy on white paper that incorporates the revisions (HRC 8.7). Sellery and Harris do not list its publication. The essay perhaps appeared in *Homes and Gardens*, a magazine edited by Lady Georgina Coleridge between 1949 and 1963. In a letter dated 2 August 1955, Phoebe, an employee at Curtis Brown, wrote to Bowen: "so very glad that you are willing to do something for the Times and also for Lady Georgina. I am sure there is no deadline. She would like anything from you at any time, and I will let her know that she can expect the article round about the beginning of October. I take it this is along the lines she suggested about preposterous heroines. October 1st would be too late for anything Christmasy" (HRC 11.3). "Preposterous heroines" might refer to "Outrageous Ladies." I paged through *Homes and Gardens* for 1955 and 1956 without locating this article. From 1956 to 1963, the magazine was known as *Home*. Unable to find the published version, I have used the typescripts as a base text.

1. Florence Barclay (1862–1921): best-selling British author of eleven books, mostly novels of undying love. Her second novel, *The Rosary* (1909), inspired five different film versions. *The Broken Halo* (1913) concerns a young man who loses his faith, then recovers it with the help of a pale, little lady, many years his senior.

2. Ethel M. Dell: see note under "James Joyce."

3. *The Green Hat*: Michael Arlen's *The Green Hat* (1924) was first a novel, then was adapted as a play starring Tallulah Bankhead, then a film, re-titled *A Woman of Affairs*, starring Greta Garbo.

4. Scarlett O'Hara: the protagonist of Margaret Mitchell's *Gone With the Wind* (1936).

A Way of Life

"A Way of Life" appeared in *Vogue* 110 (1 December 1947): 145, 210, 212. It was reprinted in British *Vogue* (January 1948): 44, 92, 96. The American version has been used as the base text. Whereas Bowen maintains that catching a glimpse of oneself unexpectedly in a mirror induces a sense of strangeness, in the essay "Mirrors Are Magic," written two decades later, she claims that she *does* recognize herself in public mirrors. "A Way of Life," in its movement from individual estrangement to national estrangement, responds to social changes in the postwar period: women's roles, Labour government, house and home, wages.

1. Goodbye-to-all-that attitude: Robert Graves's autobiographical account of trench warfare during the First World War, *Good-bye to All That* (1929), stirred much anti-war sentiment.

The Forgotten Art of Living

"The Forgotten Art of Living" appeared in *Contact: Good Living* 13 (December 1948): xxvi–xxviii, 1. This issue of *Contact* focused on happiness. The editorial "Comment on Contents" elaborates: "This is the thirteenth Contact Book: it deals with good living – with hedonism, happiness and pleasurable activity in its broadest sense: with the material means or 'tools' of pleasure; and with the experience of those who have found satisfaction in widely differing occupations" (iii). The biographical note on Bowen in this issue emphasises her comparative angle on happiness: "Elizabeth Bowen, the distinguished novelist, opens the book with an essay on what does and does not constitute happiness in the nineteen-forties, compared with the delights of former ages. She finds reason to regret the past, but without self-commiseration" (iii). In the same issue of *Contact*, William Sansom wrote about a colony of nudists on a French island and James Pope-Hennessy addressed the topic of hidden villages in Provence. The syntax slides around, with unusual emphasis on certain phrases that require, therefore, to be read twice. Moreover, Bowen uses a curious passive voice from time to time, that gives the impression of prose translated from French: "Outside one class, it [the gift for living] was to be come upon only in the exceptional person." "Was to be come upon" shifts emphasis away from who comes upon this quality. Erratic hyphenation has been amended.

1. Mary and the children: passage unidentified and possibly a pastiche invented by Bowen. The style is strongly reminiscent of Reverend Francis Kilvert's Victorian diary: "Came to Hawkchurch for three days. A pleasant and lovely journey with the air cleared and cooled by the storm. Uncle Will

met me at Axminster Station with Polly and the dog cart" (Kilvert 221). William Plomer edited three volumes of Kilvert's diaries between 1938 and 1940, and a one-volume selection in 1944. Bowen discusses Old Cheriton in *Pictures and Conversations* (9–19).

2. *The Artamonov Business*: Maxim Gorky's novel, published in 1925 in Russian, was translated into English in 1948. Ever watchful of foreign developments in fiction, Bowen reviewed Gorky's *A Book of Short Stories* in 1939 (*Collected Impressions* 153–6).

3. *Embusqués*: shirkers, with a military connotation of "those who lie in wait or ambush."

The Art of Respecting Boundaries

"The Art of Respecting Boundaries" exists in published and unpublished versions. Five sheets of typescript with blue ink revisions bear the title "The Art of Reserve or, The Art of Respecting Boundaries" (HRC 1.5). The essay was published as "The Art of Respecting Boundaries" in a series called "Arts of Living" in *Vogue* 119 (1 April 1952): 116–17. It was reprinted in *Arts of Living*, edited by Ernest Dimnet and others (New York: Simon & Schuster, 1954): 140–7. The *Vogue* version has been used as the base text. The rhetorical "we" in the first paragraph has no clear identity until Bowen specifies that she belongs to an era that respected intimacies and long-term friendships. To claim that generations in the 1950s do not respect boundaries or reserve is, as the title gives out, not just a breach of etiquette, but also a breach of art.

The Virtue of Optimism

"The Virtue of Optimism" appeared in *House and Garden* 104 (October 1953): 151, 228. It was the second article in a series on "the Homely Virtues – or the art of getting the most out of life," as a headnote to Bowen's article states. In this regard, it expands the definition of "art," as do the essays on "The Forgotten Art of Living" and "The Art of Respecting Boundaries."

Disappointment 1

In 1953 and 1954, disappointment preoccupied Bowen as a subject of psychological, even psychoanalytic, proportions. In this substantial essay, never published, she addresses adult disappointments. In the companion essay that follows, also called "Disappointment," she dwells on childhood disappointments. For the sake of identifying them, I have numbered these two essays consecutively. "Disappointment 1" exists as a corrected eight-page yellow carbon with a pencilled note in the upper right corner on the first page: "Reader's Digest (30/9/1953)" (HRC 2.6). Despite paging through American and British editions of *Reader's Digest* for 1953 and 1954, I could find no trace of this essay. In fact, Bowen's business correspondence with Curtis Brown indicates that *Reader's Digest* cancelled a contract for this article. In a letter dated 23 October 1953, Bowen's secretary wrote to Colin Young:

> You will have had from Mr. Ferguson of The Reader's Digest, a copy of his letter to Mrs. Cameron of the 20th October on the subject of her article on *Disappointment*.
>
> While she will gladly abide by your decision in the matter, Mrs. Cameron does feel there is a great deal to be said for accepting the fee of 100 guineas, "for trying," and leaving it at that. And perhaps, when she is in America next February, she could see Mr. Ferguson about the possibility of attempting another article. As it now stands, *Disappointment* represents about a week's work, and now, when she is devoting every available minute to the novel, she can ill afford to spend further time on it.
>
> If you agree that the matter can be left like this, the article will be available for you and Mrs. Haggard to try to place it elsewhere – although Mrs. Cameron feels there is little likelihood of either of you succeeding in doing so. (HRC 10.5; original punctuation)

In a letter dated 23 December 1946 to Dorothy Daly at Curtis Brown, Bowen wrote about her trouble meeting the expectations of editors at *Reader's Digest*: "I must say that I do not find the *Reader's Digest* highly concentrated style easy to hit off: I did, at their instigation, try to write for one of their series once. The result, which did not make the grade, was, I think, subsequently sold elsewhere by you under the title *Tipperary Woman*" (HRC 10.5). She apparently never published anything in *Reader's Digest*, despite being asked at least twice.

1. A comma has been added.

2. The typescript reads "profession," but the plural seems more likely.

3. The typescript reads "sooner or late." "Later" seems likely, unless Bowen intended "soon or late."

4. The word "a" has been added.

5. In the typescript, "manuscript" is abbreviated as "M.S."

Disappointment 2

This version of "Disappointment" exists in three versions: an unpublished draft and two published versions. As a base text, I use the essay published under the title "Disappointment" in *Family Doctor* 4.3 (March 1954): 145–46. In an abridged form, the essay appeared under the title "The Badge of Courage" in *Parents Magazine* (February 1954): 35. Although the *Parents Magazine* version is substantially the same as the *Family Doctor* version, it omits the opening two paragraphs and two sentences in the conclusion. I have compared the published version of "Disappointment" with the three-page typescript on pink carbon (HRC 2.6). Variants between typescript and published versions are minimal. Paragraphs are shorter in the *Family Doctor* version than in the typescript. Occasionally the editor substituted full stops for Bowen's colons, semi-colons, and em-dashes. Something of a connoisseur of disappointment, Bowen writes aphoristically in *The House in Paris* that "Disappointment tears the bearable film off life" (219).

   1. In the typescript, there is no paragraph break.

   2. In the typescript, there is no paragraph break.

   3. In the *Family Doctor* version, the semi-colon is mistakenly placed after "enter." In the typescript, the semi-colon correctly appears after "in."

   4. In the typescript, there is no paragraph break.

   5. The question mark is omitted in the *Family Doctor* version. In the typescript, Bowen uses a semi-colon.

   6. In the typescript, there is no paragraph break.

How to Be Yourself – But Not Eccentric

"How to be Yourself – But Not Eccentric" was written for *Vogue* 128 (July 1956): 54–5. Bowen concentrates on outward conformity and inward identity. In this regard, "How to be Yourself" makes a companion piece to "Disloyalties," where Bowen claims that "The novelist's subject is not society, not the individual as a social unit, but the individual as he himself is, behind the social mask" (*Afterthought* 195). The friction between acceptance of social norms and inner dissent from those norms fuels creativity for the novelist, who "is often the product of an intensive environment – racial, local or social. What he creates takes character from his own strongly personal and often also inherited sense of life" (*Afterthought* 197). Instead of speaking about creativity in "How to be Yourself," Bowen concentrates on the fulfilment and uniqueness of personality as it emerges through time and self-knowledge.

The Thread of Dreams

One of Bowen's very last non-fiction pieces – she wrote only a few reviews after this – "The Thread of Dreams" was published in the English edition of *Réalités* (February 1969): 656–9. The single paragraph that constitutes this essay may have been an editorial decision rather than Bowen's. In the magazine, the margin meanders down the page in a sinuous curve and onto the next two pages of text. The essay, however, logically could break into intelligible paragraphs. The international English edition of *Réalités* (the magazine was founded as a French publication) targets a jet-setting, art-collecting audience. Features on foreign travel to Portugal, Marrakesh, Japan, and Prague address a cosmopolitan readership. The February 1969 issue is devoted to India. Illustrated with three photographs, the essay conveys something of Bowen's preoccupation with the spiritual dimensions of existence.

Works Cited

Archives

The Elizabeth Bowen Archives, the A. E. Coppard Archives, the John Lehmann Archives, and the Knopf Archives are all held at the Harry Ransom Humanities Research Center at the University of Texas at Austin. Throughout this volume, those separate archives are designated by the abbreviation "HRC," followed by a box and file number. The Bodleian Library, Oxford University, holds the Isaiah Berlin Archives. The William Plomer Archives are held at the Palace Green Library, Durham University.

Books and Articles

Attlee, C. R. "Each Must Make His Contribution." *The Listener* 23.594 (1940): 1036.

Berlin, Isaiah. *Letters 1928–1946*. Ed. Henry Hardy. Cambridge: Cambridge University Press, 2004.

Bowen, Elizabeth. *Afterthought: Pieces About Writing*. London: Longmans, 1962.

—. "Alfred Knopf." HRC 1.2.

—. "Autobiographical Note." HRC 1.5.

—. *The Bazaar and Other Stories*. Ed. and intro. by Allan Hepburn. Edinburgh: Edinburgh University Press, 2008.

—. *Bowen's Court and Seven Winters*. Ed. and intro. by Hermione Lee. 1942, 1943. London: Vintage, 1999.

—. "Britain in Autumn." HRC 2.2.

—. *Collected Impressions*. London: Longmans, 1950.

—. "Coming to London." *Coming to London*. Ed. John Lehmann. London: Phoenix, 1957. 74–81.

—. "Eire." *New Statesman and Nation* 21 (12 April 1941): 382–3.

—. "Fiction." Rev. of *Finnegans Wake*, *At Swim-Two-Birds*, and *Hope of Heaven*. *Purpose* 11.3 (1939): 177–80.

—. "First Writing." *Mademoiselle* 32 (January 1951): 57, 117–20.

—. *The Heat of the Day*. 1949. New York: Anchor, 2002.

—. *The House in Paris*. 1935. Intro. by A. S. Byatt. New York: Anchor, 1998.

—. "Hungary." HRC 6.2.

—. Radio Interview, 1959. With John Bowen, William Craig, and W. N. Ewer. BBC Broadcast, 11 September 1959. Transcription HRC 2.3.

—. Introduction to *An Angela Thirkell Omnibus*. London: Hamish Hamilton, 1966. vii–ix.

—. Introduction to *Pride and Prejudice*, by Jane Austen. London: William & Norgate, 1948. vii–xv.

—. "Ireland Makes Irish." *Vogue* 108 (15 August 1946): 180–1, 214–17.

—. "Mental Annuity." *Vogue* 126 (15 September 1955): 108–9.

—. *The Mulberry Tree: Writings of Elizabeth Bowen*. Ed. Hermione Lee. New York: Harcourt, 1986.

—. "A Passage to E. M. Forster." *Aspects of E. M. Forster*. Ed. Oliver Stallybrass. London: Edward Arnold, 1969. 1–12.

—. *Pictures and Conversations*. Foreword by Spencer Curtis Brown. New York: Knopf, 1974.

—. "Portrait of a Woman Reading." *Chicago Tribune Book World* (10 November 1968): 10.

—. Preface to *Frost in May*, by Antonia White. London: Eyre & Spottis-woode, 1948. v–x.

—. *The Shelbourne*. 1951. London: Random House, 2001.

—. *A Time in Rome*. New York: Knopf, 1960.

—. "What We Need in Writing." *Spectator* (20 November 1936): 901–2.

Bryant, Heather Jordan. *How Will the Heart Endure: Elizabeth Bowen and the Landscape of War*. Ann Arbor, MI: University of Michigan Press, 1992.

Connolly, Cyril. *Ideas and Places*. London: Weidenfeld & Nicolson, 1953.

Ellmann, Maud. *Elizabeth Bowen: The Shadow Across the Page*. Edinburgh: Edinburgh University Press, 2003.

Gellhorn, Martha. *The Face of War*. Rev. ed. 1959. New York: Atlantic Monthly, 1988.

Glendinning, Victoria. *Elizabeth Bowen: A Biography*. 1977. New York: Anchor, 2005.

Kilvert, Rev. Francis. *Kilvert's Diary 1870–1879*. Abridged. Ed. and intro. by William Plomer. London: Cape, 1944.

Lane, Jack. "Introduction." *"Notes on Eire": Espionage Reports to Winston Churchill, 1940–2*. Aubane, Ireland: Aubane Historical Society, 1999. 5–9.

Proust, Marcel. *Remembrance of Things Past*. Vol. 3. Trans. C. K. Scott Moncrieff, et al. Harmondsworth: Penguin, 1981.

—. *Le Temps retrouvé*. Ed. Pierre-Louis Rey, et al. 1927. Paris: Gallimard, 1989.

Reynolds, Sir Joshua. *Discourses on Art*. Ed. Robert R. Wark. 1769–90. New Haven, CT and London: Yale University Press, 1997.

Ritchie, Charles. *Diplomatic Passport: More Undiplomatic Diaries, 1946–1962*. Toronto: Macmillan, 1981.

—. *The Siren Years: A Canadian Diplomat Abroad, 1937–1945*. Toronto: Macmillan, 1974.